International
Relations
in Transition

International Relations in Transition

Robert Wesson

Senior Research Fellow
Hoover Institution

Professor Emeritus
University of California, Santa Barbara

Prentice Hall, Englewood Cliffs, New Jersey 07632

Library of Congress Cataloging-in-Publication Data

Wesson, Robert G.
    International relations in transition / Robert Wesson.
        p.   cm.
    Includes index.
    ISBN 0-13-471699-X
    1. International relations. 2. World politics--1945-   I. Title.
JX1391.W48 1990
327'.09'048--dc20
                                              89-8792
                                                 CIP

Editorial/production supervision and
  interior design: Merrill Peterson
Cover design: Wanda Lubelska Design
Manufacturing buyer: Peter Havens

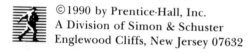
Printed in the United States of America

10 9 8 7 6 5 4 3 2 1

ISBN 0-13-471699-X

Prentice-Hall International (UK) Limited, *London*
Prentice-Hall of Australia Pty. Limited, *Sydney*
Prentice-Hall Canada Inc., *Toronto*
Prentice-Hall Hispanoamericana, S.A., *Mexico*
Prentice-Hall of India Private Limited, *New Delhi*
Prentice-Hall of Japan, Inc., *Tokyo*
Simon & Schuster Asia Pte. Ltd., *Singapore*
Editora Prentice-Hall do Brasil, Ltda., *Rio de Janeiro*

Contents

Preface

The traditional contentions of nations, called "powers," are rapidly giving way to a new kind of international relations more appropriate to an age of high technology and sophisticated civilization. The bipolarity that dominated world affairs from 1946 into the 1980s is outdated. The outlines of international politics of coming decades are unclear, but economic and social problems to a large extent displace military questions. Japan figures more prominently, the Soviet Union less so.

Change swirls so rapidly that much of whatever may be stated of the contemporary world will be irrelevant or invalid before this book can reach the reader. But this only makes it the more necessary to review the evolving scene. Dealings with the world continue to be as important as ever for our country and our lives, although the ways in which they affect us change.

To try to get a fix on modern international relations would be difficult even if they were not in a confusing flux. For some understanding of the ways in which countries deal with one another, it is essential to deal with an enormous amount of information and many unanalyzable relationships. It is also necessary to have a deep feeling for human nature; foreign policy is made by fallible people. Those who speak for nations may be thoughtful, well studied, and selfless; they may also be shortsighted, prejudiced, and self-centered. Diplomacy is not a science but an art, subject to all the vagaries of personality and ideas; in few other fields of human endeavor is there such a high ratio of failure to success. There is no real expertise in international relations; and as the world and the problems of international dealings become more complex, leaders become less competent to cope with them.

This book hopes, withal, to present some insights. Without laying out details about the actions and structures of the United Nations, the ways of diplomacy, nuclear strategy, or the evolution of the international system, it explores the essentials of the contemporary world system. It stresses the obvious but sometimes neglected fact that conditions and needs are different from what they were a generation or even a decade ago. It outlines some notions of what is at stake and what might be done better.

For these purposes, most attention goes to the United States, on which international politics center. This is the power that most others see as a leader, although some regard it as a threat or cause of problems. Only the United States has a hand in all manner of problems nearly everywhere; and the study of U.S. foreign policy is not far from the study of the international system.

The Soviet Union, although it would very much like to qualify as a global power, has little to do with events in much of the world, such as the Western Hemisphere and Southeast Asia. It remains, despite its problems, a major factor in world equations; and it is of special current interest because it has entered a period of flux after long rigidity. Japan occupies an increasing part of the attention of the United States, but its political role, although expanding, is still modest. The European powers, joining in the Economic Community, play an important part. China and India are too huge to be ignored. Many complications arise from relations with these and more than a hundred other theoretically independent and sovereign polities. The lesser powers must adjust to the ways of their superiors, but highly unequal relations present difficult problems for both sides. In sum, ours is an international system of utmost complexity.

Yet through our examination of the international relations of today there runs a single broad fact; namely, that concerns of power give way to a range of new problems of adjustment to modernity. It is consequently the basic plan of this book to examine first the old international relations (through Chapter 4) and then the new (through Chapter 11).

After some notes in the Introduction about the study of our subject, Chapter 1 deals with the development of the international system through the world wars. Chapter 2 treats the traditional conflictual nature of interactions of sovereign states and the U.S.-Soviet bipolarity. The expression of conflict through nuclear confrontation, conventional defense policies, and alliances is discussed in Chapter 3. Chapter 4 deals with competitive policies of the United States and the Soviet Union in regard to weaker nations of the Third World. Chapter 5 summarizes how the world and its values have changed: war is no longer a serviceable instrument of national policy, territorial acquisition has ceased to be rewarding, and ideology has receded. As detailed in Chapter 6, a major aspect of change is that forces of cultural and economic internationalization cause modification of the Marxist-Leninist states. A parallel change, discussed in Chapter 7, is the mitigation of the hostile bipolarity that dominated postwar decades. Chapter 8 notes how new kinds of relations and concerns come to the fore, international action of many kinds becomes more important, and common concerns partly replace power rivalry. Economic matters claim more and more attention, with their political ramifications, as outlined in Chapter 9. The economic and social inequalities that complicate the international order are considered in Chapter 10. The concluding chapter sketches the uncertain world panorama dominated by economic change, seemingly evolving toward a looser system of international institutions interwoven with national states.

Those who have read part, most, or all of the manuscript include Stephen Kull, Jan F. Triska, Robert C. North, Carlos J. Moneta, Alexander L. George, and Paul Kreisberg, all of whom made valued comments, although it is not implied that they necessarily agreed with its ideas. Sarah Blair and Margaret Smith were very helpful in pruning the text.

International
Relations
in Transition

Introduction

The Problem of Understanding

Our nation is caught up in a web of relationships with other sovereign powers of this globe, mostly friendly or neutral, sometimes hostile, potentially calamitous. These multifarious interactions have a large impact on our lives. Foreign economic relations—the balance of trade and the flow of investment—may be decisive for the prosperity of the nation. "Defense," whether to assure the physical safety of the nation or to enable it to oppose inimical foreign actions or to promote whatever may be considered "national interests," consumes enormous sums. It has been about as costly as all the education that should form the new generation and enable the nation to compete in the world.

Important as foreign affairs may be, hardly anything within the common ken is less comprehensible. Appreciation of the issues and problems requires analysis of the politics of various nations and understanding of their decision-making process, their history, inherited mentality, and ideas, little of which do we really comprehend, even if we have mental energy really to try. The subtle and intricate interactions of the international system, with complex background trends and environmental factors, from demographic problems to economic pressures and technological developments, are beyond our mastery. We are understandably inclined to simplistic approaches.

Understanding is deficient not only where there is lack of study. For example, the political structures and ideological motivation of the Soviet Union made it seem a great menace to the United States; and they have been investigated more intensively than those of almost any other nation. But no one faintly anticipated the extraordinary changes in Soviet affairs beginning in 1985. Enlightened American citizens even have trouble comprehending why their own government behaves as it does. In a different vein, no one has any real sense of what the computer revolution may eventually do to international relations.

In their preoccupation with immediate problems, leaders do not seem much concerned with a broad perspective or a long-range view. They are seldom familiar with foreign lands and peoples. Myths and ideologies are influential in foreign policies; clichés, stereotypes, and fixations are more powerful and persistent in foreign than in domestic questions. Those engaged in a policy or program are biased in favor of continuing it. If the medicine isn't working, the response is usually to prescribe bigger doses. To change is to admit failure, and it is nearly always possible to make some kind of case for what is being done. Misinformation abounds; there is probably more of it in regard to questions of international politics than in any other department of ordinary life. It is easy to select evidence to confirm prejudices, as was done egregiously, for example, in official reports on the war in Vietnam. Foreign affairs are like fortune-telling: those engaged in the business talk and act as though they know a great deal more than they really do.

The foreign policy bureaucracy is trained and paid to write current reports, give briefings, and get over today's problems. Many of the lower-level professionals are quite sensible and well-informed, but they are not asked to give reasoned judgments. Those who select applicants for the American Foreign Service look for ability in administration, not international relations. Chiefs at the top of the pyramid are necessarily amateurs in foreign affairs, since expertise in this realm is not a major qualification for domestic political success anywhere. Decision-makers deal with complex distant matters about which they have read a briefing paper containing a few bits of the enormous mass of information that should rightly be taken into account. They probably make little effort to see how the other side views questions, act for domestic political ends, and often do not know what they really intend.[1] Incidentally, in international relations, as in other spheres of life, big decisions are less likely to be rational than little ones.

---

[1]As observed by Sidney Weintraub, *Economic Coercion and U.S. Policy* (Boulder, CO: Westview, 1982), p. xi. Concerning difficulties of rationality in international relations, see Robert Jervis, *Perception and Misperception in International Politics* (Princeton: Princeton University Press, 1976), p. 383 and passim.

An important secondary difficulty is that statements made by actors on the scene of world politics may be truthful or they may not be. It is assumed that assertions of a chemist about chemistry will be correct so far as reasonably possible; if they are not, the maker is unscientific. But political leaders are not judged according to the veracity of their utterances; and where emotions are as important as facts, broad declarations are difficult to prove wrong. The management of international affairs is essentially political, and understanding requires looking behind stated purposes to try to discern real motives, gains hoped for and costs feared, both domestically and abroad. To appreciate how completely partisanship can shape perceptions one needs only to compare the treatment of events by different groups—those in favor of a hard line in Central America and those opposed, for example—or in different countries, as the treatment of Israeli-Palestinian clashes in the United States and Europe.

An additional reason for irrationality in foreign relations is that we are prisoners of the past and fail to adjust ideas and policy to the onrushing world. Much as generals prepare for the bygone war, which is the war they know about, statesmen and their advisors reason in terms of the dramatic experiences of their predecessors. They apply history uncritically, seeing chiefly whatever conforms to a desired image,[2] pointing to dramatic and seemingly clear-cut but often misleading examples.

In 1956, the British foreign secretary, Anthony Eden, thought that the Egyptian strongman Gamal Abdel Nasser was a reincarnation of Hitler, and that permitting him to keep the Suez Canal, which he had nationalized, would be dangerous appeasement. The events leading up to the Second World War—the failure of collective security, appeasement at Munich, and the nightmare of Hitlerism—weighed upon the thinking of a half century later, although nothing like the events leading to WW II can possibly recur. Congressional reluctance to support antigovernment forces ("Contras") in Nicaragua in 1987 has been denounced as parallel to the betrayal of the democratic government of Czechoslovakia to the Nazis in 1938; and a leading American columnist compared the Reagan-Gorbachev summit of December 1987, at which an agreement was signed to abolish intermediate-range nuclear missiles, to that notorious failure to prevent world war.[3]

Foreign policy making also goes its own way because individuals promote their own ideas, disregarding the wishes of higher authority. For example, one of the greatest decisions of history, the opening of the First World War, was promoted by officials exceeding their proper roles. The German chief of staff, Helmuth von Moltke, pressed Austria-Hungary to go to war against Serbia while German Chancellor Theobald von Bethmann-Hollweg

---

[2]Ernest R. May, *"Lessons" of the Past: The Use and Misuse of History in American Foreign Policy* (New York: Oxford University Press, 1973), p. xi and passim.

[3]*Newsweek*, December 21, 1987, p. 78.

was urging caution; and the French ambassador to Russia assured Tsar Nicholas II of French support without authorization from his government. In the 1973 Middle East war, Henry Kissinger acted almost independently of President Nixon. Admiral John Poindexter in 1985–1986 deliberately kept President Reagan uninformed of dealings with Iran.[4]

It is a further complication that the satisfaction of national or individual pride is quite as influential as national security or other "vital interests." For example, in 1982 the British government of Margaret Thatcher responded to the Argentine invasion of the Falkland Islands with alacrity and gusto, not to regain a colony they would be glad to be rid of but because of anger and concern for prestige. The prize of victory was not the retention of the nearly valueless territory with fewer than 2,000 inhabitants but the warm feelings of a people conscious of lost imperial greatness, a glow that gave the government victory in the next election. In a different manner, the American decision to embargo trade with Nicaragua in May 1985 seems to have been made because of developments not in Central America but in Washington: after the Congress refused to vote funds for anti-Sandinista forces the administration had to do something. Likewise, the effort in 1987–1988 to remove General Manuel Noriega from power in Panama, after many years of toleration of his narcotics trade, was apparently motivated by frustration at inability to remove Daniel Ortega from power in Nicaragua.

Like writers about foreign affairs, the practitioners may be brilliant or dull; and it is not easy to certify which are which.[5] How much of the high politics of world affairs should be considered irrational, in terms of the purposes of the leaders or the well-being of the community, is unknowable. We like to suppose that our destinies lie in wise hands, and some may feel that the assessments of foreign policy making in this book are overly negative. With a little imagination one can find purposes for anything and thus make policies seem understandable. But if one looks coldly at the record, the dominant impression is of thoughtlessness. World history may well be regarded as a sad chronicle of the follies of the great. [Stalin's self-blinding (although its import was defensive) was an extreme example. On the eve of the Nazi attack in June 1941 he issued an order forbidding that intelligence about the coming attack be circulated or brought to his attention.[6]] If a decision defies rational understanding, it may be simply erroneous. Leaders

---

[4]Richard N. Lebow, "Clausewitz and Nuclear Crisis Stability," *Political Science Quarterly* 103, Spring 1988, 95–104.

[5]Interviews reported in Steven Kull, *Minds at War: Nuclear Reality and Inner Conflicts of Defense Policy Makers* (New York: Basic Books, 1988) give some idea of the uneven intellectual level of eminent strategic analysts.

[6]Alexander Dallin, "World War II as a Soviet Plot," *New York Times*, November 15, 1987, Book Review, p. 35.

of developed and less developed nations alike make mistakes, and they are more prone to do so in foreign than in domestic affairs.

The Study of International Relations: "Realism"

There is no theory, properly speaking, of international relations. There can be none that makes reliable predictions. Turbulence and chaotic interaction would make it impossible to project the future from the present with any confidence, even if we knew vastly more than we do and had the intelligence to handle the infinite data. The theories, or approaches to theory, that have been propounded may give some feeling of making sense of the past; but they are more like intellectual exercises than guides to action or aids to foresight. It is not even certain that history offers any definite lessons for today's problems. We can do little more than note some generalities, such as the unpredictability of affairs, or read the present in terms suggested by the past. We might have some idea how things ought to turn out if conditions remained constant and leaders were reliably rational, but conditions are always in flux and international affairs are riddled with novelty and inconsistency.[7]

At best, we can try to place actions within a general framework that determines what kind of explanations we are looking for; and analysts emphasize various ordering principles or approaches. They may treat international affairs on the basis of the expressed interests of the parties, or "real" interests, which may be different. They may look at sources of irrationality, personal, organizational, or political. The collective psychology of interacting policymakers plays some part.[8] Bureaucratic urges commonly carry the day; the U.S. bombing of Libya in 1986 had to be mostly staged from England, despite attendant difficulties and complications, because the air force couldn't let the navy have all the glory.

Some writers stress the structure, dynamics, and accepted rules of the system, or international regimes, as they are often called. Others try to analyze the actions of the actors, mostly nation-states. Those with a different philosophy may see influences lurking behind the scenes and pulling strings, more or less in line with the Marxist interpretation of government as a front for economic interests. Others psychoanalyze the nations or responsible individuals. For example, deep roots of Nazism have been found

---

[7]For a survey of the discipline of international relations, see Stanley Hoffmann, *Janus and Minerva; Essays in the Theory and Practice of International Politics* (Boulder, CO: Westview, 1987), pp. 3–22.

[8]The thesis of Irving L. Janis, *Victims of Groupthink: A Psychological Study of Foreign Policy Decisions and Fiascoes* (Boston: Houghton Mifflin, 1973).

in German culture; and if Hitler had been an emotionally sound personality, Munich might have gone into history as a sensible accommodation. Lyndon Johnson's paranoia is cited as a cause of U.S. miscalculations in Vietnam.[9]

There are different levels of analysis: the systemic, treating the interactions of powers within the framework of the international community; the national, studying how individual nations formulate policies and react to foreign events; and the individual, dealing with persons who make decisions. These are often treated separately; their realities, however, are inseparable. One may lay the blame for conflict on the international system, with its anarchic invitation to struggle for advantages or security at the expense of other states. Or one may fault the inherent aggressiveness of nation-states, or the bad ones. But the international system would surely be placid if its participants were not truculent, and states could not be aggressive if the system were not conducive to truculence and if groups and leaders within the nation were not perverse, vicious, or weak.

There are thus many crosscutting approaches. However, the great philosophic divide of traditional international relations theorizing has been between those who consider themselves "realists" in that they stress the facts of force and power, and their critics. Many of the latter may be called "idealists," or better, "modernists," as they emphasize the aspects of international relations that are becoming more important in the contemporary world.

The former emphasize the amoral side, seeing humans as primarily power-bent and the struggle for power as the dominant fact of relations among sovereign states. They focus strongly on the nation; sovereignties are deemed to have selfish and competitive interests that they promote so far as they are capable. Scornful of ideas of international law or morality, the "realists" follow somewhat in the tradition of Machiavelli, who understood politics as a ruthless contest in which the dagger and poison cup were ordinary instruments. In their view, any nation is to be trusted only to use its power for its advantage. They look back to Thomas Hobbes, who considered "the war of all against all" to be the natural condition of humanity.

The leading modern prophet of the "realist" approach was Hans Morgenthau, who felt that a nation should guide itself simply by pursuit of "national interest," which in practice seemed to amount to the pursuit of power, mostly military.[10] The "realists" do not deny that other motives than coldly conceived national interests, including ideals, play an important part in the interactions of states; but they urge the nation to be self-centered—

[9]Richard N. Goodwin, "The War Within," *New York Times Magazine*, August 21, 1988, p. 35.

[10]Hans J. Morgenthau, *Politics among Nations: The Struggle for Power and Peace*, 5th ed. (New York: Alfred A. Knopf, 1978).

an admonition that would hardly seem necessary in a world where abnegation is uncommon.[11]

The "realist" approach is largely conditioned by the study of history, and it assumes that the nature of states and their interactions have not substantially changed and are not likely to do so soon. A leading writer, K. J. Holsti, asserts, "Most main issues and characteristic forms of interaction are not significantly different from those in the European state system [of the 19th century]."[12] The balance of power, the guiding principle of European affairs in the 18th century, lingers in the thinking of the late 20th century; scholars love its logic and neatness. Statesmen see themselves in roles like those of their honored predecessors.

In this approach, there is hardheadedness graced by clarity and simplicity. To study international relations as a dramatic contest of power is intriguing for writers of textbooks, professors, and students, doubtless for many of the same reasons that the makers of foreign policy like to see the world in such terms. The assumption that power is what it is all about represents economy of thought; it gives us a handle on the whole affair. The seemingly simple (but in reality complex and ambiguous) notion of power has a scientific air: we are looking at stark facts, setting aside idealistic illusions. Most of all, it appeals to competitive instincts.

But this "realism" is unrealistic. The projection of the past onto the much changed present is misleading, and the "realist" view is outmoded and receding, although it lingers in the thinking of many. The world and its problems have steadily evolved since the end of the last world war (which may indeed be the last), and most rapidly since 1985.

Nations are not mere predators, and use of force among great powers would be insane. It is a truism that actors on the world stage ought to pursue national interests; no doubt all formulators of foreign policy would claim to be doing so. But national interests include not only what may be wrested from another state but also benefits to be secured in cooperation; and the political and economic condition of the world and the nation can be considered a national interest, perhaps the highest national interest the foreign office can hope to promote. The shared interest may be clearer than the competitive interest: there is no doubt of the value to the United States of a reduction of the threat of chemical warfare, but it is unclear whether an improvement of the Soviet economic outlook is desired or not.

Treating the interaction of states as a zero-sum game, in which the gain of one (in terms of power) equals the loss of another, is the more unrealistic

---

[11]See Daniel Mahoney, "Notes on Political Philosophy and Contemporary International Relations," *Teaching Political Science* 15, Fall 1987, 4–9.

[12]K. J. Holsti, *International Politics: A Framework for Analysis*, 5th ed. (Englewood Cliffs, NJ: Prentice Hall, 1988), p. 59.

because it has become hard in the power-oriented game for anyone to gain significantly. This is true not only of war, but also in regard to everything related to defense, wherein the more one spends on means of destruction the more others feel they have to spend. A realistic foreign policy would strive less to register doubtful gains by threat or use of force than to reduce the likelihood of its use.

International dealings and human needs include many matters, economic, cultural, and social, in regard to which the ability to employ violence is hardly relevant. The United States cannot rectify its trade imbalance with Taiwan by hints of nuking Taipeh. Neither the United States nor the Soviet Union would appear to have gained much if anything from its strategic arsenal in recent decades; investing more in the economy and less in arms would possibly have enabled them to avoid the decline they have suffered in terms of shares of world production and trade. In fact, the ability of the strongest states to get any return from their military expenditures, or to manipulate weak states by any means, military or nonmilitary, seems quite limited.

Everyone seems to regard power as desirable, but it seems to be desired not so much from concrete gains expected as from the luxury of having and enjoying it. It is not clear how its various aspects should be weighed. The military has been treated as the chief measure,[13] although the chief or only utility of modern strategic weapons is psychological. Japan and Germany, without nuclear forces, are weighty by virtue of economic strength. China is regarded as one of the very greatest powers because a large fraction of the world's population is Chinese.

The division between those who stress power and those who are more prone to think in terms of other values corresponds roughly to that between hawks and doves. Makers of foreign policy side with the "realists" of international relations theory insofar as they tend to rely on force or threat of force and are prone to action, unilateral if necessary, without much attention to intangible consequences. Their opponents stress consultation and broad acceptability of policies.

From the modernist point of view, true realism should begin with the fact that modern civilization is dominated by phenomenally expanding technology. Nations have very little to gain from injuring one another, very much from working together to meet growing common needs. The threat of force, especially mass-murderous, potentially suicidal nuclear destruction, is not to be understood as a natural component of the relations of powers but as a morbid aberration.

The two approaches correspond to the old and new in international relations. The traditional preoccupation of foreign policy, especially that of

---

[13]As by Karl W. Deutsch, *The Analysis of International Relations*, 3rd. ed. (Englewood Cliffs, NJ: Prentice Hall, Inc., 1988), pp. 20–40.

European powers of the 18th and 19th centuries, was ceaseless complicated maneuvering for position and influence, including territorial gain if possible. The more modern concern is for economic and other matters in which cooperation is better for all sides than contest. The former aspect, although declining, will doubtless persist indefinitely; the latter aspect, although rising sharply in recent decades, is as old as diplomacy. Historians of the future will probably place the crossing of the two curves in the Reagan administration, which saw the shift from regarding the Soviet Union as chief source of international ills to a strong inclination to seek settlement of differences with that power.

Chapter 1

Development of the State System

The Coming of the Modern Era

The international system that we know began when, after centuries of slow material progress through the Middle Ages and the Renaissance, there emerged a set of independent national units. The introduction of artillery made nobles' castles vulnerable and led to the consolidation of most of feudal Europe into nation-states, France, England, Spain, Austria, and so forth, which dominated Europe (then a fairly self-contained universe) from the end of the 15th century. The nation-states formed the rising European system that eventually produced modern science, technology, and industry.

From the 15th into the 20th century, the European nations jousted, most intensively in the area around France and Germany. The principal contestants were about a dozen, including, in addition to those mentioned, Poland, Hungary, Prussia (which made itself the leading component of Germany), Netherlands, and Sweden. They seemed virtually immortal through all their potentially deadly quarrels. Theirs was the balance of power, theirs the glory of vying for world leadership, perhaps supremacy. From time to time, a near-hegemonic power, such as Austria under Charles V, Spain under Philip II, or France under Louis XIV and Napoleon, would make a bid for domination. But the would-be unifiers were always defeated, and the balance of power (whereby states would combine against any one that seemed to be acquiring sufficient strength to threaten the independence of all) sustained an unsteady equilibrium. This allowed considerable freedom for the strong and some for the weak.

The stalemate Peace of Westphalia (1648) ended generations of bitter religious conflict (ideological, in modern terms), and the nation-state system entered a period of relative calm and refinement. War became a game of monarchs and small professional or mercenary armies, trained more for the parade ground than for the battlefield, fighting by conventional rules for usually unimportant territories. The outcome of conflict was ordinarily inconclusive; a victorious power did not want to eliminate the enemy or make allies too strong.[1]

This moderation was possible because the aristocrats of Europe formed a community. They spoke French, copied the styles of Versailles, welcomed foreigners to the court, and cherished no strong national prejudices. Many statesmen had careers in various capitals. The elite of different nations had much more in common with each other than with the uncouth plebeians of their own nations, who bore the costs of princely ambitions. It was realistic to regard war, in the phrase of Clausewitz, as a continuation of politics, usually not much more destructive than its other forms.

The mores of genteel combat and ceremonious battle broke down in the conflicts following the French Revolution of 1789. The contest was no longer to satisfy the vanity of a prince or to acquire a small fiefdom, as new forces of democracy and nationalism raised emotions of confrontation. The state, having made itself the embodiment of the people, commanded its sons to march into battle, to kill or die for liberty and equality.[2] Those who rejoiced in liberation from feudal tyranny fought for their new sacred rights, while the princes and their followers defended a precious traditional way of life.

After a generation of nearly continuous warfare, the armies of monarchic Europe marched into Paris, put Napoleon to flight, and then crushed his attempted return at Waterloo. The victors, who stood for the old order, tried to put the pieces back together by the Peace of Vienna in 1815. Fearful of revolution-breeding war, they sought not merely to restore the status quo ante but also to erect a permanently stable system. They managed excellently in that Europe remained at peace, with minor interruptions, until 1914.

During that most ironic century of history, the industrial revolution grew up, and technological change eroded the bases of the European nation-

---

[1]Evan Luard, *War in International Society: A Study in International Sociology* (London: I. B. Tauris, 1986), pp. 50–51.

[2]Michael Walzer, *Just and Unjust War* (New York: Harper & Row, 1977), p. 35.

state system. Better guns took precedence over massed manpower, railroads became essential for strategy, and the telegraph put diplomats under close control by foreign ministries. Conscription provided large peacetime armies, and military costs rose with improving weaponry. Concurrently, liberal forces recovered from defeat, and the democratic mode and mentality spread. Foreign policy became increasingly subject to pressures of opinion.

Meanwhile, industrial civilization was spreading beyond its West European heartland. Across the Atlantic, the United States rose rapidly following its civil war; after 1890 it was the world's strongest economic power, although it remained for a long time almost a nonparticipant in world politics. Japan undertook rapid modernization after mid-century, when the United States forced it to open its doors and abandon two centuries of isolation. It made its debut on the international stage by seizing Taiwan from China in 1894. Russia, with a population growing to far outnumber the nations of Western Europe, accelerated economic development in the latter part of the 19th century, especially in the 1890s.

The major West European powers, as though in recognition of the rising importance of the overseas world, set out between 1870 and 1900 on a binge of land-grabbing, carving up almost all of the Afro-South Asian world not previously staked out. In three decades, Britain, France, and Belgium acquired 8 million square miles of new colonies, and Germany and the United States sliced off smaller portions.[3]

This thrust reflected a vastly increased ability, thanks to modern weapons, to work their will against non-European peoples. It was also competitive. Territory was desirable, but it was easily obtainable only overseas. When one country claimed lands, others felt they had to reach out for their share. It was assumed that modern states had to ensure their future by fencing off markets and sources of raw materials overseas, although most colonies had little of either. One acquisition led to another: to control the route to India, Britain had to dominate Egypt; to protect Egypt, it was necessary to secure the Sudan. Empire building also answered the urge of the modern states to expand not only their economic and political influence but also their culture worldwide.

Despite crises from time to time, Europe felt itself to be relatively happy and self-confident, with faith in endless progress, responsible government, and peace. At the beginning of this century, the nation-state was beloved as never before or since.[4]

---

[3]For an account of the acquisitions, see Daniel Chirot, *Social Change in the Modern Era* (New York: Harcourt Brace Jovanovich, 1986), pp. 76–80.

[4]Henry M. Pachter, *The Fall and Rise of Europe: A Political, Social, and Cultural History of the Twentieth Century* (New York: Praeger, 1975), p. 3.

The Great Wars

The peacekeeping balance between the leading powers was undermined by the 1870 victory of Prussia over France and the rise of a united Prussian-led Germany. In its growing industrial prowess, Germany demanded a grander place for itself and motivated a counteralliance of France and Russia. These secured the support by Britain, in large part because of the insistence of Germany on building a navy threatening to the insular United Kingdom. Germany formed its alliance with Austria-Hungary. Flexibility of maneuver was replaced by a standoff of two armed camps.

The unstable equilibrium broke down in 1914, and the long peace was followed by three convulsive decades until a new international system emerged after 1945. The proximate cause of World War I was the assassination of the crown prince of the Austro-Hungarian empire by a Serbian nationalist. That empire was a leftover of times when dynasties, not peoples, made states (it was built mostly by strategic marriages); and its rulers saw their multinational realm being torn apart by the forces of nationalism spreading from Western to Eastern and Southern Europe. Fearful of creeping dissolution, they resolved to take advantage of the act of terrorism and remove what they saw as the source of trouble, nationalistic independent Serbia, the magnet of the discontented Slavs in the empire, who had been left out of the Austro-Hungarian power structure.

The destruction of Serbia was intolerable for the Russians, who held themselves to be protectors of Slavs in general and had traditional interests in the Balkans. Moreover, the tsarist foreign minister had been humiliated a few years earlier by the Austrians' cavalier annexation of a disputed province. Hence, despite misgivings, the Russians mobilized to support Serbia. The militaristic German goverment felt duty-bound to reaffirm the old order by supporting its only important ally, Austria-Hungary; it also welcomed the opportunity to realize dreams of greatness and win the primacy it merited in world affairs. Consequently, Germany declared war against Russia and Russia's ally, France. When Germany marched into Belgium as the easiest road to Paris, Britain was brought into the conflict as semi-ally of France and guarantor of Belgian neutrality.[5]

With no memory of large-scale war, Europe stumbled into a general contest. Hardly anyone foresaw more than a few months of fighting, and there was much more huzzahing than foreboding. Although some statesmen

---

[5]On the calculations of the time, see Jack L. Snyder, "Perceptions of the Security Dilemma in 1914," in Robert Jervis, Richard N. Lebow, and Janice G. Stein, eds., *Psychology and Deterrence* (Baltimore: Johns Hopkins University Press, 1986), pp. 153–79.

were apprehensive, people in all belligerent capitals seemed "relieved that the strain of the armed peace was at last broken."[6]

The fighting dragged on with tremendous losses for over four years. Although people mostly regarded the struggle as being simply defense of their nation from the enemy, it was also a contest between traditional aristocratic authoritarianism and "bourgeois" liberalism, between monarchy and the new democratic nationalism.

For several years, thanks to German military prowess, the old order seemed to have the upper hand. The more modern-liberal Allies were victorious only with the help of the new trans-Atlantic giant, whom the Germans heedlessly brought into the fray. The United States entered the war in April 1917 ostensibly because of German submarine warfare, in reality because of sympathies for the freer societies of Britain and France, together with a feeling that it was time for the United States to play a fitting role in the world.

The victors sought to lay the groundwork for a new and better international order. The terms of peace were purportedly based on the principle of self-determination of peoples; and an international body, the League of Nations, was established to promote justice and security. Yet the peace brought less euphoria than malaise. The punishment of Europe was the more demoralizing because the enormous suffering seemed a purposeless fratricide. The dearly-bought victory produced disillusionment, bringing accepted values into question as never before. The way was opened for revolutionary movements, especially in the broken Russian empire. Economic troubles following the end of hostilities added to the discredit of the regnant order, even in the victorious countries.

For a few years, however, it seemed that the world might have come out of the war into relative tranquillity. Democratic governments came to power, albeit briefly in many lands, over all Europe west of Russia. In most countries, especially in France and Britain, pacifism flourished. The 1925 Locarno Pact between the principal West European nations seemed to mark genuine reconciliation of victors and vanquished. Most competition was in naval construction; but in the 1920s the chief naval powers, including Japan, reached agreements limiting their fleets. For a few years, the idea of war between modern states seemed unrealistic.

The outcome of the terrible contest was not decisive, however. The authoritarian, one might say antimodern, structures and mentality were set back but not destroyed; and they reasserted themselves in conditions of political and economic disorder. In Italy, Benito Mussolini's "March on Rome" in 1922 raised a growing specter of international thuggery, as Il Duce and his blackshirt militia shouted the new doctrine of fascism and

---

[6]Walter C. Langsam, *The World Since 1914* (New York: Macmillan, 1948), p. 19. [A German newspaper headlined, "It is a joy to be alive!" Barbara Tuchman, *The Guns of August* (New York: Macmillan, 1962), p. 121.]

their dreams of remaking the Roman empire. Various smaller countries of Eastern and Southern Europe also fell under fascistic or dictatorial rulers. In 1933, the depression brought Hitler, an imitator of Mussolini but a more fanatical racist-nationalist, to power in Germany. In reaction to defeat, humiliation, and unemployment, he mobilized the Germans to conquer Europe and whatever else he might. Britain and France showed their devotion to peace by attempting to satisfy the demands of the truculent power, but forthcomingness ("appeasement") only encouraged more demands. In 1939 the Nazis, in league with Italy and militaristic Japan, unleashed a new, truly global conflict.

The second round of the titanic struggle was materially more destructive than the first because of technological progress, but it was morally less devastating because the issues were clearer. On the one hand, the allies who called themselves "United Nations" not only defended their independent existence but also upheld ideals of decency, freedom, and constitutional government or democracy against would-be enslavers. On the other side, the Axis, or fascist, powers were battling rather frankly for domination over peoples they held inferior. The Germans showed remarkable strength of will and organization, and they reaped even more glorious triumphs than in WW I. In 1940–1941, the Hitlerites seemed to have virtually won the game, as Britain held out alone, thanks to the Channel, and the Soviet Union was cooperative with Germany. With a little moderation and political intelligence the Nazis might well have fixed their rule on the continent of Europe.

But dogmatic authoritarians are not usually gifted with moderation and political tact, and they willfully added to their enemies the Soviet Union and the United States. Russia, mobilized by Leninism and partly industrialized by Stalinism, together with the United States, aroused by Pearl Harbor, made possible the victory of what may reasonably be called the progressive side.

The New State System

This time the outcome was decisive. The old order was crushed, and the Europe-centered nation-state system was laid low. Two very large countries that before 1939 had played only a marginal role in international politics became superpowers, in the new terminology, and assumed almost unchallenged world dominance as none had ever done before. The international system became bipolar and truly global.

The downfall of the European system also brought an intellectual or spiritual shift from an essentially national focus to universalism. WWI began in the spirit of national rivalry; but because of the need, especially on the part of the liberal powers, to justify the sacrifices to their peoples, the cause was idealized. Wilson and the United States renounced territorial goals that other powers took for granted and proclaimed freedom ("self-determination") for all nations, in harmony with traditional American values. This idealism revived the morale of the weary Allied nations and did much to advance victory. The Russians also promoted a powerful and appealing universalist ideology. The Leninists stridently announced the passing of the nations and the supremacy of the universal class cause of the downtrodden masses, a modernized and popularized version of the old Russian mission of bringing civilization to many peoples.

The fascist powers were reacting in the 1930s against both of these ideals, asserting exaggerated and overbearing nationalism (Nazi racism being hypernationalism with a little pseudoscientific varnish), finding inspiration in imperial glories of the past, and glorifying arbitrary power. The Nazi episode of political and moral primitivism expressed profound negativism associated with the worst economic depression of modern times, which struck Germany harder than any other country. But defeat and the colossal atrocities of the Holocaust—Hilter's "final solution" for the Jews and other "inferior races"—discredited the consecration of narrowness and left the field to the claims of universal justice and rights for all, as exalted in different ways by the United States and the Soviet Union.

The quashing of the militarist-chauvinists in WW II and the downfall of the European power-political system opened the way to the unification of the once so jealously independent European nations. The European Economic Community (EEC) was inspired by the resolve that there must never again be an internecine European conflict. The values of *Deutschland über Alles* or *La Belle France* were not forgotten, but they retreated to the background. The *grandeur* of France, despite de Gaulle's efforts to resuscitate it in the 1960s, seems antiquarian, like the glories of the British empire.

In the EEC, Europe became an economic power equal to the United States; but it virtually renounced a world-political role. The European countries permitted their grand and hard-won colonial empires to be broken up in the generation after 1945. Their offspring were a host of mostly powerless states, multiplying several fold the number of "independent" actors. In the novel global system that emerged, the ability to project important physical power well beyond the national borders was practically limited to the two states known as superpowers. The international system thus became unbalanced as never before, with two players holding almost all the ultimate destructive power, some two dozen possessing nearly all the wealth, and more than a hundred-fifty claiming full legal rights as sovereign entities.

The Great Contest

At the end of WW II, it was not difficult to understand that it would be to the benefit of all powers, especially the United States and the Soviet Union, to cooperate in the maintenance of world order and the building of better international relations. It was possible for the superpowers to agree on a few things, principally the zones of occupation of the respective armies and the establishment of a somewhat strengthened version of the old League, a formalization of the wartime alliance called "United Nations." However, the political philosophies and values of the Soviet Union, led by Stalin, and the United States and its allies (chiefly Britain) were so different that meeting of minds was difficult and misunderstanding was very easy. Even if the two sides had been political brothers, there was ample cause for contention in rivalry for influence over the vast regions whose political institutions had been destroyed by the war, especially in Central and Eastern Europe. When the two sides claimed general validity for completely incompatible ideas of how society should be organized, contestation was inevitably bitter.

The first and one of the most important areas of competition was Germany, about three-fourths of which was occupied by the Western powers, one-fourth (after the transfer of extensive territories to Poland) by Soviet forces. It was proposed that the United States, Britain, France, and the Soviet Union set up a joint government with its capital in Berlin; but the two sides desired completely different political futures for the Germans. The occupying forces imposed their conflicting institutions, and two Germanies went opposite ways in ill feeling; what was dubbed the "Iron Curtain" was drawn across the land. Further friction was caused by differences over Eastern Europe. The United States accepted that the Soviet Union was entitled to have friendly neighbors but not that it had the right to impose its rule and its economic and political system on the countries it occupied. This feeling was strongest in regard to Poland, the state in defense of which the Western powers had gone to war in 1939.

The Soviet Union, however, moved step by step, by unfree elections and elimination of oppositions, to make East Germany, Poland, Hungary, Romania, and Bulgaria into something like small copies of itself under little Stalins. In 1948, the Communists of Czechoslovakia, feeling that the country was turning against them, carried out a coup and extended the Iron Curtain along their western border. Moscow seemed to have acquired a rich new empire. The Western powers, especially the United States, were angered but unwilling to go to war to press the Soviets back.

The Soviets and their allies tried to round out their dominion of Eastern Europe with Greece, where a Communist-led rebellion came near toppling a pro-Western government. In response, the United States proclaimed in 1947 the Truman Doctrine, a promise of support not only for Greece and Turkey (from which the Soviet Union was demanding territory) but for all peoples threatened by foreign-supported communism.[7]

---

[7]For an account, see John L. Gaddis, *The Long Peace: Inquiries into the History of the Cold War* (New York: Oxford University Press, 1987).

Not easily deterred, the Soviets in 1948 tried to force the Western powers out of the sections of Berlin they held, on grounds that they were not entitled to share in what was not the capital of a united Germany. Instead of driving a column overland to the relief of the besieged part-city, the United States organized an impressive airlift; and the Soviets were compelled to back down. Still the Soviets found it hard to give up hopes of getting the Western powers out of Berlin, and they pressed their demands from time to time even after Stalin died in 1953 and Khrushchev gave a somewhat more enlightened look to Soviet foreign policy.

By 1955 it was possible, however, to agree on the neutralization of Austria, until then jointly occupied by the victor powers. The partitioning of Europe between the two spheres was fairly well settled and accepted, as was shown by the American acceptance of Soviet crushing of the Hungarian uprising in 1956.

The contest went on in less developed regions, which came to be called the "Third World," especially in the new nations coming out of the former colonial empires that covered a large part of the globe at the beginning of WW II. Although the imperial powers would have liked to hold onto their possessions, they had been too much weakened (or had been removed as in the case of Asian colonies conquered by the Japanese) and had lost much of their will to rule alien lands. Moreover, the peoples of the colonies had heard about rights. In the 19th century, Asians and Africans submitted more or less passively to small European forces; in the postwar period they organized "national liberation movements" or, if agitation did not move the colonial power, undertook guerrilla warfare.

There consequently appeared on the world scene scores of new sovereignties whose political complexion was uncertain. The effort to influence them, or the anxiety to prevent the other side from dominating them, led to a prolonged rivalry between the superpowers. This brought war in Korea and Vietnam and dangers of war elsewhere, as in the Near East. Mostly, however, the competition was nonviolent. The United States sought to help countries develop in a manner that would keep them from turning in desperation to communism. The nations of the world were called upon to decide between good and evil; Secretary of State John Foster Dulles proclaimed that neutrality was "immoral." The Soviet Union was at first concerned only with contiguous lands; but after the passing of Stalin in 1953 it strove to lure uncommitted nations to adhere to its "camp of peace" and follow its model of development, thus swinging an ever-larger part of humanity to the Soviet side.

The "free world," or the West, was much the stronger, for many years militarily and always economically; but the East, or Soviet block, was willing to spend a larger part of its resources on military power and upheld a doctrine of universal class conflict mixed with Russian-inspired messianic authoritarianism. The Soviet-led side was not notably successful, but it was sufficiently dynamic to rouse the United States from relaxation in victory to partially remobilize and make "containment" of communism the focus of its foreign policy. This implied something new in the history of international relations, a prolonged conflict without military engagement of the principals, or the "cold war."

This was intense through the 1950s, and it was heightened by hot war in Korea. It reached a climax in the missile crisis of October 1962, when the superpowers came nearest, in the postwar era, to armed conflict. It was somewhat eased as the United States pulled back in disillusionment over the fiasco of Vietnam and the Nixon administration came to a degree of detente with Leonid Brezhnev's Soviet Union in 1972. Antagonism revived in the latter 1970s because of the Soviet arms buildup and Soviet success in using conflicts in Africa to win the adherence of Mozambique, Angola, and Ethiopia. The invasion of Afghanistan in December 1979 further aggravated relations between the United States and the Soviet Union. It was followed by the election of a forthright anticommunist as American president in 1980, and the cold war seemed perhaps more bitter than ever.

Thus for more than 30 years it was generally believed that superpower bipolarity was the great fact of international affairs, that this represented a contest between radical and conservative forces, and that this was a permanent feature of world politics. These beliefs were all erroneous. The bipolar clash did not have a great deal to do with developments on the world scene except sporadically and in the first years of the cold war. As regards political purposes, neither side was progressive in the sense of being disposed to institutional reform or experimentation; the difference was between the more regimented-authoritarian East and the more open-individualistic West. And bipolarity, stable as it seemed, was always artificial, resting solely on military power that was essentially unusable. It had eventually to wear out and give way to a configuration more consonant with economic reality.

Classic International Relations

The highest obligation of the state has traditionally been to protect the homeland and its people from foreign attack, which could mean enslavement or death. Externally, the chief, sometimes almost the only, business of the state was defense, which was treated as equivalent to power and prestige, although these did not necessarily contribute to security. The acquisition of a territory was desirable, regardless of enmities it might cause.

As the nation-states contended on the European scene through the 18th and 19th centuries, there was some feeling like that of rival teams of a football league. It was accepted that states had enemies, whatever the cause of hostility; at the same time, the competing sovereignties saw themselves as civilized Christian states set off against a culturally and morally inferior outside world. Their contentions were part of the national being, always interesting, seldom very dangerous. They energized the society and occupied the otherwise unengaged highborn. In the late Middle Ages, kings felt they had to undertake campaigns from time to time to occupy restive nobles; in later centuries, naval buildups and colonial wars to some extent served parallel purposes.

Leadership in war was the original title to kingship, and the conduct of foreign affairs has been peculiarly the province of the ruler. British monarchs, for example, insisted through the 19th century in having a say in foreign policy long after they had quite surrendered domestic policy to the ministers approved by parliament. Dealing with foreign powers is the most intriguing business of government; and rulers, with their cabinets, assuredly liked it, as they still do. Foreign affairs well into this century were for the aristocrats, who provided the high officers and diplomats even in relatively democratic countries such as Britain and France. The two categories worked together and complemented one another, making alliances, war, and peace.

Traditional Diplomacy

The detailing of envoys to other countries is as old as history, but the practice of permanently stationing official representatives in foreign capitals arose in the Renaissance, about the same time as the European state system was taking shape. The role of the diplomat rose to its highest courtly refinement in the 18th century.[8] A large body of custom has grown up around diplomatic (and consular) representation in order to define procedures and to avoid misunderstandings. Like the military, the diplomatic profession is steeped in tradition and etiquette or protocol—wars have been threatened over whose carriage went in front of whose. Formalities may become overpowering even in recent times. Negotiations with the North Vietnamese in 1972 were stalled for 10 weeks by a dispute over the shape of the conference table—whether it was to be square, oval, or circular, because it was thought that the seating arrangement might give a symbolic advantage to one side or the other.[9] Yet not merely was the geometry of the table irrelevant; the agreement laboriously hammered out had no effect except to serve as a cover for the withdrawal of American forces from Vietnam.

The rules of diplomatic protocol are usually observed scrupulously because powers realize that it is in their interest to maintain the procedures of their dealings. Even in wartime, diplomats and their rights have almost

---

[8]Concerning the history, see Harold Nicolson, *The Evolution of Diplomacy* (New York: Collier Books, 1966).

[9]Morgenthau, *Politics among Nations*, p. 81.

always been fully respected. Diplomatic immunity extends not only to diplomats and their baggage but also to family and servants, to the annoyance of those charged with enforcement of traffic and parking regulations. Diplomatic pouches have been abused for smuggling of drugs and arms for terrorists, even wanted persons; yet their integrity is respected. It was a shocking lapse when, in November 1979, Iranian militants backed by their government took over the American embassy in Teheran and held the diplomats hostage.

Diplomatic immunities are intended in part to protect secrecy, confidentiality of communications between diplomats and governments being deemed essential. Secrecy has always been traditional in foreign affairs, since they were the province of kings and their private cabinets. In the age of democracy, it is commonly felt that the people have the right to know what is being connived behind closed doors. However, negotiations become difficult if the negotiators speak to the public at home and abroad and take positions for their media value. President Wilson called for "open covenants openly arrived at," but when he became chief negotiator of the peace treaties, he forgot this idealistic position.[10] On the other hand, it is politic to keep the public informed so far as possible and to involve interested parties. If Wilson had done this, the Senate would hardly have committed what most historians regard as the error of refusing to ratify the Treaty of Versailles.

The tradition of diplomatic professionalism persists today. Foreign offices and foreign services are highly trained and rather exclusive. Some of this tradition, coming from the practice of the tsarist empire, carried over into the Soviet Union, or was revived by it; the Soviet specialists in foreign affairs are decidedly more professionalized than the American. The United States, feeling little threatened through most of its history and distrustful of aristocratic ways, has been and to a considerable degree still is more amateurish.

Nationalism

"International" relations refer to nations, and we often speak of powers, countries, and nations as equivalent. The safety and prosperity of the nation is supposedly the supreme desideratum. But it is often unclear what constitutes a nation.

There are two aspects, the formal and the informal. A nation on the world stage is a government, recognized as sovereign over a fixed territory and its inhabitants. This has usually sufficed. But when in modern times the feelings or opinions of a large number of persons has to be taken into account, the other aspect comes to the fore: a nation is a population that

---

[10]John Stoessinger, *The Might of Nations: World Politics in Our Time*, 6th ed. (New York: Random House, 1982), pp. 203-4.

feels itself to belong together apart from other peoples. This feeling has been based commonly on language: Swedes are those who regard themselves as Swedish, mostly because that is their native language, even if they reside in Finland. The Japanese know very well who is Japanese, and they deny that classification to families that may have lived for generations in Japan (unless, in recent times, they take prescribed legal steps to assimilate themselves, which includes assuming a Japanese name). Nations may also be based on a shared history and the corresponding sense of community. The best example is Switzerland: Swiss are very much Swiss although they speak French in Geneva, German in Zurich, or Italian in Lugano, because they have stood together for centuries in defense of their independence and freedom. Belgium is not such a good example, as the French-speaking Walloons coexist somewhat uneasily with the Flemings, who speak a variant of Dutch; nonetheless, having formed a state since 1830 has sufficed to mold a Belgian nationality.

Nations of Spanish America, sharing language and the Hispanic cultural heritage, have had only a political basis. When the region became independent early in the 19th century, administrative divisions of the Spanish empire set themselves up as independent entities, and people gradually became accustomed to regarding themselves as Venezuelans, Peruvians, or Mexicans. The nationality, nonetheless, is not totally distinct but a subdivision of the Latin American category. Countries of sub-Saharan Africa are still more artificial, being based on arbitrary colonial boundaries taking little or no account of a great variety of ethnic-linguistic groups. The nation is rather superficial; for many years to come, the inhabitants of Uganda (for example) are not likely to feel themselves as a single people but as members of the Ganda, Soga, Acholi, or another of the many ethnicities. People of Nigeria refer to themselves as Nigerians when outside the country; at home, they are rather Yoruba, Igbo, Fulani, and so forth.

The difference between nation as state and as community is critical in the case of Yugoslavia, which is a federation of eight rather autonomous republics, each with its own language (although all are South-Slavic and fairly closely related) and two autonomous regions, with Hungarian and Albanian majorities. Under a strong leader, Tito, with a degree of ideological commitment, the country was governable; in his absence and in the decay of internationalist-communist ideology, it seems ungovernable. People regard themselves as Serbs, Croats, Slovenes, and so forth, not as Yugoslavs; and it is difficult to secure agreement on anything. The Soviet Union faces a similar problem, as many peoples have little love for the Russians, who are less than a majority. This problem plagued the old Russian empire; Lenin tried to solve it by proclaiming his new state not a nation but an international movement of the proletariat. But no one believes any longer in proletarian internationalism.

Nationalism is the feeling that we are different from others; it is consequently hard to distinguish cultural separatism from racism. Cultural as-similation may override racial difference; Guatemalans of Indian race be-come acceptable to the mestizo rulership by speaking Spanish, dressing in European fashion, and acting like non-Indians, or ladinos. One can hardly guess how much of the antagonism between Chinese and Malays is due to difference of language, religion, and customs, and how much to physical appearance. The would-be internationalist ideology of Marxism is equally powerless to surmount nationalism and racism; African students encounter bitter anger when they date native girls in Moscow. The joy of helping the underprivileged of the world does not deter Chinese students from rioting fiercely against Third World fellow-students, who get larger stipends.[11]

The United States has been more successful than any other nation in overriding the differences of ethnic background and race by a common American nationality based on faith in freedom and democracy, a faith for-tified by the prosperity and power of the conglomerate nation and its proud standing in the world. It is easy to be loyal to the richest and most respected of nations, where life becomes ever more abundant. Yet even in the United States, nasty manifestations of prejudice recur. Serious differences might emerge if the national ideal should lose its strength and its capacity to ce-ment the union of diverse elements.

The diversity of America's people is a primordial fact limiting or shap-ing its foreign policy. For example, it was a deterrent to mixing in European affairs prior to WW I. When the United States entered the war, it had to be on the basis not of a strictly national interest, which would be differently interpreted by people of different ethnic origin, but of defending freedom and democracy. As further immigration alters the character of the United States as a nation, with the growth of minorities of African, Hispanic Ameri-can, and East Asian background, the character of American foreign policy—possibly the ability to have a coherent foreign policy—must be affected.

In sum, the concept of sovereign nations, each with its own language and culture, grew up in the European state system, especially in the 19th and early 20th centuries. It has now lost some of its validity in its homeland, as nations of Western Europe transfer part of their sovereignty to the Eco-nomic Community. In time there may develop something of a European identity, with a sense of superiority to Russians and Americans, but this is not likely to be intense. Many peoples around the world have taken up the principle of nationalism, at times with great feeling. The Koreans, for example, have a very strong idea of Koreanism. On the other hand, nation-alistic divisions within the state may be ruinous. In Sri Lanka, being Tamil or Sinhalese is cause enough to murder or be murdered. On the other hand, for many countries the lack of any real sense of nationhood makes much

[11]*New York Times*, December 27, 1988, p. 1.

more difficult the integration of society and the construction of a sound political order.

Nationalism is generally thought of as a good thing, or at least acceptable; to act on nationalistic grounds is proper, as long as other nations are not assaulted. If the Soviet Union is seen pursuing ideological purposes, this raises profound distrust; if it seeks strictly nationalistic goals, it is at least understandable. Nationalism may be necessary for the integration of society; we do not know how well we could manage without the social bond of feeling ourselves akin in an important way, as we are Americans, or British, or Brazilian, set at least a little apart from the other peoples of this planet. In the world at large, however, the national idea seems increasingly ambiguous; it may be argued that nationalism is somewhat backward, a contradiction to modernism. It is a doubtful basis of international practice.

Chapter 2

The Conflictual World

Aggressiveness

Throughout history, whenever independent states of comparable strength have been in close contact, there have been competition and friction, culminating from time to time in wars, frequently purposeless in terms of material interests. This has been the case even when the sovereignties were rather similar, sharing language, culture, and religion. For example, the numerous ancient Greek city-states worshipped the same gods, recited the same epics, had fairly similar political institutions, and met in pan-Hellenic festivals, such as the Olympic games. Yet they warred frequently, sometimes changing alignments but never finding a stable peace, although their contests were usually not desperate and did not ordinarily threaten the lives of either civilians or states. Similarly, the little republics of medieval and renaissance Italy, although they had very much in common, were perpetually bickering and intriguing against one another and often fighting, sometimes as though for fun. In the postwar period, it has been very difficult for the United States and the Soviet Union to recognize that they have every reason to compromise whatever differences may exist, no reason to threaten one another with annihilation.

The underlying reason for this perversity is the same as that which keeps the lion from coexisting idyllically not only with the lamb but also with lions of other prides. Tribal-aggressive instincts and territorial imperatives seem to be rooted in the human as well as in the animal psyche. Some psychologists believe aggressive drives are inborn and instinctual, independent of culture or reason, related to the will to power, akin to but beyond libido. The failure to release the psychic energy of aggressiveness supposedly causes psychopathologies and neuroses.[1]

Although most societies are rather peaceful and socialization and education inhibit physical aggression,[2] competitiveness is everywhere. Whether or not there is actual fighting or will to injure or destroy the opponent, contest is part of life, from the deadly wars of ant colonies to those of great powers, from the duels of elk at rutting season to the mutual battering of the boxing ring. There is rivalry and ill feeling between neighbors, colleagues, siblings, and sometimes spouses.

Competitive-aggressive urges find different outlets. The semiritualized conventional vengeance of families in Sicily, Appalachia, or Pakistan doubtless owes much to the pleasures of the hunt. The mores of the vendetta would not be upheld if many people did not find it interesting and exciting, like the duels of honor of early modern Europe. Juvenile gangs fight for turf or for the thrills of fighting. According to a columnist, prisoners in a Los Angeles jail carry on the hatreds of the slums; "as in the neighborhoods, Crips, who wear blue accessories, would slaughter on sight Bloods wearing any of their trademark red. Why? No reason is required. Atavism often is a sufficient explanation for the random 'drive by' shootings that are a favorite mode of self-expression. There is, of course, the traditional territorial imperative, the gangs' struggle for 'turf'."[3]

It is pleasant to get the better of others, to join in a team contest of some kind, or to fight for a cause; it is most gratifying if one can humiliate or injure others while doing good. CEOs fight to get ahead of rivals, both personal and corporate. Market share may mean as much as profits, and takeover magnates show something of the motivation of colony grabbers of the 19th century. If one doesn't like a fight, there is no point in getting into politics.

Hatred is a powerful and satisfying emotion, not only against those who have wronged us but often against those whom we have wronged. As in the classic vendettas, it persists long beyond its utility. The United States, for example, remained unflinchingly hostile to Communist China ("Chicoms") a dozen years after the Sino-Soviet split made it sensible realpolitik to improve relations with the less threatening of the communist giants.

---

[1]Konrad Lorenz, *On Aggression* (New York: Harcourt Brace and World, 1966), passim.

[2]Samuel S. Kim, "The Lorenzian Theory of Aggression and Peace Research," in *The War System: An Interdisciplinary Approach*, ed. Richard Falk and Samuel S. Kim (Boulder, CO: Westview, 1980), pp. 84–97.

[3]George F. Will, "A 'West Coast Story'," *Newsweek*, March 28, 1988, p. 76.

Communism had to be simple, united, and changeless; and the apparent division had to be a charade to deceive the West. Enmity toward Vietnam has similarly outlasted the reasons for it. On the other side, the entire Soviet approach of antagonism toward the "capitalist" world, which was cultivated during the early revolutionary period and the Allied anti-Soviet intervention of 1918–1919, became pointless after the failure of the revolutionary movement in Europe in the early 1920s; but it has taken the Soviet leadership decades to grow out of it.

The visceral feeling that we are different and in some indefinable way superior is universal. So far as Russians retreat from Leninism, they tend to reassert Russianism. Melanesians and Indians in Fiji remain separate and antagonistic communities through generations, like Africans and East Indians in Guyana. In Malaysia, the Chinese are denied full citizenship. The United States is rare in welcoming immigration and taking pride in a multiracial society. Until humans change character, relations among tribes and nations will not lack animosity.

Coexistence is most contentious when a group that regards itself as superior feels threatened in its existence or status by inferiors. For example, South Africans of European extraction are terrified by the idea of giving power to the Black majority; Jewish Israelis fear an eventual Arab majority that would bring to an end the Jewish state. When different races have little in common, even relatively cultivated and moderate peoples, such as Americans and Australians, have shown themselves capable of sadistic cruelty and brutal massacres.[4]

The goal may be less to gain something for ourselves than to have the satisfaction of injuring the enemy, to make him cry "uncle" or run away in disgrace, if not to die ignobly. If we were merely seeking material gains, we would endeavor to make our desires acceptable to the other side. But when we are aroused to win the game, it is preferable to rub in the victory, whatever the cost. For example, the Allies insisted on the costly and ineffective firebombing of German cities in WW II partly because the policy was never critically evaluated, partly because of the pleasure of dishing out punishment to the enemy. The United Nations also proudly refused to consider anything short of unconditional surrender of the Axis powers in WW II, enabling Nazi propagandists to convince their people that they could only fight on because surrender was equivalent to death. It would have been enough to propose terms sufficient to disarm the enemy; when he was disarmed, one could impose whatever conditions necessary. (Japanese surrender was actually made conditional on respecting the position of the emperor.) Unconditional surrender may have cost millions of lives, but it satisfied the thirst for total triumph.

The international contention of our day has some of the spirit of a

---

[4]Jared Diamond, "In Black and White," *Natural History* 97, October 1988, pp. 8–14.

game, with contenders forever looking at the scorecard.[5] Many writers on international relations use the word "game" to describe their subject, without intending to detract from the seriousness and realism of it all.[6] In the "razzle-dazzle ground game," as one writer has it, "Moscow's strategy for Super-Summit, the biggest football game of the season, can be summed up in three words: Move the ball. The Moscow Maverix, under the leadership of Mike 'Gorby' Gorbachev will try to keep the pressure on veteran Gipper Reagan and his Washington team, gaining yardage wherever possible. The stakes for defeat are high, since under the unique rules of this league, the following game will start with the score and field position with which this game leaves off ... "[7] Fans will travel a thousand miles to a crucial game and celebrate wildly the triumph of the team with which they identify without ever having had any personal contact; in international rivalries, the fascination of cockfighting or hockey is compounded by patriotism, idealism, and feelings of nobility. If there is synthetic drama in organized sports, there is far more human drama in the great game of nations.

We do not have to ask why we play; the competition is the why. As we become fully engrossed in winning, the enemy is dehumanized, although we like to think of him as always cunning and dangerous. Violence attracts and fascinates even as it sometimes horrifies. Love of it is reason enough to pay huge prices to watch two men pummel one another for a minute or so in the boxing ring. Those who are captivated by it or accept it are the admirable toughies; those who would deny it or try to avoid it are the softies, to be scorned as men of action scorn impractical intellectuals and mushy idealists.

This predilection had much to do with the extraordinary concentration of American policy in the 1980s on military conflicts in El Salvador and Nicaragua. The administration chose to assist the military opposition to the leftist government of Nicaragua instead of the moderate domestic civilian sectors, who had better chances of bringing change. It would be more charming to see the Sandinistas chased out of Managua by our heroes than to have them overcome by economic hardships or tamed by political processes. Meanwhile, the administration took some interest in the economic and social problems of Central America only because of their relation to the military problem; and much larger difficulties of South America, such as the foreign debt, were neglected.

A neat bombing of an unpopular power, such as Libya or Iran, is popular; and a democratic politician who prefers caution risks appearing weak.

[5]Robert Ehrlich, *Waging Nuclear Peace: The Technology and Politics of Nuclear Weapons* (Albany: State University of New York, 1985), p. 16.

[6]For example, Zbigniew Brzezinski, *Game Plan: The Geostrategic Framework for the Conduct of the U. S.-Soviet Contest* (Boston: Atlantic Monthly Press, 1986).

[7]Frank J. Gaffney Jr., "Soviet Playbook: Razzle-Dazzle Ground Game," *Wall Street Journal,* December 8, 1987, p. 28.

In the 19th century, when there was little fear of serious warfare, the press, public opinion, and parliaments were usually more belligerent than governments.[8] People admire macho leaders, at least as long as costs are low.

Indeed, they may be persuaded to accept very high costs and terrible suffering with remarkable passivity when they have become inured; violence has great inertia when it becomes part of life. No one could move to stop the senseless slaughter of WW I; the war of attrition became simply a contest to see who would have the most survivors, with no possible positive gain proportionate to the torment. The Germans kept fighting and dying in WW II long after it was evident that no purpose was served by doing so, sheepishly obedient to Hitler when he had obviously become the greatest failure of German history.

Groups seeking to assert their identity, such as Sikh or Basque separatists, often believe violence useful or indispensable. Terrorists exaggerate what they can gain by bombings and assassinations; they could probably achieve more by peaceful agitation and gradual enlargement of their rights. But they feel the need to draw lines, to compel commitment, even to invite the countermeasures of the enemy. Radicals have often justified terrorism on grounds that it would provoke the tyranny to repression, which would lead the people to join the terrorists in revolution. This is not a reason but an excuse; the record shows that the people are repelled by the terrorism and view the repression as justified.

Seeking to define its cause by violence, the South in 1861 began hostilities by attacking Fort Sumter. It could almost certainly have withdrawn peacefully from the union by negotiation and simple refusal of cooperation. There had been strong inclinations in Lincoln's government to evacuate the fortress, which posed no threat to South Carolina. No one in the North would have demanded a war to collect federal taxes in recalcitrant states. But many were prepared after the attack to answer the call to arms. The shelling and bloodshed shocked the North and thrilled the South, and the war was on.[9]

War

It has often been said that war is inevitable, or at least that conflict is inherent in the nature of humans and nations.[10] It is reminiscent of the territorial

---

[8]Evan Luard, *War in International Society: A Study in International Sociology,* (London: I. B. Tauris, 1986), p. 220.

[9]Peter J. Parish, *The American Civil War* (New York: Holmes and Meier, 1975), pp. 76–78.

[10]Stephen Kull, *Minds at War: Nuclear Reality and the Inner Conflicts of Defense Policymakers* (New York: Basic Books, 1988), pp. 238–43.

instincts extremely common in birds and mammals. Our nearest relatives, the chimpanzees, stop fighting viciously among themselves to make forays against neighboring bands and murder the vanquished.[11] There seems to have been much conflict among paleolithic hunter-gatherers, and primitive peoples are usually warlike. Their clashes may be very brutal; raiders sometimes slaughter anyone they can, including women and infants.[12] Their warring has a great variety of motives, including fear and dislike of strangers, or no real motive at all. Some primitive societies seem very pacific, but they are few.[13]

War is sometimes an outlet for energetic men desirous of displaying valor without too much danger of death, like a tournament with no judge in the stands.[14] Warfare among primitives is often a traditional and stylized social activity, calling for prolonged preparations, body painting, dancing, and shouting; it is quite different from intragroup aggression.[15] When the stakes have been low, as in the battles between cities of the Italian Renaissance and the parade-style wars of Europe in the 18th century, there is little need for bloodshed. When men become convinced that they must kill or be killed, war becomes mass murder.

Even if there is no real thought of slaughtering people, possession of military force is the most impressive way of asserting the national claim to right and prestige in the world. It can be openly displayed or subtly brandished; but particularly for the less sophisticated, destructive power is the most impressive measure of standing.[16]

Until this century, war was usually regarded as rather healthy, an exercise in which virtues combine.[17] According to Ralph Waldo Emerson, "War educates the senses, calls into action the will, perfects the physical constitution, and brings men into such swift and close collision that man measures man."[18] In the 19th century some saw war as the Darwinist means of selec-

---

[11]Michael Ghiglieri, "War among the Chimpanzees," *Discover* 8, November 1987, pp. 66–78.

[12]Irenaus Eibl-Eibesfeldt, *The Biology of Peace and War* (New York: Viking Press, 1979), pp. 127–31, 170–74.

[13]Seyom Brown, *The Causes and Prevention of War* (New York: St. Martins Press, 1987), p. 14.

[14]Michael Walzer, *Just and Unjust War: A Moral Argument with Historical Interpretations* (New York: Harper & Row, 1978), p. 25.

[15]As in New Guinea. Edward Li Puma, "War in the Guinea Highlands," Diane McGuinness, ed., *Dominance, Aggression, and War* (New York: Paragon House, 1987), p. 184.

[16]For an exhaustive study of war, see Quincy Wright, *A Study of War*, 2nd. ed. (Chicago: University of Chicago Press, 1965); see also Michael Howard, *The Causes of War and Other Essays* (Cambridge: Harvard University Press, 1983), and Brown, *The Causes and Prevention of War*.

[17]As noted by William James, "The Moral Equivalent of War," in *William James, The Essential Writings*, ed. Bruce W. Wilshire (Albany: State University of New York Press, 1984), pp. 353–54.

[18]Ralph Waldo Emerson, *Complete Works*, vol. XI (Boston: Houghton Mifflin, 1876), p. 152.

tion of the fittest, without considering whether those slain were really to be deemed unfit. In our time, war or readiness for it serves to some extent as the certification of technological prowess.

Nations have been more driven to war by emotions than lured by goals, as observed by Clausewitz.[19] War is thrilling in absolutism, when our destiny is at stake and all are called upon to give their utmost for the greatest cause. Soldiers hate its suffering but love its excitement and the most moving camaraderie of which humans are capable.[20] The zest of arms fills the pages of such magazines as *Soldier of Fortune* and *Military*. In war, differences and divisions disappear, and the highest altruism—self-sacrifice for nation or buddies—comes to the fore.[21] As soon as the horrors fade from memory, the hankering for heroic violence returns.

War legitimizes forbidden things. Not only is the soldier invited to kill; he is pardoned for rape and robbery (looting). War gives emotional security in physical danger; it is the antidote to the tedious, wearisome boredom of civilized life. Even in the midst of the gore, many have found joy in battle.[22] The soldier of today is not likely to have the pleasure of plunging steel into the guts of the vile enemy, hardly even that of popping off a man with a well-aimed rifle shot; but there are thrills for those who handle marvellous machines like modern aircraft.

With tales of peril and great feats, of good battling evil to the death, war and martial glory serve modern television as they served Homeric bards. Most of us have had no direct experience of war; but it competes well, as material for melodrama, with amorous triangles. The American civil war has evoked thousands of books, and it has its cultists 125 years after its end. Scholars like to study and recount the martial deeds of characters so unlike themselves and feel themselves sharing the fellowship of the strong and manly.[23] Children love toy tanks and rayguns. Young men, and many not so young, delight in war games, as nearly real-life as possible. The scheming of violence is entrancing; for the more adventurous, there may even be some unconscious enjoyment of the risk of unspeakable destruction.[24]

[19]Richard N. Lebow, "Clausewitz and Nuclear Crisis Stability," *Political Science Quarterly* 103 (Spring 1988), p. 90.

[20]J. Glenn Gray, *The Warriors: Reflections on Men in Battle* (New York: Harcourt Brace and Co., 1959), pp. 28, 52.

[21]Erich Fromm, *The Anatomy of Human Aggression* (New York: Holt Rinehart and Winston, 1973), p. 214.

[22]Sam Keen, *Faces of the Enemy: Reflections of the Hostile Imagination* (San Francisco: Harper & Row, 1986), p. 69.

[23]Robert Nisbet, *Twilight of Authority* (New York: Oxford University Press, 1975), pp. 154–74.

[24]As Stephen Kull contends in "Nuclear Arms and the Desire for World Destruction," *Political Psychology* 4, no. 3, 1983.

The conflict preferably revolves around ideologies and personalities; we love to hate a Hitler or a Stalin, a wicked personality who is the odious incarnation of a vile idea. It was unfortunate in WW II that Americans had no particular Japanese individual to hold up as symbol of the wickedness of the nation. Emperor Hirohito was chiefly interested in marine biology, and Prime Minister Tojo was too colorless. On the other hand, we exalt and identify with noble figures on our side, such as the inspiring courage and determination of a Churchill in the cause of freedom. With less reason, Germans and Russians in WW II had the deepest faith in Hitler and Stalin.

The decision to sacrifice lives is bound up with rage and pride. The Austrians opened the First World War not only because they calculated that crushing Serbia was necessary to preserve their dilapidated multinational dominion but also because they were angry. The Russians had no strong material interest in coming to the aid of Serbia, and Austria was no conceivable threat to their territory, but they resolved to stand by a small Slavic state assaulted by a Germanic power, and the Austrians were archrivals. Warned that war might mean the end of his dynasty, Tsar Nicholas hesitated but felt that honor required action. The German Kaiser could have let Austria and Russia fight it out, but he deemed it unworthy not to support his ally. He also wanted to call the tsar's bluff. Hitler did Roosevelt a favor after Pearl Harbor by declaring war on the United States, indulging his fury with no benefit to his cause.

We must stand together as a team, and doubters are next to traitors. When preparations for the Bay of Pigs affair were under discussion (1961), those who asked the wrong questions were told abuptly to stand up or get out.[25] President Johnson heaped scorn on the "nervous Nellies" in debates about Vietnam.

The prize of victory is the gratitude of the nation and the praise of history. For this, President Johnson became obsessed with selecting targets in a poor and backward Asian country that had no desire to be part of any general Sino-Soviet conspiracy (when these powers were spitting at each other), had nothing against the United States (to which Ho Chi Minh once looked as a model), and was of no particular importance to this country.

If there were no need to stand up to foreign power, would society cohere? An absence of sense of national engagement and danger, leading to superficiality of nationalism and disinclination to sacrifice personal for national welfare, may be a major cause of the social and political problems of Latin America. For the Philippines, lack of national pride makes an unproductive or self-destructive culture.[26] Foreign policy occupies much more popular attention than warranted by the material effects of ordinary inter-

---

[25]John Ranelagh, *The Agency: The Rise and Decline of the CIA* (New York: Simon and Schuster, 1986), p. 367.

[26]James Fallow, "A Damaged Culture," *Atlantic* 260, November 1987, pp. 49–58.

national affairs on our lives; and if the domestic scene is tranquil, foreign engagement may be the more necessary as an energizer.

Nonetheless, war is not essential for the health of the nation. Such admirable countries as Switzerland and the Scandinavian countries have escaped it for a very long time, and others have been involved in war only when they have been assaulted.

The Truculent State

Aggressiveness tamed within the group is turned outward. Organizations contend with one another, seeking to expand their spheres or increase their influence; bureaucratic agencies and churches do so no less than industrial corporations and trade unions. The most encompassing and compelling of organizations are sovereign states; and conflict is built into any system of independent states interacting and seeking advantages without legal restraint. Leaders promote the political, economic, and strategic interests of their respective nations and thereby their own prestige and legitimacy, in a contest for advantages if not for supremacy. Strength, even if it cannot rationally be put to use, asserts national greatness.

War in modern times is always nominally defensive. All contestants in 1914 claimed and probably believed they were acting for the salvation of the motherland. In 1939, Hitler proclaimed that he was driven to invade Poland in response to Polish incursions, and he had Germans in Polish uniform fake a raid to prove it. He was driven to attack the Soviet Union to remove a terrible menace. As soon as fighting begins, of course, we have to kill those who would kill us. All military purpose is commonly called "defense"; there are no ministries of offense.

Sometimes, as in Hitler's case, the claim of acting defensively can be dismissed as hypocrisy. But ordinarily, each side sees a different set of facts or supposed facts. Each places the worst interpretation on the other's intentions and capabilities, and it is easy for both to regard themselves as acting in legitimate self-defense. Moreover, a state may be drawn into taking a bellicose initiative not because it is expansive but because it is declining and fears future dangers. Such a feeling, of course, lay behind Austria-Hungary's decision for war in 1914.

Under modern conditions the chief cause of conflict is the demand for more security.[27] But my security is your insecurity. Each side fears not only what the other may be doing but whatever it might be capable of doing now or in the future.

---

[27]Stanley Hoffman, *Janus and Minerva: Essays in the Theory and Practice of International Politics*, (Boulder, CO: Westview, 1987), pp. 318–19.

In this spirit, it is necessary to keep up a military establishment suitable for our status in the world. Whatever the meaning of strength in this context, we do not want the antagonist to be stronger than we are. In the contest of power, if we do not stand up for ourselves and our rights, the consequences may be unimaginable. And power raises the feeling of need to exert power in the world.[28] The idea that we sacrifice something valuable by reducing any weaponry is deeply embedded in the nationalistic outlook.

Leaders may have all the money or fame they want, but they never have enough power. Hunger for power combines with idealism, the desire to serve the cause. For those who have reached the summit of national authority and can aspire to little more on the domestic stage, power means wielding influence and doing good on the world stage. Premiers and presidents measure themselves against other premiers and presidents, seeking to assert personality and ideas. Responsibility for "national security," that is, for guiding the nation in its contest with other powers, is the strongest rationale for executive authority and for a free hand and immunity from hampering checks and annoying criticism. It is in foreign affairs that the chief has most freedom of action, finds most satisfaction, and can most easily earn plaudits.

It is better to contend with foreigners than with domestic opponents. Leaders can take up the cause of improvement of education or welfare reform, but it is much simpler to defend the nation against a foreign menace. There are endless differences about monetary policy or assistance for the poor, but no one will disagree with the need to safeguard security and national vital interests. Most will accept the leader's version of the situation; who else is so qualified to assess the menacing circumstances?

American presidents seem increasingly enamored of a world role; foreign affairs gives them high visibility with low political risks, at least at the outset. They thrive on crises and conferences with foreign leaders, especially "summits," and they see the prestige of their nation as their best claim to fame.[29] They may enjoy being feared. They usually prefer to find reasons for action than for avoiding action; it is much better to be seen as too resolute or hard than too soft in the confrontation with evil.

No one can well assess how much of the spirit of confrontation is due to genuine concern for the security of the community, how much to competitive zeal and pride. Broadly speaking, those who are more satisfied with their condition at home are more disposed to favor undertakings abroad, while those who are discontented with domestic management see foreign adventures as unnecessary or burdensome. External threat makes better in-

---

[28]Karl W. Deutsch, *The Analysis of International Relations* 3rd ed. (Englewood Cliffs, NJ: Prentice Hall Inc., 1988), p. 98.

[29]Nicholas B. de Katzenbach, "Foreign Policy, Public Opinion, and Secrecy," *Foreign Affairs* 52, October 1973, p. 9.

ternal order, for the benefit of all to some degree, but more strongly of the well placed. Conservatives or rightists are consequently more assertive in foreign affairs than reformers or leftists, who are less concerned with bringing people together morally, more with attacking economic privilege and standing for the disadvantaged against the advantaged. In Japan, West Germany, Britain, and Italy, the leading anticonservative party tends to be critical of military expenditures. Intellectuals, who take pleasure in attacking constituted authorities, are especially disposed to deplore the costs of contention. Impressed by the injustices of their own government, they may even idealize the adversary, or at least overlook his sins, because he is opposed by an authority they dislike. The praise of Western writers for the likes of Stalin and Mao is sad reading.

In the human ambivalence, there is no likelihood that the continuing international struggle will disappear. The macho position never lacks arguments: we have to keep our guard up at all costs, lest the enemy take advantage; we cannot slacken lest we give appearances of weakness; we have to exert pressure to make the other side behave or to keep it from worse behavior, or to assure our friends that we mean business and are to be relied on.

The danger to national security may, of course, be more or less imaginary. For example, the shah of Iran in the 1960s and 1970s armed his country very heavily and expensively (ultimately at the cost of his throne), allegedly against the danger of a Soviet attack, when such danger was nonexistent. There seems to have been little or no likelihood of Soviet invasion in 1987, when Iran was helping Afghan guerrillas fighting Soviet forces and was at war with Iraq, which was friendly to the Soviets. Moreover, Iran was vulnerable because of its enmity toward the United States.

Warlike postures and actions serve a moral-psychological purpose although the conflict may be meaningless from the point of view of material interests. The clash between Argentina and Britain over the Falkland Islands (which the Latins call "Malvinas") is instructive, the more so because there were no important ideological or economic issues (aside from rumors of possible oil). Nothing except prestige was at stake, and it would be more advantageous economically to lose than to keep the islands.[30]

The Falklands are treeless, eternally windswept, always chilled, without mineral resources, of only synthetic strategic significance, and of more interest to biologists (because of abundance of birds and seals) than to men of action. They had some importance as a waystation in the days of sailing vessels, and Britain, France, Spain, and Argentina had a few men there before the British expelled them in 1833. Argentina never renounced its

---

[30]See Richard N. Lebow, "Miscalculation in the South Atlantic: The Origins of the Falkland War," in Robert Jervis, Richard N. Lebow, and Janice G. Stein, eds., *Psychology and Deterrence* (Baltimore: Johns Hopkins University Press, 1986), pp. 89–124.

claim; but little was made of it for nearly a hundred years, during which relations between Britain and Agentina were mostly close and friendly.

After the overthrow of Argentina's nascent democracy by military coup in 1930, rightist groups revived the claim as a political tactic. They elevated the forlorn islands into the national irredenta, the lost province, the recovery of which was a national duty, although the Falklanders were entirely British. The injustice was drilled into schoolchildren, promoted by patriotic associations, and made the subject of books and celebrations. It sometimes appeared that recovery of the long-lost and only briefly held territory would be the key to restoration of Argentina's strength and prosperity. The thesis became the more compelling as Argentines found it difficult to understand the failure of the glorious destiny that once seemed theirs.

The British would apparently have been willing to be relieved of the islands but could not simply give away British subjects. An Argentine policy of gradual strengthening of relations between the islands and the mainland would probably have led eventually to obtaining them pacifically.

This was precluded, however, by the lack of tact and patience of the military government that undertook in 1976 to restore Argentina to greatness. In 1982, when the generals found their "national renewal" faltering and opposition rising, they resolved to regain popularity by boldly seizing the lost province. Like many other governments opting for brave resolutions, they grossly overestimated their capacities, failed to take account of reactions to their assault, and overlooked the effects of breaching international norms. One is reminded of Austria's opening WW I or of Japan's error at Pearl Harbor—when the Japanese had the good luck that the Americans were asleep.

Britain had shown some disinterest in the islands; the Argentines were confident that it would not even try to defend them from 8,000 miles away. The Reagan administration would be sympathetic in its general fondness for "limited authoritarian" anticommunist regimes and gratitude for Argentine cooperation in supporting anti-Sandinistas in Central America. The world would look with favor on an anticolonial action; and the Soviet Union, then the largest buyer of Argentine grain, would assist the anti-imperialist move and bar anti-Argentine measures.

All those assumptions were erroneous. The government of Margaret Thatcher reacted vigorously and won great popularity thereby; her firmness helped the Tories win the next election. The Reagan administration, after rather frantic efforts to mediate, with the secretary of state commuting between London and Buenos Aires, stood by its vital NATO ally. The Soviet Union did nothing of importance to help the Argentine anticommunists, doubtless seeing costs greater than any likely dividends. Latin American countries gave only vocal support.

The generals were right in one calculation only: their action aroused the enthusiasm of all sectors and parties of the nation, as even the bitterest opposition groups joined in cheering the great national enterprise. But enthusiasm for the fight gave way to the bitterness of defeat. The military rulers, their incompetence exposed, had to turn the government over to an elected president, Raul Alfonsín, in December 1983.

The cause was national, however. After the failure, the Argentines were less prepared than previously to admit the whole idea was a mistake and that the islands would be only burdensome for them; they do not give up a foreign cause toward which to divert discontent. The British, for their part, undertook to prepare for the war they had just won and spent large sums on defense of the islands—a defense not made more necessary by the 1982 war but less so. Each Falklander costs the British treasury about $100,000 per year, apparently permanently.

In March 1988, when the British engaged in a military-naval exercise around the islands involving less than a thousand personnel, Argentina took it as a great affront and felt, or pretended to feel, threatened with invasion, necessitating a military alert. The two sides, with everything to gain from cooperation and nothing from contention, are trapped in opposition over an insignificant issue.

International conflict is seldom so devoid of real stakes, but social-political benefits play a major part, as competition and confrontation stimulate our efforts, sustain national morale, and cement social peace.

The Military

A major element of the state is the oganization holding its physical power to coerce or destroy. Virtually all states (except ministates) have armed forces, regularly including army, air force, and navy, in the manner of great powers, even though they may have no external ambitions and face no dangers, or none against which they could defend themselves. A state has to maintain armed forces since other states have them. The military establishment is also the guarantor of internal order as well as, perhaps more than, external security. It is in many lands a major reason for its own size; a civilian president would find himself unemployed if he should try to reduce the soldiers' budget.

Most armed forces are quite pacific, and one cannot assume that the existence of armies causes wars and dangers of war. But the needs of the armed forces undeniably create an interest in international ill will. Not only is the great contest of powers a source of visceral satisfaction, an expectable outcome of misunderstandings and conflicts of interest, and an occupation of chiefs of nations; it also represents a huge intellectual and much more an economic activity. The careers, prosperity, livelihood, and self-esteem of millions ride on the foreign danger; and those whose business it is to protect against if not destroy the enemy must have moral justification for their profession.

In the United States, those who have a stake in the confrontation of powers are not only the 3 million employees of the Department of Defense and its suppliers, the approximately 300,000 officers of the armed services, and the numerous and well-financed "intelligence" community, but also the defense or military theorists, observers, and commentators of all kinds, supported by defense contractors and politicians, as well as amateurs of things martial—the endlessly proliferated military-industrial-bureaucratic-intellectual complex. The direct economic outlay has been some $300 billion yearly in the United States, not much less in the Soviet Union. The defense establishment is woven into the national society, economy, and mentality; and many interests become dependent on defense contracts and assuredly resolved to resist cutting them.

The defense budget defies rational management for many reasons, including its size and elaborateness, uncertainties regarding any future war, controversies as to what is to be accomplished, inter- and intraservice rivalries, and the complexity of weaponry and tactics. Research creates pressures to improve weapons or build new ones. The Stealth (B-2) bomber is an example of the passion for technology. The purpose of the plane seems to be more a demonstration of virtuosity than to "clean up" in a Soviet Union reeling from a nuclear assault; but the cost of a fleet, approaching $100 billion, would provide a large permanent endowment for a hundred major new universities. Whatever weaponry can be constructed should be because the other side may do as much; but it is seldom clear what equipment should serve which mission.

Budgetmaking becomes an open-ended scramble. Advocates of appropriations not only look to the national strength but also to political gains (how much is to be spent in whose district), the well-being of contractors, and the promotion of personal and organizational ambitions. It is very difficult to organize procurement efficiently; there is no free market for military hardware, and many problems arise with both competitive bidding and negotiated contracts. Not surprisingly, the incidence of corruption in defense contracting seems to be higher than in most government spending.

Defense expenditures are affected only slowly by changes in the international atmosphere. The forces insist on their new weapon systems, even if this means reducing active units and maintenance—the toys are as important as is fighting ability. If fewer units are to be produced, the price per unit rises, while it is more important that the weapon be technically perfect than that it be deployable with the maximum effect. Since there is no good way to assess the effectiveness of weapons, they are assumed to give strength more or less in proportion to their cost; consequently, it becomes a function of the military organization to spend money. For such reasons, the Stealth bomber sells for some $650 million per copy. It would be cheaper made of pure gold.

The tightly organized military is subject to bureaucratic infighting; each service branch sees its goals as the national goal. Parity of forces in the Department of Defense is almost as important as parity with the Soviets. Each branch must have the finest vehicles for its officers and personnel to fly, drive, or sail. Force levels depend to a large extent on tradition. The Navy's insistence on 15 carrier groups goes back to the naval agreement of 1921, fixing the number of American capital ships at 15—then battleships, now carriers.[31] The admirals would hate to lose one of the flagships on whose bridge they love to stand.

The military profession is unique. The soldier's life has charms of masculinity, loyalty, comradeship, and symbolism, as well as the sense of struggle for an incontestable value. The soldiers and sailors cherish their honors, pageantry, ceremonies, and traditions, from brass bands and military funerals to the regimental colors and the history of the corps. Military organizations are inward-looking and self-regarding, with a mentality distinct from that of civilian society. The lives of the officers—commonly living in barracks, socializing with themselves, enjoying their own recreational facilities, attending military schools—are more bound together than those of any other profession except perhaps a priesthood. They tend to regard themselves, the guardians of the nation, as the repository of patriotism as well as the model of dedication, with every right to make themselves heard on questions of national security or the standing of the nation in the world.

The military profession does not shine for innovativeness, practicality, or general good judgment. The common quip that military intelligence is an oxymoron is somewhat overstated, but some follies of the past give pause. Before the First World War, the French army insisted on conspicuous, bright red pantaloons, supposedly essential for morale, which the generals held more important than guns. Throughout the war, generals ordered millions to their death in mass charges against trenches armed with machine guns. The scientifically minded Germans in 1914 sent horse cavalry into battle armed with lances. On the eve of WW II, the U.S. Cavalry favored horses and was indifferent to mechanization.[32]

Not many exercises are so futile as pitting noble horses against automatic weapons or tanks, but it is difficult to alter military doctrines defended by vested interests. A strong group will protest loudly against ending

[31]Richard A. Stubbing, *The Defense Game*, (New York: Harper & Row, 1987), p. 73.
[32]Edward L. Katzenbach, Jr., "The Horse Cavalry in the Twentieth Century," in *The Use of Force: International Politics and Foreign Policy*, ed. Robert J. Art and Kenneth N. Waltz, 2nd. ed. (Lanham, MD: University Press of America, 1983), p. 219.

any mission and find ample cause to justify it; and officers resist technological innovations that render their organization and customs obsolete.[33]

It is characteristic of the military organization that, even more than other governmental agencies, it pulls a cloak over itself. The desire to conceal matters that would contribute to the military capacities of the potential enemy, especially information about weapons and disposition of forces, is understandable. But documents are wantonly overclassified, frequently even papers dealing with matters in the public domain. Access to official information is denied in principle so far as feasible, and the military bureaucracy tries to seal the mouths of its employees. Secrecy is part of the bond of brotherhood; and the possession of confidential information, regardless of its possible irrelevance, is a source of pride. Those who possess information denied to ordinary persons do not have to explain their judgments. They also enjoy some immunity; the secrets that most have to be guarded are those of failures and incompetence. The accuracy of material usually is in inverse proportion to its classification.[34]

An example of the love for secrecy is the military dislike for and restrictions on civilian satellite photography. It reduces the value of their secret holdings; the outsiders learn things (which the Soviets very well know) that the defense officials would like to keep to themselves. As they interpret it, the national security is imperilled. Yet it is arguable that the new technology serves peace by bringing facts about military developments on both sides into the open and exposing false claims.[35]

The custodians of the national safety, feeling that the less known by outsiders the better, seem to regard the press as an enemy. Thus during the 1983 Grenada operation reporters were entirely excluded for no evident reason; it was stated that it was for their protection, but warning shots were fired when they approached.[36] During the truly dangerous world war, reporters were welcomed to the front lines, where some were killed.

If the safety of the nation were the only concern and safety were reasonably interpreted to mean primarily the avoidance of nuclear conflict, it might be recognized that openness is desirable in principle. If each side felt better informed about the other there would be less need to prepare for all

---

[33]Many examples are given by Arthur T. Hadley, *The Straw Giant, Triumph and Failures: America's Armed Forces* (New York: Random House, 1986).

[34]John L. Gaddis, "Implementing Flexible Response: Vietnam as a Test Case," in *The Use of Force: International Politics and Foreign Policy,* ed. Robert J. Art and Kenneth N. Waltz (Boston: Little, Brown, 1971), p. 364.

[35]William J. Broad, "Private Cameras in Space Stir U. S. Security Fears," *New York Times,* August 25, 1987, p. 17.

[36]Gary M. Quester, "Grenada and the News Media," in Peter M. Dunn and Bruce W. Watson, eds., *American Intervention in Grenada: The Implications of Operation "Urgent Fury"* (Boulder, CO: Westview, 1985), pp. 109–28.

possibilities, less suspicion, and less tension. The argument can be made, as it has been made by physicist Edward Teller, that the attempt to keep information secret is in principle misguided and counterproductive, because it deprives people of information, penalizes allies, and retards science.[37]

Secrecy contributes to military competition. Because the soldiers envision the nation as perpetually in conflict, albeit of low intensity, defense planners proceed on worst case assumptions, that the enemy is wholly unscrupulous and indefinitely ambitious. If the enemy seems momentarily less menacing today, it may be a deceit; we cannot be sure what they are covertly scheming for the day after tomorrow, and we have to plan for defense needs that may appear seven or ten years from now.

The closed nature of the military establishment makes it difficult to guess to what extent it is responsible for an adversarial approach to foreign policy. Its general tendency is conservative, as it upholds order, obedience, and tradition. It likes to take control where it becomes involved, as in Vietnam,[38] but wants to carry out policies in its own way. In countries with weak political systems, the military commonly assume full responsibility for the political direction of the nation; in the United States, they feel entitled to be consulted in the broad area of security policy. Despite the American peculiarity of having a civilian in charge of the military department (with civilian deputies), the Joint Chiefs act to some extent as an independent power. For example, in 1972 they demanded B-1 bombers and Trident submarines as the price for endorsing arms control; in 1979 they got MX missiles in return for supporting SALT II.[39]

The armed forces, like the CIA and other intelligence agencies (the Defense Intelligence Agency, National Security Agency, Army Intelligence, Office of Naval Intelligence, and Marine Corps Intelligence), are prominent in foreign policy councils and among the advisors of the president. The insiders have the advantage that they possess information that no others are in a position to check or contradict. Although the relations of military power to foreign policy are unclear, the methods of force are simplistic, and its practitioners are not likely to be much interested in the philosophic nuances of foreign relations and the subtler means of achieving national ends. The forces—the military intelligence organs more than the CIA—can be counted on to take the general approach that our world is dominated by a contest of military power.

They do not underestimate the need for their product and the hazards

---

[37]Edward Teller, *Better a Shield than a Sword: Perspectives on Defense and Technology* (New York: Free Press, 1988), pp. 118–20.

[38]David Halberstam, *The Best and the Brightest,* (New York: Random House, 1972), passim.

[39]*New York Times,* January 29, 1988, p. 1.

of disarmament; estimates of the Defense Intelligence Agency are regularly more alarming than those of the CIA. When the CIA estimated Soviet military expenditures to have increased by 2 percent yearly from the mid-1970s, the Defense Intelligence Agency put the figure at 6–7 percent.[40] High estimates of the Soviet military buildup not only tell the political authorities that the Soviets are aggressive and dangerous; they also justify generous appropriations.[41]

The Department of Defense is considerably less inclined to permit exports of high-technology wares than is the Department of Commerce; and in a crisis the Pentagon probably takes a more anxious view, the State Department a more relaxed one (thereby earning the scorn of the warriors). The DOD wants to denounce alleged Soviet arms treaty violations when State sees them as dubious or unimportant. For the State Department, an agreement generally represents a victory; for Defense, it is a doubtful matter.

This does not mean that the armed services are adventurous and eager to fly into a fracas. In case of fighting (short of an attack on American cities), their people are the chief sufferers. For the most part, they are conservative; and they seem to prefer the routine of training and preparation. They may not much hate the enemy—soldiers tend to respect their professional adversaries. Moreover, the generals learned in Vietnam the penalty of an unpopular war. Cold war suits them, not intervention; and they have been less disposed to activism in the 1980s than some of the State Department, who would like the soldiers or sailors to solve their problems. Civilians in the Department wanted American forces in Panama to depose Gen. Antonio Noriega in 1988; the soldiers saw such action as a misuse of their facilities.

The goal of military preparedness in our day is less war capability than prestige, more the satisfaction of strength than actual use of weapons. If the generals are not spoiling for battle, however, they are not likely to strive diligently to cool the international temper. It is unrealistic to ignore their influence on both sides in encouraging an atmosphere of confrontation. The huge conglomerate cannot fail to exert great weight.

This is also true of the Soviets, although it is more difficult to assess the behind-the-scenes influence of the military in the Soviet than in the American system. Guesses as to Soviet defense expenditures are unreliable and subject to different interpretations. For example, the CIA includes in Soviet costs what Soviet conscripts would receive if paid the stipends of

---

[40]Stubbing, *Defense Game,* p. 5; Dale R. Herspring, "Gorbachev and the Soviet Military," in *Soviet Foreign Policy,* ed. Robert F. Laird (New York: Academy of Political Science, 1987), p. 49.

[41]The Department of Defense publishes a glossy annual *Soviet Military Power* (Washington: Government Printing Office), giving a dramatic view of Soviet military strength.

American volunteers instead of chewing-gum money. As a result, Soviet defense expenditures are calculated to rise (disproportionately because Soviet forces are larger) when Congress gives American soldiers a raise.[42] However, it is clear that the military is even more important for the Soviet economy and much more of a burden for a feebler industrial base, taking about double the American military's share of GNP. Potentially at least, it has far more effect on the national character, as shoolchildren have military training and exercises from an early age, military-patriotic ceremonies and themes are omnipresent, and 2 or 3 years' military service is obligatory for males.

Yet from the time of the revolution, the Soviet rulership has taken great pains to minimize the political role of the soldiers, rightly fearing that they were best able to snatch power from the party leadership. The Leninists compared their revolution to the French and wanted to forestall their Napoleon. They put political officers alongside strictly military officers, sacrificing some military efficiency to political reliability. The regular hierarchy is paralleled to this day by a secondary set of officers under the command of communist party bodies, responsible for morale, indoctrination, and assuring the reliability of commanders. They are supplemented by KGB officers throughout the forces.

The control apparatus has been very successful in maintaining the subordination of the armed forces to party leadership. Stalin in 1937 gave a demonstration of his authority by executing a large majority of the higher officers without an audible murmur. In the war, he had to give the generals some leeway, but he claimed full credit for himself and after victory shunted the most eminent generals aside. Khrushchev had some problems with the most famous wartime commander, General Georgi Zhukov; but he was able to carry out large reductions of the armed forces. Since then, there has been little evidence of military influence in Soviet politics, although the minister of defense (a marshal) has usually had a seat on the politburo and there is a sprinkling of officers in the central committee of the party.[43]

Under Gorbachev, military influence seems to have been checked. The armed forces are no longer represented on the politburo.[44] They had to withdraw from Afghanistan. They accepted a treaty reducing Soviet missiles much more than American, a unilateral reduction of Soviet armed forces, and partial pullback from Eastern Europe. High commanders who seem to have opposed such moves have been retired. Worst, the media have criticized the sacred armed forces as never before.

---

[42]Stubbing, *The Defense Game,* p. 9.

[43]Gordon R. Smith, *Soviet Politics: Continuity and Contradiction* (New York: St. Martins Press, 1986), pp. 177–86; for history, see Albert Seaton and Joan Seaton, *The Soviet Army, 1918 to the Present* (New York: New American Library, 1986).

[44]F. Stephen Larrabee, "Gorbachev and the Soviet Military," *Foreign Affairs* 66, Summer 1988, pp. 1002–26.

U.S.-Soviet Antagonism

Two powers in a single political sphere, sufficiently equal to represent a challenge of each to the other, are natural adversaries. Such a confrontational relationship has recurred many times through history. For example, England and France, the leading neighbor-powers of the West, were for centuries at odds, often fighting. After the unification of Germany in 1870, England and especially France began to feel more threatened by Germany; and until the end of the Second World War, France and Germany were classic opponents, much aware of their differences and of the menace of each to the other. There was no such antagonism between France and Belgium or between Germany and the Netherlands.

Even relatively weak powers come into opposition so far as they would feel dominant within a region. India and Pakistan, the big powers of their subcontinent, have had many clashes and several wars since they became independent in 1947. Their chief reason for quarreling would seem to have disappeared when Pakistan lost the majority of its population to the poverty-stricken new state of Bangladesh and the superiority of India became incontestable. But in October 1987 Indian and Pakistani armies were shooting at each other over a stretch of glacier at 20,000 feet in the Himalayas.[45]

Argentina and Brazil were half-enemies for generations, sometimes rather bitter rivals, with occasional mumblings of war. Up to 1930, Argentina could look down on Brazil as relatively poor and consider itself the regional hegemon; but since about 1960 Brazil has raised itself to predominance. By 1987 the Brazilian GNP was four times the Argentine, the competition was decided, and enmity has been replaced by amity. Cooperation was in order, moreover, because both nations had become more troubled by relations with the United States.[46] Even more modest powers may be prone to regard the nextdoor neighbor as the national antagonist. For example, Venezuela and Colombia occasionally mobilize forces over intrinsically unimportant scraps of territory and make warlike noises, although everyone knows they cannot really fight.

It is inevitable that the two leading powers in the close-knit modern world oppose each other. Each represents the only danger to the other and the chief political restraint to its will. Only they are capable of first-class strategic forces, and only they regard themselves as global powers. The Soviet state, covering a sixth of the earth's land and containing a multitude of nationalities, seems to itself more than an ordinary state.[47] The United

---

[45]*Time*, October 12, 1987, p. 45.

[46]Wayne A. Selcher, "Brazilian-Argentine Relations in the 1980s: From Wary Rivalry to Friendly Competition," *Journal of Interamerican Studies and World Affairs* 27 (Summer 1985), 25–54.

[47]On Soviet capacities, see James Sherr, *Soviet Power: The Continuing Challenge* (London: Macmillan, 1986).

States likewise, because of its history and its mixture of peoples and races, takes its success as evidence of the universal validity of its philosophy. There have been no weighty material disputes between the superpowers, no territorial or important economic questions; but the free-for-all called international politics is mostly between the two strongest players.

Many leaders of anti-Sovietism, such as James Burnham (*The Coming Defeat of Communism* and *Suicide of the West*), were defectors from the cause; that is, they accepted the values, methods, and mentality of the struggle for communism but turned their artillery around. For them, it has been much more important to be anticommunist than to be in favor of the open society. Enthusiasts for the "Contras" fighting the hated Nicaraguan regime have generally been unworried about whether their clients were properly democratic or not. Generally speaking, the more anticommunist, the less inclined to require democratic credentials, the more inclined to excuse repression by avowedly anticommunist authoritarians, as in Chile or South Africa.

The basic ideological claim of Leninism, that the Russian Revolution represents the triumph of the good side in the universal and inevitable class struggle, has hardly been taken seriously for many years; but Soviet leaders formerly liked to talk of the "world correlation of forces" evolving to their benefit and of their rise to parity with the United States, leaving open the possibility of turning parity into superiority. When Khrushchev in 1959 said "We will bury you," he was not threatening murder but bragging that the Soviet system would persuasively outperform the American and witness its demise. Since then, the desirability of converting other countries has been undermined by unpleasant experiences, especially the defection of China and other countries; and optimism has been dissolved by economic failures. On the other side, American authorities sometimes seem to have felt that an absence of American influence anywhere was an invitation to Soviet penetration, which had to be countered by the conversion of the whole world to democracy and free enterprise.

The ethical foundation for a claim to leadership is moral superiority. Leaders would present their nations and by implication themselves as representatives of a happier and better society that deserves to prevail in the world. Even as he states that he would not "be hemmed in by our values,"[48] General Secretary Gorbachev seems to believe, like his predecessors and doubtless his successors, that his country has special worth, regardless of relative poverty. This is in the millennial Russian tradition shared by Dostoievsky and Solzhenitsyn, revived in a modernized form by Lenin, and basic to the Soviet character.

As a multinational state, the United States has seen not a national but an abstract enemy, a generalized plague called "communism." Because of this feeling, many persons refused for a long time to acknowledge the re-

[48]*New York Times*, December 8, p. A6.

ality of the Sino-Soviet split. American conservatives, even the well-informed Joint Chiefs of Staff, could not perceive it until Soviet troops massed on the Chinese border.[49] Viewing the world as bipolar gives a simple frame of reference for understanding complicated affairs.

Former President Nixon warned in 1988 that, "Under no circumstances should the United States allow its foreign policy to be affected by changes in Soviet domestic policy,"[50] although it had been long maintained that Soviet domestic policy, its tyranny and oppression, was good reason for opposition to Soviet purposes. Soviet reforms are attributed not to internal dynamics of that state but to the American military buildup of the Reagan years, apparently on the assumption that Soviet leaders feared an American attack. In the judgment of the sober *Economist,* "Russian good behavior comes from Western firmness, not Western concessions," and Russia has changed only tactics, not purposes.[51] As George Bush's national security advisor, Brent Scowcroft, put it, "The challenge is, how do we maintain our skepticism and agnosticism toward the Soviets when they are smiling at us?"[52]

Thousands of careers have been built on U.S.-Soviet hostility, and organizations strive to keep up the causes that are the reason for their existence. The strategists look forward to an indefinite arms race and do not contemplate that their profession will become anachronistic. Governments, as political entities, prefer political-military to economic competition. Very big powers like to have an antagonist worthy of their attention, and we love flagwaving, although we are doubtful about dangerous actions. In the 1988 U. S. electoral campaign, George Bush insisted on the necessity of maintaining military strength to deal with Gorbachev, and Michael Dukakis tried to reassure voters that he also loved the military and would only allocate expenditures more efficiently. Something like a "cold war" comes naturally to the leading nations.

[49]Halberstam, *The Best and the Brightest,* p. 245.

[50]Richard M. Nixon, "Dealing with Gorbachev," *New York Times Magazine,* March 13, 1988, p. 78.

[51]*The Economist,* September 17, 1988, p. 17.

[52]*Business Week,* November 21, 1988, p. 39.

Chapter 3

Defense Policies

Strategic Arms

The spirit of conflict finds nightmarish expression in nuclear explosives, which give a bomb a million times the destructive force of the blockbusters of WW II and represent the great terror of our age.[1]

The nuclear arsenals have cast a long shadow over world affairs ever since they burst on the scene in 1945, yet they may have a positive side. Nuclear weapons are credited with preventing war these many years, on the reasonable grounds that fears of mass murder-suicide have kept statesmen sober and restrained them from actions that could escalate uncontrollably. No quarrel of postwar times has been worth risking nuclear conflict.

Whether or not the superweapons merit esteem as peacekeepers, they have had the virtue of promising mutuality of devastation since the Soviets acquired a respectable arsenal in the 1960s. A nuclear war would not be like a duel of honor but like a high-speed collision of two automobiles loaded with dynamite.

Although the nuclear forces, astronomically more potent than chemical explosives, dramatize the dangers of the clash of sovereignties, modern

---

[1]For a survey, see McGeorge Bundy, *Danger and Survival: Choices about the Bomb in the First Fifty Years* (New York: Random House, 1988).

technology menaces in many ways, from fantastically deadly gases to self-propagating biological agents. A few molecules of nerve gas, cheaply manufactured and easily spewed almost anywhere, bring quick death; and the possibilities of bacteriological warfare, the agents of which may have the virtue of multiplying themselves, can only increase with the progress of genetic engineering.

Fortunately, such products of the laboratory are much less attractive to the military mind than more visible and violent agents of death. Remarkably, poison gases were not employed in WW II, possibly because Hitler was gassed in WW I. But in its war with Iran, Iraq used chemical weapons rather freely and effectively, killing many thousands, soldiers and civilians, with primitive substances like those that brought misery to WW I. This success may raise the temptation to resort to such means in the future, although there is strong feeling against them. The superpowers keep up capabilities and have stockpiles capable of cleansing the earth of humanity many times over, but negotiations go on to outlaw them. It is difficult because verification is nearly impossible. The potentialities of old-fashioned warfare, forces shooting metal at each other, have also progressed marvelously. A nonnuclear war between superpowers could be totally calamitous.

The megadeaths from an hour-long nuclear exchange might be fewer than from six years of WW II, but they might conceivably be much more, with daily tolls in the tens of millions instead of thousands. The superpower arsenals are said to contain the equivalent of more than half a million bombs of the type that incinerated Hiroshima, estimated to total about 15,000 megatons in about 50,000 warheads, the equivalent of 15 billion tons of high explosive, 3 tons for each inhabitant of the earth. Each superpower could launch thousands of times the destructive energy contained in all the bombs showered on Germany in WW II.

Nuclear explosions have a triple value: the explosive force of the blast shattering buildings; heat of the explosion igniting everything combustible in a city; and radioactive fallout capable of killing millions of people, quickly or slowly. Clouds of deadly dust would encircle the globe; water would be poisoned, in large areas for years or decades; and the smoke from enormous firestorms might cause something of a "nuclear winter" and failure of agriculture. No leaders could contemplate a nuclear exchange with confidence that they and theirs could be safe.[2]

The annihilation in 1945 of Hiroshima and Nagasaki by primitive A-bombs, with about 150,000 fatalities in each, has often been criticized. Yet

---

[2]On technical aspects of the nuclear confrontation, see Dietrich Schroeer, *Science, Technology, and the Nuclear Arms Race* (New York: John Wiley and Sons, 1984); on presumed consequences, see Nicholas Wade, *A World Beyond Healing: The Prologue and Aftermath of Nuclear War* (New York: W.W. Norton, 1987); also, James Thompson, *Psychological Aspects of Nuclear War* (New York: John Wiley, 1985).

the decision is fairly understandable in terms of the mentality of the time and the desperate Japanese defense of Pacific islands. It followed the fire-bombing of German and Japanese cities, which suffered approximately equal although less instantaneous devastation. Revisionist historians have contended that it was planned in order to intimidate the Soviet Union,[3] but this seems unlikely. In the heat of the war with Japan the American leadership was not so farsighted as to be scheming for the cold war that would not really begin until two years later.

The leveling of two cities left a healthy distaste for the weapon. Since then, nuclear weapons have been perfected, endowed with hundreds or thousands of times greater power, and provided with means of accurate delivery (within a few hundred feet) at any distance; but their use has been inhibited. In the Korean war, for example, nuclear weapons would have been convenient, and some advocated their use; but even in a parlous military situation, with American forces in headlong retreat from the Yalu river, the United States abstained.

Around 1948, there was some talk that the United States should keep the world safe by preventing the Soviet Union from developing a nuclear capacity, using nuclear weapons for this purpose if necessary.[4] This was not totally illogical and would certainly have been done if the United States had cherished grand imperial designs, but it does not seem to have been seriously considered. After the Soviet Union acquired the bomb in 1949, talk of preemption died out.

There have never been definite public threats of the use of nuclear weapons in crisis situations. Inevitably, however, hints of nuclear action have been dropped, perhaps effectively enough to modify behavior.[5] The United States has at various times pointed to its nuclear capacity: to hurry up the delayed Soviet withdrawal from Iran in 1946, in the Suez crisis of 1956, in 1958 to deter Chinese Communist seizure of the offshore islands of Quemoy and Matsu. In 1954 Eisenhower considered and vetoed a nuclear strike to help the French forces in Vietnam. From time to time in the late 1950s, Nikita Khrushchev indulged in rocket-rattling and boasts of Soviet nuclear capacities; he vaguely threatened annihilation to prod the Western powers to withdraw from Berlin, and he claimed that Soviet missiles would protect Cuba from the United States—bravado when the Soviets were at a disadvantage of ten to one in nuclear weapons. It seems that Strategic Air Command officers were dismayed in 1962 at the failure of President

---

[3]As argued in detail by Gar Alperovitz, *Atomic Diplomacy: Hiroshima and Potsdam,* (New York: Simon and Schuster, 1965).

[4]Michael MccGwire, *Military Objectives in Soviet Foreign Policy* (Washington: Brookings Institution, 1987), pp. 16–17.

[5]That is the theme of Michio Kaku and Daniel Axelrod, *To Win a Nuclear War: The Pentagon's Secret War Plans* (Boston: South End Press, 1987).

Kennedy to take the opportunity of the missile crisis to launch a strike on the Soviets.[6] Nuclear parity did not prevent Nixon from bringing up a first-use threat; an alert was ordered to warn the Soviets in the Arab-Israeli war of 1973. American nuclear forces have been placed on alert many times, although Soviet forces have never been.[7]

Nuclear weapons have been brandished without apparent thought as to how they would really be used, and evidence of the effect of the nuclear balance or imbalance on foreign policy on both sides is ambiguous.[8] They cannot be politically useful unless there is some confidence of winning a war.[9] There has been little indication of proposed nuclear escalation of quarrels over Third World issues, as the superpowers have left the fighting to Third World parties.

Whether employed as a threat or not, the U.S. monopoly of nuclear weapons from 1945 until 1949 and large superiority until well after the Cuban missile crisis of 1962 doubtless tempered Soviet ambitions at a critical time. Fresh from victory, the Soviet Union was imbued with a mixture of Russian messianistic expansionism, leftovers of Leninist revolutionism, and enormous self-confidence; Stalin or Khrushchev might conceivably have been tempted to use military means to give more nations the benefits of Sovietization if there had been no nuclear danger. Through the Eisenhower era, U.S. nuclear superiority was a generalized deterrent to adventures. "Brinkmanship," or the suggestion that this country might go to (or over?) the brink of nuclear war to counter Soviet expansionism, served as a partial substitute for conventional military forces prepared to deal with Korea-like troubles.

After the humiliating 1962 missile crisis, the Soviet leadership undertook to close the gap. Since the mid or late 1970s, it is assumed that the United States and the Soviet Union have been in a condition of "parity," which does not mean strict equality of nuclear strength but a sufficient equivalence that neither has clear superiority.[10] This brought about a situation of permanent threat with no strategic answer.

In this situation, a nuclear war could come only by miscalculation.

[6]Richard N. Lebow, "Clausewitz and Nuclear Crisis Stability," *Political Science Quarterly* 103, Spring 1988, p. 96.

[7]Morton H. Halperin, *Nuclear Fallacy: Dispelling the Myth of Nuclear Strategy* (Cambridge, MA: Harper & Row, 1987), pp. 25–32; Charles R. Morris, *Iron Destinies, Lost Opportunities: The Arms Race between the U.S.A. and the U.S.S.R., 1945–1987* (New York: Harper & Row, 1988), p. 367.

[8]As judiciously discussed by Richard K. Betts, *Nuclear Blackmail and Nuclear Balance* (Washington: Brookings Institution, 1987).

[9]Colin S. Gray and Keith Payne, "Victory Is Possible," in *Thinking about Nuclear Weapons: Analysis and Prescriptions*, ed. Fred Holroyd (London: Croom Helm, 1985), pp. 197–207.

[10]For a history of the arms race, see Charles R. Morris, *Iron Destinies*.

This is conceivable. The computers have several times raised false alerts, as when the rising moon gave the signal that Soviet rockets were on the way. One is reminded of the Cuban missile crisis of 1962, when the world supposedly teetered on the brink of hell for several days and when alternative policies, seriously proposed in the White House, might have had the gravest results. The danger of war was probably much less in reality than it seemed at the time, because of an American nuclear superiority much larger than Kennedy and his advisors knew; but it is not impossible that Soviet leaders might have become convinced that they were about to be attacked and decided on preemptive moves. Various events added to the hazards. The premier American spy in Moscow, Colonel Oleg Penkovsky, who was about to be arrested and executed, managed to send a message to Washington that the Soviet Union was going to launch a nuclear strike; if the CIA had taken up the alarm, American countermeasures would have certainly redoubled the tension level. The United States very nearly struck at Soviet bases in Cuba when a U-2 reconnaissance plane was downed, although the Soviets probably had nothing to do with it. A U.S. intelligence ship happened to be just off the Cuban coast, a U-2 plane violated Soviet airspace, and the U.S. Navy accidentally damaged a Soviet submarine; any of these circumstances could have had dangerous repercussions.[11]

Much thought has been given to avoiding a calamitous error.[12] The Soviets have even taken lessons from their American antagonists about reducing risks of accidental war and prevention of accidental firing. But the danger of accidental nuclear war is proportional to the reliance on nuclear weapons; and it is commonly assumed that nuclear war might come through misunderstandings in a tense political situation. One side might decide that preemptive action was less dangerous than awaiting an attack. But preemption would be a desperate gamble, because no one could be sure of a first strike disabling the adversary and preventing a devastating counterblow from submarines or bombers. A fully successful mass launching would require much practice; the fact that weapons are likely to malfunction complicates nuclear planning.[13] Humans hate uncertainty, but perhaps it has kept us alive.

---

[11]Richard N. Lebow, "Clausewitz and Crisis Stability," *Political Science Quarterly* 103, Spring 1988, pp. 91–94; Raymond L. Garthoff, "Cuba: Even Dicier than We Knew," *Newsweek*, October 26, 1984, p. 34; Raymond Garthoff, "The Cuban Missile Crisis: The Soviet Story," *Foreign Policy* 72, Fall 1988, pp. 61–80. On instabilities in control of nuclear forces, see Paul Bracken, *The Command and Control of Nuclear Forces* (New Haven: Yale University Press, 1983).

[12]Paul Bracken, "Accidental Nuclear War," in *Hawks, Doves, and Owls: An Agenda for Avoiding Nuclear War,* ed. Graham T. Allison, Albert Carnesale, and Joseph D. Nye, Jr., (New York: Norton, 1985), p. 25; Henry S. Rowen, "Catalytic Nuclear War," in *op. cit.,* pp. 148–66.

[13]Arthur T. Hadley, *The Straw Giant, Triumph and Failure: America's Armed Forces* (New York: Random House, 1986), p. 199.

U.S. Nuclear Strategy

Much as nuclear bombs substituted for an army invading Japan, the United States has regarded nuclear weapons as a suitable way of countering a large Soviet superiority of ground forces in Europe. This has meant that this country had to be prepared under certain circumstances to initiate nuclear war.

The implied first use by the United States seemed satisfactory for so long (despite the inhumanity of the proposed massacre of millions) that it became ingrained in strategic thinking and has been left more or less in place in the very different condition of Soviet parity, some say superiority. Doctrine has evolved, however. From the early 1960s the threat of nuclear retaliation seemed implausible for communist misdeeds less grievous than a massive attack in Europe, and the Kennedy administration developed two complementary ideas: that the assured ability of the superpowers to destroy each other, "mutual assured destruction," appropriately known as MAD, would deter nuclear war; and that the United States had to develop means of handling something less than an all-out attack, that is, "flexible response."[14]

The United States has never abandoned the idea of nuclear weapons functioning as a deterrent. But it is hardly credible to threaten mutual suicide. The United States supposedly would employ strategic missiles only for the gravest cause, in response to a Soviet strike against this country or a Soviet ground assault against NATO Europe that could not otherwise be contained. But in nuclear matters it is impossible to distinguish defensive from offensive use; and it would be dangerous to convince the Soviets that the United States might use nuclear weapons in a deterrent fashion, that is, in a first strike. The Soviet Union would be very unlikely to consider a missile assault on the United States unless it believed that this country might be about to attack and thus felt driven to get the large advantage of the first blow.

To diminish such a possibility, the United States has given much attention to the invulnerability of forces. Defense planners have insisted on the so-called triad, the three-pronged panoply of land-based missiles (with recently 2,300 warheads), submarine-launchable missiles (6,700 warheads available, although only a fraction are at sea at any given time), and bombers (carrying about 5,000 missiles, including cruise missiles). This insistence follows from interservice rivalry; army, navy, and airforce each have to have their share.[15] The submarines are not only mobile but also difficult to de-

---

[14]Roman Kolkowicz, *The Logic of Nuclear Terror* (Boston: Allen and Unwin, 1987), p. 5.
[15]Morris, *Iron Destinies,* p. 440.

tect, especially if deeply submerged; for this reason, the United States has half its warheads, although only about 10 percent of its nuclear megatonnage, on submarines.[16] The Soviet Union, which has less access to the oceans and can keep submarines on duty for a smaller fraction of the time (about 20 percent, against 50 percent for the American vessels), keeps about two-thirds of its striking power in land silos.

It is helpful for strategic stability that submarine-launched missiles are less accurate than land-launched and are hence less capable of a disarming strike against enemy launchers. But nuclear submarines suffer the disadvantage of unreliability of communications. To avoid complete dependence on them and to retain the ability to hit precise targets, the United States continues to rely heavily on land-based systems. As a supplement to the submarines, the Carter administration proposed to build powerful new land missiles, the MX, with mobile basing, as a stabilizing weapon. No satisfactory basing mode was worked out, however; and the MX was finally adopted as a fixed, that is, destabilizing weapon. Other new weapons systems also tend to be destabilizing. The Stealth bomber, if it can evade radar, would be suitable for a surprise attack. Cruise missiles, launched from submarines off the coast and flying under radar, could also strike with minimal warning.

Complications arise from the tactical nuclear weapons held ready on the battlefield. There is a continuum from the smallest to the largest warheads; the psychological leap is from chemical to nuclear explosives, and crossing the nuclear threshold seems to imply readiness to go all the way. The most appropriate use of short-range nuclear weapons by NATO would seem to be to preempt Soviet use of nuclear weapons; the Soviets would presumably then be obliged to launch on warning, and the holocaust could be on its way in minutes.

Such problems led to a reconsideration of MAD and to vague ideas of limiting damage in a nuclear exchange so that the nation could claim victory, even though tens of millions might have perished and many of the living would be doomed. It also led to the proposal for a strategic defense. Nuclear-tipped missiles seemed to give complete dominance to the offense; but it is hoped that sophisticated technology can create a shield even against the superweapons. However, no real defense, space-based or land-based, is likely for many years, if ever. No defense is considered fully effective against bombers, which are many times slower, larger, and more fragile—probably hundreds of times easier to knock out. It is ironic that the United States should at the same time work on the costly Stealth bomber and a hypothetical antimissile system.

[16]Robert Ehrlich, *Waging Nuclear Peace: The Technology and Politics of Nuclear Weapons* (Albany: State University Press of New York, 1985), pp. 110, 294.

Soviet Nuclear Doctrine

Soviet nuclear doctrine has seemed fairly similar to American.[17] There are differences arising from different conditions, such as more limited Soviet access to the open oceans; but weapons and basic problems are much the same on both sides, just as tanks and artillery function about the same in the hands of any professional soldiers. As in the United States, there is a fundamental division between those who reject the idea of nuclear war and those who are comfortable planning for it. Formerly, the greater secrecy of Soviet society made Soviet silos less vulnerable; satellite photography has equalized the two sides in this regard.

There are, however, differences of outlook reflecting the different character of the two political systems. The Soviet leadership has made few statements about proposed or possible use of nuclear weapons, except more or less public-relations pronouncements against first use and for disarmament proposals. Soviet ideas must be inferred from theoretical writings, which are informative, because Soviet nuclear strategizing (unlike the bulk of American writing) is the work of officers writing for the military press, that is, for other officers.[18] Soviet discussions on the subject are less detailed and scholastic than American, perhaps largely because they are by men of action, not critical academics, who are far fewer in the Soviet Union. So far as civilian writers express themselves, they are inclined to be more dovish than the generals.

Soviet strategists tend toward practicality; they have considered American ideas about nuclear war hopelessly scholastic and unrealistic.[19] Since the times of the uneducated Khrushchev's blustering, the Soviets have shown growing sophistication along with greater concern for the impact of policies on public opinion at home and abroad.[20] Arms control negotiations have greatly contributed to Soviet understanding regarding nuclear weapons.

Since Stalin, it has been the Soviet position, like the American, that nuclear war could be avoided but that it was necessary to be prepared for it. Both sides regard nuclear weapons as a deterrent against nuclear weapons, although the Soviets have been inclined to see a nuclear war as just a much bigger war.

---

[17]David Holloway, "Thinking about Nuclear War: The Soviet View," in *Thinking about Nuclear Weapons,* ed. Holroyd, pp. 45–72; Stephen Kull, *Minds at War: Nuclear Reality and the Inner Conflicts of Defense Policymakers* (New York: Basic Books, 1988), pp. 248–95.

[18]Roman Kolkowicz, *The Logic of Nuclear Terror,* p. 29.

[19]Freeman Dyson, *Weapons and Hope* (New York: Harper & Row, 1984), p. 250.

[20]Rose E. Gottemoeller, "Arms Control Decision Making since Brezhnev," in *The Soviet Calculus of Nuclear War,* ed. Roman Kolkowicz and Ellen P. Mickiwiecz (Lexington, MA: Lexington Books, 1986), pp. 85–89.

The general idea is to build up forces for an uncertain future without definite game plans. There is no notion of limited or controlled nuclear war; it is believed that there can be no rules or limitations. Any nuclear war can be expected to be total; and its only purpose can be to destroy the enemy, for which maximum forces are desired. From the Soviet viewpoint, at least as publicly expressed, the idea of limited nuclear war is a shameful attempt to legitimate nuclear first use. If the United States would look to first use of tactical nuclear weapons to overcome conventional inferiority, the Soviets have seemed to think in terms of first use of strategic weapons for preemption of an attack being prepared. This approach may be conditioned by the sufferings of the country in WW II and consequent determination to minimize destruction on Soviet territory in a future war.

The Soviets seem to have had some idea that nuclear war should be winnable, and the idea of MAD was rejected as defeatist. It is unclear how far this was a reasoned conclusion or deduced from the ideological postulate that Lenin's revolution must be irreversible, hence that there must be victory or at least survival. For many years after the revolution, it was official dogma, as Lenin had laid down, that war between capitalism and socialism was inevitable because of the main fact of history, the class struggle. This teaching was partly renounced in 1952 by Stalin and definitely in 1956 by Nikita Khrushchev, who replaced it with the thesis of Peaceful Coexistence—that the two worlds could get along, even cooperate in some matters, while carrying on a competition that should lead to the eventual victory of the Soviet-socialist cause.

Since 1977, it seems to have become standard doctrine that no one could win a nuclear war.[21] Quite probably, the Soviets have been more apprehensive of nuclear war than Americans. Americans may fear their devices might not work, but the Soviets have the highest respect for American capacities.

The reform wave initiated in 1985 by Mikhail Gorbachev has gradually permeated Soviet strategic thinking, leading not only to much more flexible policies regarding arms control and disarmament but also to a general shift to more flexibility and realism, toward defensive postures instead of the preemptive threat, on the basis, according to Gorbachev, that we must "totally rule out any outward-oriented use of force."[22] Soviet officers were reported to be apprehensive over cuts in the forces, but on personal rather than political grounds: they expressed fears not for their nation but for their jobs and pensions.[23]

---

[21]F. Stephen Larrabee, "Gorbachev and the Soviet Military," *Foreign Affairs* 66 (Summer 1988), p. 1020.

[22]*New York Times,* December 8, 1988, p. A6.

[23]*New York Times,* December 23, 1988, p. A3.

Nuclear Theorizing

There has been an enormous amount of thinking, talking, and writing about nuclear strategy, but the chief product is confusion. The theorists are like zoologists trying to predict the behavior of animals they have not seen in conditions they do not know. We have no idea how real people would react under catastrophic conditions that we cannot imagine; the best guess might be that in the holocaust of holocausts they would behave irrationally.

Many nuclear-related concepts have been elaborated, such as deterrence stability, crisis instability, massive retaliation, limited war, tactical compulsion, escalation dominance, escalation control, assured destruction, counterforce targeting, countervalue targeting (a gentle term for planning the slaughter of tens of millions), war-ending techniques, and decapitation (destroying or incapacitating the enemy leadership). There are fundamental contradictions: some see dangers only in the sinister enemy, some see the danger arising from the doomsday weapons and the competition in deploying them. Some say that nuclear arms should be maintained because they have kept the peace successfully; others feel that we are lucky to have survived in spite of the nuclear overhang. Some find it perilous to change, others are afraid to fail to change.

There are many dilemmas of threshold, response, escalation, targeting, and linkage to political conditions. Should we liquidate the enemy leadership or leave an authority with which to negotiate? Is it desirable to act rationally, in order not to provoke the enemy, or to be seen as irrational, so that the enemy could not count on our reluctance to make a retaliatory strike? Should we impress the other side with our readiness to launch, to maximize deterrent effect, or would this make the enemy more likely to launch preemptively?

To aim at cities is not only inhumane but also militarily inadvisable, because enemy cities can't hurt us in the short time a nuclear war is likely to last. But aiming at launch facilities would compel the enemy to unleash their rockets. It would seem expedient to use nuclear weapons against the weapons threatening us; yet to plan to do so brings instability because of the advantages of hitting first. A first strike is dictated by multiple warheads: a single missile can deliver ten or more reentry vehicles, each potentially capable of knocking out an enemy silo.

A first strike might well be effective in a military sense, because retaliatory action would be more or less lost in the confusion. A half dozen nuclear bombs on the United States would cause chaos; the effect of a few hundred would be unimaginable. It would be very difficult to maintain the command structure, and communications might be overwhelmed by electric forces from an atmospheric explosion hundreds of miles away, an electronic storm disabling communications and unshielded computers. The proposed airborne command center would be especially vulnerable to the electronic pulse. While submarines would supposedly be fairly safe, it might be impossible to communicate with them.

If only fixed launchers were involved, a nation, seeing nuclear war about to begin, would presumably "launch out from under" in order to neutralize as much as possible of the enemy force; this becomes easier as tracking capacity improves. Yet the enemy would be under the same compulsion; the greatest calamity would be to hesitate and allow the enemy to preempt. The probable result would be that the two sides would race and launch about the same time. Then both would destroy mostly empty silos. But the effort would not be wasted; the blasts and radioactive fallout would kill a considerable fraction of the respective populations.

A blow against enemy forces must be immediate, while cities can wait for their turn. Countervalue targeting would represent a degree of inhumanity that would beggar historical comparison. Yet it would contribute to stability if both sides aimed at populations, as neither would have much to gain and very much to lose by initiating a nuclear exchange. A related question is whether the strategic force should be planned for strength or stability. Strength supposedly makes a valuable deterrent; but to minimize dangers, it would be logical to give priority to reducing the advantages of a first or preemptive strike and the pressures to risk it. Should missiles be made mobile, at great expense, for invulnerability, thereby compelling the enemy to target cities? Would it be better for the United States if Soviet submarines were undetectable and so contributed to the stability of deterrence? So far as it is important to avoid nuclear war, high accuracy of rapidly launchable nuclear weapons is undesirable.

Present (1989) stocks of deliverable warheads would suffice to destroy the United States and the Soviet Union as functioning societies some twenty times over; is there any point to having more, or would be it better to have less? The commonest argument for a big arsenal is that there will be malfunctions, failures of communications, and possibly large losses to an enemy first strike. Moreover, there are an indefinite number of objectives to be targeted. The military in principle probably want more of whatever may be had, tanks, ships, or missiles. It has been said, the more nukes the safer.[24]

There was an inclination in the early years of the Reagan administration to believe that it was best to plan in terms of nuclear victory over the totalitarian evil.[25] But even if most of the population escaped immediate death from explosions and radiation (deaths from which would continue over weeks and months), it is hard to imagine that our highly interdependent civilization could carry on with a large fraction of its facilities ruined. What would happen to transportation and communications? Who would feed the cities? Would farmers get fuel to harvest crops? Would there be

[24]Ehrlich, *Waging Nuclear Peace,* p. 295.
[25]Kull, "Nuclear Nonsense," p. 38.

electricity to pump water? Would anyone keep order, or would gangs armed with handguns roam around taking whatever they could find? To equip the population to confront countless such problems and others undreamed of, it would be necessary to make immense preparations, which are not likely to be made. Perhaps victory would be symbolic; according to a T-shirt motto, "He who dies with the most toys wins." Or as an American general put it, "At the end of the war, if there are two Americans and one Russian, we win!"[26] it mattering not who was right but who was left.

Questions of nuclear strategy cannot be resolved without deciding to what extent nuclear arms are desired for strength, to keep up with or outdo the opponent, as a political deterrent to check aggressive behavior, or simply to dissuade from a possible nuclear attack. Do we seek war-fighting capacity or minimal insurance? The latter would be less expensive, less dangerous, and in the opinion of many sufficient.

It has been fascinating to think about the unthinkable, to speculate about megadeaths and mass annihilation through weapons that represent the culmination of human intelligence, or its perversion; and the fantasies have pushed aside the realities.[27] Theoreticians have presented their lucubrations as calmly as though they were dealing with volcanoes on Mars instead of the fate of everything they hold dear. In the great sport of planning the superwar, it is easy to forget what one is planning for. Logic cannot be imposed on something inherently so illogical as nuclear combat-suicide of the greatest powers. The anonymity of the presumed victims makes it possible for aggressive imagination to be indulged without troubling the conscience.[28]

The fundamental contradiction of nuclear arms is that they serve not military but psychological purposes. In practice, it makes no difference if the warheads were filled with lead instead of uranium and plutonium. Nuclear weapons can be employed as a "continuation of politics," in the phrase applicable in the 18th and perhaps the 19th centuries, only as display. The important nuclear fact is essentially psychological, the perception of one side or the other being ahead, which is relevant so far as both sides think it is relevant. To accept inferiority would show weakness and lack of resolve.[29]

The question, "What can be gained by risking nuclear war?" hardly seems to be asked. If the Soviets had no nuclear weapons, would the United States leap at the chance to occupy Moscow? It did not even issue an ultima-

---

[26]Kull, *Minds at War*, p. 84.

[27]Kull, *Minds at War*, p. 306.

[28]As suggested by Konrad Lorenz, *On Aggression* (New York: Harcourt Brace and World, 1966), p. 283. Much of the confusion of nuclear thinking appears in the interviews reported by Kull, *Minds at War*.

[29]Philip A. Sabin, *Shadow or Substance? Perceptions and Symbolism in Nuclear Force Planning*, Adelphi Papers No. 222 (London: International Institute for Strategic Studies, 1987).

tum for the Soviets to withdraw from Eastern Europe when it had a nuclear monopoly. If the United States had no nuclear weapons, would the Soviets occupy the West? They do not apparently profit from hegemony of Eastern Europe.

Infinitely destructive weaponry has been perceived as the crown of world leadership. It is assumed that Japan, for example, cannot be really great without a nuclear arsenal. But nuclear weapons can serve only to create the uncertainty that engenders caution, and perception is in practice more important than reality.[30] The nuclear arms buildup makes sense only if one realizes that it is an industry and a game independent of any possible military use. The capacity for mass murder should have no relevance to standing in a civilized community of nations.

Nuclear Proliferation

Gargantuan piles of explosives cannot be made absolutely safe in a world of frequently ill-informed and emotional actors. Although some have argued that wider dispersal of the ultimate weapon would help to keep the peace,[31] it is generally assumed that the likelihood of an explosion is greater if a larger number of governments, including some that have shown a disposition for terrorism, are nuclearly armed. The possibilities of catastrophe by accident, miscalculation, or devilish calculation would presumably be enhanced.[32]

For such reasons or because they like to keep their special powers for themselves, the United States and the Soviet Union have been at pains to restrict the membership of the nuclear club. Britain and Canada shared in the production of the first atomic weapons. The United States cut them out at war's end, but British scientists cracked American secrets. The Soviet Union tested an A-bomb in 1949, well before the West expected. The French joined the club by 1960.

The French entry was unwelcomed by the United States, but the French "force de frappe" (with about 300 warheads, roughly of the magnitude of the British force) has come to be regarded as a NATO asset. Along with the British nuclearly armed submarines it is an adjunct of the Western strategic deterrent and some reassurance to West Europeans skeptical of the American umbrella. It might not be sane for the French or British to

---

[30]For a general discussion, see Sabin, *Shadow or Substance?*

[31]As Kenneth N. Waltz, *The Spread of Nuclear Weapons: More May Be Better*, Adelphi Papers No. 171 (London: International Institute for Strategic Studies, 1981).

[32]In the general view. See Joseph S. Nye, Jr., "The Diplomacy of Nuclear Nonproliferation," *Negotiating World Order*, ed. Alan K. Henrikson (Wilmington: Scholarly Resources, 1986), pp. 79–94.

invite national obliteration by hitting Soviet cities, but the possibility of their not being sane might be effective. In order to counter a German drift toward neutralism, the French have extended their nuclear umbrella to cover the Federal Republic.

The Soviet Union has been at least as reluctant as the United States to see nuclear weapons in the hands of its allies. Refusal to support the Chinese effort was a reason for the breakup of that alliance in 1960. The Chinese nuclear capacity, demonstrated in 1964, may have dissuaded the Soviet Union from trying to apply to China the doctrine of limited sovereignty of socialist countries.

No other power has openly armed itself nuclearly, and the superpowers strongly desire that they should not. However, the secrets are no longer secret; and nuclear power generation can be engineered to give byproduct plutonium usable for nuclear explosives.

To discourage development of nuclear weapons, the United States and other exporters of uranium and other requisites for nuclear reactors have placed complex stringent conditions on them, at the cost of much friction. U.S. law would also cut off military and economic aid to countries acquiring nuclear weapons.[33] The International Atomic Energy Agency, with headquarters in Vienna, tries to oversee controls and check on nuclear facilities. This is very difficult, however; and a number of nations have broken formal pledges to restrict their nuclear operations to peaceful purposes.[34]

The superpowers also tried to close the gates by the Nuclear Non-Proliferation Treaty of 1968. This has been signed by a large majority of the nations in a remarkable display of willingness to renounce a sovereign right with no more compensation than the vague understanding that the superpowers would reduce their nuclear holdings.

Generalized dislike for nuclear arms has found expression in many proposals and some agreements banning nuclear weapons from particular regions, such as the Treaty of Tlateloco, signed by nearly all Latin American nations. South Pacific states have agreed on the goal of a nuclear-free corner of that ocean, and Southeast Asian nations have a similar pact. What effect the pious wish could have in the event of war is not clear.

Antiproliferation policies have not been wholly successful. Israel, which has a deep sense of insecurity and welcomes any means of impressing its Arab neighbors, may have about 100 atomic weapons, with shortrange missiles. There has been little publicity of the Israeli nuclear force: the Israelis wish to avoid the opprobrium of nuclear proliferation; the United States keeps it quiet in order not to embarrass Israel; the Arabs do not like to admit their inferiority. India, which exploded an atomic device in 1974, can

[33]Efforts to check nuclear proliferation are discussed by Joseph A. Yager, ed., *Nonproliferation and U.S. Foreign Policy* (Washington: Brookings Institution, 1980).

[34]Gary Milhollin, "Heavy Water Cheaters," *Foreign Policy* 69, (Winter 1987/1988), pp. 100–119.

produce some 20 bombs yearly. India claims that its nuclear explosives are for civilian purposes, but no nuclear power has found any such utility. Pakistan, which is desperate to measure up to India, probably has the makings of several A-bombs. South Africa possibly has 10–20 weapons. Argentina, Brazil, Iran, Iraq, Taiwan, Libya, and North Korea have done more or less toward acquiring nuclear capabilities.[35] It is remarkable, however, that more countries have not sought the satisfaction of possessing the superweapon.

If nuclear weapons in many hands create a certain likelihood that sooner or later someone might use one or a few, the leading powers would do well for their own safety to try to reduce conflicts everywhere. They could also, by cutting their own stockpiles of nuclear weapons, diminish the legitimacy of smaller powers imitating them; the chief reason for wanting nuclear weapons seems to be that the big players in the world league have them. If the Soviet Union and the United States were to eliminate nuclear force as a factor in their relations, they would be in a position to demand that other countries renounce something so inhumane as nuclear weapons. The case for using political and economic pressure against the nuclear threat is certainly stronger than the case for intervention against human rights violations. It should not be difficult to join in demanding an end to the threat to everyone.

Arms Control

Whether or not a nuclear arms race adds importantly to the danger of war, it is expensive and raises the sense of danger. Can the superpowers agree to limit or reduce their arsenals? The call is worldwide; almost everyone regards disarmament as virtuous. Taxpayers of the West join with idealists of peace in wishing an end to the arms buildup. Soviet citizens are reported to be unanimous in the desire to reduce the nuclear burden. Third World leaders beg that a little of what is wasted on potential destruction be spent to rescue their countries from poverty.[36]

Disarmament negotiations are much older than atomic bombs. The Hague Conference, convened in 1899 when Europe was near its most peaceable, took steps to regulate the conduct of war, including the outlawing of poison gases. The Covenant of the League of Nations in 1919 promised

[35]E. A. Wayne, "Undeclared A-Bombs Spread," *Christian Science Monitor,* November 17, 1988, p. 1.

[36]For a general discussion, see Christopher J. Lamb, *How to Think about Arms Control, Disarmament, and Defense* (Englewood Cliffs, NJ: Prentice Hall Inc., 1988); Paul F. Diehl and Loch K. Johnson, eds., *Through the Straits of Armageddon: Arms Control Issues and Proposals* (Athens, GA: University of Georgia Press, 1987). Soviet views are given by *Disarmament and Security 1987 Yearbook* (Moscow: U.S.S.R. Academy of Sciences, Institute of World Economy and International Relations, 1988).

disarmament, which should have complemented the disarmament imposed on defeated Germany by the Treaty of Versailles. The interwar years saw lengthy negotiations of naval treaties, which led to the scrapping of a few ships but which did nothing to check the coming of the Second World War. At the opening of the atomic age, the United States proposed the "Baruch Plan" to place atomic energy under an international (probably U.S.-dominated) agency; but the Soviets would have nothing of it. Much talk of disarmament in the 1950s and early 1960s was highly propagandistic, an exercise performed better by the Soviets, who presented grand proposals for banning nuclear weapons or all weapons, than by the United States.

Since the cold war began running down, however, arms control has been the chief subject of East–West negotiations, or a dual subject, nuclear matters having been kept separate from the less publicized discussions of reduction or pullback of nonnuclear forces ("Mutual Balanced Force Reduction"). There have been many agreements, including the Limited Test Ban Treaty (1963) banning aboveground nuclear tests; the SALT I accord (1972) freezing some offensive weapon levels; the Antiballistic Missile (ABM) Treaty (1972); a treaty limiting the size of underground nuclear tests to 150 kilotons (1974); SALT II (1979), limiting some offensive weapons, never ratified but observed; and the Stockholm Agreement (1986) providing for notification and observation of large-scale maneuvers. Most significant has been a treaty banning intermediate range missiles in Europe (1987).[37]

Progress has been difficult and slow. There are ample suspicions on both sides, and negotiations are primarily entrusted to persons whose business it is to maintain military strength. Weapons systems are built as bargaining chips to get concessions from the other side; but once built, they are not readily bargained away. The problem of guaranteeing fulfillment (verification) is formidable; there is no separating offensive from defensive weapons; and without considerable goodwill, it is impossible satisfactorily to weigh one weapons system against another.

The improvement of satellite and other means, however, has eased the problem of verification. It is possible not only to count silos with considerable reliability but also to detect any significant underground nuclear test from a considerable distance. Telescopes in the sky can pick out objects the size of a basketball from 500 miles above.[38]

Equally important for the improved prospects is the extension of *glas-*

---

[37]For details of negotiations see Albert Carnesale and Richard N. Haas, eds., *Superpower Arms Control* (Cambridge, MA: Ballinger, 1988); Alexander George, Philip J. Farley, and Alexander Dallin, eds., *U.S.-Soviet Security Cooperation* (New York: Oxford University Press, 1988); Bruce D. Berkowitz, *Calculated Risks: A Century of Arms Control, Why It Has Failed and How It Can Be Made to Work* (New York: Simon and Schuster, 1987); Leon Sloss and M. Scott Davis, eds., *A Game for High Stakes* (Cambridge, MA: Ballinger, 1986); and Lynn F. Davis, "Lessons of the INF Treaty," *Foreign Affairs* 66, Spring 1988, pp. 720–34.

[38]William E. Barrows, "Why Verification Can Be Solidly Trusted," *New York Times*, December 28, 1987, p. 19.

nost, or "openness," to the Soviet military, the setting aside of what seemed to be paranoid addiction to secrecy, in keeping with the changes brought by the Gorbachev leadership. The December 1987 Intermediate Nuclear Force (INF) agreement rests on an extensive program of regular and short-notice inspections on both sides that would have been inconceivable a decade earlier. Although the gains from elimination of a category of nuclear weapons (about 4 percent of the total) are estimable, it is perhaps more important that foreigners have access to secret Soviet facilities.

Even if it should be possible to reduce the number of missiles threatening each superpower from the territory of the other, a tenth of the nuclear stockpiles would suffice to destroy all major cities in both countries. The primary gain from any disarmament agreement is political or psychological, a feeling that shared interests can prevail and a reason to seek more grounds of cooperation. Any understanding tends to make it seem less urgent to build up the armories. A total ban on nuclear testing would have the same effect; it would do nothing to reduce stockpiles but would weaken the feeling that it is necessary to continue to improve them. So far as arms control means detente, the Soviets may gain from it by improved access to Western markets and credits and a decreased willingness of allies to cooperate with the United States. On the other hand, this country cannot afford to be seen as willfully rejecting disarmament.

The record of compliance with arms control agreements has been generally good. There have been dozens of complaints, but they have almost all been the result of ambiguities and have mostly been corrected. The Soviet record has improved since Brezhnev and especially since Gorbachev took power in 1985.[39] The only clear-cut violation to date has been the Soviet radar near Krasnoyarsk, in contravention of the 1972 ABM treaty; it is of no great military importance and has not been completed. In December 1988 Gorbachev offered to internationalize it.[40]

There is some feeling within the American government (and presumably the Soviet government) that the other side is certain to cheat; it is feared that agreements, no matter what the terms, will sap the national resolve, leading us to disarm while the enemy pretends to do so. It has been contended that the arms race is actually desirable because it is a substitute for the real thing.[41] But arms control agreements seem to have reduced the dangers of nuclear war,[42] and they may weaken the attachment to nuclear weapons, making it possible to believe that it is not necessary to outdo the antagonist in nuclear capacities, only to have enough to make a nuclear war excessively risky. In the 1950s, a few hundred looked like overkill; the tens of

[39]Gloria Duffy and others, *Compliance and the Future of Arms Control* (Cambridge, MA: Ballinger Publishing Co., 1988).

[40]*New York Times,* December 8, 1988, p. A6.

[41]Kull, *Minds at War,* p. 246.

[42]Duffy, *Compliance and the Future of Arms Control,* p. 27.

thousands in strategic stockpiles represent not the reality of international relations but a morbid aberration. If this is accepted, nuclear—and nonnuclear—weaponry may gradually lose its psychological value, and the nuclear shadow over humanity may fade away.

"Conventional" Military

Much more is spent on conventional armaments, including navies and air forces, than on the more spectacular strategic arms. By far the greatest concentration of nonnuclear as well as nuclear power is piled up in Europe near the western borders of East Germany and Czechoslovakia. The great threat that the armed forces of the United States and its allies, like those of the Soviet Union and its allies, are intended to counter, is an attack across this frontier, although "Armed conflict in Europe appears less likely than in almost any other part of the world."[43] Most strategic scenarios in the West, and we may assume most in the East, are based on this improbable circumstance.

Apprehensive Americans have feared that the Soviets might add the industrial power of Western Europe to their military-political might and gain world supremacy; and the Soviet forces, evidently structured for a westward assault, have given grounds for such fears. But this may be a holdover from the days when ground superiority was the Soviets' counter for American nuclear monopoly. It also seems to answer a belief that the Soviet Union could deter the United States by looking fearsome, in the manner of fish and lizards that puff themselves up when they sense danger. It would make sense for the Russians to launch an attack only as a counter to an attack on the Soviet Union. Even if they could march to the Atlantic without opposition and without risk of nuclear devastation, populous and advanced Western Europe would be harder to manage than the rather ungrateful vassals of Eastern Europe.

A surprise attack, in any case, would seem impossible in the face of continual close surveillance; the Soviets have needed in the past about three months to mount movements far less ambitious than the conquest of Western Europe, such as intervention in Czechoslovakia (1968), the invasion of Afghanistan (1979), and the threat against Poland (1981).[44] A Soviet assault on Western Europe would make sense only as reprisal for a nuclear attack, which is the probable meaning of Soviet planning.[45]

---

[43]James Berry Motley, "Low Intensity Conflict: A Global Challenge," *Teaching Political Science* 15, Fall 1987, p. 15.

[44]Richard A. Stubbing, *The Defense Game* (New York: Harper & Row, 1987) p. 22.

[45]MccGwire, *Military Objectives,* p. 372.

It may be that the military planners do not take seriously the idea of a Soviet army flooding across the East–West divide. Fortification of the West German border would greatly reduce the advantages of any Soviet numerical superiority and would improve nuclear stability.[46] This is not done, however, because of German unwillingness to underline the permanent division of Germany.

Yet here, along the border between the two Germanies, is the only place where the forces of the two sides of the world glare at one another. The confrontation is visible and dramatic. Here we measure ourselves face to face against the enemy. Nowhere else is there an important target within marching distance of the very large Soviet forces. Most of the periphery of the Soviet Union is guarded by mountain barriers, with sparsely settled or unproductive lands beyond; and an invasion of Japan would require an amphibious capacity the Soviets lack. Moreover, only here is the Soviet Union open to conquest. It was over the North European plain that German armies marched to Moscow and the Volga, and Soviet armies drove into the heart of Europe. One imagines a new war on the same stage as the best-remembered war.

No one has any idea whether a nonnuclear war in Europe would be like WW II, when German armored columns made spectacular breakthroughs, or like WW I and the Iran-Iraq war, when armies pounded each other for years with little movement. But it is commonly believed that the Eastern conventional forces are grossly superior to the Western, presumably capable of sweeping rapidly from the Elbe to the Atlantic. Recent figures indicated 22,200 NATO tanks against 53,000 of the WTO; 2,865 attack aircraft against 2,330; 2.34 million ground troops against 2.14 million; and so forth.[47] Western analysts say, with varying emphasis, that the Soviet-WTO forces are much superior; the Soviets say they are roughly equal, their tank superiority being balanced by NATO's attack aircraft and antitank weapons.

The Pentagon admits comparisons only in numerical terms. There is evidence that the Soviets are catching up in technology, evidence strongest at budget time in Washington; but U.S. weapons are evidently generally superior. Many Soviet weapons, including a large part of their tank force, are obsolete. Adding up WTO against NATO forces is unrealistic insofar as East German, Czechoslovak, or Hungarian troops are unlikely to fight doggedly under Soviet command to perpetuate their national subordination.

The principal purpose of the conventional forces on both sides in Europe, like the nuclear forces, is to stand tall as a deterrent. Elsewhere, it is difficult for democratic powers to use military power, except perhaps for an occasional reprisal. It even seemed too costly to have Marines chase out

---

[46]Jervis, "Strategic Theory," in *The Logic of Nuclear Terror*, ed. Kolkowicz, p. 57.
[47]*The Economist*, October 22, 1988, p. 51.

the government of an annoying and pitifully weak power, Nicaragua, in the nearest thing to a U.S. sphere of influence. The United States has desired a capacity for intervention in the unstable Near East (a "Rapid Deployment Force"), but anything more than a naval presence seems to be too expensive. The United States is not likely to field a large army into Asia, Vietnam-style, for a very long time. It is unclear what the role of big armies should be, outside the European theater.

Soviet armies have the minor task of maintaining the political integrity of the bloc, as they have done in East Germany, Hungary, Czechoslovakia, and (by threat) Poland. The Soviet Union can hardly contemplate a conquest of Iran or Turkey, especially after the unhappy experience of Afghanistan. An invasion of China could be considered only in the unlikely event of a Chinese civil war—and probably not even then. Elsewhere, as in Angola and Ethiopia, the Soviet Union has been able to take advantage of conflictive conditions only through furnishing arms and advisors, letting a Third World country, Cuba, supply troops.

Secondary powers may be freer to employ armies.[48] The Cubans have deployed the largest expeditionary forces of the lesser powers, having had some 50,000 shoring up the government of Angola in 1988. The Castro government must have found the venture rewarding, although it was unclear what Cuba gained beyond satisfactions of "internationalism" and perhaps Soviet gratitude. It had a high cost in U.S. hostility and had to be given up when the Soviets decided it did not pay; it was agreed that the Cubans would be withdrawn in return for South African evacuation of Namibia. In 1978–79 the Vietnamese occupied Cambodia (Kampuchea), and in 1979 the Chinese undertook to "punish Vietnam" by an invasion. But the Vietnamese, like the Cubans, in 1988 agreed to pull out. The South Africans have conducted many smallscale operations, mostly to intimidate neighboring states; their results are hard to assess. Iraqis and Iranians battled 8 years and suffered perhaps a million deaths and another million casualties, not to speak of enormous material losses, for nothing. The Israeli invasion of Lebanon in 1982 was militarily successful, but instead of the expected peace it brought the near-destruction of the government of Lebanon and a disorderly situation complicating the problems of Israel.

If the ground forces of the superpowers have seen little activity, U.S. naval and air forces have occasionally been employed. A stated purpose of the U.S. Navy is to protect sea lanes,[49] although it is not clear why anyone except pirates would attack American shipping short of war, and for dealing

---

[48]For details of armaments of all countries, see *The Military Balance 1986–87* (London: International Institute for Strategic Studies, 1986 and subsequent years). Also, *World Armaments and Disarmament: SIPRI Yearbook* (Stockholm: Stockholm International Peace Research Institute).

[49]According to Secretary of the Navy, James H. Webb, Jr., *Wall Street Journal*, January 18, 1988, p. 12.

with pirates, frigates are more useful than capital ships. The Navy wants new killer submarines to protect convoys across the Atlantic, WW II style.

To a large extent, the fleet is for display. U.S. naval actions in the Persian Gulf in 1987 and 1988 showed the world that we were there and that the Soviets were almost excluded. Imposing vessels, especially aircraft carriers, should inspire admiration and perhaps a bit of apprehension, whether on a friendly call or a coercive mission. It may be for this reason that the American navy prefers to buy behemoth carriers instead of a much larger number of utility vessels, and consequently found itself practically without minesweepers for duty in the Persian Gulf.

It has seemed important to the Soviet Union to have a naval presence in the South Pacific and Indian Oceans, as it is for the United States. Planes of both spend much time cruising over the endless waters. On one occasion, after Soviet military flights came undesirably close to Alaska, U.S. planes were sent on a beeline run toward a Soviet Pacific port, veering away only ten minutes short of the mock target.[50]

The postwar record of the superpowers' use of military threats shows mostly failures. For example, Stalin failed to browbeat Yugoslavia in 1948 and China in the 1960s. Soviet-Japanese relations sagged when the Soviets built up their forces on the Kurile Islands after 1978 and paraded their power off the Japanese coast. Finding that military power fails to translate into corresponding political influence in the Asia-Pacific region, the Soviet Union has made multiple moves toward economic development projects, collective security conferences, environmental efforts, and expansion of trade, supplementing but not replacing its military presence.[51] U.S. naval maneuvers off the Central American coast and repeated "exercises" in Honduras had no apparent effect in modifying the behavior or mentality of the Nicaraguan government. U.S. naval and Marine deployment in Lebanon in 1983 was likewise futile. For battleships to lob shells into Lebanese villages was not a cost-effective way of fighting terrorism.

The superpowers have been militarily successful only when not seriously opposed. Soviet troops, for example, were able to repress deviation from orthodoxy in Hungary (1956) and Czechoslovakia (1968) in the absence of organized resistance. Similarly, in Grenada (1983), Libya (1986), and the Persian Gulf (1988), the United States could carry out successful, or at least low-cost operations. Determined foes have checked the superpowers in Vietnam, Afghanistan, Korea, and Nicaragua; the prospect of real battle probably deterred the Soviet Union from sending armies into Romania (1968 and after) and Poland (1980–81).

---

[50]*Christian Science Monitor,* November 24, 1987, p. 2.

[51]Hiroshi Kimura, "Soviet Focus on the Pacific," *Problems of Communism* 36, May–June 1987, pp. 1–16.

Although conventional forces are more usable than nuclear arms, they have not proved much more useful.

Alliances

George Washington's valedictory exhortation to avoid "entangling alliances" was a guidepost of American foreign policy for most of the national existence, even when this country had achieved unequalled economic power. With the coming of the cold war, however, this advice was forgotten in eagerness to maximize entanglements, building and keeping up alliances, seeking new allies or near-allies and friends who might become allies.

The first important move toward building the worldwide American alliance system was the Rio Pact (1947) for the defense of Latin America.[52] This was an outgrowth of the Pan-American system patronized by the United States since the beginning of the century and a multilateralization of the Monroe Doctrine. It was designed not to counter a threat of invasion, which was nonexistent, but to preserve something of the political solidarity generated by the war. It was followed by the NATO alliance, which was put together in 1949 less to defend against possible Soviet invasion than to fortify Western Europe against muscular communist parties, especially in France and Italy. It became the most successful alliance in history.

Having done so well in Europe, the United States undertook to cobble NATO clones in less hospitable areas. The Southeast Asia Treaty Organization (SEATO, 1954) was designed to halt the spread of communism from China, and the Bagdad Pact (which became the Central Treaty Organization, CENTO, after Iraq pulled out and the United States formally joined in 1959) to protect the Near East. Neither was a genuine alliance, none of the regional members being expected to make any real contribution beyond furnishing sites for American bases. This was also true of security guarantees extended to Japan, South Korea, and Nationalist China (Taiwan) in the early 1950s.

Postwar "pactomania" climaxed in the 1950s and ebbed as it became evident that the alliances formed only under pressure from the United States had no substance. SEATO and CENTO have long since faded. In the 1980s the United States has paid very little attention to the Organization of American States (OAS), which has sunk into inanition for lack of funds. The ANZUS Pact (1951) between Australia, New Zealand, and the United States

[52]L. Ronald Scheman, "Rhetoric and Reality: The Inter-American System's Second Century," *Journal of Inter-American Studies and World Affairs* 29, (Fall 1987), pp. 1–32.

has lapsed because of New Zealand's barring vessels carrying nuclear weapons.

The important remaining multilateral alliance, NATO, has a rather elaborate structure capped by the North Atlantic Council made up of ministers of all member states, assisted by a civilian secretary general and international staff. Under the Council is a Military Committee of chiefs of staff of members, with various commands, including Supreme Headquarters Allied Powers Europe. The commander has always been American. As a going concern, with staff, procedures, assets, and vested interests, NATO has a sense of permanence.

Even NATO has problems. Nuclear policy is always controversial; and Europeans have difficulty deciding whether they want U.S. missiles on the ground, making their countries prime targets, or want not to have them, in which case they feel unprotected. They are torn between fears of being drawn into a war they do not desire and of being abandoned by their American protector, between fears that it may respond too energetically and that it will hesitate to respond.[53]

It is the silent hope of the United States (and expressed fear of Europeans) that a nuclear war might be decided in Europe and spare the United States; it is the Europeans' hope that the war might be fought over their heads,[54] although they tend to doubt that the United States would risk the destruction of New York and Washington to avenge Berlin or Paris. They become nervous when the United States and the Soviet Union get together to deal with grand questions without consulting Europe, as in the summit meeting at Reykjavik, Iceland, in October 1986.

The allies have varying attitudes toward the alliance. Britain, although reduced in relative weight among nations, still enjoys a "special relation" with the United States, which gives it a somewhat superior role. De Gaulle pulled France out of the military structure of NATO in 1966, and his successors have shown no wish to return, but France is a good and a respected ally. Lesser powers, such as Spain and the Netherlands, have a tendency to feel that the U.S.-Soviet quarrel is not their affair. Greece, seeing not the Soviet Union but its fellow NATO-member Turkey as the foe, is least cooperative of all.

West Germany, denied nuclear forces and fearful of becoming the battleground of any conflict, has serious doubts. The center-rightists in power mutter about American unreliability, if not abandonment, and show no enthusiasm for nuclear modernization. The oppositionist Social Democrats

---

[53]Jane M. O. Sharpe, "Arms Control and Alliance Commitments," *Political Science Quarterly* 100, (Winter 1985–1986), pp. 650–51; Carl H. Amme, *NATO Strategy and Nuclear Doctrine* (New York: Greenwood Press, 1988).

[54]Donald C. Hendrickson, *The Future of American Strategy* (New York: Holmes and Meier, 1987), pp. 74–75.

are among the most Marxist of major European parties and would apparently like to get out entirely.[55] With about a million foreign troops in their small country, with NATO jets sending sonic booms and tanks tearing up fields, Germans see themselves treated as inferiors nearly half a century after their defeat. For such reasons, West Germans are decidedly friendly toward the Soviet Union. Bonn encourages German banks to lend to the Soviets and German firms to enter joint ventures and hopes for closer ties with East Germany and Eastern Europe, where Germans have long seen their destiny.

The European allies dedicate a much smaller fraction of their wealth to defense, 3.8 percent on average against the 6.5 percent of the United States. The one that spends most generously is the poorest, Greece, which arms against Turkey. Next is Britain, which cherishes some old sentiments of world responsibility. Small powers, such as Denmark, are least disposed to spend for the alliance.

It should not be difficult for European NATO powers to match the military capacity of the Soviet bloc, as they have about the same population and more than double the economic product—assuming that the East European countries can be counted as full assets for the Soviet side. Canada, in a geographic situation like that of the United States, carries a defense burden only about a third as heavy in terms of proportion of GNP (2.1 percent) and of the labor force dedicated to the military.[56] Neutralist Sweden spends 2.8 percent of GNP on defense.

The United States keeps 320,000 American troops in Europe and devotes to it a great deal of money (over $100 billion yearly, or as much as half the total defense budget if forces in the United States assigned to NATO are included), a burden that makes it difficult to pare the federal deficit. Consequently, "burdensharing" has acquired great popularity in U.S. politics, and a large majority of Americans seem to feel that Europe should pay more. It is also irksome that allies criticize U.S. actions outside Europe, as in Central America, even give aid and comfort to leftists, although the United States sees itself fighting the common ideological enemy. NATO allies are much more disposed than the United States to cut deals and promote trade with the Soviet Union.

On the other hand, the NATO allies add in their troops (90 percent of the ground forces on the spot), the real estate they provide, and the inconveniences they suffer for serving as America's first line of defense, and believe they are doing quite enough.[57] Unless they feel more threatened

---

[55]For German attitudes, see Wolfram F. Hanrieder, ed., *Arms Control, the F.R.G., and the Future of East–West Relations* (Boulder, CO: Westview, 1987).

[56]Jean Edward Smith, "Restructuring Canada's Defense Contribution: A Possible Way to Western Security," *Political Science Quarterly* 102 (Fall 1987), pp. 441–49.

[57]Karen DeYoung, "A 'Fair Share' for our NATO Allies," *Washington Post National Weekly Edition*, May 2–8, 1988, pp. 8–9.

they will not be persuaded to do more. Nor do they apologize for differing with U.S. policy in the Third World, regarding this as a distraction from the primary engagement and fearing embroilment in conflicts of slight interest to them.[58]

Some in the American defense and foreign policy establishment would prefer for this country to make its way like a self-willed superpower with much less regard for allies unless they are willing to make greater sacrifices. But it is rather heretical to propose pulling back to "fortress America." The level of U.S. defense expenditures is fixed by this country for its purposes, not to comply with the wishes of Europe. Bearing the greater military burden means enjoying the greater influence; and the United States, having become habituated to a sort of protectorate, seems to prefer Europe not to be too self-reliant.[59]

If the need for large American forces in Europe may be questionable, it is less clear why the Republic of Korea needs an American force of 43,000, with an American general in command of the joint army. The ROK has twice the population and about 6 times the economic strength of North Korea; and one might suppose that the people of the thriving, rather free country would be quite as patriotic as those ground down by one of the most intense tyrannies of the world. There is no prospect of the Soviet Union or China backing a North Korean assault on the South. The American presence is an irritant for the people of the republic, some of whose annoyance surfaced in boos for Americans and cheers for Russians at the 1988 Olympic Games. It is also the chief basis of North Korea's claim to represent Korean nationalism. Some Koreans say that the United States brought about the war in 1950 and since then has prevented reunification.[60]

No one would urge having an American army in Korea if it had not gone there in the 1950s. However, since the forces are there, it is seen as weakness to consider paring their numbers. On becoming president, Jimmy Carter proposed first a withdrawal, then a reduction; but two years later, he backed away under pressures from the armed services, Congress, South Korea, and Japan.[61]

Allies are valued as means of projecting military force abroad. If Japan and various European allies will share the cost, so much the better; if necessary, we will pay rent for a forward locale for our forces. Bases in Western

---

[58]Lawrence S. Kaplan, "The United States, NATO, and the Third World," in *East–West Rivalry in the Third World: Security Issues and Regional Perspectives,* ed. Robert W. Clawson, (Washington: Scholarly Resources, 1986), p. 12.

[59]For a general study, advocating radical revision of the alliance system, see David P. Calleo, *Beyond American Hegemony: The Future of the Western Alliance* (New York: Basic Books, 1987); for a historical view, see Lawrence S. Kaplan, *NATO and the United States: The Enduring Alliance* (Boston: G. K. Hall, 1988).

[60]*The Economist,* June 18, 1988, p. 35.

[61]Chae-jin Lee and Hideo Sato, *U.S. Policy toward Japan and Korea: A Changing Influence Relationship* (New York: Praeger, 1982), pp. 117–27.

Europe, Spain, Greece, Turkey, Italy, and the Philippines provide a site for deployment of troops and airpower and for naval or intelligence operations. (Other countries hosting American forces in 1987 included Australia, Bahrain, Diego Garcia, Honduras, Iceland, Netherlands, Panama, Portugal, South Korea, and above all West Germany, with more than all others combined.)

Yet the number of U.S. bases abroad has decreased gradually, as one or another becomes obsolete or succumbs to nationalistic pressures, from over 2,000 shortly after WW II to about 700 in 1987.[62] How useful or necessary they may be is not clear. Colonies at the beginning of this century were something of an unprofitable pretext for the armies and navies needed to protect them.[63] Bases nowadays serve not only to support operations but also to justify the forces stationed on them. The costs are often high, and their wartime use is commonly restricted. Although they inject much money into the local economy, nationalists demand large sums as rent to overcome patriotic qualms. Whenever a base agreement comes up for renewal there is haggling, which becomes difficult as Congress cuts foreign aid allocations.

The largest U.S. installations overseas, Subic Bay Naval Base and Clark Air Field near Manila, are regarded as invaluable, although it is not apparent just what function they serve beyond a satisfying projection of U.S. power to that part of the world.[64] They enable the U.S. to act as policeman for the South China Sea, although it is not clear why and against whom the United States has to police this area.

Some Filipinos feel that they can achieve self-respect only if they shed the dependence implied by the foreign presence. From the American viewpoint, to the contrary, the Filipinos should pay part of the cost of the common defense, as the Japanese do. Negotiations in 1988 for extension of the lease on the Philippine bases were complicated. Knowing that relocation would be difficult and expensive, the nationalist parties demanded over a billion dollars yearly rent. However, the bases are the second largest employer in the country (surpassed only by the government), and their closure would be costly for the economy quite apart from the loss of the rental fee (called "aid").[65] The Filipinos settled for less than half a billion.

To some extent, the network of foreign bases forms a single web. If the rent rises in one country, others take note; if U.S. forces are required to leave Greece, their presence in Spain is made a little doubtful. Their status also depends on the world political climate; if there is more tension, coun-

---

[62]Jed C. Snyder, "Security Slips at NATO's South Flank, *Wall Street Journal*, November 18, 1987, p. 33.

[63]Henry M. Pachter, *The Fall and Rise of Europe: A Political, Social, and Cultural History of the Twentieth Century* (New York: Praeger, 1975), p. 25.

[64]James Fallow, "The Philippines: The Bases Dilemma," *Atlantic*, 261, February 1988, pp. 18–30.

[65]*The Economist*, August 6, 1988, p. 11.

tries are more hospitable to the foreign presence; in times of relaxation, it seems less tolerable.

Alliances complicate the strategic standoff. If there were no problem of reassuring allies, the United States and the Soviet Union might well be satisfied with something more like a minimum deterrent; a counterforce capability is desirable chiefly because of commitments abroad. But alliances are valued beyond anything they are calculated to achieve. For some in Washington, NATO makes a reasonable level of international tension desirable; too much calm would lull the Europeans into feeling less need to look to the United States and Soviet influence would increase.

Washington posits the interdependence of commitments; if we fail in any, those who depend on us will see us as weak and will yield to hostile forces. Stress on commitment rather than interests reduces flexibility;[66] but we want responsibility, which is the mark of greatness. We seek to assure clients of our steadfastness, although the more they rely on us the less they need to rely on themselves or to take into account the wants of their own people.

The United States begged Southeast Asian countries to accept American protection against the North Vietnamese aggressors in the 1960s. The Reagan administration was much more exercised about radical Nicaragua's threat to its neighbors than the Central American countries directly exposed. If the real issue were their safety from foreign aggression, they would be grateful for whatever support they might receive and more anxious to be defended than the patron would be to defend them. That was the case, for example, in 1939, when Britain and France felt more threatened by Nazi aggression than did the United States, which, despite their pleas, came only slowly and reluctantly to their rescue.

Alliances have a political function; NATO helps the moderate or conservative parties in Europe. This has an economic side; to be an ally of the United States implies affiliation with the Western economic system. Alliances with the more advanced countries also help to check the flow of militarily useful products and technology to the Soviet bloc. The Coordinating Committee for Multinational Export Control, or COCOM, has from the beginning of the cold war worked to prevent the Soviet Union from compensating for its technological lag by imports. An informal grouping based on understanding only, it is composed of NATO members plus Japan and minus Iceland, and it cooperates with other advanced countries, such as Sweden and Switzerland.

COCOM's task of blocking exports of thousands of products to the Soviet Union—or other destinations from which they might be forwarded to the Soviets—is not easy. In the volume and complexity of international

---

[66]Bruce W. Jentleson, "American Commitments in the Third World: Theory vs. Practice," *International Organization* 41, August 1987, 667–704.

transactions, falsification and smuggling can never be foreclosed entirely. A single sample of a new product may be enough to give away its secrets. There is no agreement as to where lines should be drawn; and the tendency, in times of relative relaxation, is to reduce the list of controlled articles and expedite export permits. Even if violations are discovered, it is difficult to punish the guilty. Competitive allied nations are generally more loath to renounce profitable business than is the United States. Apart from the political and economic costs of enforcement, there is some question whether the endeavor is rational; some believe that trying to limit the export of technology hurts American industry more than it hampers Soviet industry.[67]

Balancing Alliances

The biggest purpose of NATO is probably symbolic. It served effectively to check the once menacing communist movement in Western Europe; it continues in place to maintain a degree of political unity of Western Europe and the United States. It is also a counterbalance to the Soviet-led Warsaw Treaty Organization, which was formed in emulation of NATO in 1955, much more to bind the Soviet-dominated countries of Eastern Europe than for strictly military purposes. That is, the WTO represents an institutionalization of the party-mediated bonds of the Soviet bloc; and it is more necessary for the Soviet bloc than NATO is for the West.

The Soviet Union has acquired allies, if they may be so called, only by virtue of military occupation in or immediately following major war, most importantly in Eastern Europe—Poland, East Germany, Hungary, Czechoslovakia, Bulgaria, and Romania—which were occupied by Soviet forces in 1944–1945. A primary reason or excuse for the Soviet sphere in Eastern Europe was to obtain a defensive glacis against such an attack as the Soviets suffered in 1941, putting Soviet troops several hundred miles in advance of the borders. This at least makes an overland invasion of the Soviet Union more impracticable.

Soviet hegemony has been successful in that the Soviets have institutionalized their system in East Germany, Czechoslovakia, Hungary, and Bulgaria, less effectively in Poland and Romania. They have not, however, been able to make themselves well liked; and loyalty has been assured only by having forces on the ground. The only one of the satellites without a Soviet military presence, Romania, is the most deviant, although it is nearly surrounded by Soviet power. Management of the bloc is not easy. Not only have East European governments been decreasingly disposed to follow meekly the Soviet lead; economic costs seem to have been rising.

Like NATO allies, WTO members spend much less on the contest than the senior partner, roughly the same percentage of their GNP (about 4–7

---

[67]Eugene B. Skolnikoff, "Technology and the World of Tomorrow," *Current History* 99, January 1989, p. 6.

percent) as the NATO allies,[68] and only about one-third of the Soviet percentage. The East Germans spend the most and are militarily the most important.

The Soviet Union is able, however, to use its position as hegemon of the East European bloc to promote a high degree of interdependence. This is institutionalized in a multitude of agreements, not only the military collaboration of WTO but also political bonds among both governments and communist parties. Its economic organization is the Council for Mutual Economic Assistance (CEMA, sometimes called Comecon). Half to three-quarters of the East European partners' foreign trade is within the bloc.

The Soviet bloc or sphere in Eastern Europe in the 1950s was virtually an unacknowledged empire, whose satraps were entirely obedient to the Kremlin. As the ability of Marxist-Leninist parties to work their will has been eroded, it has become more like a genuine alliance. The Soviet Union can no longer simply dictate, although it dominates WTO much more effectively than the United States dominates NATO. The coherence of the bloc seems increasingly to rest on the common interests of political elites in the satellite countries and the Soviet Union.

Alliances, however, are essentially outmoded. In their 18th century age of glory, they were a crucial part of the international system; easily made and unmade, they were the means of upholding the balance of power. When they became hardened early in this century, they set the stage for war. In the 1930s the fascist powers proclaimed aggressive alliances to frighten the world. In the postwar period, alliances have been the incarnation of the cold war. So far as the bipolar confrontation ebbs and Europe feels unthreatened, alliances must lose importance and coherence.

NATO and WTO retain a certain utility, however, as long as there are major political differences between Western and Eastern Europe. For the Soviet Union, military collaboration is an essential means of upholding a special relationship with the countries of its sphere; it does not desire to dissolve the bloc just as it does not wish to permit minorities of the Soviet Union to break away. For the United States, NATO is the anchor of political influence in Europe, even though it may shed much of its military character and become a simple club of like-minded powers. Essentially, however, alliances, like nuclear weapons and conventional military forces, belong to the world that is receding.

---

[68]*The Military Balance 1986–1987* (London: International Institute for Strategic Studies, 1986) p. 212.

Chapter 4

Contesting
the Third World

Problems of Influence

There is a military confrontation in Europe only because the Western and
Soviet spheres meet there. But great powers have seldom in history and
never in modern times come to blows because of demands directly against
one another, and control of Europe is not at issue. Soviet hopes of gaining
sway over European lands beyond where the Red Army marched in WW II
faded rapidly after the Marshall Plan and NATO were put in place. The
United States and the Soviet Union sparred for decades, however, for influence in or hegemony over weaker, generally economically backward nations. There the United States feared that the Soviet Union might gain an
advantage, with probably dreadful consequences. American writers have
felt that it is dangerous for the Soviet Union to have influence anywhere
outside its accepted sphere; and any Soviet penetration is considered a challenge for the United States.[1]

In retrospect this fear seems exaggerated, because efforts to reorder
less developed countries have proved unprofitable and influence in them,
so far as gained, has added little to the power of either side in the cold war.

[1]See, for example, Joseph G. Whelan and Michael J. Dixon, *The Soviet Union in the Third
World: Threat to World Peace* (Washington: Pergamon-Brassey's, 1986).

But the angst was not sheer folly. Many regarded the Soviet system as highly successful—it had performed admirably in the war after staggering in the first months—and it was not hard to believe that the Soviets had, as they boasted, the potent recipe for rapid modernization and industrialization through central planning. If the Third World were widely Sovietized, with the bulk of the world's population, the long-term outlook for political freedom in the world would be grim.

Moreover, in seeking to win or hold the allegiance of weaker powers, the superpowers have been impelled by vocation of leadership and desire to affirm their way of life. Both are more than ethnic groups or nationalities incorporated as states; they are superstates legitimated by an ideal. They have from their beginnings wanted to spread the faith, to see other nations become like themselves, to be an example for the world and to forward their political-social-economic constitution, which is part of their being. The superpowers in the postwar period thus set themselves the task of shaping the conduct of less developed societies.

Economic Pressure

Means of influence or compulsion have been many. One has been economic pressure, ranging from denial of trade preferences or suspension of an assistance program to an embargo on trade. In 1948, the Soviet Union cut off exchanges with rebellious Yugoslavia, which had been selling 50 percent of its exports to the Soviet bloc and buying 95 percent of its imports from it. But the Western powers came to the rescue, and Yugoslavia survived and prospered. In 1955, the Soviet Union began trying to lure the Yugoslavs back into their orbit by encouraging trade, making a few loans and promising more; but there was no reestablishing the old dependence. The lesson was not easily learned, however. The Soviets proceeded in somewhat the same negative way against other breakaway states, China and Albania, with the same negative results.

The United States, with far greater economic power, had more reason for confidence in an embargo on trade with Cuba in 1960 and after; but again results were poor. The Soviets stepped into the gap and Cuba became economically dependent on them. The allies of the United States were willing to sell whatever nonmilitary goods the Soviets could not supply. The United States has also prohibited transactions with Vietnam, Albania, and North Korea, without much apparent effect on the conduct of those states. In recent years, the United States has imposed economic sanctions of some degree on the Soviet Union (for the invasion of Afghanistan), Poland (for the imposition of martial law), South Africa (for apartheid), Libya (for support of terrorism), Nicaragua (for revolutionism), and Panama (for drug trafficking). In none of these cases was much achieved.

Economic coercion is probably useful only if it is quiet and measured, especially if measures are elastic and graduated, offering incentives as well as punishing. Holding back on high-tech exports to China, with the support of other industrial nations, persuaded the Chinese to halt shipments of missiles to Iran in 1987. But when economic penalties are made a political issue, they are more likely to strengthen the resolve of the targeted state and increase its popular support.[2] Unilateral embargoes are almost always ineffective. Publicity raises the resistance of the target state and brings it moral support against "economic imperialism"; it also increases the political cost of failure, as in the case of General Noriega.

Much of the value of an embargo is moral, to make clear our repugnance for a regime by shunning it. The completeness of the prohibition of trade with Castro's Cuba, including food and medicine, much exceeds the importance of denying it militarily useful goods or depriving it of foreign exchange. It was at one time forbidden to import cancelled postage stamps of the People's Republic of China. It is desirable to be seen as doing something when nothing else can easily be done; for this reason, trade with Nicaragua was halted in 1986 when aid to the "Contras" was blocked. It may be conjectured that Soviet boycotts of China and Albania were imposed mostly because of pique at ingratitude. Economic measures against South African apartheid are prompted more by the desire to take a visible stance than by considerations of likely effects on South African policies.

The commoner and more esteemed approach to seeking influence is to give aid. Scores of nations have received the largesse of the United States and the Soviet Union (and others), many billion dollars and rubles in programs of economic betterment, along with armaments and military training. The political payoff has been disappointing, however. Donors have had little success in purposefully reshaping alien societies or causing other countries to do things desired by the donor but not by the client.

Limits of Influence

Economic aid at best gives the donor nation a certain standing and the assurance that its views will be considered. For example, a huge assistance program for Egypt compensated that country for divorcing itself from the Arab boycott of Israel. When the United States was constructing power plants and establishing universities in India and also contributing importantly to the Indian diet, during the 1950s and 1960s, American prestige in that country was high. It was largely lost by leaning toward Pakistan in the India-Pakistan war of 1971.

Governments receiving aid are sensitive to the likelihood that it may be reduced, and the United States has used this threat with some success to influence countries not to build nuclear weapons, to cooperate in suppression of drug traffic, to vote in certain ways in the United Nations, or not to

---

[2]Sidney Weintraub, *Economic Coercion and U.S. Foreign Policy* (Boulder, CO: Westview, 1982), pp. xvi, 9, 25, and passim.

become friendly with Libya.[3] But the demand is irritating, and compliance is not likely to be wholehearted and effective. Third World countries will accept gifts, but they do not propose to change their ways to please others, and they do not like to appear to have been bought. They easily come to take assistance as a right, the termination of which is seen as an injustice. The sense of obligation has to be continually reinforced. Recipients have no illusions regarding the generosity of the givers, who usually make their interests clear.

The effectiveness of programs is also diminished by the fact that those administering them are likely to be poorly informed about politics, needs, and culture of the countries that they should be influencing. This is truer of the decision makers. If academic specialists are puzzled by alien societies, it is not to be expected that leaders of great powers should have much comprehension of the psychology and politics of the less developed countries. This is not a subject of interest to the rising politician in the United States or elsewhere in the modernized world; those who are expert in their own political system are less qualified to judge motives and characters in a very different system, in which they have neither experience nor interest. It may be that the United States and the Soviet Union are equally ineffective in this regard. If the United States has the advantage of much more systematic study of the Third World, the Soviets have sometimes done better by relying more on nationals.

Officials of the receiving state say what they are expected to say or what helps to bring in foreign bounty. Local representatives of the great power in turn report in terms to please the authorities at home. They are called upon to perform assigned tasks, not to demonstrate sensitivity to local needs and feelings. In the Angolan civil war, the CIA, which should represent the highest level of sophistication in the American government, allied itself with South Africa, the target of hatred of almost all Black Africans. It thereby legitimated Cuban-Soviet intervention and facilitated the victory of the Marxist-Leninist party, which had seemed very doubtful. Prior to the revolution that toppled the shah of Iran in 1979 the United States had no idea what was going on in his country and made little effort to learn.[4] Leaders of rich, strong powers easily form a poor opinion of the character of Third World peoples and institutions, whatever the requirements of diplomatic language, regard them somewhat as children, and make little effort to reach understandings with them.

Both the United States and the Soviet Union, prone as they have been to see the world in terms of their own preoccupations, have regularly assumed that the other exercised much more control over its clients than was

---

[3]Roger C. Riddell, *Foreign Aid Reconsidered* (Baltimore: Johns Hopkins University Press, 1987), p. 207.

[4]R. K. Ramazani, *United States and Iran: Patterns of Influence,* (New York: Praeger Press, 1982), pp. 150–55.

the case. As stated by Jan Triska, "domination, as practiced in the past, is no longer in the interests of the dominant powers . . . [which] will eventually have to yield, however grudgingly, to the subordinate powers." In any case, "The symbolic value of hegemony is out of proportion to its intrinsic value."[5]

In regard to specific policies, the weaker power may exercise more influence over its patron than vice versa. For example, Israeli pressure on the United States has seemed highly effective; Israel has had something like a veto on U.S. arms sales to Arab countries, causing the loss of profitable business. American pressure on Israel (as in disapproval of the invasion of Lebanon in 1982 or treatment of the Palestinians in 1987–1988) has not shown much effect. Taiwan, completely dependent on U.S. support, checked American policy toward mainland China for many years and kept Washington opposed to the seating of Beijing in the United Nations until 1971.

The superpower may be most frustrated where it seems to have most advantages. For example, in 1978 the Soviet Union had a large presence in Afghanistan, a backward bordering nation rather isolated from the Western world. There was an extensive Soviet economic program; and the government, including many Soviet-trained persons, was very friendly. Yet the people rebelled, provoking the misbegotten invasion. The Soviet Union has lost what seemed to be strong positions in Yugoslavia, China, Albania, Indonesia, Iraq, Egypt, Ghana, Guinea, Mali, Sudan, and Somalia.

The Central American-Caribbean region, where the United States is dominant as nowhere else, has given this country many headaches. Although early in this century simple nonrecognition would suffice to topple a government disapproved by the State Department, in the 1980s a long and costly campaign to destabilize the Marxist-Leninist government of Nicaragua failed. Several billion dollars left El Salvador no less poverty-stricken, turbulent, and leftist-threatened than before. The United States proved entirely unable to persuade the rulers of Haiti, the poorest country of the hemisphere, even to adopt a democratic facade after the collapse of the Duvalier dictatorship in 1986. The very closeness of American relations with Cuba before 1959 probably contributed to the bitter enmity that developed under Castro's leadership.

An unpopular and ill-reputed dictator of Panama, not long ago practically a puppet state, was able to defy the determination of the American administration to get rid of him. Panama was so closely linked with the American economy as to use the dollar for its national currency, and it was almost an occupied country with numerous American bases and forces far superior to the Panamanian Defense Force. But the withdrawal of economic

---

[5]Jan F. Triska, "Summary and Conclusions," in *Dominant Powers and Subordinate States: The United States in Latin America and the Soviet Union in Eastern Europe,* ed. Jan F. Triska (Durham, NC: Duke University Press, 1986), pp. 441, 464.

aid and imposition of strong economic sanctions in 1987 and 1988, including freezing of assets and prohibition of American citizens and companies
making payments to the government of General Manuel Antonio Noriega,
stiffened his resistance. It enabled the previously despised dictator to present himself more effectively as defender of the national sovereignty.

No people owe more to the United States than the Koreans, and under
the American umbrella they have had an amazing economic upsurge; yet
anti-Americanism has become rampant.[6] For many Koreans, it is obvious
that the Americans are in Korea for American purposes, not as friends but
as occupiers, an "imperialist" presence more threatening than the despotism of North Korea. Politicians use anti-Americanism while taking advantage of the alliance and counting on American support for democratization.
They certainly do not wish to irritate their principal customer, but Koreans
resent U.S. complaints of trade imbalance and pressures on them while they
are struggling toward modernization and democracy. American officials
find the Koreans ungrateful.[7]

In many cases the failure of influence seems to have been due to the
fact that relatively few persons in the less developed society shared American (or Soviet) purposes. They were more or less corrupted by foreign support, a movement against them turned into a movement against their patron, and their loss of power meant loss of U.S. (or Soviet) influence. For
example, the United States had a willing junior partner in the Iranian shah
for many years, but its supporters were strong only in the palace, police,
and armed forces; the revolution of 1979 brought powerful anti-U.S. forces
to the top.

Something similar seems to have occurred in Afghanistan. The Soviets
worked with a small group of persons, especially in the army, alienated from
the traditional society. The Soviets seem to have accepted that their clients
represented the masses longing for liberation from tribal chiefs, landlords,
and mullahs. But forces rose up akin to those that rebelled against the Am-
erican-backed regime in Iran.

The United States and the Soviet Union encounter somewhat similar
frustrations in dealing with alien peoples, who can be assisted but have to
make their own destinies.

U.S. Influence

Energetic revolutions uphold broad principles of justice. Somewhat like the
Leninists in 1917 and the French revolutionaries of the 1790s, who felt that

[6]Nicholas D. Kristof, "Anti-Americanism Grows in South Korea," *New York Times,* July 12,
1987, p. E3.

[7]*Wall Street Journal,* September 23, 1987, p. 30.

they had to give their neighbors similar libertarian-democratic regimes, the United States saw itself at its birth as the "New Order of the Ages" ("Novus Ordo Seculorum," as proclaimed on the Great Seal). The democratic republic was a brave innovation; it would be builder of the New World and model for the Old. Spreading across the open continent, it found swelling pride in its "Manifest Destiny" and became aspirant to almost boundless mastery.

Through most of its history, the United States has concentrated on its own affairs and hoped that the good example would be persuasive; but it early declared, by the Monroe Doctrine, a sort of protectorate over the weaker republics to the south. In the First World War, the United States crusaded for freedom and self-determination, which it assumed would be attained by crushing the forces of iniquity. The results were disappointing, and the country turned inward until the late 1930s when, under the goading of the fascistic-militaristic powers, it became deeply concerned with the condition of the world. Since the Second World War the nation has sought, with variable consistency, to promote democracy, or at least freedom from communist totalitarianism.

In dealing with other advanced industrial democracies, the United States counts on shared interests and has felt little need to offer special inducements or to threaten reprisals in political matters. But Third World countries have commonly seemed to require direction, expressed by either inducements or pressures. Their interests should fundamentally coincide with those of this country; however, because they often fail to recognize this, the United States has felt compelled to lend a guiding hand.

The long-term interest of the United States has been seen as the development of stable open societies, more specifically the prevention of communist power, which was believed permanently to preclude proper political development. For the United States, the reliable friends and desirable partners are the stable democratic states. These are little tempted by extremism of any kind, generally sympathize with ideals of freedom, and are good members of the international economic community.

The goal of democratization has never been pursued systematically, however. Although the United States likes to have orderly client states, it prefers not to assume much responsibility for their political health and virtue; and interest has been more in appearances than in the reality of democracy. The administration has often seemed to prefer the practical advantages of dealing with governments capable of preserving order and making a good climate for business. Most amenable to American wishes have been dictators without much thought for the needs of their own people; democracies are not likely to be subservient. A cooperative dictator, such as General Mohammad Zia of Pakistan before his assassination in August 1988, is an esteemed asset; the more democratic alternative was a hazardous unknown.

Because of the reactive character of American policy-making, little attention and resources have been given to causes without immediate political returns; and emphasis has been on stability, the chief aspiration of the bureaucracy. This has meant concern primarily with security and a propensity to view events in military-strategic terms, which in many cases has implied support for an unpopular social order and toleration for militocracy.

Uncertainty as to the balance between immediate strategic and longer-term political aims has led to a division of American opinion, with "practical" or "realistic" ideas opposing "idealistic" or "progressive." In the past, the "realists" have usually prevailed. The results have been mixed. For example, U.S. policy in Iran, exercised through a shah who relied very heavily on this country, was decidedly successful from 1953 to 1979: Iran acted as a U.S. surrogate in the region, was the best arms buyer in the world and so recycled a large quantity of petrodollars (even as the shah led the way in raising oil prices), welcomed U.S. investments, permitted use of its territory for military and intelligence purposes, and at the same time forwarded an ambitious program of modernization. Yet the close embrace ultimately contributed to the downfall of the shah, who became excessively dependent, held power too tightly, overemphasized the military, and became alienated from his own society. The successor government of the Ayatollah Khomeini was even more fiercely hostile to the United States ("The Great Satan") than the shah's had been friendly.

Although support for dictatorship is problematic, to impose democracy is contrary to the democratic spirit, and nations that are willing to acknowledge economic backwardness resent being told how they should organize their government. The promotion of human rights is more acceptable; almost everyone will subscribe in principal to human rights. But even talk of human rights, so far as it implies superiority, has ruffled not only partisans of authoritarianism but also nationalists. The Carter administration's preaching of human rights to Latin American military governments, although welcomed by intellectuals, alienated traditional elites and caused the active distrust of the military establishment.

In the 1980s, the atmosphere had changed sufficiently to make possible more frank official promotion of democratic institutions, to the general approval of the world and the embarrassment of the more sensitive nondemocratic governments. The United States set up the National Endowment for Democracy overtly to support democratic movements in the Third World, not only in democratic countries but also in others that did not welcome it, such as Nicaragua and Chile. It subsidizes organizations, financing travel, helping publications, and so forth; but its feeble funding (under $20 million) indicated its low priority. The West Germans were spending more than six times as much for this purpose.

After Carter in 1978 pressured the Dominican army to respect electoral results, the United States found satisfaction in the democratic tide sweeping Latin America, although it is not clear how much is really changed if the military rulers of Guatemala, for example, are persuaded to permit the election of a civilian government. The dictatorship of Augusto Pinochet in Chile was reprobated, and his defeat in a plebiscite in 1988 was welcomed, although at an earlier time his anticommunism and exemplary adherence to free enterprise would have won Washington's approval. The chief charge levelled at the Sandinista government of Nicaragua was failure to fulfill its promises of democracy. The principal concern, of course, was its anti-U.S. attitudes and close ties with Cuba and the Soviet Union; but it was reasonably assumed that if it were more responsible to independent political forces it would be less hostile to the United States.

The promotion of the American way is complicated by the fact that it has two main components, the political, or democracy, and the economic, or the free enterprise-capitalistic system based on the market economy. Emphasis on one or the other varies, but favor for economic freedom has been more consistent than promotion of democracy. Very little is said and less is done against strong-arm government in Singapore because its economic performance and business climate are splendid. In Guatemala (1954), Brazil (1964), and Chile (1973), the United States looked with favor on the replacement of legally elected governments by military rulers because of socialistic policies of the former. The international financial community, acting in conformity with U.S. policy, has required countries desiring loans (which most countries desire) to adopt policies of free enterprise or market economics but has ignored political institutions.

There has been no consistent long-term strategy, however, to promote economic freedom. The policy in practice has usually been to seek immediate advantages or to meet the needs of the day. Trade negotiations have regularly neglected systemic effects; it has been a matter of little concern that economic aid has gone to governments and official agencies and has consequently served to enlarge the state sector.

If foreign aid has done little to build the kind of societies favored by the United States, it has not had much more success in winning adherents; and in the 1980s there was a rising sense of disillusionment.[8] Economic aid has consequently been scaled down or phased out in most countries. The total amount spent, about $10 billion in recent years, remains about the same or grows, but it has been concentrated on immediate political objectives. In the 1980s, about 40 percent of foreign aid and an equal fraction of military assistance has gone to Israel and Egypt, mostly because of the political importance of the friends of Israel in the United States and the desire to underwrite the uneasy peace between Israel and its strongest neighbor. Attention and expenditures have also been focused on Central America because of the violent struggles of radical leftists against traditionalists (or

---

[8]David H. Blake and Robert S. Walters, *The Politics of Global Economic Relations*, 2nd ed. (Englewood Cliffs: Prentice Hall, 1983), p. 139.

pro-Soviet against pro-U.S. forces, as seen from Washington) in El Salvador and Nicaragua, to the neglect of problems of the remainder of Latin America, which has over 90 percent of the population and wealth of the region. For the rest, aid has mostly amounted to rent paid to countries for hosting American bases, or has been emergency relief, or has financed particular programs, such as drug eradication.

Military assistance programs have shrunk. Large numbers of Latin American officers once attended American schools, both in Panama (until 1984) and in the United States; but many thousand U.S.-trained officers in Peru, Colombia, and many other countries have not made officer corps pro-U.S. or even brought about effective antiguerrilla forces. The program has virtually lapsed. At its peak in 1966, the United States had 769 military advisors in Latin America; in 1988, there were 92 (exclusive of 55 trainers in El Salvador), mostly concerned with delivery of matériel.[9]

Arms deliveries have also faded as a means of influence. In the 1960s and into the 1970s it was a privilege to be permitted to purchase armaments from the United States, and this country felt able to use military sales as a lever. Now, however, only in the most advanced categories is there a sellers' market. The Soviets, French, British, Chinese, Brazilians, West Germans, Italians, Spanish, Taiwanese, Israelis, and others are eager to sell almost any weaponry Third World countries could use, including copies of Soviet or American missiles. France is more competitor than ally, offering arms to the Third World as an alternative to superpower entanglement.[10] Brazil went into arms manufacturing because of U.S. reluctance to sell to the former military regime and has made itself an important exporter; it operates strictly on a business basis and has done very well in the violence-prone Near East.

Provisions that American arms should not be transferred to a third country without permission and should be used only for external defense have proved difficult to enforce. To stay in the market, the United States had to become a more liberal provider, making less effort to restrict the use of the arms that it delivers. Greater willingness has not sufficed to beat the competition, however; total U.S. sales have decreased steadily from $22 billion in 1982 to $5 billion in 1987 (while total Third World purchases have decreased from $55 to $30 billion).[11]

For such reasons, the official effort to develop American influence in the Third World has had limited success, and whatever may have been

[9]Richard Halloran, "U.S.-Latin Military Contact Withers," *New York Times,* April 3, 1988, p. 8.

[10]Mark R. Rubin, "French Arms and the Third World," in *East-West Rivalry in the Third World: Security Issues and Regional Perspectives,* ed. Robert W. Clawson, (Washington: Scholar Resources Inc., 1986), pp. 173–82.

[11]For details of the business, see Michael Brzoska and Thomas Ohlson, *Arms Transfers to the Third World* (New York: Oxford University Press, 1987).

achieved by aid programs has been more than offset by disliked policies. African states, for example, have been alienated by equivocal American relations with South Africa; Arabs and others by partiality toward Israel; Latin Americans by unilateral interventionism, as in the anti-Sandinista campaign.[12]

The American successes have been largely nongovernmental, informal, cultural, and economic. The nation has done well when the government has done poorly; foreigners have admired American ways even when they disapproved of official policies. For example, the Arabs have found the United States offensive, not only because of its support of Israel but also because of insensitivity to their needs and concern only for its own (and Israel's) security needs. But an Arab official remarked, "What do we want with Russia? We don't go there, we don't send our children to study there. It's natural for us to look to the States, if only you wouldn't keep pushing us away."[13] He might have added that Russia neither buys their oil nor supplies the capital and consumer goods they need.

Soviet Influence

The Russian revolution was made in large part by minorities oppressed by the tsarist state, but the new rulers were unwilling to dissolve the union represented by the huge empire. Lenin's answer to this dilemma was to proclaim a brotherly union of all peoples, rationalized by the Marxist idealization of class over all other bonds.

The Leninists were able by force of arms to impose their government on nearly all of what had been the tsarist domain. But the proletariat of the rest of the world almost completely ignored the call from the Russian brethren. Soviet proselytizing for class warfare and revolution had some momentary successes in the troubled times of 1918–1919, and more or less Soviet-style governments ruled briefly in Hungary and Bavaria. But thereafter the vision of universal revolution faded, and hopes of early revolution in the advanced countries of Europe were moribund after 1923. In order to survive, the Soviet state was compelled to behave as a state among many, for a long time as a weak one.

But it could not renounce pretenses of world revolutionary leadership, which was the basis for its claim to be more than an ordinary state, a new form of society; only on the basis of this claim could it insist on the justice of the rulership of the Russian center over the many non-Russian

---

[12]From J. Farer, "International Law: The Critics Are Wrong," *Foreign Policy* 71 (Summer 1988), p. 34.

[13]*Wall Street Journal*, November 17, 1987, p. 30.

peoples. To carry on the mission of revolutionary transformation, the Leninists tried infiltrating leftist organizations and organizing mostly clandestine parties in Europe. Attention also turned to making trouble for the capitalist powers in their colonies. However, the Soviet-sponsored revolutionary movement achieved practically nothing in the interwar years, and communist parties had very little success in raising the masses of colonial empires against their master. But diplomacy gradually brought the Soviet Union acceptance in the concert of nations.

If no great war had come, the revolutionary-expansionist idea might well have died by the 1940s. However, thanks to the advances of Soviet armies in the last months of the war, the Soviet Union found itself in possession of something between a sphere of influence and an empire, which required ideological rationalization.

For a decade the Soviets, fully occupied with reconstruction of the devastated land and the consolidation of their dominion in Eastern Europe, paid rather little attention to distant lands. Stalin, moreover, distrusted nationalist leaders and regarded the independence of the new nations as fictitious. Only in 1955 did the Soviet Union renew its interest in the Third World, when First Secretary Nikita Khrushchev opened a campaign to win friends in southern Asia. Thereafter, Soviet activity was generally increasing for 20 years in Asia, Africa, and to a much lesser extent in Latin America.[14]

Soviet influence, however, has made itself strongly felt in only a small fraction of potentially convertible nations, chiefly in very backward ones. It has never brought about a revolution anywhere, only taken advantage of conflicts arising without its intervention; it would probably be fatal for a Third World revolutionary outbreak if the Soviet Union took a hand directly in it. Moscow has chalked up gains for the Soviet way mostly because leaders such as Castro of Cuba or Agostinho Neto of Angola turned to it for help. The Soviet Union in the 1960s and 1970s claimed that about a score of countries, mostly in Africa, were of "socialist orientation" or "revolutionary democratic" character, while various others were said to have taken the "non-capitalist path of development." By the late 1980s, however, fewer than a dozen Third World countries theoretically subscribed to the Soviet ideological way, and only one convert since 1970 (Ethiopia) was seriously trying to put it into practice.

The Soviet campaign in the Third World has been supported by loyal, disciplined communist parties in many countries, instruments with advantages and disadvantages. It also has had the ideological sympathy of many anti-Americans not formally affiliated with the pro-Soviet movement. But the Soviets have always been ready to set ideology aside to deal with governments and factions, offering material or political support, favorable trade

---

[14]For a general account, see Andrzej Korbonski and Francis Fukuyama, eds., *The Soviet Union and the Third World: The Last Three Decades* (Ithaca, NY: Cornell University Press, 1987).

deals, or arms in return for opportunities to establish desired connections or to get a place in the political picture. In less developed countries, the Soviets have built hospitals, sold cheap books, offered scholarships for study in Moscow, invited radical and nonradical leaders to international meetings, tried to gain control of trade unions and other organizations, and helped rulers set up a political security apparatus.

In the 1960s, the Soviet Union made an effort to compete with the United States in large-scale economic aid, but its capabilities were inadequate. The most important vehicle of Soviet influence—its only effective instrument in recent years—has been the provision of armaments to parties or governments finding them more affordable than those proffered by Western countries. Weapons on credit or gratis may mean survival and victory, and the Soviets have usually been the largest suppliers of arms to the Third World since the late 1970s. Their sales have been economically important, amounting to 20–30 percent of Soviet exports and hard currency earnings.[15] They have also helped the Soviet munitions industry to expand its runs, while the armed forces shed obsolete equipment.

Tens of thousands of advisors have accompanied Soviet arms, especially to Cuba, Libya, Syria, and Vietnam, while many officers from these countries go to the Soviet bloc for training. Arms deals have even brought a little-noted Soviet presence (about 100 officers) in Peru. The Soviets have not sought formal alliances with noncontiguous countries, but they have acquired bases or facilities in Cuba, Vietnam, Angola, South Yemen, and Syria. Among the most important of these is Camranh Bay in Vietnam, although it is unclear what real benefit the Soviets derive from the large base developed by Americans in the Vietnam war. In wartime, it would be irrelevant; in peacetime, the Soviet naval presence in the Southeast Asia hardly brings commercial profits or advances the fortunes of pro-Soviet parties. In the "new thinking" of the Gorbachevites, it is not important.[16]

Supplying weapons has done more for presence than for influence, but it has been effective in conflictive situations. The Soviet Union acquired influence in Algeria from the fight for independence, although it was subsequently dissipated. It also gained by assisting rebels against the former Portuguese colonial empire in Africa. It saved the new governments of Angola and Mozambique from probable defeat. It may have been decisive for the survival of the radical regime of Ethiopia in its struggle with both Somalia and Eritrean insurgents. Revolutionary regimes in Cuba and Nicaragua could hardly have held out against the United States without its economic and military help.

---

[15]Mark N. Kramer, "Soviet Arms Transfers to the Third World," *Problems of Communism* 36, September-October 1987, pp. 55, 62.

[16]*New York Times*, December 23, 1988, p. A3.

The Soviets have also been able to work through surrogates of one kind or another, especially personnel of communist states, Cuban or East European, desirous of earning credits and playing a world role by cooperation with the Soviet big brother. Tens of thousands of Cubans protected communist governments in Ethiopia and Angola; small detachments of Cubans and East Germans serve as palace guards for Soviet-dependent dictators, mostly in Africa; and the East Germans have specialized in organizing political police in many countries.[17]

But the settled Soviet rulership does not share the enthusiasms of fresh revolutionaries. Pragmatic, skeptical of the "socialist orientation" that it hails, and wary of revolutionism in an increasingly conservative Third World, the Soviet Union has rather sought, even before Gorbachev, to restrain ideological zeal. It has kept its distance from the unreliable Ghadaffy of Libya, although he seems to have wanted a Soviet alliance after the American bombing in 1986. It has never been eager for Castro's liberation of Latin America; in 1962 Khrushchev was more cautious than Castro. The Soviet-oriented communist parties in Latin America have usually been uncooperative with pro-Castro guerrillas. The Soviet Union has committed almost no personnel to Nicaragua beyond normal embassy staff.

The Soviet Union has more than the United States been disposed to favor anyone, "bourgeois nationalists" or not, who would cooperate with its foreign policy. Soviet support for parties has borne little relation to their class composition, proletarian or bourgeois, but much to their attitude toward the Soviet Union. Unlike the United States, the Soviet Union will have a diplomatic presence anywhere.

Since the early 1980s, Soviet efforts to expand influence in the Third World have subsided. Withdrawal from Afghanistan was the result of change (loss of ideological drive and ruthlessness and growth of independent opinion) and a cause of more change. More important symbolically than practically, it seems to write an end to the old messianism. The failure also made it difficult to win adherents in the Third World, while the cramped Soviet economy has discouraged assumption of new responsibilities, such as ailing Nicaragua. Moreover, there are fewer troubled waters in which to fish as the new nations have become consolidated; the last important opening came with the breakup of the Portuguese empire.

The returns have been disappointing. Only two states, Cuba and Vietnam, are firmly aligned with the Soviet Union. Sovietization has been a partial success in Cuba, although Cuban dependence on the Soviet Union derives directly from American policy. The Soviets were never able to win any real influence over Egypt, despite 20,000 troops on the ground at one

---

[17]Carol R. Saivetz and Sylvia Woodby, *Soviet-Third World Relations* (Boulder, CO: Westview Press, 1985) p. 200.

time, large arms aid, and strong political support; the withdrawal in 1972 was humiliating.[18]Considerable expenditures produced only slight signs of Soviet influence on Indian policy.[19] For a long time, India was dependent on Soviet arms; but it has developed its own production and found other suppliers in the West.

It has proved very difficult to reconstruct alien societies, even with the assistance of a political party rather closely modeled after the Leninist pattern. For example, extensive military assistance to the Yemen Arab Republic (North Yemen), including supervision of modernization of the army, never had any impact on Yemeni social, economic, or political institutions.[20] Angola, often regarded as committed to the Soviet way and dependent on a large number of Cuban troops, has sought and procured arms and advisors in the West. Although it does not have diplomatic relations, the United States is Angola's chief trading partner. Mozambique, although nominally Marxist-Leninist, has even more strongly shown its desire to improve relations with the West.

The greatest bar to the broadening and deepening of Soviet influence among the less developed nations is inability to supply their economic needs, especially at a higher technological level; disillusionment has been widespread.[21] The Soviets have accounted for less than 1 percent of African foreign trade; they have been most successful with very poor nations, Ethiopia, South Yemen, and Angola, as provider of military, not civilian wares.

Equally discouraging for Third World admirers of the Soviet Union is the failure of efforts to apply the Soviet economic model. Before communism, Cuba was near the top among Latin American countries in various socio-economic indicators; more than a generation later, it is middle-ranking; and it manages to keep afloat only thanks to a Soviet subsidy roughly equivalent to a quarter of the Cuban national product. Mozambique was poor when it became a Marxist state in 1975; it is now destitute. Nicaragua and Ethiopia under Marxist-Leninist governments have suffered much more impoverishment than can be attributed to military problems. Most striking is the case of Vietnam, which, after its military victory in 1975, suffered economic defeat. Mismanagement brought impoverishment, and the country has sunk into far greater poverty than its neighbors, with a per capita national product among the world's lowest, about $100.[22]

---

[18]Alvin Z. Rubinstein, *Red Star on the Nile: The Soviet-Egyptian Influence Relationship since the June War* (Princeton: Princeton University Press, 1977), pp. 334–35.

[19]Robert C. Horn, *Soviet-Indian Relations: Issues and Influence* (New York: Praeger Publishers, 1982), p. 218.

[20]Stephen Page, *The Soviet Union and the Yemens: Influence in Asymmetrical Relationships* (New York: Praeger, 1985) p. 206.

[21]Robert I. Rotberg, "Africa, the Soviet Union, and the West," in *East-West Rivalry in the Third World,* ed. Clawson, p. 230.

[22]*New York Times,* April 7, 1988, p. A3.

Covert Operations

Nations pursue their ends abroad not only by conventional means but also by secret actions, ordinarily illegal and certainly unscrupulous. Unacknowledged operations, miscalled "intelligence," are often violent. They are also commonly criminal, a reason for keeping them secret. Typically intended to bring about political results in a foreign country that are not desired by the government affected, they infringe the principle of independent sovereignty. As carried out in weaker or less developed countries, they are a contemporary substitute, on a small scale, for old-style imperialism.

The great powers hardly undertake clandestine actions in fellow advanced countries (except information-gathering, which is in a different category), because they can achieve less in a well-ordered society and they would be more likely found out and embarrassed. There could be nothing in Europe like Nixon's secret bombing of Cambodia; no one would propose a little clandestine war on the frontier of East Germany, like the originally covert "Contra" operation against Nicaragua.

Third World countries, with less effective news-gathering and lawkeeping and more susceptibility to corruption, offer a relatively inviting field of action. Moreover, the sense of superiority to Third World peoples invites discarding the restraint that would be felt in dealing with cultivated Europeans. The Iran-Contra affair showed the ease with which secret policy could be carried on in the Third World outside the view of the media; it became public only because of Iranian dissent.

Where clandestine operations are feasible they will be found necessary, and the KGB and CIA point to each other as proof of their own indispensability. But the foreign section of the KGB (which is mostly a domestic agency, like the FBI but far more powerful) is either much less effective than the CIA or else much more skillful in hiding its work. It is not known ever to have engineered a coup. It seems to be engaged abroad mostly in gathering useful information; the Soviet preoccupation is less overthrowing noncommunist governments than appropriating their technical secrets.[23] The KGB, however, works with and subsidizes local communist parties. It also has specialized in disinformation, typically planting stories in Third World papers to discredit the United States.

Other powers, including Britain, France, Israel, Cuba, and East Germany, have highly regarded undercover agencies. The British M-15 is kept very much under wraps; the government would like to deny its very exis-

---

[23]Recent writings include William R. Corson and Robert T. Crowley, *The New KGB: Engine of Soviet Power* (New York: William Morrow, 1985), p. 223; Amy W. Knight, *The KGB: Police and Politics in the Soviet Union* (Winchester, MA: Allen and Unwin, 1988). For insider accounts, see Ilya Dzhirkvelov, *Secret Servant: My Life with the KGB and the Soviet Elite* (New York: Harper & Row, 1988); and Stanislav Levchenko, *On the Wrong Side: My Life in the KGB* (Washington: Pergamon-Brassey's 1988).

tence.[24] Cuban and other communist agencies are said to work closely with the KGB; the connection is an important channel of Soviet influence. The East German secret service has taken the lead in assisting the political controllers of Third World Marxist-Leninist states, from Nicaragua to Ethiopia. Israel's Mossad has acquired a formidable reputation by virtue of successful operations, both in the capture of Nazi war criminals and in the rescue of Israelis held hostage. It has also dealt with enemies of Israel abroad. It has been called the world's best.

For some ambitious Third World nations and for impassioned political groups without a government, such as the Irish Republican Army, terrorism serves some of the purposes that "intelligence" serves for major powers. Terrorism in the modern sense began in the struggle of revolutionaries against the tsarist regime in the latter part of the 19th century; and it has been the mainstay of many a "national liberation movement," including that of the Zionists against British colonial authorities prior to the establishment of the state of Israel in 1948. Doctrinaire regimes are most prone to terrorism, their ideology justifying ruthlessness and duplicity; it has become the tool of otherwise weak tyrannies, such as Libya.[25] North Korea has carried out a number of unpleasant actions, such as blowing up a South Korean airliner in 1987 in poorly calculated hopes of discrediting the South Korean government. Even poverty-stricken Ghana engaged in subversion in half a dozen African countries in the early 1960s under Kwame Nkrumah.[26]

Terrorism is facilitated by modern devices; virtually undetectable plastic explosives are a dream (or nightmare) weapon, like almost metal-free and consequently undetectable handguns. Modern organization and communications also make covert operations more attractive. The importance of terrorism, however, is inflated by the attention of the press. Aside from the sabotage of airliners, the number of victims worldwide is only about 1/200 of the number of highway fatalities in the United States alone. There is not much evidence of direct Soviet involvement, a fact not surprising in view of the danger that terrorism might be turned against Soviet officials.[27] The possibility of terrorists using a nuclear bomb has been often mooted but is apparently not great; it would probably require the expertise of a cooperating government.[28]

---

[24]The British government was much disturbed by the revelations in Peter Wright, *Spycatcher: Autobiography of a Senior Intelligence Officer* (New York: Viking, 1987).

[25]Walter Laqueur, *The Age of Terrorism*, (Boston: Little Brown, 1987), pp. 321–22.

[26]J. K. Holsti, *International Politics: A Framework for Analysis*, 4th ed. (Englewood Cliffs, NJ: Prentice Hall Inc., 1982), p. 243.

[27]Stephen Segaller, *Invincible Armies: Terrorism into the 1990's*, (London: Michael Joseph, 1986), pp. 3, 122.

[28]Laqueur, *Terrorism*, pp. 317–18.

The Role of the CIA

Estimates of the agency's budget range from $1 up to $9 billion, hidden in the appropriation of the Department of Defense. It has from 15,000 to 18,000 employees, about a third of them overseas, mostly with official missions. In the early years of the Reagan administration, some 40 covert operations were underway, most of them unimportant.[29]

What fraction of the CIA budget is devoted to "operations," in contrast to the gathering of information can only be guessed. However, it engages in many activities, including bribing journalists and supporting right-thinking newspapers, working with labor leaders and politicians of all shades, and bugging communications. The CIA may help a political group or any of a variety of organizations. It frequently becomes involved in elections in Third World countries where there is a perceived U.S. interest, as there usually is. It not only makes trouble for unfriendly rulers but also helps friendly ones, providing advisors, training police and other operatives, and giving information. It is forbidden to operate in the United States, but this prohibition has been breached; for example, in the Vietnam war it infiltrated and kept tabs on protest movements.[30] It seems to have worked energetically, mostly through the National Security Council, to influence U.S. opinion in favor of the Nicaraguan "Contras."[31]

With claims of expertise and need for secrecy, the CIA and other branches of the "intelligence community" are generally exempt from outside supervision, and they are peculiarly "the president's men."[32] Legal requirements for reporting covert actions to congressional committees are not stringent or effective. The degree of presidential control depends entirely on the feelings of the chief executive. Since the revelations of dealings with Iran in 1985–1987, operations have been subject to the review of the National Security Council; but this is a rather permissive check.

Overt foreign policy has to be defended and can be hobbled if support is inadequate; clandestinity gives freedom of action. Leaders may prefer secrecy even when it is unnecessary, just as mountains of government documents are labeled "confidential." It is not clear why it had to be the CIA that financed Radio Free Europe and Radio Liberty for many years, thereby causing them embarrassment when the CIA's involvement came to light, as it eventually had to.[33] In many cases, such as book publication, the chief

[29]John Ranelagh, *The Agency: The Rise and Decline of the CIA,* (New York: Simon and Schuster, 1986), pp. 16, 20, 677; Gregory F. Treverton, *Covert Action: The Limits of Intervention in the Postwar World* (New York: Basic Books, 1987), p. 14.

[30]E. Drexel Godfrey, "Ethics and Intelligence," *Foreign Affairs* 56, April 1978, p. 634.

[31]Robert Parry and Peter Kornblub, "Iran-Contragate's Untold Story," *Foreign Policy* 72, Fall 1988, pp. 3–30.

[32]Ranelagh, *The Agency,* p. 18.

[33]Scott D. Breckinridge, *The CIA and the U.S. Intelligence System* (Boulder, CO: Westview, 1986), p. 221.

reason for the CIA's responsibility must have been that it has more freely disposable funds than the USIA.

Secret operations may be rather innocuous; the CIA has sponsored perfectly decent organizations, and it has given much attention to semilegitimate manipulation of opinion by unacknowledged propaganda.[34] The agency seldom operates on its own; it is easier, less risky, and more effective to turn responsibility over to formal or informal native organizations that share its outlook. But clandestine "intelligence" commonly involves bribery, almost certainly falsifications, and very likely murder (although this method has been officially placed off limits) or more dignified paramilitary operations.[35] On a few occasions, persons accused of terrorism against Americans or drug traffickers have been abducted abroad.

It is difficult to marry ethics and secrecy. But the permissibility of foreign policy actions that are inherently illegal and unethical is hardly questioned outside the United States and not very strongly in it. In the congressional hearings on the Iran-Contra affair in 1987, there were many denunciations and lamentations of lawbreaking and foolish policies damaging to the United States; but the utility of covert actions in principle was hardly questioned.[36]

However, not many of the CIA's essays in clandestinity can really be counted successes. One might be its intervention in the critical Italian general election of 1948, when a communist victory could have caused great difficulties for the Western powers. No one can be certain whether the CIA made the critical difference, but neither can anyone prove that it did not. The kudos are clearer in the case of the Salvadoran election of 1985, when Napoleon Duarte, thanks to the CIA, defeated a rightist candidate who seems to have received a majority of the votes but who had a reputation as an organizer of murder, including that of Archbishop Romero. The general conviction that Duarte's mandate was illegitimate seems to have weakened his government, however. The CIA engineered a mini-invasion of Guatemala in 1954 to overthrow the government of Jacobo Arbenz, but most credit goes to the Guatemalan army. It could easily have crushed the invader force of a few hundred but turned against the leftist president for its own reasons. A clearer triumph was the return of the shah of Iran to his throne in 1953, courtesy of CIA organization and logistics. The arming of anti-Soviet mujahideen in Afghanistan was, of course, highly successful; but the

---

[34]Stansfield Turner, *Secrecy and Democracy: The CIA in Transition* (Boston: Houghton-Mifflin, 1985), p. 81.

[35]Kenneth E. Sharpe, "The Real Cause of Irangate," *Foreign Policy* 68, (Fall 1987), 22, 26–27.

[36]For accounts of secret operations, see Bob Woodward, *Veil: The Secret Wars of the CIA* (New York: Simon and Schuster, 1987), and Constantine Menges, *Inside the National Security Council* (New York: Simon and Schuster, 1988).

operation, which was too large to be kept secret, might well have been handled by military personnel.

The gain from successful operations has by no means been unalloyed. The overthrow of the legitimate government of Arbenz, who was never shown to have been linked with the Soviet Union,[37] was followed by decades of military tyranny; and it remains a permanent discredit on the reputation of the United States in the eyes of Latin America. In all probability, if the American administration had been patient, Arbenz would have been ousted in due course by the conservative officers with a less negative sequel. The United States likewise earned lasting opprobrium for assisting the opposition to the socialistic government of Salvador Allende in Chile before the 1973 military coup. Like Arbenz, Allende would almost certainly have been toppled by Chileans if Washington had felt able to let Chilean politics take its course. Some Latin Americans approved of both actions, but many more were angered, and their children in the universities continue to damn the Yankees for such sins. Would-be secret actions in Vietnam and Cambodia in the early 1970s (such as "Operation Phoenix" killing persons considered sympathetic to the communists) contributed to the revulsion of public opinion against the war. The CIA-directed Nicaraguan "Contra" operation, which began secretly but quickly became public, hardly gave encouraging results. The idea that the CIA was the proper agency to establish democracy would not occur to many people; and the Sandinista government was happy to treat its enemy as a creature of the CIA. The "Contras" became highly controversial, less a means to an end than a political object.[38] Incidentally, costs have risen remarkably. The successful operation in Guatemala in 1954 engaged about 200 men; the unsuccessful operation in Nicaragua 30 years later engaged over 10,000.

"Intelligence" operations generate a mythology; not very sophisticated Third World peoples are inclined to believe that the CIA is capable of anything and to blame it for any mysterious misfortune. Rajiv Gandhi, who surely knows better, blames India's woes on it. It is even charged with manipulating the weather. In 1988 some Pakistanis credited the CIA with the assassination of General Zia, although he had been very cooperative with the United States and the American ambassador and two generals perished with him.[39] Operations of the CIA have doubtless sometimes helped democracy, but they also make it problematic; what is the point of elections or freedom of the press if they can be manipulated by a foreign power? Covert activities cannot really be in the democratic spirit.

Human nature is such that covert operations are seldom wise or well-

---

[37]Ranelagh, *The Agency,* pp. 268–69.

[38]For a general account, see Roy Gutman, *Banana Diplomacy: The Making of American Policy in Nicaragua, 1981–1987* (New York: Simon and Schuster, 1988).

[39]*New York Times,* August 21, 1988, p. E2.

conceived, and a policy that cannot be defended publicly is not likely to be good policy in the long run. Those undertaking to act in secrecy seem rarely to give thought to secondary and longer-range costs, overestimate what they can achieve, and underestimate risks and difficulties. To operate in the under-world of secrecy means to collaborate with dubious characters, such as smugglers, would-be assassins, and drug traffickers. The CIA worked with the Panamánian dictator General Manuel Noriega many years, fully aware that he was a drug trafficker and double-dealer. It may have been legitimate to give assistance to anti-Sandinista forces in the 1980s; putting the opera-tion in the hands of the CIA involved bribery, smuggling, secret raids, hid-den airstrips, and drug trafficking.[40]

The lies to which secrecy leads cannot but be demoralizing as their influence spreads in the administration, and they are a serious discredit as they become known. When secrecy and deceit are legitimized and accepted, it is hard to control administration effectively; people both inside and out-side the government may give up the effort to follow what goes on, just as the secretaries of defense and state backed away from the secret arms deals with Iran in 1985–1987. Thrilling capers detract from considering sounder approaches and encourage arrogance and disregard for law, as well demon-strated in the arrogance of Lt. Colonel Oliver North and Vice Admiral John Poindexter in their accounts of Iran-Contra dealings.[41]

The difficulties of the Reagan administration in Lebanon, Iran, and Nicaragua arose not from being hampered by democratic controls but from lack of openness and consultation.

In the age of active journalism and official leaks, practically everything of importance sooner or later comes into the public view. Hardly anything is more important for effective foreign policy than credibility, but it is an easily wasted asset. The knowledge that statements are often nonfactual makes all manner of actions suspect; and if a major democratic nation in-dulges in unacknowledgable operations, this goes far toward making them acceptable practice for all.

A former attorney general and undersecretary of state, Nicholas B. de Katzenbach reflected in 1973, "We should abandon publicly all covert operations designed to influence political results in foreign countries. Spe-cifically, there should be no secret subsidies of police or counterinsurgency forces, no efforts to influence elections, no secret monetary subsidies . . . We should confine our covert activities abroad to the gathering of intelligence information."[42] According to Clark Clifford, who drafted the 1947 law set-

---

[40]As detailed by Leslie Cockburn, *Out of Control* (New York: Atlantic Monthly Press, 1987).

[41]See *Report of the Congressional Committees Investigating the Iran-Contra Affair* (Washington: Government Printing Office, 1988); John Tower, Chairman, *The Tower Commission Report* (New York: Bantam Books/Times Books, 1987); Patricia A. O'Connor, ed., *The Iran-Contra Puzzle* (Washington: Congressional Quarterly Inc., 1987).

[42]Nicholas B. de Katzenbach, "Foreign Policy, Public Opinion, and Secrecy," *Foreign Af-fairs* 52, October 1973, p. 15.

ting up the CIA, "I believe that on balance covert activities have harmed this country more than they have helped us."[43]

The more important function of the intelligence agencies is the gathering and analysis of information, in order to give leaders means of sound judgment; and this seems to account for the greater share of the CIA budget. Logic and good management would at least dictate the separation of operations from information-gathering. This would make it much easier to maintain an atmosphere of rationality in the agency. If the CIA were confined to information and analysis, it would be better able to recruit qualified personnel, could collaborate freely with research and scholarly institutions, and ought to be an important national cultural asset.

The CIA's understanding of world affairs is not improved if it is "entwined with the machinations and frustrations of presidents . . . [regarded] as hit men and spies and wiretappers and blue movie makers and gumshoes."[44] It would also be advisable to take the CIA out of the White House basement and to separate it from foreign policy making, giving it as much independence as the FBI.[45] Such a divorce, however, is unlikely. It would be contrary to the desires of the gatherers of data to have a hand in the more exciting affairs; people become far more emotionally involved in operations than research.

There have been doubts within the Agency itself about the suitability of covert actions.[46] It cannot be easy to draw a line between what is legitimate and what is not. The sound rule would be to say no to covert operations in case of doubt; the inclination has been to say yes.

Interventionism

Prior to World War I, intervention in the narrow sense—the exercise of force on the territory of another state—was casually undertaken in the less developed areas. "Gunboat diplomacy" and colonial wars were too frequent to cause much notice. By the 1920s, such actions were becoming more difficult; U.S. occupations in Nicaragua, Haiti, and the Dominican Republic were widely questioned, although casualties were few. Costs have risen sharply since the Second World War, as Third World nations have become better armed and more determined to assert independence. Worldwide publicity about any violent action anywhere is also a constraint; many parties are prepared to propagandize the sins of the superpower.

[43]Patrick J. Leahy, "CIA, Covert Action, and Congressional Oversight," *New York Times*, March 31, 1988, p. 13.

[44]Ranelagh, *The Agency*, pp. 512–13.

[45]Leahy, "CIA."

[46]Turner, *Secrecy and Democracy*, p. 85.

The chief restraint is the modern aversion to bloodshed. People are very sensitive to loss of lives, even if they are trivial in terms of the total population of the country. In the case of Vietnam, for example, fatalities that were one-tenth of those caused by vehicular accidents revolted public opinion. The death of 239 marines in Lebanon in 1983 sufficed to compel withdrawal. Moreover, there is always fear of possible escalation of conflict and involvement of the other superpower, with inconceivable dangers.

Hence significant military interventions since 1945 have been intended to be low-cost.[47] Following the Vietnam experience, American forces have gone only where little resistance was anticipated, such as Grenada. Other interventionist actions, as against Libya, Lebanon, and Iran, have avoided ground combat.

Intervention is deemed appropriate only within a sphere of influence—indeed, the modern sphere of influence of a superpower may be defined as the region in which it can reasonably use military force without much danger.[48] In this sense, the United States has a sphere of influence in the Caribbean and Central America, less clearly over all Latin America; and it has exercised its prerogative in the Dominican Republic (1965), Grenada (1983), and less directly in Nicaragua (1980s). The willingness to use naval and air force in the Near East would seem to amount to a claim that the region is a U.S. sphere of influence; it would certainly be strongly disapproved if the Soviets acted similarly in the area, for example, in defense of Lebanon against Israel.

Eastern Europe is counted as a Soviet sphere of influence, and the Soviet Union has used force in East Germany (1953), Hungary (1956), and Czechoslovakia (1968) and threatened force in Poland (1981). Proximity is not decisive in defining spheres of influence, however. Finland, the country nearest the main centers of the Soviet Union, is not pro-Soviet; Cuba occupies a similar position in relation to the United States.

The use of force to rescue a beleaguered regime is ordinarily regarded as legitimate and is probably not to be considered intervention. A government is free to request help, including armed forces, and a great power may properly accede. Thus in 1950 the United States came to the rescue of the South Korean government that it had established; and the world community gave general approval, even some military cooperation. Noncommunist Latin American opinion viewed the effort in the 1980s to protect the government of El Salvador against guerrillas much more charitably than the effort to use guerrillas to overturn the communist government of Nicaragua. The Soviet Union has claimed to be invading in response to a plea from national authorities, as in the cases of Czechoslovakia and Afghani-

---

[47]Evan Luard, *War in International Society: A Study in International Sociology,* (London: I. B. Tauris, 1986), p. 177.

[48]On spheres of influence, see Jan F. Triska, ed., *Dominant Powers and Subordinate States.*

stan; but the claim was falsified by the installation of a new pro-Soviet leader.

The Soviet Union has been much more cautious about engaging its own forces far from the homeland than has the United States. This caution is understandable because of naval weakness and the old Russian tradition of overland instead of overseas expansion. Moreover, the Russians have avoided criticism by letting Cubans do the fighting in Africa, as they left the fighting in Korea to Koreans and Chinese, in Vietnam to Vietnamese. Until Afghanistan, Soviet troops were never killing people of a Third World country. The Soviets threatened intervention to save Syria in 1967 and Egypt in 1970 and 1973,[49] but it is uncertain how solid the threat may have been.

The impulse to intervene mounts as the superpower sees an emergency getting out of control. The Soviet Union acted rashly in Afghanistan when it feared the communist regime might collapse. The Johnson administration, receiving alarmist reports of revolution from the Dominican Republic in 1965, took fright that delay might mean a new Cuba in the Caribbean. Officials huddle anxiously and leave critical thought behind in the anxiety to act. Intervention comes easier when it has an ideological rationale, but it suffices that an evil character is to be slapped.[50] That they were noncommunists did not save Libyan, Iranian, and Panamanian dictators from the wrath of the American government and public.

In 1981 the Reagan administration made a major issue of revolution in Central America in the belief that a significant victory over communism was to be had at minor risk and cost. Likewise, support for anti-Sandinistas was to be a cheap way of punishing an unfriendly government without consideration of the costs either of defeat (a major political setback) or victory (a new responsibility for a dependent government in bad circumstances) or a prolonged war (which meant spending political capital to support it in Congress, the nation, and the world).[51]

World opinion is much more tolerant of an intervention that amounts only to a reprisal than of an effort to occupy a territory or overturn a government. Thus in April 1986 the United States suffered little political loss for bombing Libya for supporting terrorism. The relative guilt of Libya and Syria was unclear; a dance-hall bombing with one American fatality (responsibility for which was doubtful), was not a convincing reason; and about 100 non-terrorist Libyans were killed. But condemnation of the American action was minimal because of the poor reputation of Muammar Ghadaffy

---

[49]Richard Hermann, "Soviet Policy and the Arab-Israeli Conflict," *Political Science Quarterly* 102 (Fall, 1987), p. 423.

[50]H. W. Brands, Jr., "Decisions on American Armed Intervention: Lebanon, Dominican Republic, Grenada," *Political Science Quarterly* 102, Winter 1987/1988, pp. 612–13, 623–24.

[51]Regarding limitations of military action, see Stephen T. Hosmer, *Constraints on U.S. Strategies in Third World Conflicts* (New York: Crane Russak, 1987).

and because no one suspected that the United States was interested in occupying Libyan territory. Happily for the reputation of the United States, the mission failed in its chief object, to murder Ghadaffy, and thereby make him a martyr of anti-imperialism.

Likewise, the world did not widely sympathize with Iran's fury at American chastisement for attacks on shipping in the Persian Gulf in 1987. Whatever reprobation there might have been was removed by Iranian shelling of neutral vessels. It is difficult for those who show little respect for international law to seek its protection. The Eastern Caribbean states could support the U.S. invasion of Grenada because the nearest thing to a government was a clique of the assassins of the recognized government of Maurice Bishop.

Small countries may also take advantage of the disrepute of tyrannical governments to use force against them. Thus Tanzania was hardly criticized for ousting the notorious Idi Amin of Uganda in 1979, and many Ugandans welcomed the action. Vietnam, invading Kampuchea in 1979, might have been applauded by the world at large and by most Kampucheans for getting rid of the execrable Khmer Rouge regime; however, it stayed on to earn the dislike of the "liberated" people and the poor opinion of a large majority of nations.

The political cost of low-level military actions may thus be slight or moderate, and an intervention that is judiciously handled and minimally violent may discourage irresponsible conduct. Benefits, however, are also likely to be low and probably mostly internal-political. For example, putting Kuwaiti tankers under the American flag and sending a large naval contingent to escort them in and out of the Persian Gulf contributed more to moral gratification than to its ostensible purpose of assuring an important oil flow. In 1987 the Soviets offered to join an international force to protect shipping in the Gulf; this might have solved the problem, but the basic point was to prevent a Soviet takeover of the Gulf—how the Soviet Union could dream of control of the Gulf at the time when it was being pressed to withdraw from Afghanistan was not explained. Little more than a year earlier it had been deemed necessary to court Iran by arms deliveries to thwart the Soviets; but the United States preferred, mostly because of pique over the Irangate fiasco, practically to take the Iraqi side in the war.

In 1987, the U.S. secretary of defense, Caspar Weinberger, gave an impressive litany of reasons for defying Iran and showing the flag in the Persian Gulf:[52] 1) to maintain freedom of navigation on the high seas, 2) to preserve free world access to oil resources, 3) to promote stability and security of moderate Arab states, 4) to prevent domination by any hostile power, 5) to thwart Soviet aims for a warm-water port, access to oil, and world domination, 6) to keep allies, 7) to sustain the forward deployment essential

---

[52]In a speech at the Naval Postgraduate School, Monterey, CA, November 2, 1987.

for the strategy of deterrence, 8) to remain credible in the face of a military threat, and 9) to uphold a nonpartisan foreign policy despite the vacillations of Congress and the impractical or unconstitutional War Powers Act. No good citizen could doubt the need thus to protect the vital interests of the United States.

The result was not brilliant. Violence in the Gulf was considerably worse after the American vessels moved in than before. Naval operations cost about $2.50 for every $1.00 of oil escorted out of the Gulf.[53] Other anti-Iranian actions undercut American efforts to get international backing for an arms embargo against Iran. An accidental byproduct was the downing of an Iranian airliner with over 200 fatalities. For the navy, however, action in the Gulf was the best justification in 40 years for spending taxpayers' money. More vessels were dispatched to the area weeks after the war ended, and they stayed for many months. Ironically, the Iraqis, far from being grateful to their semi-ally in the war, turned violently anti-American.[54]

Intervention is always more complicated than expected. It is difficult to deal with the people in the country supposedly being helped; the Soviet Union was plagued by quarrels among Afghan communists in the same way the United States found its South Vietnamese unmanageable. The Soviets, like the Americans, tried and discarded a series of local leaders. No gratitude can be expected, and it is difficult for the outsider to solve the internal problems that motivated the intervention. The Soviet Union, moreover, has had lessons in Afghanistan remarkably like that of the United States in Vietnam. Soldiers did not understand what they were fighting for and were shocked to find themselves treated as invaders instead of saviors as the propaganda had it. There was antagonism between soldiers and officers, as in Vietnam. Drug abuse was widespread, and morale dropped as it became evident that the war was not being won.[55]

El Salvador typically confounded the planners of Washington. The guerrillas remain undefeated, and it is not certain how badly the Salvadoran army wants to end the civil war that brings it money and weapons far beyond previous dreams. The government also knows that an end to the war would mean winding down the munificent subsidy. The party favored by the United States has seemed incapable of leading the nation, and the United States has won little love.

Public opinion in the United States seems prepared to support intervention only if it is short and successful, and the Congress is less inclined to be hawkish than the executive. Distrust of intervention found expression in the War Powers Act of 1973, which requires notification of Congress

[53]Richard Halloran, "What Price U.S. Patrols in the Gulf?" *New York Times*, February 21, 1988, p. E2; Barry Rubin, "Drowning in the Persian Gulf," *Foreign Policy* 69, Winter 1987/1988, pp. 120–34.

[54]*Wall Street Journal*, December 5, 1988, p. 1.

[55]Bernard E. Trainor, "Study on Afghan War Cites Low Soviet Morale," *New York Times*, June 5, 1988, p. 8.

within 48 hours of the introduction of U.S. troops into hostilities and their withdrawal within 60 days unless the action is approved by Congress. The validity and value of this measure are disputed, however. The Congress is inhibited in trying to check the president's powers abroad, but it has ample means of doing so if public opinion unequivocally turns against an action.

The autonomy of nations within the spheres of influence of the superpowers seems to increase with the domestic problems of the latter. Vexation and intervention are natural reactions to the insubordination of those who have been subordinates, but the expense and poor success of American policy concentrated on the poverty-stricken and intrinsically weak Central America region may be educational. Latin America has grown more willful during the years when the United States has been trying to bring Central America into conformity, although Washington failed to notice the fact.

Third World countries are not much afraid of intervention, as they have shown by freely expropriating foreign assets, even valuable oil fields in countries of small population and no military power. In the fuel crisis of 1974, some Americans called for a military solution,[56] but sanity prevailed.

The United States has adjusted to the slide from the total dominance of the late 1940s about as gracefully as might be expected. Albeit somewhat unwillingly, it has accepted limits on its power even in the most sensitive area of Central America and the Caribbean. If halfway measures are not successful, as in Nicaragua and Panama, the administration does not raise the stakes by military action but shrugs and turns to other concerns. The Soviet Union has likewise shown itself able to adapt realistically to a major failure on its border. It has proceeded to reassessment of policies in the Third World and the search for better ways of influence. If very great powers can always retreat decently from difficult positions, the world will be safer.

The American public is said to believe, by a margin of more than three to one, that "Economic power is more important than military power in determining a nation's influence."[57] Yet to let affairs evolve and count on gradual development is contrary to the instincts of leaders, perhaps counter to their political interests in engaging popular opinion for a national cause.

The Challenge of Revolution

The superpowers from time to time have seen friendly governments overturned by hostile movements.[58] The Soviet Union has thus far been able to

[56]Robert O. Kaolin and Joseph S. Nye, *Power and Interdependence: World Politics in Transition*, (Boston: Little Brown, 1977), p. 28.

[57]Hobart Rowen, "The Democrats Are Muffing It," *Washington Post National Edition*, November 30, 1987, p. 5.

[58]Jonathan R. Adelman, ed., *Superpowers and Revolution* (New York: Praeger, 1986).

meet this challenge except in Afghanistan. For the United States it has proved more difficult.

The problem is acute when the revolutionary movement is potentially expansive within the region of special U.S. concern, as in Cuba (1960), Chile (1970), and Nicaragua (1979). Every administration since 1945 has believed itself obliged to prevent or overthrow leftist revolutionary regimes in this hemisphere,[59] even though this required risking the establishment of a rightist authoritarian regime.

It is easy to support authoritarian friends. Yet an effort to maintain an undemocratic regime may assure that eventual and perhaps inevitable change is violent and unfavorable. Antidictatorial movements take an anti-U.S. turn if they see this country cooperating with the unpopular rulership; they hold the foreign influence responsible for the national affliction. If a radical anti-U.S. party overthrows a dictator and comes into control of the government by violence, the new rulers, who strongly want to break with the past, think in terms of breaking with the United States, which they regard as responsible for the old regime.

For example, the New Jewel Movement taking control of Grenada in 1979 did not want good relations with the United States that might interfere with going its leftist way.[60] The Sandinistas came to power seeing the United States as responsible for the tyranny against which they fought; to defy "the enemy of humanity," as it is characterized in the Sandinista anthem, was made an article of faith. Feeling themselves mortally at odds with the U.S.-dominated order, revolutionaries welcome U.S. hostility—a sentiment that rises not from the masses but from the leadership, which uses it to bind the masses to themselves. The Sandinistas exaggerated fears of invasion, even talking of grandiose plans to counter a U.S. attack in 1987 when the ability of the Reagan administration to send in American forces had fallen near zero.[61]

Insurgents against U.S. influence have almost automatically turned toward the Soviet Union as the alternative power in the world. This occurred in Cuba, Nicaragua, Grenada, and Ethiopia. For the new rulers in all of these, it was important to see themselves not as isolated rebels but as part of a general struggle for world change, freedom of peoples, or the new order of socialism.[62] According to the formal policy statement of the Grenadan ambassador to Moscow, "Our revolution has to be viewed as a world-wide process with its original roots in the Great October Revolution [of Lenin]. For Grenada to assume a position of increasingly greater impor-

[59]Sharpe, "The Real Cause of Irangate," p. 41.

[60]Robert Pastor, "Does the United States Push Revolutions to Cuba?" *Journal of Interamerican Studies and World Affairs* 28, (Spring 1986), pp. 1–34.

[61]*New York Times*, December 17, 1987, p. 8. On U.S. policy, see Roy Gutman, *Banana Diplomacy: The Making of American Policy in Nicaragua, 1981–1987* (New York: Simon and Schuster, 1988).

[62]For Ethiopia, see Marina Ottaway, *Soviet and American Influence in the Horn of Africa,* (New York: Praeger, 1982), p. 159.

tance, we have to be seen as influencing at least regional events."[63] The Castroites set about trying to extend their revolution to all Latin America; the Sandinistas felt it was their duty or right to give theirs to Central America. The Salvadoran guerrillas, comparing the stages of their revolution with those of Lenin's, envisioned themselves as partners in revolution with Cuba and Angola, looking to the awaited crisis of world capitalism.[64]

There are three possible ways of dealing with such a politically undesirable movement. One is to crush it by force. Another is to express enmity and harass it without taking decisive actions to liquidate it. The third is to treat it as a fairly understandable exaggeration, check its possible spread (the likelihood of which is exaggerated by both the revolutionaries and their enemies), but continue reasonably normal relations.

The first of these is not ordinarily available for a democratic government answerable to public opinion. Many people reject interference in the internal affairs of another state, perhaps sympathize with the revolutionaries or claimants to revolutionary virtue, and ask why their boys should be sent to die in bad causes. Since 1917 there have been a dozen communist revolutions or takeovers of one kind or another, and in most cases it would have been militarily feasible for the United States or other anticommunist powers to quash them. But this has actually been done only in the 1983 intervention in Grenada, which was defended by a few hundred armed Cuban workers and Grenadan troops. This action, trivial as it was militarily, was politically possible only because of the disintegration of the Grenadan regime and the excuse of protecting about a thousand foreign, mostly U.S. medical students in an anarchic situation.

The opposite course is patience, carrying on normal relations so far as possible and taking a slightly lofty position toward the radicals in power, as though confident that they were subject to influence and inducements to good behavior and would come to their senses in due course. If the regime is hostile to private enterprise, the private sector will punish it by withdrawing. It may be guessed that such an accommodative approach to Russia in 1918, to China in 1949, to Vietnam in 1954, to Cuba in 1959, and to Nicaragua in 1979 would have avoided a siege mentality and led to an evolution of the respective communist regime unburdened by fear.[65]

Suavity, however, has usually been unattractive for leaders of state. It was more from neglect than conscious policy that this line was partly followed in Mozambique, which the American administration in the 1980s found not to be irretrievably communist. Elsewhere in Africa, the Marxist-

---

[63]Seabury and McDougal, eds. *The Grenada Papers*, p. 207.

[64]Document prepared for the November 1986 meeting of the General Command of the FMLN entitled "Preparatory Phase of the Strategic Counteroffensive," mimeo. American Embassy, San Salvador, 1987.

[65]Tony Smith, *Thinking like Communists: State and Legitimacy in the Soviet Union, China and Cuba* (New York: Norton, 1987), p. 192.

Leninist line of various countries, such as Benin or Cameroon, has also been more or less ignored, a course that was easier because their radicalism was largely rhetorical and had no particular effect on their neighbors and their economic importance was negligible.

The middle road lies between forceful action and tolerance. It has usually seemed imperative to do something about communists seizing power, especially if anticommunists raise a banner of counterrevolution and plead for help. It comes easiest to enter the fray, although it can be done only halfheartedly and sacrifices the options of decisive action or of diplomatic management.

In the case of the Russian Revolution, Britain and France, with a little support from the United States, intervened desultorily in 1918–1920. They wanted to "strangle Bolshevism in its cradle," an understandable urge considering that the Leninists declared war on everything they deemed sacred; their anger was multiplied by the Soviet betrayal of the Allied cause. The Leninist revolutionaries not only proclaimed the overthrow of all existing governments and the end of religion and other traditional values but also broke the national pledge not to make a separate peace with the German enemy and were somewhat subservient to them as long as the war lasted. But the Allies were too exhausted from the World War to make a major exertion. They gave supplies to anti-Soviet forces in the Russian civil war and sent a few troops, who did almost no fighting but greatly assisted Bolshevik propaganda and moral. This ineffectual meddling turned the conflict into something of a Russian national struggle against the foreign interventionists, helped to solidify the Bolshevik party, hardened the Leninist state as it otherwise could never have been hardened, and ended by giving the communist forces a memorable victory over what they called the league of world capitalist-imperialists.

The Western powers, especially the United States, have often followed this middling course of treating a communist revolution as unacceptable, menacing it, and becoming allied with its domestic enemies, but failing to act strongly enough to liquidate it. The results have always been, as they were in Russia, the opposite of the intentions.

For the United States, the most painful example of this unhappy approach was the effort to safeguard the southern part of Vietnam from the stronger regime of the communist part of the country.[66] The United States was originally drawn in by the desire to please the French, who wanted to restore their rule after the defeat of Japan. After France was defeated and departed, however, the policy had its own momentum: we could not abandon those whom we had helped to power. The basic idea, that Vietnam was an instrument of Chinese expansionism, which was a projection of Mos-

[66]On the involvement, see George McT. Kahin, *Intervention: How America Became Involved in Vietnam* (New York: Knopf, 1986).

cow's, was wrong at both junctures: Vietnam was never inclined to give China anything, and the Chinese had no mind to do anything for the Russians, with whom they had broken well before the American involvement became massive. It was also difficult to make a proper anticommunist crusade of the war while maintaining fairly good relations with Moscow, the fountainhead of the movement.

There was no serious effort to assess probable costs and gains. Entanglement deepened because of secrecy, confidence in American omnipotence, and willingness to become entangled. After the spurious Gulf of Tonkin incident and the famous nearly unanimous congressional resolution authorizing retaliation—the nearest equivalent to a declaration of war—there was a moral commitment. The war was made a test of will, hence the harder to reconsider. It was assumed that massive application of technology should solve all the problems—Vietnam was subjected to far more tonnage of bombs than devastated much of Europe and Japan in WW II.

The Vietnam experience exemplifies the difficulties of an attempt by a democratic state—or by any state—to impose its will in a recalcitrant country of which it knows very little. The chiefs in the Pentagon and the White House had little means of learning how their orders were being carried out and how the war was going, so they demanded statistics. For many of these, the Americans in Saigon would turn to the Vietnamese, who would raise or lower the figures as desired. Since it was required to report the number of "search and destroy" operations, they were preferentially carried out where the enemy was not. When forays were to be made into Viet Cong territory, the enemy would be warned by an artillery barrage, so they melted back or prepared ambushes. Body counts were demanded; any bodies would do, and only a small fraction seem to have been of combatants.[67] To justify the war to the public and itself, the Johnson Administration had to generate optimism. This required accepting the optimistic appraisals and ignoring or repressing negative reports from the field. The skeptical American press was regarded as the enemy.[68]

The war had to be fought as a test case of something. Although it was. going badly, the policymakers were worried that their Saigon dependents might prefer to make peace with Hanoi and thus make the American effort unnecessary.[69] It was reasoned that a greater U.S. effort would lead to a greater South Vietnamese effort; but when the superpower assumed respon-

---

[67]On the conduct of the war, see John L. Gaddis, "Implementing Flexible Response: Vietnam as a Test Case," in *The Use of Force: International Politics and Foreign Policy,* ed. Robert J. Art and Kenneth L. Waltz (Boston: Little Brown, 1971), pp. 343–63; see also Halberstam, *The Best and the Brightest* (New York: Random House, 1972), especially pp. 202–7.

[68]On the decision making, see Halberstam, *The Best and the Brightest;* and Leslie H. Gelb and Richard K. Betts, *The Irony of Vietnam: The System Worked* (Washington: Brookings Institution, 1979).

[69]Halberstam, *The Best and the Brightest,* p. 355.

sibility the clients felt less need to exert themselves. Advisers around the president were more hawkish than President Johnson himself. But the war became impossible when both the public and the soldiers, high and low, came to regard it as wrong or futile.

The costs of military concentration on an unimportant target included a deterioration of the strategic abilities of the armed forces—if the Soviets had a mind to take aggressive action, there would have been no better time than when the U.S. was caught up in the Vietnam excursion. President Johnson's "Great Society" program was wrecked. The defeat caused an unexampled erosion of the American social fabric. The nation, especially its opinion leaders, contracted a guilt feeling such as the United States had never felt before, which for many years after the withdrawal strongly inhibited foreign adventures that suggested a comparable involvement.

The communization of Vietnam, it was many a time predicted, would send a Red tide over Southeast Asia and shift the world balance against the United States. But the domino really fell only in Laos, the most backward and least important country of the region; although Cambodia (Kampuchea) was taken over by communists, it was invaded and occupied by Vietnamese forces, who found it indigestible. There was little effect on Southeast Asia generally.[70] The victorious Vietnamese communists proved incapable of managing their economy, sank into exemplary poverty, and by 1987 were reduced to begging for international assistance to avert famine.[71]

Even less rationalizable has been the U.S. treatment of Castro.[72] Castro apparently felt a visceral dislike for the power that had dominated Cuba economically and politically since 1898; aware of his attitude, the CIA was scheming his elimination when he was still in the hills.[73] But the Cuban people were not anti-U.S. when he came to power, and violence and bloodshed inflicted by this country were necessary to make anti-Yankeeism acceptable. Castro did not have to be pushed into the Soviet embrace, but he could make Cuba dependent on the Soviet Union only because successive American administrations gave him every assistance. The cancellation of Cuba's sugar quota and subsequent ending of all commercial relations, following various measures of Castro against American interests, forced or enabled Castro to shift economic ties from Cuba's chief market and suppliers to the Soviet bloc and facilitated the establishment of a socialized economy. The breaking of diplomatic relations in January 1961 (in retalia-

---

[70]James Fallow, "No Hard Feelings?" *Atlantic* 262, December 1988, p. 76.

[71]*Wall Street Journal*, May 11, 1988, p. 18.

[72]For accounts of relations, see Wayne S. Smith, *The Closest of Enemies: A Personal and Diplomatic History of the Castro Years* (New York: W. W. Norton, 1987); Alan H. Luxenberg, "Did Eisenhower Push Castro into the Arms of the Soviets?" *Journal of Interamerican Studies and World Affairs* 30 (Spring 1988), 37–72; M. Morley, *The Imperial State and Revolution: The United States and Cuba, 1962–1986* (Cambridge, MA: Cambridge University Press, 1987).

[73]Ranelagh, *The Agency,* p. 356.

tion for Castro's limitation of U.S. embassy staff but also to prepare for the recognition of an anti-Castro government) deprived the United States of much of its remaining leverage.

A critical step was the April 1961 Bay of Pigs landing, a botched effort to overthrow the Castro government by an exile group organized by the CIA (and correspondingly discredited in the eyes of most Cubans). The assault enabled Castro to rout out oppositionists and assert total control in the name of military emergency, while the militias were set to watching out for enemy planes from the rooftops. Castro thereupon declared Cuba to be a socialist state and took credit for having been Marxist at heart while he had been pretending to be a democrat fighting against the Batista dictatorship for free elections and constitutional government.

Succeeding American administrations followed a sterile policy for three decades. President Kennedy, infuriated by the Bay of Pigs failure, gave the CIA the task of killing Castro. Some 30 schemes were considered, from an exploding cigar and a poisoned wetsuit to a hefty gangster contract.[74] (Ironically, Castro is said to have been grieved by the assassination of Kennedy.) Pinpricks, such as the CIA's setting canefields afire, helped to keep Castro's movement spirited and dynamic and his masses loyal. Exclusion of Cuba from the Organization of American States and pressure on Latin American states to break diplomatic and commercial relations (until given up in 1975) did not soften Castro. Isolation excluded, so far as possible, the influences that would have made it more difficult to press Cuba into the very alien Soviet mold or would have pulled Cuba back toward the more congenial ways of its neighbors. Negotiations were refused unless the Castro government would make substantial prior concessions, divorcing Cuba from the Soviet Union or renouncing its "internationalist" role in Africa.

It was feared that Castro's revolutionary message to Latin America was stronger than Latin America's example of moderation for Cuba. But probably more decisive for U.S. policy was the desire to punish a misbehaving small power in what should have been the immediate sphere of influence of the United States. Its temerity was the more exasperating because Cuba had been, of all foreign nations, perhaps the most cooperative with U.S. purposes. But if one assumes that the purpose of Castro and his close followers was to make Cuba a solidly anti-U.S. and pro-Soviet bastion, American policy suited them excellently. The refusal to sell consumer goods to Cuba helped Castro impose spartanism, blaming economic troubles on the "blockade," and the inability of Cuba to import U.S. movies (legally) made it easier to keep out what the communists regard as moral pollution. U.S. enmity made Cuba relevant to world politics and important in the politics of the hemisphere. Castro was given the image of a David standing up to

[74]Ranelagh, *The Agency,* p. 386.

the Yankee Goliath; the dictator of an inherently unimportant country became an important figure on the world stage, even, for a term, president of
the "non-aligned" movement.

The United States, while assisting cultural exchanges with the Soviet
Union and favoring trade in nonmilitary goods, forbade virtually all contacts
with the communist power potentially most subject to its influence. The
authorities who demanded that the Soviets live up to their agreement to
buy large amounts of American grain would not even permit antibiotics to
be sold to Cuba. The U.S. interest in having a friendly Cuba on the doorstep
was sacrificed to essentially emotional urges, as the near neighbor of the
United States was converted into a Soviet military outpost. There is no reason to suppose that Castro would have obtained Soviet military support if
he had not been threatened.

The problem will probably never recur in anything like the same form.
There will certainly be uprisings against repressive, corrupt, and above all
incompetent regimes; but Marxist ideology can hardly play an important
role. Future revolutions are not likely to be important, or even to seem
important, for the world balance of power. It should be possible to regard
them calmly, acting in concert with other powers so far as they may conceivably seem menacing to the world community. Revolutions may have to take
care of themselves.

Chapter 5

The New World System

The New Society

In times when the jousting of knights was the favorite sport and manhood included swordplay, war was a natural part of an uncomplex existence. Life was hazardous at best and if a few people were killed on a campaign, it did not much trouble the community. In the highly ordered and dynamically interactive modern world, to the contrary, huge stockpiles of weapons capable of destroying civilization are incongruous. The use of force between sovereign powers makes little sense, and traditional international relations based on force or the threat of force are obsolete.

It is evident, as the 1980s come to an end, that the outlook fundamentally changes: the bipolar standoff has wound down, the contest for the Third World has lost significance, and more diplomacy revolves around economic than political affairs. These changes, like many others all operating together, are the logical outcome of the enormous growth of technology, production, information, communications, and the circulation of goods, people, and ideas in the postwar world.

It is a truism that we are carried breathtakingly forward by the achievements of science and engineering, at a seemingly ever-quickening pace, in directions unknown. Science is said to double its stores of knowledge every fifteen years. Much of it has no immediate practical application; but very much goes to remaking ways of living and doing, in an intensity of flux novel in human history. There was not a great deal in the life of the Romans that would have been incomprehensible to the Babylonians two thousand years earlier. Even in the 18th century, daily life was recognizably like what it had been for many centuries. But from the beginnings of the industrial revolution in England in the latter part of that century, ever-expanding technology has increasingly modified human existence. Now a generation grows up with little understanding of the world of the previous generation.[1]

Nowhere is the potential of science more striking than in the processing and transmission of information. The speed and capacity of computers zoom ever higher, and they not only imitate more and more of the capacities of the brain but also accomplish many things of which humans are incapable. Crisis scenarios are played out on computer screens. A disk not much larger than one's hand can contain the equivalent of 200,000 printed pages; it is impossible to prevent the transportation of enormous quantities of information anywhere. New techniques open up unpredictably. Moderate-temperature superconductivity, for example, promises manifold applications that would have seemed miraculous a few years ago. How genetic engineering may change crops, animals, and perhaps humans is beyond speculation. Technology remakes both the way people indulge their desires and the ways they earn a living. It is predicted that within a generation half the work force of advanced countries will sit in front of computer terminals. "Reality is leaping ahead of fantasy," in the words of a chip designer, who foresees ten times more progress in hi-tech in the next dozen years than in the last dozen.[2]

Many innovations, from automatic dishwashers to intelligent-seeming toys, may make little apparent or immediate difference to the tenor of life; but one can be sure that they affect patterns of thought and action. Household appliances have greatly changed the role of women, and talking toys must do something to the minds of children. The automobile has probably had a good deal to do with democracy; a society of persons able to move about freely is surely harder to discipline.

New dimensions of communication have had profound effects on society and politics. Radio in the 1920s and 1930s enabled a politician to speak to millions instead of those within the range of his voice. Without radio, Hitler could never have become master of Germany. Television, with much more immediacy and impact, has been far more revolutionary. A paradigm of the technological age, it is cheap enough to be universally available in the richer countries and broadly in the poorer. It levels society, as rich and poor, ignorant and learned, receive much of the same informational input.

---

[1]Alvin Toffler, *Third Wave* (New York: William Morrow, 1980) has graphic comments on the effects of the new technology.

[2]*Fortune*, July 18, 1988, p. 92.

Supplemented by videorecorders and cassettes, television fills the largest single fraction of the leisure time of most adults; in industrial countries, it presents more material to form the character of children than does school or parents.

Humans, in brief, have made for themselves a new environment, with profound effects on the personality, the ways individuals relate to society and the state, and the interactions of nations. To a degree that can be sensed but not clearly set forth, institutions change both outwardly in form and inwardly in content and meaning. The technological revolution, while in some ways swallowing up the individual, increases mental and physical mobility, self-awareness, and expectations. Partly released from material wants, people find a multitude of new needs. Expectations rise in the age of technological marvels. In some ways, modern men and women are conformist, slaves to moods and fashions; in other ways they are individualistic, skeptical, demanding, at times rebellious, certainly unpredictable.

The meaning of authority is altered. Many a government, from South Africa to Poland, must be puzzled why people under its power are so stubbornly rebellious. The Israelis have been astonished to find how difficult it is to convert superior force into effective control. In the 1930s the idea was prevalent that the modern government, armed with the tools of propaganda and indoctrination and looming overwhelmingly over the citizenry, was becoming all-powerful. This proved to be shortsighted. People are not, or refuse to remain, automatons; and minds are ultimately uncontrollable.

The power of the state is enlarged with its vastly expanded responsibilities and greater means of action, yet its ability actually to manage many things decreases. This is evident in the difficulty not only of prohibiting indulgences considered illicit, such as narcotics, but also of trying to guide thinking. Everywhere, in theoretically regimented countries as well as in the looser societies, people show great ingenuity in evading rules imposed on them.

The state is unable to handle the economy, which outstrips the ability both of economists to analyze and predict it and of bureaucrats to regulate it. Problems of trade flows, currency imbalances, interest rates, unemployment, and so forth, are baffling. Governments seemingly must assume a new role in the guidance or protection of production, but their ability to do so rationally is questionable. Economic questions assume a new importance. It becomes obvious that the future role of the United States depends on such economic factors as debt, trade flows, and capital movements, which the government does not know how to control. Industries rise and decline with unprecedented rapidity. The status of nations changes with novel rapidity in ways no one predicts; the recent upsurge of East Asia has changed the face of the world.

The interrelations of nations are altered in countless ways, directly or indirectly. It is all too familiar how the new weaponry has remade the

potentialities of combat, especially for the strongest powers, although governments have yet to draw the full conclusions. It is an innovation of profound significance that any major power can photograph any part of the
world in great and increasing detail with orbiting telescope-cameras. There
can be no more closed, or hidden societies. The volume of global communications has grown enormously. By virtue of the ease and speed of travel
and transportation, countries and cultures impinge on one another in a
multitude of ways and to an unprecedented extent. Interchanges of nations
expand continually, mostly, it seems, to their mutual benefit.

As never before, people are aware of events and problems, not only
in their own society but around the world; Californians react to brutalities
in Africa or the Philippines. The modern individual is increasingly a citizen
of the world. The new problems, too, are increasingly global; for those who
swelter in a heat wave exacerbated by the accumulation of carbon dioxide
in the atmosphere, the interdependence of nations is all too real.

The new age brings not only new complications of existence but opportunities as well. The abundance of communications and richness of
modern education and learning provide the means for better approaches.
Nations, too, must learn new ways of dealing with one another.[3]

The Subsidence of War

A signal development, sometimes overlooked in the publicity given to violence, has been a fairly steady decline in warfare since the armageddon of
1939–1945. There has been much ideological antagonism in the postwar
period; and many clashes of hostile spheres, in which the future of humanity was thought to be at stake, might well have led to catastrophe. Yet the
contemporary peace among great powers has already been the longest in
the historical record, and it seems less threatened now than at any previous
time.

Between states standing near the pinnacle of technological and cultural development there is not even any important political conflict. This
is unique in world history and a key distinction of the new international
condition. In earlier times, the most highly civilized sovereignties, such as
ancient Greek city-states, the republics of medieval Italy, or the nation-states
of early modern Europe, were chronically sparring and occasionally warring. The rich and strong did most of the fighting against each other; today,
violence is for the poor and weak. Europe for centuries was the most war-

---

[3]As pointed out by Edward L. Morse, *Modernization and the Transformation of International
Relations* (New York: Free Press, 1976).

ridden of continents; now it is the most pacific, without even the minor conflicts that slightly roil the Americas, Africa, and Asia.

In the less developed world, in the absence of a nuclear deterrent, there have been many, mostly minor wars. Some have been fought by former colonial rulers trying to retain control of various territories. But the colonial or semicolonial wars ground down with the retreat of France from Indochina (1954) and Algeria (1962), the loss by Portugal of its last African colonies of consequence (1974), and the failure of the U.S. effort to salvage Western influence in Vietnam (1975). There can be no more such conflicts between advanced and less developed nations.

War has been left to preindustrial societies, such as India and Pakistan, Iran and Iraq, Libya and Chad. Its commonest cause has been disputes over arbitrarily drawn boundaries. Territorial quarrels may be also religious, such as the Iran-Iraq war (1980–1988) and the Israeli-Palestinian-Arab conflicts. European colonial masters having gone, there are many "national liberation" struggles against Third World rulers. Tamils feel oppressed by Sinhalese in Sri Lanka, Eritreans do not understand why they should be under the rule of Ethiopia, and there is no satisfactory way to settle the jurisdiction of large stretches of the Western Sahara.

From Burma to El Salvador, dozens of small wars simmer at any given time ("little war" being the literal meaning of *guerrilla*); and hundreds of thousands have been killed in Third World insurgencies in the last decade. But the word "war" is used rather loosely to include many disturbances fomented by groups not organized as states; and little wars are lumped with big ones. Violence within the state is a different species from the duels of states.

The numerous guerrillas, ranging from banditry under a political flag to full-scale civil war, carry on usually rather desultory low-intensity conflicts. They mostly represent social disorder, and no international peacekeeping mechanism could possibly put an end to them. Outside powers may take advantage of the weakness of a state to support a rebellious faction, as in Angola, Mozambique, Sudan, or Nicaragua; but this does not constitute international conflict unless the armed forces of two governments are involved. For the most part, weaker powers prefer security to aggrandizement; of the scores of unnatural and irrational boundaries in the Third World, only a tiny fraction are contested. Thus the sub-Saharan African states have agreed on mutual support of territorial integrity, no matter how the boundaries came to be drawn.

These wars and guerrillas, too, seem to be easing as the atmosphere of world politics calms and violence appears unrewarding. By 1989, the fairly big war between Iran and Iraq and smaller wars between Libya and Chad, Angola and South Africa, and Vietnam and Kampuchean nationalists were ended or seemed to be on the way to pacification; and the civil war in the Sudan had lost intensity. Guerrilla conflicts, in the Western Sahara and Sri Lanka, simmer down. Edenic tranquillity is far away, but the violence seems increasingly unrewarding.

Although governments have been reluctant to realize that war is not a usable institution for modern countries, it has really been obsolete since the industrial revolution and modernization of weaponry began to change its character. In the 1830s Carl von Clausewitz, the great military theoretician, saw war becoming impractical even as he was treating it as an extension of politics.[4] In the latter part of the 19th century there was some tendency to glorify war, partly because there had been no very bloody fighting for a long time, partly because Darwinism and the exaltation of "survival of the fittest" were taken to rationalize battle as the means of assuring that the fittest or best of men and nations should prevail. The mild-mannered British philosopher Herbert Spencer saw war as eugenically necessary. On the eve of WW I, General Friedrich von Bernhardi wrote, "The efforts directed towards the abolition of war must not only be termed foolish but absolutely immoral and must be stigmatized as unworthy of the human race. To what does the whole question amount? It is proposed to deprive men of the right and the possibility to sacrifice their highest material possessions, their physical life, for ideals, and thus to realize the highest moral unselfishness."[5]

This was a minority opinion, however. There was enough fear and repugnance of war that a great international conference met in 1899 at the Hague to talk disarmament and the moderation of war; it outlawed some types of weapons. As tensions were rising a few years later, a British economist, Norman Angell, pointed out that pacific nations were more prosperous and little was to be gained even from victorious war. Arms races, he noted, were futile, the costs of governing a subjected land were greater than the returns, and trade was not subject to conquest.[6] He failed to take into account the inertia of old ways; and when the great war came in 1914, his vision seemed to be a sad illusion. But he was correct in his appreciation of the trend of civilization.

The euphoria that greeted the coming of war in 1914 was short-lived and soon gave way to grim determination to avoid the unspeakable disaster of defeat.[7] Shocked by the slaughter and suffering, enlightened world opinion came to regard armed aggression as a crime; and war was held justifiable

[4]Richard N. Lebow, "Clausewitz and Nuclear Stability," *Political Science Quarterly* 103 (Spring 1988), 83.

[5]Cited by Stephen Kull, "Nuclear Arms and the Desire for World Destruction," *Political Psychology* 4, no. 3 1982, p. 568.

[6]Normal Angell, *The Great Illusion* (London: G.P. Putnams Sons, 1913).

[7]Erich Fromm, *The Anatomy of Human Destruction* (New York: Holt Rinehart and Winston, 1973), p. 213.

only for the salvation of the nation. Guilt for starting the war was written into the peace treaties of 1919, all the defeated governments were overthrown, and there were shouts of "Hang the Kaiser." The League of Nations was established in hopes of underwriting eternal peace. In 1928 almost all the nations of earth solemnly renounced war by the Kellogg-Briand Pact.

WW II was greeted with gloom, in contrast to the cheers for its predecessor. Even Hitler's indoctrinated masses, as they saw troops leaving for the front, were silent and somber, to the chagrin of the glory-minded Fuehrer. The British and French went to war with great reluctance, despite the moral crudity of their enemy and the need to halt the Nazi onslaught. They refrained from serious fighting until the Nazi offensive in the west in the spring of 1940.

After WW II, captured leaders of the Axis powers were put on trial and executed, not only for crimes committed during the war but also for the planning of the war itself. A major war is now a gamble of the rulers' lives. It is significant that the formal declaration of war, a leftover of the ceremonious challenge to combat, is outmoded; there has been no officially declared war since 1945.

The recent great wars started by miscalculation. In 1914, it was assumed that the war would be more or less like the brief and fairly bloodless conflicts of the preceding century, and the boys would be home for Christmas. In 1939 the Nazis counted on a splendid blitzkrieg to grab Poland, after which it should be easy to make peace. Britain and France, having failed to move to save Czechoslovakia less than a year before, would surely accept the loss of Poland as an irreversible fait accompli, especially after the Soviets had swallowed half the country. The British and French, on the other hand, declared war in the expectation that blockade would suffice painlessly to bring the Nazis to terms; they hoped somehow to manage victory through a "phony war" of minimal casualties. In 1941 the Japanese reckoned that by destroying the American fleet at Pearl Harbor they would induce the United States to desist from a useless effort to interfere with Japan's campaign for dominion over East Asia and its fabled riches.[8]

In the 1930s civilized nations opted for war; but it is no longer possible even for a foolish and ill-intentioned leadership to feel confident in the gamble. A nuclear war might not produce more fatalities than either world war, but it would more likely cost many times more, and no rational statesman elects a course sure to kill millions in short order. The superweapons can neither protect from a counterblow nor secure a useful gain. There is no certainty that there will not be another great war, but the possibility exists only so far as minds are embedded in the past or subject to madness.

---

[8]George Sansom, "Japan's Fatal Blunder," in Robert J. Art and Kenneth N. Waltz, eds., *The Use of Force: International Politics and Foreign Policy* (Boston: Little Brown, 1971), p. 260.

The Decline of Expansionism

Not only has war become infinitely more dangerous; the traditional goal of war, territorial conquest, has lost its value.

International relations have seemed like variations on a changeless theme from the dawn of history until the nuclear age because of the fact or belief that wealth and power came from control of lands and people. Power in the past has served to enlarge the state through acquisition of territory, thereby increasing power. Aggrandizement was vitally important especially as nation-states were being put together in the 15th to 17th centuries, and the habit of mind was retained.

"Imperialism," which in current discourse is a crime, a century ago was seen as good. In the 19th century European powers coveted lands of neighbors, or if these could not be had, lands of weaker peoples. Russia was expanding into areas of weakness around its perimeter, the United States cherished its "Manifest Destiny," and Japan saw empire building as the certificate of world stature.

But expansionism has been losing utility for a long time. Although Lenin thought colonies so necessary to capitalist countries that they had to fight over them, less ideological observers had concluded by the beginning of this century that colonial holdings were on balance unprofitable.[9] The Boer war (1899–1902) was practically the last important colonial campaign of the Western powers, and in 1909 Britain surrendered its gains by giving South Africa self-rule. In WW I, major powers cherished their old territorial objectives and added some new ones, such as Germany's desire to hold Belgium; but the governments, for the sake of fighting spirit, played down such aspirations[10] and stressed the need to save the homeland from the terrible enemy. At the end of the war, although the victors bickered about overseas spoils, they made few changes in Europe that could not be justified on grounds of national self-determination. The United States gave a lofty example by renouncing territorial gains.

In the troubled 1930s land hunger resurged. The Japanese went into Manchuria in 1931 and later into China proper, and Mussolini overran Ethiopia in 1936 for no reason but vainglorious ostentation. The idea that greatness was to be achieved by conquest reached its climax in the Nazi program, of which it was the heart: to make Germany ever more glorious and prosperous by acquiring new lands to populate by breeding the master race. But the discredit and failure of the Nazis totally discredited such ideas.

No victorious power acquired significant territory after World War II,

---

[9]Henry M. Pachter, *The Fall and Rise of Europe: A Political, Social, and Cultural History of the Twentieth Century* (New York: Praeger, 1975), p. 25.

[10]Fromm, *Anatomy of Human Destructiveness,* p. 213.

although the potentialities were enormous. As a result of the war, the Soviet Union came into control of most of Eastern Europe; in accordance with the principles proclaimed at its founding, the peoples liberated from capitalism should have been joined to the "workers' state" of the Soviet Union. This was also the clear implication of the Soviet party program and the first Soviet constitution. Yet Stalin annexed only a small part of East Prussia, from which the natives had been expelled. The East European countries were left as nominally entirely independent states.

One reason for restraint was reluctance to affront the Western powers; Britain and France had gone to war to defend Poland, and the United States was much concerned for the independence of Eastern Europe. But it would certainly have been possible to meld the East European states gradually into the Soviet political system without formal annexation. Far from being ever more tightly bound, the vassal states have gradually enlarged their autonomy. Moscow must have felt it would be too burdensome to try to rule directly the East European peoples, with their traditions of independence—in addition to the non-Russians who are over half the population of the Soviet Union.

The Soviets sent an army into Afghanistan in 1979, but their failure showed how the world had changed in half a century. In the early 1920s a very weak Soviet Union incorporated huge Central Asian territories formerly under tsarist protectorate without difficulty; in the 1980s the powerful Soviet Union was frustrated by small and poor Afghanistan. On the one hand, the determination of the settled Soviet system to expand had weakened; on the other, the will of the Asians to resist had risen and was fortified by the support of the United States and the international community. What would have been treated in the 1920s as a minor matter of the Soviets intervening in an isolated backward country on their borders raised nearly universal feelings of outrage a half century later and was condemned overwhelmingly by the United Nations.

Vietnam has had a similar experience in Kampuchea (Cambodia), which it invaded about the same time that the Soviets went into Afghanistan. Under pressure from China and its other neighbors, and probably from the Soviet Union, Vietnam undertook to withdraw its forces by 1990. The decision must have been painful, because Vietnam has long considered Kampuchea as its protectorate; but the occupation became too costly in terms of chronic guerrilla fighting, the disapproval of the world community, and economic costs of $2–$3 billion yearly.[11]

West European countries, Britain, France, Netherlands, and Belgium, not only gained no new territories in the wake of the victorious war but surrendered their empires. Britain hated to give up Malaya, a magnificent dollar earner through exports of tin and rubber; France found the loss of

[11]*Wall Street Journal,* December 19, 1988, p. A14.

Algeria, with over a million European settlers, traumatic. Portugal, a less modernized country, practically had to be driven by force from its important African colonies. But the anticolonial movement gathered momentum as it proceeded; and the former lords of immense overseas dominions retained only a few scraps, chiefly strategic islands. Something of their postwar prosperity is doubtless due to this form of liberation. The United States has even surrendered territories of military value with small native populations (as Okinawa) or none (as the Panama Canal Zone).

Reunification was a strong motivation for North Vietnam until it was achieved in 1975; and territorial change is an issue for the nations that remain divided as a result of WW II, Korea and Germany. But it seems no longer very advantageous for rulers to add to their domains or to hold onto lands inhabited by unwilling people. Territorial expansion has ceased to be a significant cause of conflict even for the Third World; there has been virtually no effort since 1945 to gain territory except where boundaries were unsettled.[12]

The cooperativeness of subjects has become more important than having bodies to command and tax, and unwillingness to accept foreign domination has grown everywhere.[13] The urge to control raw materials has also decreased. One rationalization of Nazi demands in the prewar years was the injustice of Germany's being deprived of the minerals and other natural wealth that other European powers allegedly possessed in their colonies; the fascists called themselves "have-not" powers, like an international proletariat, with moral claims to a redistribution of riches. In a neo-Marxist interpretation fairly popular until recently, desire to secure raw materials has been a major reason for imperialism and wars. In fact, however, neither raw materials nor any other economic factor has been the clear cause of any conflict since the Boer war (1899–1902).[14]

It is far easier and cheaper to buy raw materials, producers of which are eager to sell, than to annex them. Synthetics have replaced many natural products; after Pearl Harbor, the United States was concerned by Japanese seizure of the chief sources of rubber, silk, and quinine—for all of which man-made substitutes were found. Only oil is still important for international quarrels. The United States has been highly sensitive to events in the Near East since the fuel crisis of 1974; and nations squabble about presumptive oil-bearing seafloor, as in areas between China and Vietnam. But the producing countries have been quite pleased to sell their oil; and the Japanese, lacking energy resources, have shown how well a nation can do without.

[12]Evan Luard, *War in International Society: A Study in International Sociology* (London: I.B. Tauris, 1987), p. 172.

[13]Louis J. Halle, "Does War Have a Future?" *Foreign Affairs*, 52, October 1973, pp. 25–26.

[14]Hans J. Morgenthau, *Politics among Nations: The Struggle for Power and Peace* (New York: Alfred A. Knopf, 1978), p. 53.

As design and sophisticated technology become more important, the relative importance of material inputs decreases. A multimillion dollar computer needs only trifling amounts of raw materials, mostly inexpensive. Curiously, the most important ingredient in computers, silicon, is one of the most abundant elements in the earth's crust. Technology makes power today and will surely do so more fully tomorrow, but it is much less practical to annex brains than mines or wheatfields. How much could a conqueror extract from Silicon Valley?

Because of the weakness of incentives for landgrabbing, the multiplication of independent states, the democratic ethos, and fears of possibly escalating disorder in international relations, the principle of formal sovereignty is more compelling than ever before. For example, the U.S. intervention in Grenada (population 120,000) in 1983 was justified by the virtual lack of a government, those in power having just murdered the prime minister and much of his cabinet; by the need for protection for a considerable number of American citizens (medical students); by the support of nearly all of the neighboring Caribbean states; by the plea of the governor-general of Grenada; and by fears of a communist security threat in what has been considered as nearly a U.S. sphere of interest as any in the world. Before the Second World War, such an action would hardly have raised an eyebrow. Yet condemnation, in the United Nations and around the world, was general, even among NATO allies of the United States.[15] In the General Assembly, 108 voted to condemn; only 9, chiefly the United States and eastern Caribbean ministates, opposed.[16] Likewise, the United States was inhibited from direct action in Nicaragua throughout the Reagan administration, despite the high priority given by the White House to the overthrow of the Sandinista government. Early in the century, it caused no political problems when the Marines were several times sent to Managua for trivial reasons.

Aside from the absorption of South Vietnam by the North, not one of the more than 150 sovereignties in the world has been extinguished in the postwar period. Territorial acquisition is outmoded even in the Third World. Most African countries are highly artificial, with boundaries arbitrarily drawn by colonial powers, and they have suffered many internal quarrels; no boundary has been changed. Pakistan was truncated in 1971 because the two parts were not only very different but were separated by the breadth of India; yet India did not take East Pakistan, as it could easily have done, but let it become Bangladesh. There is no military obstacle to India's annexing Sri Lanka, where Indian forces have been on the ground

---

[15]W. Raymond Duncan, "Soviet Interests in Latin America: New Opportunities and Old Constraints," *Journal of Interamerican Studies and World Affairs* 26, May 1984, p. 173.

[16]Anthony Payne, Paul Sutton, and Tony Thorndike, *Grenada: Revolution and Invasion* (London: Croom Helm, 1984), pp. 168–176.

helping to fight Tamil insurgents; but India does not apparently think of doing this. It has trouble enough in holding its diverse peoples together. It is contrary to the nature of the democratic state to impose undemocratic rule on others. The only important recent case in which a modernized conqueror has insisted on ruling directly a conquered people is the Israeli dominion over occupied Arab territories, the Gaza Strip, Golan Heights, and West Bank. Israel has done so because of the conviction that these lands were divinely bestowed on the Jewish people, together with the desperate urge, in its feelings of insecurity, to keep hostile forces at a distance from the heart of the nation.

Economically, Israel has gained something from taxation and expropriations in the occupied territories;[17] but whatever has been gained is greatly outweighed by multiple costs, including the expense of policing the areas. Israel has also suffered considerable external economic costs; for example, it is denied concessions by the European Parliament, and it is excluded from what should be very profitable interchanges with its neighbors. Tourism, an important industry for the small country, fell sharply. By the time the Palestinian uprising was a year old, the Israeli economy was in crisis from loss of exports and other revenues.

Moral-political costs have been heavier. Potential immigrants to Israel have shied away. Repressive measures have marred Israel's image in the world; and it suffers considerable moral isolation, having no real friend in the world except the United States. Even in this country, its image has been badly tarnished. There is little gain for security; Israel cannot rest comfortably until it comes to terms with the Palestinians. Worst are the political costs of commanding people without rights. It is an understatement to say that Israeli politics has been complicated.

If annexation is passé, indirect control, or sphere of influence, is not. However, it seems difficult to compel obedience or to secure much advantage from it. Clients become claimants. The Soviet sway over a half-dozen countries of Eastern Europe apparently is economically negative.[18] Shortly after WW II, the Soviet government could exploit its satellites for the benefit of its own reconstruction, but it has become increasingly necessary to make concessions to keep the East Europeans loyal. Control of the bloc nations is militarily convenient, but it may well decrease the security of the Soviet state, since it is a major reason, possibly the strongest single reason, for anti-Sovietism in the United States and Western Europe. The chief value of its sphere of influence for the Soviet Union is testimony to the strength

---

[17]John P. Tarpey, "The Economics of Israeli Occupation," *Christian Science Monitor,* May 4, 1988, p. 13.

[18]Largely because of an energy subsidy. J.F. Brown, *Eastern Europe and Communist Rule* (Durham, NC: Duke University Press, 1988), p. 140.

and future prospects of the Soviet system. But it is an asset only if it is fairly contented.

It is not apparent that the Soviets can count much return of any kind from billions of rubles spent on a disreputable regime in Ethiopia; they urge it to improve relations with the United States.[19] They support the withdrawal of Cuban forces from Angola. The patronage of Marxist-Leninist Cuba has been very expensive, and it is questionable whether the strategic value to the Soviet Union has been worth the damage to U.S.-Soviet relations. The price of sustaining the Cuban economy has probably discouraged the Soviet Union from the much smaller sacrifice of supporting the economy of Nicaragua.

Whatever strategic gains there may be from the use of the territory of client states, they are not overwhelming when missiles can go accurately around the world and submarines freely roam the seas. Foreign bases carry both economic and political costs. The United States has learned this in Spain, Greece, the Philippines, and elsewhere, however desirable far-flung facilities may be as a means of spreading military might.

The relation of the United States to what was once a sphere of influence in Latin America is somewhat different from that of the Soviet Union to Eastern Europe. Commercial relations with the Latin republics are advantageous, but it is not clear that U.S. economic interests benefit markedly from political superiority. Military relations have greatly declined; politically, the Latins have learned how assertive they can be without risk. The dominant power is blamed for anything, admired for little. Thus the United States is much better liked in Eastern Europe than in Central America. The democratic state has not invented adequate or feasible means of transmuting political superiority into comfortable and profitable dominion—nor, it seems, has the authoritarian state.

If the value of territorial dominion underlay the character of international relations through the ages, its passing means that they are fundamentally changed. It is still desired to control lands and peoples, or to prevent other powers from doing so; the United States has gone to great efforts to prevent a pro-Soviet guerrilla alliance from coming to power in El Salvador. Snatching Grenada from the Soviet orbit in 1983 was a great symbolic victory for the American way, whatever the unimportance of the nutmeg isle. But defense budgets are justified by the idea that someone has a great deal to gain from forcible control over foreign lands. So far as it is recognized that there is little value in territorial aggrandizement, the contest of nations ceases to be a struggle for existence. It becomes more of a game, in which the score is registered partly in terms of territories over which we can claim some kind of sway.

---

[19]*New York Times*, November 28, 1988, p. 1.

Waning Ideology

Part, recently most, of the desire to control foreign lands is the desire to see them organized our way, in accordance with our ideas of politics and society, our ideology. This predilection, like the urge for territorial aggrandizement, is outdated.

An ideology gives simplistic, emotionally appealing answers for overly complex multidimensional problems. An attempt to fit reality into an easily understood formula, it is antitechnical and antiscientific. Modern political drives have no single direction, and ideological monism does not fit a modern pluralistic society. It is a useful rationale for absolute power, but absolutism has no place in the technological world.

The premodern counterpart of ideology was politicized religion. The century of religious wars following the Reformation and ending in the exhaustion of the Thirty Years' War (1618–1648) was followed by comparatively dispassionate politics. For reasons related to improved communications and organization of the state as well as to the philosophy of the Enlightenment, the French Revolution introduced a new ideological temper, exalting universal freedom and equality. Revolutionary war, however, led to Napoleonic empire-building.

After the defeat of Napoleon, the broad aspirations of the French Revolution revived in libertarian and reformist or radical movements; a not very violent revolutionary wave swept over Europe in 1848. Discontents were nourished by the maladjustments of early industrialization, and the expansion of journalism and education encouraged aspirations for justice. Hegel, Marx, Mill, Fourier, Owen, Bentham, and others, socialists and nonsocialists, formulated novel and stirring political themes and gave voice to the principal ideological motifs that rose to their height in this century.

The First World War was the great maker of ideological passion. Dramatic physical destruction, desperate struggle, danger, and suffering engender violent thought, the sense of absolute right and wrong, and unconditional commitment. At the same time, the wartime role of the state as master of all and coordinator or controller of activities, mobilizer and planner of production, sanctions the idea that the state should solve all problems—and ideology becomes important as a program of political action. War gives the state responsibility for the economy and justifies socialism or statism, for which ideology mobilizes people.

Leninist communism took shape as a reaction to the defeat of Russia. It represented an effort to build a new authority in a great but afflicted country, promising a new bliss combining collectivist virtues with modern technology. But it was not so much Marxist theory as Germany's successful wartime mobilization and gave Lenin the idea of the state-managed economy; "Prussian socialism" pointed the way to the Soviet state-owned economy. Centralized management melded with the inspiration of Russian messianism gave rise to one of the major movements of our time. Through the interwar period a much-feared league of intransigent radical parties, the Communist International, or Comintern, trampled—at least oratorically—on all that conventional folk thought sacred, not only property rights but also patriotism and religion, and trumpeted universal social revolution in the name of equality and justice.

In opposition or imitation, less radical movements of dissatisfaction proclaimed what purported to be revolutionary doctrines. Mussolini, exalting a sort of political gangsterism as the means of restoring Italian imperial greatness, renounced socialism and invented a new garb for old tyranny, which he baptized "fascism." His movement owed much to the brutalization of the war, and ex-soldiers were its early champions; it represented bitterness at the outcome of the conflict (Italy felt cheated by the peace terms) and the urge to have another go at it. It became something of an international mode. Mussolini's more powerful and more dynamic imitators, Hitler and his followers, who called themselves "National Socialists," came to power in a depressed and demoralized Germany in 1933. They found admirers in many nations despite the extreme narrowness and incoherence of their doctrines. There were fascist parties in Britain, France, Belgium, East European and Balkan countries, and elsewhere; and in the war not a few persons were prepared to collaborate with the conquering Nazis against their own people, some even to risk their lives fighting for Nazism in Russia. The emperor-worshipping Japanese, too, claimed to stand for a higher order in building their "Greater East Asia Co-Prosperity Sphere."

Fascism having been crushed by defeat, Marxism-Leninism carried on, thanks to the momentum of victory. But it subsided under Stalin into crude tyranny and an essentially nationalistic outlook. After a little reawakening under Khrushchev, it came to doze in the Brezhnev doldrums (1964–1982) and was effectively put to sleep by Mikhail Gorbachev.

Elsewhere, ideology has been vigorous only where fertilized by war. In China, for example, Maoism was an effort to keep alive the purer communism of the civil war that ended in 1949. But it spent its idealism in the Cultural Revolution (1966–1969) and subsided after the death of the Helmsman in 1976. Deng Xiaoping, who was purged in the Cultural Revolution for indifference to ideology ("Black cat, white cat, what matter if it catches mice?" was his motto) moved steadily away from ideological commitment. In 1988 the Chinese closed the main ideological journal, *Red Flag,* which had fallen on hard times, and replaced it with *Seeking Truth.*[20]

In WW II the communists played a strong role in resistance movements. For many years subsequently, Soviet-aligned communist parties had a large following in Western Europe. But by the latter 1980s they

[20]*New York Times,* May 2, 1988, p. A3.

had lost importance. Once-promising parties have become irrelevant splinters, in many cases (as in Finland and Spain) much divided. Only in Italy has the communist party maintained some, although declining, influence, by virtue of moderation and divorce from Soviet influence. The more genial policies of General Secretary Gorbachev have improved the image of the Soviet leadership but not of the system, least of all of Marxist-Leninist ideology.

The notion of class revolution is incongruous for modern society, as is the idea of power of the workers expressed through the self-selected vanguard party. Socialist parties in Western Europe no longer propose rapidly to remake society or to do much that is unacceptable to conservatives. While calling themselves "socialist" they do nothing to terrify bankers and industrialists. Socialists and conservatives are not much farther apart than Democrats and Republicans in the United States. Even in France, bitterly divided ever since the revolution of 1789, the biggest parties advocate policies differing only in emphases. In developed countries, the idea of instant happiness through revolution is dead.

Ideology has resurged only in conditions of revolutionary violence, as in Central America and Iran in 1979 and afterwards; and doctrinaire Marxism suits less developed countries, such as Cuba and Nicaragua, so far as they have the United States as their adversary. To underline their moral independence and rejection of a hated past, the Sandinistas teach grade school children not only the glory of their movement but also such irrelevancies as Marx's analysis of the revolution of 1848.[21] The Soviet Union and its European bloc, however, seem to be impatient with the Sandinistas for their impracticality and dogmatism.

Neither of these ideological flareups has prospered. The Sandinistas, far from enveloping Central America in revolutionary socialism, had to retreat both politically and economically, permitting some political opening and a more market-oriented economy. No movement has been more passionate than the Iranian revolution led by Ayatollah Khomeini, but it had no great resonance in the Islamic world and after less than a decade seemed worn out by unsuccessful war and by political and economic realities.

Ideologies in general have become dilapidated or irrelevant.[22] The big issues seem to have largely worked themselves out, or at least to have lost most of their emotional force; and the quarrels are over matters less rending than the makeup of society. Not only is fascism defunct and socialism exhausted; the meaning of "progressive" has become clouded, aside from association with egalitarianism. "Liberal" in the United States has become a term of scorn suggestive of governmental extravagance. Even the welfare

---

[21]Barbara E. Joe, "Revolutionary Education in Nicaragua," *Nicaragua in Focus* (Puebla Institute, 1988), pp. 4–11.

[22]As indicated a generation ago by Daniel Bell, *The End of Ideology* (New York: Free Press, 1960).

state is an uncertain concept; all modern states, while assuming large responsibilities, admit that the amount of welfare the state can provide is finite. The left-right cleavage, which dominated politics for generations, has been largely replaced by such issues as democracy vs. dictatorship, religious vs. secular values, individualism vs. communitarianism, and nationalism vs. internationalism.

There has been less call for dramatic change as the mood of the world has quieted. Politically speaking, not much has really happened since 1945. The biggest confrontations have affirmed the status quo: the Berlin blockade, the Korean War, the Cuban missile crisis, and other trials of strength left things much as they were before. Even the Vietnam War merely gave the leaders of Hanoi what had been promised to them by the Geneva Conference in 1954. No names of world shakers stand out in the postwar period comparable to those of the first half of the century, such as Lenin, Stalin, Hitler, Churchill, and Roosevelt. The great happenings have been undramatic and pacific, such as the exhaustion of ideological politics in China and the Soviet Union, the unification of Europe, and the rise of Japan from direst poverty to the world's second largest economy.

Although ideological commitment is passé as inspiration, it is alive as distortion. There are many cults and intellectual fads in the United States and other countries at the forefront of the postindustrial age. Small neo-Nazi organizations stubbornly exalt one of history's most egocentric murderers. Here and there, fiercely emotional in-group attachments prevent what seems to an outsider to be a rational approach; for example, Afrikaners have their private defensive values, in which apartheid is justice. There are exotic guru-led communities and religious fundamentalisms. The modern world, however, does not spawn firm political movements with a plausible agenda for changing society.

This skeptical and materialistic age dissolves certitudes. Patriotism has become rather shallow for many, especially intellectuals. A political ideology calls for state action, but modern thinking cannot idealize the state, with all its flaws and limitations. Political parties no longer have the old-time discipline; one result is the decline of the communist parties, whose forte is discipline. Even the Catholic Church finds it difficult to require obedience. In many countries, "Liberation Theology," a doctrine looking to justice less in the hereafter than on earth, vexes the conservatives; in the United States, a majority of Catholics are at odds with teachings of the pope on birth control, the role of women in the Church, and related matters; and the bishops decry the strictures of the Vatican.

Moods are more important than ideologies; an example is anticommunism. Another widespread mood is anti-Americanism, variously popular in many countries.[23] The "Green" movement is more attitude than theory,

---

[23]Alvin Z. Rubinstein and Donald E. Smith, eds., *Anti-Americanism in the Third World: Implications for U.S. Foreign Policy* (New York: Praeger, 1985).

more emotional than ideological. The Greens are prominent in Germany and have allies in many lands. Their chief theme is protection of the environment; but they wave banners of disarmament, anti-nuclear power, feminism, and general protest; they are almost anti-industrial. They have no real program and divide when confronted with practical problems.

An ideology proposes to change the makeup of society; the broadest mode of the 1980s calls for the state to desist from trying to manage society. Its idea is simply to let people have their way to increase production and enjoy life. This is also much of the message of the contemporary movement favoring extension of democracy. It has little of the egalitarianism of the French Revolution; it is not messianism but rejection of tyranny.

Perhaps ideology has never been really decisive. Catholic France fought on the Protestant side in the Thirty Years' War to thwart the ambitions of the Holy Roman Empire. Republican France in 1893 became allied with autocratic Russia. Hitler and Stalin, the great champions of bitterly antithetic ideologies, or antithetic propagandas, embraced to start a war on August 23, 1939; and they subsequently split not over doctrine but over incompatible territorial ambitions. Ideology did not keep the Soviet Union and Yugoslavia united after the war, and it did not prevent America from helping Tito to make good his independence. It could not hold the Sino-Soviet alliance together, despite the awesome promise of power of that combination. Ideology has in the past usually been more pretense and rallying cry than genuine motivation. In our day grand visions have ever less to do with international contentions.

Objectives of Foreign Policy

It is questionable how much the makers of foreign policy can achieve in the contemporary world. In distant times when international relations were consummated by the intrigues and maneuvers of European foreign ministers, there were big stakes in the engrossing game. Diplomacy was commonly associated with a threat of force, although leaders preferred to achieve their ends without fighting. For example, Bismarck brought the smaller German states under the Prussian aegis and made the new Reich the leading power of Europe by shrewd diplomacy and three minor wars. Hitler acquired Austria and Czechoslovakia by negotiation with Britain and France; he probably could have subjected Poland likewise peacefully if his scant patience had not succumbed to his impatience for military glory. Hitler scored a great coup when in the summer of 1939 he secretly outbid Britain and France for the support of the Soviet Union, trumping their guarantee of the independence of Poland by offering the Soviet Union the eastern half of the country.

In the postwar period, however, the threat of force has been much less usable, especially between the superpowers. The United States was able to press the Soviets to withdraw from Iran in 1946 by a quiet threat when the atomic monopoly made this impressive; and in the early years of the cold war there was a strong inclination—doubtless a continuation of the wartime mentality—to think in terms of possible military action. For example, in 1947 the Soviets hinted that they might take certain Turkish territories; and in 1948 they blockaded West Berlin. Khrushchev indulged in something like ultimatums from time to time, but such bluffing had no result and was dropped after the 1962 missile crisis.

More recently, intimidation, or attempted intimidation, has played little part in the relations of the great powers. It also appears that the threat or use of force has lost utility in their relations with small powers. The Soviet Union has been able to make effective use of its army only to maintain the status quo in its sphere. Since Vietnam, the United States has felt able to carry out only small scale operations, such as sending marines to Lebanon with no clear mission or cleaning up a messy situation in Grenada.

The power game remains important, of course. For example, the ability of the United States to balance relations with the Soviet Union and China, avoiding a pitfall in Taiwan, will have more effect on the political balance than several aircraft carriers. Yet it would seem that the stakes have been largely psychological, the winning of friends and supporters; and gains or losses are temporary or reversible. Not much power is to be gained by diplomatic moves.

Few doubt that power is a proper goal of national leaders; and power is usually conceived as one will prevailing over another. But there is little reason other than satisfaction to seek to impose our will on other nations. We do not fancy taking their land or forcing them to buy our goods or otherwise pay tribute; there is not much of value we could possibly extract from them. Whatever military power can achieve for commerce is not commensurate with the cost. We might wish other nations to be more friendly and trustworthy; but this can hardly be obtained by coercion. It remains the very important task of statesmen and diplomats to control frictions and forestall misunderstandings.

We can insist on imposing our will in the limited sense that we would not permit another power to injure us. The highest priority goes to national security, that is, the physical safety of the community within its accepted boundaries and its ability to live as its people wish, without undue pressures or coercion from without. But we seem less threatened by a greedy or recklessly domineering power wishing to infringe on our freedom than by many maladies of civilization.

The national interest or "vital interests" may be variously understood, just as the values of individuals are varied, depending on traditions, personalities, and the character of the society and the political system. The universe of makers of foreign policy has been greatly broadened, encompassing innumerable concerns and requiring expert understanding of countless issues, from airline regulations to biological warfare. More than ever, nations need to work in long-range perspectives. The whole world interacts; it is impossible to separate relations with any one nation from those with others and world opinion.

In the age of image, psychology and pride are extremely important; a very great power must show its abilities in the space race, a modest one subsidizes an unprofitable national airline. But the important transformations of the contemporary world scene have been brought about by economic growth or the lack of it. Japan and, on a smaller scale, Taiwan and Korea have risen like new volcanoes on the basis of their work, not their political maneuvers, much less their military power. To the contrary, the Japanese arm mostly to please the United States; they are fearful that a buildup of their armed forces would hurt their exports in Asia. Europe has restored itself economically, while remaining politically nearly immobile. On the other hand, lack of growth has lowered some nations, such as Argentina, on the international scale of wealth and prestige. While the U.S.-Soviet political duel has been approximately a draw, economic needs have pushed the Soviet Union to new approaches to world affairs.

National strength and the basis for standing tall in the world are made by internal forces, most of all the efforts of individuals and private groups; foreign policy can help only marginally. The chief utility of the modern foreign policy apparatus would seem to be to promote official and unofficial cooperation of nations, their cultural and economic interchanges, and their joint efforts to cope with rising social and environmental problems, from drug trade to deforestation. In this time of building a new civilization, it behooves the leaders of nations, especially those that feel themselves responsible for world destinies, to give new and better thought to their priorities of needs and the values they would achieve for the good ordering of relations among nations and the making of a more secure and more humane civilization.

U.S. Foreign Outlook

It is urgent for the principal actors on the world stage to redefine their roles and purposes corresponding to the needs of the age, but they lack efficient institutions and mechanisms to do so. In bygone times, it seemed simple for the head of government with advisors to formulate the national interest in conventional strategic terms as players moved their pieces. But the complexity of the game increases more than the ability of the players to devise their strategies.

The problem is outwardly most severe for the democratic states, the looseness and dividedness of which imply incoherence of foreign policy. All manner of groups and pressures, in and out of government, push in different directions for often contradictory purposes. The United States, in particular, has no generally agreed standards for formulating national purpose, except in excessively general terms; and its public opinion is usually variable and unclear. There is no mechanism in government rationally to set priorities or to bring together the multifarious demands and choose among them. Military/political policy is completely separate from economic policy

An authoritarian state should theoretically be able, although it is difficult in practice, to focus effectively on an overriding goal, one or a few persons staking out coherent courses of action. The democracy, composed of intertwined political, economic, cultural, humanitarian and other interests, cannot and should not have one great foreign policy but many policies, some of them inevitably contradictory. It is impossible for the state to speak with a single voice for the numberless voices. Not only does the pluralistic society inject many purposes into the official positions, but many entities represent the nation in the world, from multinational corporations and traders to political and religious movements, cultural and artistic exchanges, and military outposts; and they carry on their little parts of foreign policy.

American foreign policy has seemed cumbersome in the 1980s, especially in troubled areas such as Central America and the Near East. In part, this must be attributed to the fact that the machinery of foreign policy making is especially unsystematic, even by comparison with other democracies. There has been no important improvement since shortly after WW II; and the policy making process, like much of the policy made, is obsolete. It can be generally described only by stating that the president theoretically decides matters, or determines how they are to be decided; and most of American foreign policy can be treated as a chronicle of presidential decisions. But his range of attention is limited, and he has a thousand other things to attend to. If he attempts to decide matters by himself or with a small staff, all but the most immediately pressing matters are probably neglected.[24]

In no other nation is control over foreign policy so shared between the executive and a legislative body, and the role of the Congress tends to increase in recent times as the number of persons and groups interested in foreign affairs increases. Many pressures from private groups are channeled through it, and its assent is necessary for any important continued action. However, the Congress is disposed to defer to the constitutional authority of the president to handle foreign political affairs, as long as his actions are reasonably acceptable. It does not want to be seen as sabotaging the na-

[24]For surveys, see Amos Yoder, *The Conduct of American Foreign Policy since World War II* (New York: Pergamon Press, 1986); and Cecil V. Crabb Jr. and Kevin Mulcahy, *Presidents and Foreign Policy Making: From FDR to Reagan* (Baton Rouge, LA: Louisiana State University Press, 1986).

tional leadership. It seldom injects itself into negotiations except when treaties are in question, and it tends to accept the wishes of the executive regarding allocations of money (within budgetary limitations) for military and other purposes relevant to foreign policy. Although the Constitution gives Congress the right to declare war, the president has (the War Powers Act to the contrary) almost complete freedom to make war, limited only by possible public opposition.[25]

But the Congress, like the president, finds foreign affairs interesting, has considerable staff, is subject to a multitude of pressures, and holds the power of the purse.[26] In the long run, it can bar any presidential policy it seriously dislikes. Whether the Congress or the executive is more rational in foreign policy questions it would be difficult to judge. The former is more cumbersome, the latter more headstrong; both are inclined to pursue short-term interests and to heed interest groups.

In the United States, the amateurs on top have seldom listened very much to the professionals of foreign affairs. Both Congress and the president have usually distrusted them and have regarded them as poor guardians of the national security. The Congress gives the State Department about 1 percent as much as the Department of Defense. The secretary of state is never a foreign affairs professional; and the president has generally leaned more on White House aides, especially his national security advisor, than on the secretary of state, whom he cannot easily fire. In the postwar period, Secretaries Dean Acheson (under Truman), John Foster Dulles (under Eisenhower), and Henry Kissinger (under Ford) were among the few really enjoying the confidence of the chief. George Schultz came into his own only in the twilight of the Reagan administration. The very close personal ties of Secretary James Baker with President Bush are unique.

One reason that the president has usually had less than full confidence in the Secretary of State is that the latter works with professionals who have tenure, are probably tradition-minded, and are not necessarily eager to carry out new policies the president may envision. Another reason is the divergence of outlook between the State Department and the defense or military establishment, each having a bias for what it does professionally, the one for negotiation, the other for preparation for combat (although the State Department may be quite willing to turn problems over to the military). Most important, no doubt, is the fact that the president likes to handle foreign affairs himself and has confidence in his own judgment.

Within the government, loyalty goes to the agency or organization as well as to the president. There are conflicting pressures from different departments of the administration; negotiations within the bureaucracy can

---

[25]John T. Rourke and Russell Farner, "War, Presidents, and the Constitution," *Presidential Studies Quarterly* 18 (Summer 1988), 513–22.

[26]Edwin S. Muskie, Kenneth Rush, and Kenneth W. Thompson, *The President, the Congress, and Foreign Policy* (Washington: University Press of America, 1986).

be as contentious as those between the United States and the Soviet Union, and a small bureaucratic sector may have a virtual veto because of its ability to put up substantive or procedural roadblocks.[27] The bureaucracy informally represents a multitude of interests, and its power rises because technical issues call for expert attention.

For such reasons, there have been tendencies to concentrate foreign policy in the White House. It was taken in hand in the 1980s by an irregular group around the president, an informal coterie including the secretaries of state and defense, the director of the CIA, the national security advisor, and a few others selected mostly on the basis of their personal relation with the president.[28] At times, foreign policy making centered on the National Security Council, with the collaboration of the CIA; the State Department and Defense Department were partly excluded or simply not informed. The results were not only imprudence and some misguided actions but illegality (as in Irangate). For the last part of the Reagan administration, leadership fell informally to a trio of Secretary of State George Schultz, Secretary of Defense Frank Carlucci, and National Security Advisor Colin Powell. Lack of fixity of foreign policy making, aside from the ultimate responsibility of the president, means that it is volatile, responding both to the shifts in the group of trusted aides and to political perceptions.

Just as there is no systematic way of defining priorities in the administrative medley, there is no clear notion how far a leader should follow the public, try to lead it, or ignore it. The president certainly would like to have general support for his actions, and he hopes that they will raise his popularity; on the other hand, he probably has strong notions of what the nation should be doing and certainly feels that he is much better informed than ordinary folk, perhaps better than anyone else.

Although foreign policy must ultimately rest on the people's understanding of the role of their nation in the world, public opinion is a questionable guide. Its greatest shaper, television, gives more importance to looks, performing style, and catchy phrases than to complex issues. Television also causes pressure for quick, probably inadequately considered responses and makes foreign affairs into instant issues. The habit of getting the news in bites on the screen doubtless contributes to superficiality and short-term approach to foreign affairs; policy can hardly be thought out carefully if it is made with an eye to how it plays on the evening news.

Leaders are often unsure how public opinion will treat their initiatives, especially as events take their unexpected course. People are more volatile regarding foreign than domestic issues, concerning which they probably have more direct information. On the other hand, policy may be

[27]Herbert F. York, "Negotiating and the U.S. Bureaucracy," in *A Game for High Stakes,* ed. Leon Sloss and M. Scott Davis. (Cambridge, MA: Ballinger, 1986), pp. 133–40.

[28]Martin Anderson, *Revolution* (San Diego: Harcourt Brace Jovanovich, 1988), p. 310.

fixed, perhaps more than warranted by national interests, by a voter-bloc upholding a consistent position. Basic policy toward Israel has seemed unalterable; support for this small country is a major component of U.S. world policy although it has frequently meant virtual diplomatic isolation of this country. Relations or lack of relations with Cuba have been much influenced by the strong feelings of Cuban emigres in Florida.

In regard to complicated questions, the public commonly has little more than generalized ideas of the good and bad sides. But mass opinion is not spontaneous, or even primarily based directly on the facts reported by news agencies, but is largely shaped by educated specialists. Because of the importance of world affairs, there has grown up since WW II a large unofficial foreign policy establishment comprising hundreds of academics, writers, and advisors in the media, universities, think tanks, government departments, and sundry institutes. Many are specialists in particular areas, such as the Near East. There are perhaps a hundred times more sovietologists in the United States today than on the eve of WW II. Through articles and books, lectures, conferences, and consultations, they shape attitudes that filter down through the media and seep irregularly into the government.

The judgment of the people, advised and informed by opinion-leaders, may be as sound as that of most of the top leaders. The qualifications for political success—debating flair, ability to appeal to various groups, and sensitivity to public moods—have little to do with sagacity in foreign affairs; and those who succeed are under no obligation to draw on the rich stores of knowledge in which the United States excels.

Political leaders, of course, have more and quicker access to the media than the specialists; and so far as they are persuasive, they can do a great deal to shift the climate of opinion. An eloquent presidential address to the nation regarding some danger, preferably of a dramatic nature, can raise a tide of sentiment. In the modern democratic state, however, an inquisitive press is ready to ask questions; and any forward policy, unless it proves rather rapidly successful, is likely to raise doubts. Television dramatizes actions and elicits applause, but casualties on the screen quickly cool approval for any cause that is not entirely convincing. The invasion of Grenada, like the bombing of Libya, was generally approved (after the press had been initially skeptical on moral-legal grounds);[29] but the Reagan administration did not care to try its luck with Nicaragua. If violence is thrilling, it is also repugnant, at least if associated with bodies, as was amply demonstrated in the Vietnam war. When most people became convinced that we had no interest in Vietnam important enough to justify the cost in lives, the war could no longer be waged.

Unavoidably, foreign policy issues are used or misused for domestic

[29]Payne, Sutton, and Thorndike, *Grenada: Revolution and Invasion.*

political purposes. But the involvement of the people in foreign policy is essential for the democratic state, since nationhood and the sense of community rest on the part our country plays in world affairs. Much of politics revolves around foreign policy; here leaders and masses share feelings. The latter want their leaders to express the collective feelings, the power, glory, and idealism of the nation, the greatness in which we all share. The former want support in their engagements, hope for applause, and wish to feel that they are serving the cause.

Foreign affairs interest people, and publicity compels leaders to act, as they are usually happy to do. The top American leadership probably spends more of its mental energies on foreign affairs, in which they can seldom achieve much of importance, than on the direction of the nation, to the neglect of many solvable problems. There has always been a mixture of gaming and material interest in international politicking; war has been very much the king of sports as well as the sport of kings. If the contest for power has lost most of its real meaning, it continues to be a grand show. Like commercialized sports, foreign affairs are the center of many activities and publicity, the vocation of a large number of persons, whose business it is to give them importance. Many professionals, impressed with the importance of their business of national security and perhaps of their own contribution to it, keep themselves and others convinced that issues of the greatest moment are at stake. The remarkable thing is that the sport of international competition is passably moderate and restrained.

Foreign policy in the modern democracy is an orderly chaos, unpredictable, ever subject to change although often unduly rigid, a mixture of rationality and irrationality. It depends on the education and goodwill of the people and those acting on their behalf, their ability to transcend parochial and selfish interests and to let reason check emotion. It is part of the problem of good government. The prime question of civilization is how an enlightened society can organize and manage itself to make best use of its enormous capabilities, equally in internal and external affairs.

Soviet Foreign Outlook

Foreign policy has become far more complicated for the Soviet Union since the heady days shortly after the revolution, when Leon Trotsky, named foreign commissar, said he would issue a few revolutionary summons to the world proletariat and shut up shop. The simple imperatives, first to survive, secondly to promote the cause, have given way to multiple needs of interaction, while the ability of the leadership to direct the state has shrunk.

Decision making is still institutionally relatively simple for the Kremlin, without the formal checks that restrict the American president. But the ability of the chief to dictate is far from what it was in Stalin's day, and the apparatus has long since ceased to be a wholly obedient instrument. The entrenched bureaucracy, like that of other authoritarian states, becomes difficult to move, as Gorbachev has more than once complained. It is apparently harder in the Soviet system than in the American to remove high officials who stand in the way of policies. There being no private sector to which they can go, the official career is the whole life of the bureaucrat; a position in the apparatus becomes a virtual right, which the chief, who depends on the apparatus, cannot easily take away. It being difficult to oust people, it seems to be increasingly necessary to secure the backing of stalwarts both in the state agencies and the party apparatus, perhaps the military.

Because there is no longer any clear-cut overriding priority, various agencies, none easily controlled, pull in different directions. The Foreign Ministry has other priorities than those of the Ministry of Defense; the Ministry of Foreign Trade is probably but not surely an ally of the Foreign Ministry. There are regional interests, as Central Asians, Balts, and Russians see some problems from divergent points of view. There are differences between the foreign policy bureaucracy and the communist party apparatus.

Moreover, it is by no means so easy to ignore the intellectual elite and public opinion as a few years ago. Popular sentiments probably do not count for much; but there is a still small but growing independent or semi-independent intelligentsia, which apparently has some influence although no formal power. Academic study institutes appear to have some voice in high circles. So far as Gorbachev counts on the intellectuals to check the conservatives in the party apparatus, he must listen to them.

Questions of national priorities and purpose have become at least as complicated for the Soviet as for the American leadership, and adaptation to new conditions is fully as difficult. Civilian and economic interests conflict with political-military interests, which are concerned mostly with power and image. An insoluble problem is how much to devote to armaments. The burden is heavy, capital is badly needed in the civilian economy, and decline of investment may cause future weakness.

There are many other difficult dilemmas: how can the Soviet Union maintain a modicum of ideological commitment while cultivating relations with the United States and/or other Western powers to relieve military costs and to facilitate technological and capital imports necessary for modernization? How wide should gates be opened to ease the entry of ideas and information? Is it better to try to wean Western Europe from the American alliance or to conciliate the United States? How far is it useful to support international organizations such as the U.N.? How much should the Soviets spend to gain political and ideological points in Third World countries, from which they can expect few material returns?

Questions become more confused as the Soviet state tries to find a role for itself in a world utterly different from the future it imagined when it held itself to be the initiator of a universal proletarian revolution. Recent Soviet leaders have been much more exposed to the complex realities of the big world than they were when Stalin simplified life by shutting the doors or when Khrushchev thought he could make the United States back down by blustering about his (few) missiles. They no longer enjoy the simplicity of ignorance, although the intensity of their contacts with the outside world is still much less than that of their Western colleagues.

The Soviets face such quandaries with much more limited resources than the United States, so they can less afford the luxury of waste. The Soviet state, moreover, is burdened by the need to decide many things that take care of themselves in the American system. The American administration does not have to plan levels of trade with every country; in most cases, it cannot even do much about them. For the Soviets, without a free market, all economic decisions become more or less political and hence potentially controversial and subject to political misjudgment. They also have more intractable problems in dealing with countries within their sphere of influence than does the United States. Relations with East European countries cannot be separated from the problems of minorities within the Soviet Union.

The common impression that the Soviet leadership is steadily purposeful and cunning is unjustified. It is true that foreign policy, much more than in the United States, is carried on by professionals, who are likely to have had long training from secondary school through university specialization and bureaucratic careers. And with specialization comes continuity; Soviet foreign policy leaders have stayed in place far longer than their Western, especially American, counterparts. But at the upper levels, decisions are probably made about as casually and unsystematically in Moscow as in Washington, and with less information, as the Soviet Union has only a small fraction of the number of scholars in international relations and foreign politics as the United States.[30]

Both powers have had their poorer moments. The American arms sale to Iran in 1985 and 1986 is unexcelled for foolishness, but it was a trifling affair compared to the senseless Soviet invasion of Afghanistan in December 1979. This massive military move seems to have been quite unnecessary. The government was in the hands of a thoroughgoing communist, Hafizullah Amin, whose principal fault was that he was trying to Sovietize too rapidly and was provoking a great deal of opposition. The Soviets already had access to the country and could bring in small forces at will, and Amin depended on them to protect him from conservative insurgents. If the So-

---

[30]Jerry F. Hough, *The Struggle for the Third World: Soviet Debates and American Options* (Washington: Brookings Institution, 1986), pp. 257, 266.

viets felt they had to get rid of Amin, they surely could have gradually eased him out of power.[31]

Yet they mounted a blatant invasion, undercut the communist-led Afghan army, and killed not only Amin (who they claimed had invited them) but everyone in the palace of state, typists included.[32] Such hamhandedness is incomprehensible unless one supposes that Soviet leaders, wanting to cut through a fairly sticky situation, held the inferior people of no account—a misapprehension not uncommon in American actions in the Third World. The invasion, which was apparently decided by the aging Brezhnev and a very few others in the politburo, may have been inspired partly by the ease of intervention in Czechoslovakia in 1968, or by the need for reassurance of Soviet might when the economy was in a downswing and Soviet influence in a number of Third World countries was waning. But it was an outrageous and wholly counterproductive way to prop up a zealous but wobbly communist government.

The reason for this foolishness, however, was not institutional inadequacies but an outdated mentality that thought in terms of Soviet omnipotence and ideological imperatives. The Gorbachev regime, better aware of contemporary reality, has conducted foreign affairs with a skill arousing considerable admiration in Europe and the United States—at the cost of giving up many formerly fixed Soviet positions.

Foreign Outlook of Medium Powers

A hallmark of the contemporary scene is inequality. Only the United States has a truly global reach: it has a sort of special relation with Latin America and Western Europe, it alone has a broad role in the Near East and all Africa, and it stands over Southeast Asia. It has some influence in Eastern Europe and East Asia. Everywhere, in some places feebly, in others powerfully, it can promote its political and economic ideas. By virtue of military strength, the Soviet Union is imposing; but only the United States has a global navy. The Soviet Union has friends or clients in the Americas, Africa, Near East, and Southeast Asia; but these are only spots on the map. Aside from the small states aligned with it, the Soviet Union has very limited economic and political influence. With only a very few countries, such as India, does it carry weight comparable to that of the United States. Even in Eastern Europe, Soviet hegemony is much qualified.

[31]Cf. Thomas T. Hammond, *Red Flag over Afghanistan* (Boulder, CO: Westview, 1984), passim.

[32]Timothy W. Viezer, "The Soviet Occupation of Afghanistan," in *East-West Rivalry in the Third World: Security Issues and Regional Perspectives,* ed. Robert W. Clawson, (Washington: Scholarly Resources Inc., 1986), p. 119.

A few West European nations plus Japan, China, and India, perhaps Brazil, exert some economic or political sway over weaker nations. Britain is the honorary leader of a very loose Commonwealth of former colonies and dominions. Its importance is also raised by its "special relationship" with the United States. France is more ambitious; it retains something of a sphere of influence, a sort of updating of its former empire in Africa. The currency of many countries is tied to the French franc. French troops are stationed in various countries, or enter occasionally to keep order without important protest; and French officers advise African armies. France gives more economic aid to sub-Saharan Africa than any other country. French expatriates carry on much of the administration. The use of French is spreading, even to former Portuguese and Spanish colonies. African students prefer French universities. French influence suffers, however, from the inability of France to compete economically very well with the United States and Japan. France, along with other European powers, also has a special economic arrangement with most of sub-Saharan Africa under the Lomé Agreement of 1976, giving ex-colonies commercial advantages.

Although much stronger economically than France or Britain, West Germany, as a defeated nation with fewer overseas connections, plays a more restricted politico-military role. It is also more tied by the Western alliance and is still subject to some terms laid down by the victors; most significantly, it is not allowed to have nuclear weapons of its own. More than perhaps any other power, West Germany is preoccupied with East-West relations; it stands on the edge of the Soviet sphere and looks across the Elbe to a detached part of what it wishes to think of as a single nation.

For a long time after WW II, Japan shunned foreign political involvement. Its role in the world inevitably grows; but Japan, although an economic superpower, has—and seeks—little political influence abroad. The Japanese usually defer to the United States, although their hesitation in presenting their own proposals decreases year by year. The principal purpose of Japan's foreign policy is to promote its commercial and financial interests. The Japanese naturally play a more active part in the affairs of East and Southeast Asia; Japan is fascinated by China, both as an immense potential market and as the historic source of much of Japanese culture.

A huge country like China or India is not much subject to coercion, but neither is it capable of actions beyond its immediate neighborhood. China under Mao energetically wooed revolutionary movements; but since his demise in 1976 it has dropped its missionary cause. India could intervene militarily in Sri Lanka with the agreement of that state. India naturally sees itself as something of a hegemon of South Asia, and its small but growing navy patrols the Indian Ocean. China and India both like to regard themselves as leaders of the Third World, but their leadership is the more feeble as they are antagonistic and tend to neutralize each other.

Such second-ranking powers, as nations with a glorious past, feel the need to play a part in world affairs. For the most part, they have a highly trained foreign affairs bureaucracy, and they participate actively in international meetings even though the outcome may be of no importance to them. They make some effort to expand their cultural influence and have something of a foreign aid program. Even Brazil, within its limited resources, strives to maintain a modest domination over weak countries on its borders, Bolivia, Paraguay, Uruguay, and Suriname, by cultivating cultural, commercial, and military relations.

Second-ranking powers are no threat to the independence of weak countries but help them to lessen dependence. Relations of Latin America with Western Europe are thus less tense than with the United States and less tinged with ideology. It is not regarded as interventionist when German political parties work with and help Venezuelan parties, as it would be if U.S. parties tried to do the same thing.[33]

For these politically second-level powers, however, relations with the United States are of more importance than those with any other country. Except relatively backward China, India, and Brazil, they form an American-headed club, partly formalized in various international economic organizations, partly by informal understanding, the fraternity of the rich in a mostly poor world.

Foreign Policy of Weaker Countries

Although the weaker actors formally carry on their affairs in the world in about the same way as the big powers, for them the international environment, goals, and consequent foreign policies are quite different.[34] They have limited initiative and autonomy, and they must give much attention to relations with the strongest powers, especially the United States. They cannot dream of national security by their own strength; they must trust that no great power sees fit to attack them, either because they would be indigestible or because they are protected by world opinion or because they possess nothing worth conquering (as is the case of the large majority). Their sovereignty is given by the international system, in the making of which their influence is minor or nil.

They do not much threaten one another. Except in a few unsettled

---

[33]Wolf Grabendorff, "The United States and Western Europe: Competition or Cooperation in Latin America?" in *Latin America, Western Europe and the United States: Reevaluating the Atlantic Triangle,* ed. Wolf Grabendorff and Riordan Roett (New York: Praeger, 1985), pp. 258–65.

[34]On the foreign relations of Third World countries, see Christopher Clapham, *Third World Politics: An Introduction* (London: Croom Helm, 1985), pp. 113–35; Caroline Thomas, *A Search for Security: The Third World in International Relations* (Boulder, CO: Rienner, 1987).

areas, the weak states seem to feel safer than does the mighty United States, or at least pay much less attention to external threat. There have been many conflicts in the past forty years, almost all over boundary and related matters; but they have worn out as the new nations settled down. In Latin America, various nations have occasionally growled, as Venezuela at Guyana over nearly uninhabited jungle, Peru and Ecuador likewise, Argentina and Chile over islets in the Strait of Magellan, and so forth; but there has been no major clash for more than half a century.[35] Some boundaries in North Africa remain unsettled; but sub-Saharan states respect possession, however lacking in geopolitical logic.

Since Third World countries do not have much to gain from fighting anyone and are generally discouraged from adventures, they are mostly nonmilitaristic although under more or less militocratic rule. But they feel it is necessary to have the latest hardware, so far as they can afford. The potentialities of destruction are raised by the availability of medium-range missiles (produced by China, Brazil, India, and other Third World countries), but they have little to gain by military strength. In the unstable Near East defense budgets are high, mostly because of Israeli-Arab strife. Elsewhere, a few embattled powers, chiefly Vietnam, the Philippines, Cuba, and Nicaragua spend heavily on arms. Pakistan and India devote a good deal of their scanty resources to the military. Generally, however, the armies, navies, and air forces of Latin America, sub-Saharan Africa, and much of Asia have little external purpose but serve for show and to sustain the status quo. They have little incentive to risk a war. The military adventures of Iraq, Somalia, Libya (in Chad), and Argentina (in the Falklands) have been discouraging; it is better to keep the guns at home.

Having little possibility of advancing any important policy on their own, tertiary powers are usually rather passive, as subordinate allies of a superpower (Eastern Europe, some Latin American countries), members of a regional group (Arab states, Southeast Asia), or theoretically sovereign dependents of international agencies (most sub-Saharan states).[36] Some, such as Burma and various African states, are very inward-looking, in a psychology of insecurity; many are decidedly open. The most international of all are very modern small countries, such as the Low Countries and Scandinavia, which are export-oriented, hospitable to international business, and active participants in it; they share freely in modern cosmopolitan ideas and styles.

Feelings of inferiority are a matter of cultural and economic level, not actual power. Small rich countries such as Finland and Norway are not particularly troubled by their lack of influence in the world, whereas economic

---

[35]Jack Child, *Geopolitics and Conflict in South America: Quarrels among Neighbors* (New York: Praeger, 1985).

[36]Robert H. Jackson, "Quasi-States, Dual Regimes, and Neoclassical Theory," *International Organization* 41 (Autumn 1987), 519–50.

incapacity is demoralizing for many Third World nations. On the other hand, China and India, as very large poor countries with strong cultural traditions, have a basic assuredness despite their poverty; they see greatness in the future, however unsatisfactory the present. Brazil likewise, covering half of South America, has enjoyed a self-confidence denied to smaller countries of Latin America. Those that are both small and poor have a weak self-image.

Many states have little in the way of foreign policy, not only ministates such as Trinidad and Tobago, St. Kitts, or Mauritius, but also countries such as Paraguay or Zaire. The foreign relations of most Third World states are unsystematic, if only because they cannot afford much of a professional corps, the head of state personally handles foreign policy, and there is little or no systematic study of international relations.[37] Most of the contacts of poorer states with one another take place in international forums, but many of them cannot even afford to attend numerous gatherings. They maintain permanent representatives in only a few countries, making do with honorary consulates where feasible.

Regional politics are of mostly symbolic importance. For example, the Organization for African Unity meets regularly for speeches, but its members conduct a very small fraction of their trade and communications with one another. The Arabs feel close because of their common heritage, their pride, and their shared enmity toward Israel; but they can agree on very little. The Association of Southeast Asian Nations (ASEAN) has some economic importance. Latin Americans have regional institutions and meetings from which the United States is excluded because of cultural and economic differences; but they can only give a little mutual support in relations with the advanced world, especially the United States. They are aware that their bargaining position would be strengthened by unity, but their unity is mostly rhetorical as each tries to make the best deal for itself. A notable example is the inability of debtor nations to form a union to confront creditors.

Most Third World leaders are cautious in their foreign relations. But rulers of small states, like those of the more powerful, find the world stage attractive, because the audience is so much larger and more important than the domestic crowd. It seems especially appealing for young men with abundant energy, such as Cuba's Fidel Castro (33 on coming to power), Peru's Alán García (36), Egypt's Nasser (36), and Libya's Ghadaffi (28). Resolve and dynamic personality may enable the chief of a minor power, such as Cuba, to play a conspicuous and fairly independent role, taking pride in helping guerrillas in Latin America and "leftist" dictatorships in Africa. Yugoslavia was prominent in the Third World movement under Tito, as were the Indonesia of Sukarno and the Ghana of Nkrumah; on the death of the respec-

---

[37]R. P. Barston, *Modern Diplomacy* (New York: Longmans, 1988), pp. 12–13.

tive chief, the country disappeared from the limelight. President Oscar Arias of Cost Rica achieved influence and eminence for himself and his country by promoting peace in Central America in 1987; his role in the cauldron of Central American politics brought new pride to Costa Rica. Revolutionary regimes such as those of Libya and Iran in the 1980s have found some glory or notoriety but little success in the intoxicating business of revolution.

For most countries most of the time, however, the chief purpose of foreign dealings is to secure whatever benefits may be obtainable from the richer world, in trade, aid, or other favors. Presidents or dictators of Third World nations face such an array of social, economic, and political problems at home that they take time and energy for foreign affairs only at the price of neglecting domestic needs.

Chapter 6

Erosion of Cultural-Economic Differences

Cosmopolitanization

Since prehistory, improved means of locomotion and transportation have spread ideas and improvements and thus made possible the accumulation of culture. Learning to ride horses, which must have been a miracle of progress for our ancestors, extended the human sphere far beyond the village. More efficient ships 2,500 years ago made possible the diffusion of a remarkably similar culture across thousands of miles of the Mediterranean region, from Greece and the Bosphoros to Italy and southern France and Spain.

Until rather recently, however, transportation and communication remained limited to the speed of animals or sailing vessels. Although navigational improvements in the 15th century made the extra-European world accessible, travel from London to Vienna was little faster in 1800 than it had been in antiquity, and customs of different regions of Europe were not much less diverse. Homogenization began in earnest with the invention of the railroad early in the 19th century, and it has been accelerating ever since. Now no important city is more than about twenty hours from any other, and manufacturers in the United States have goods finished half a world away in Singapore. One can play the New York Stock Exchange from Buenos Aires or Hong Kong almost as easily as from Manhattan, and the same brand of handbags is stylish from Tokyo to Paris.

Yet the erosion of differences between peoples and states has not progressed steadily in step with the mobility of persons, goods, and information. Sometimes forces of repulsion seem to be the stronger, as groups in close contact are more antagonistic than communicative. Emotions and ambitions set groups or states at odds and lead them to cultivate their differences. The Portuguese language, for example, is different from Spanish primarily because the Portuguese wanted to distinguish themselves from their powerful neighbors.

The forces of resistance are essentially conservative, seeking not to remake society but to preserve values. Much of the extremism of our day may be viewed as opposition to modern trends: to racial equality, nuclear energy, secularism, and so forth in the West; to Western cultural and economic penetration in the Third World, especially in Asia. An antimodern reaction against the spirit of liberalism underlay the ideological extremism of the interwar period. Both Nazis (who hated freedom and rationalism) and Marxist-Leninists (who rebelled against the burgeoisification of Russia) strove to separate themselves morally and politically from the mainstream of civilization. This they achieved for a number of years to a degree that would have been inconceivable for the world of 1913.

After 1945, in the calmer atmosphere of subsiding violence among the great powers and of receding ideological passions, basic trends toward erosion of differences and growth of a worldwide cultural community resumed. Modern societies are increasingly shaped by similar needs and experiences, and resistance to things foreign is strong only where narrow elites are fearful of admitting foreign ideas, as in Burma or Albania, or where new violence has erupted, as in the Near East.

Not only do new devices, from container ships to satellites and international telephone dialing, permit quicker and easier communication and movement; the industrial world has become wealthier. Those with means to do so have always liked to travel, to admire strange sights, to possess the most desirable goods from anywhere, and to enjoy the world's best art and entertainment. They wish to feel superior to native ways, products, and ideas. A century ago few but aristocrats looked to the pleasures of the cosmopolitan world; but in modern states more and more persons can indulge themselves, while the internationalist expectations of the transnational elite only grow. Every year, hundreds of millions of persons—their numbers growing perhaps 5 percent yearly—acquire at least a superficial acquaintance with strange lands and carry something of their ways to foreign peoples. Nepal is overrun with European and American tourists, and once-shrouded Tibet may soon have luxury hotels like those of Beijing.

People absorb new ideas and ways from mere exposure, sometimes no doubt because of inborn imitativeness. But they most desire to learn from those who are thought to do things better or who are richer or stronger. Countless non-Western peoples, individually or in an organized fashion, have undertaken to acquire knowledge from the more powerful or to copy them. On one level, nations adopt constitutions in a more or less international pattern; on another, economic prowess has in our day made Japanese cuisine fashionable along with Japanese electronic ware and management styles.

International commerce, expanding through the postwar period much more rapidly than domestic production, carries ideas and styles with it. In neolithic times, knowledge of faraway people probably came mostly from trade, as hill peoples exchanged flint for seashells from coast dwellers. In the Middle Ages, caravans brought the Western world not only silk and spices but also knowledge of the Orient, and the quest for exotic products led to the voyages of discovery of the 15th and 16th centuries. The leading form of contact between nations is trade, not only import/export of goods but the sending and receiving of many forms of entertainment, both gratis and commercialized. The dispensers of all kinds of goods and services bring styles, manners, and ideas from abroad.

The more wealth and influence people enjoy in their respective lands, the more they want the products of what are considered the most advanced countries, especially the United States, the language of which is widely familiar. The elite, everywhere the style leaders, are most receptive to foreign fashions and ideas. In many lands, children of the affluent classes grow up with a more or less international (or American) cultural background, learning more about celebrities of American fashion and characters of American comics or sports stars than about their national heroes.

Mexican telecasters present to their overwhelmingly swarthy audience blond or at least Caucasian models. Chinese girls have their eyelids redone to make their eyes seem larger and less Mongoloid, and even have noses and breasts enlarged to accompany their Western-style dresses.[1] In a much broader way, the American idea of the pleasant individual life erodes the Japanese custom of sticking to business long after hours considered normal in most of the world.

In a large majority of countries, U.S. films have half or more of the local market.[2] But perhaps the most influential of foreign influences is television, with imported programming, imports, rebroadcasting, cable connections, and satellite receivers. In the not distant future, thanks to satellites soaring over nations, television may be about as internationalized as shortwave radio is today. The CNN network by 1988 reached 58 countries, bringing the news to international businesspeople, officials, and journalists; it has also broadcast programs originated in 80 countries.[3] Peruvian Andean villages often get dish antennas before running water, telephones, newspa-

---

[1] *Wall Street Journal,* April 30, 1987, p. 17.
[2] *Fortune,* August 29, 1988, p. 82.
[3] *Time,* June 6, 1988, p. 77.

pers, or mail service, bringing a mixture of confusion, astonishment, and edification.[4] Videocassettes, inexpensive and easily transported (and smuggled), bring an exotic world wherever a bar or little theater can afford a player, even to river ports of Borneo, presenting images of a very different but prestigious way of living and thinking.[5]

The local culture is neglected, and the world becomes ever more like the touted "global village." Peoples increasingly dress alike, eat many of the same foods, share more of a common culture, and think less dissimilarly. Arab sheiks usually still wear their robes, but the Chinese elite have discarded Mao jackets for the business suit with necktie. Soviet apparatchiks dress like those of Europe, so far as they can afford it. The top elite have Italian tailors, and the old Russian blouses and baggy trousers are folkloric. Youth nearly everywhere, at least of the urbanized upper class, swing to similar rhythms; "heavy metal" has echoed from Khabarovsk to Buenos Aires. There is no real competition anywhere for the cosmopolitan, mostly Western styles, less because they are intrinsically fine than because they are the styles of the great modern world. Not only do the vibrant cities come to look much alike; modernity penetrates once isolated villages, from arctic shores to the headwaters of the Congo. Non-Christian countries, such as Japan and China, take up the celebration of Christmas for the fun of it.

A significant factor in the spread of an international culture is the use of English as a lingua franca by Asians, Africans, Europeans, and Latin Americans to communicate with the modern world and across the babel of a host of languages. It is the language of technology, science, business, finance, and so forth, wherever a common means of communication is needed. It is the obligatory language of international air traffic. It is the gateway to the world economy. Continental European business schools teach in English. It has the incidental advantage of hospitality; in its self-confidence, English welcomes imported words of any origin and is enriched thereby. Aside from writings dealing with strictly national affairs, anything not available in English carries less weight than it might, and those who want their voice to be widely heard must use it.[6]

A secondary factor is the effect of English on other languages. Countless terms, especially technical, are imported from English into all major languages; Japanese is thoroughly infiltrated. The borrowing of terminology, as in the social sciences, inevitably affects thinking about political and social matters. A few nations, such as France, resist; but the day is near, if it has not already arrived, when English will be indispensable for a first-class education anywhere. No scientist can afford to be without it. At the

---

[4]*Washington Post National Weekly Edition*, March 21–27, 1988, p. 19.

[5]See Gladys D. Ganley and Oswald H. Ganley, *Global Political Fallout: The VCR's First Decade* (Norwood NJ: Ablex, 1987).

[6]Commentary on the internationalization of English is given by *English Today*, a monthly published by Cambridge University Press.

same time, higher education is being considerably internationalized and, at the top level, centralized in a few, especially anglophone, countries. Highly placed Latin Americans want their offspring to boast a degree from Harvard or Stanford, MIT or the University of Chicago; Africans need a British diploma. The intellectual expansion of humanity, expressed in its lingua franca, becomes a single whole.

Only a few large and self-assured nations, such as the Soviet Union, China, India, Brazil, and Japan, can feel much confidence in a national cultural identity; and in these, too, corrosion is potent. It is possible to erect artificial defenses; for example, Iceland prides itself on the purity of the language of the Eddas and prohibits the use of surnames (one's second name is the equivalent of John's-son or Tom's-daughter). Brazil requires theater owners to show Brazilian films and play Brazilian songs. But such devices probably have little effect in preserving a native mentality, and laws favoring the home product add to the prestige of the foreign.

There is no real cultural autonomy at a high technological level. The reduction of differences among peoples and states will continue unless sharp violence comes to halt it. Past differences recede, as mountains shrink when a traveller sets out across the plains.

The Victorious Western Mode

Countless authoritarian rulers have tried to admit only what is materially useful and to keep out what they regard as poisonous. But modernity is a package, and a modernizing people will have it all. The authoritarians cannot avoid the use of English, although it is a channel for political ideas and social philosophy, carrying a message of diversity and, in diversity, of rationalism if not democracy. Attempted exclusion or prohibition makes foreign styles, wares, and ideas the more attractive, especially for youth and upper classes accustomed to having their desires, the very groups whose infection is most pernicious. Even backward countries cannot be sealed off. The military rulers of Burma tried to protect their "socialism" by practically forbidding foreign contacts; the result was not only a decline of about two-thirds in the national product but also wholesale smuggling and eventually, in August 1988, a popular (although unsuccessful) uprising.

It is ever more useful, if not indispensable, for societies, like computers, to have access to the worldwide information bank. Science is thoroughly international; its advances are made in many nations, and no scientist can keep current without following foreign developments. For example, although the laboratories of the Soviet Union and the East bloc are reasonably well equipped and have many competent researchers—according to statistics, several times more scientists than there are in the West—they have played virtually no part in many modern developments, from moderate-temperature superconductors to genetic engineering. They are held back not by jealous exclusion on the part of Western authorities but by their own governments' travel restrictions, red tape, limitations on copying machines, and the difficulty of securing foreign publications. So far as Soviet scientists are permitted to do so, they collaborate closely with American colleagues; and some of them are said to be close to General Secretary Gorbachev.[7]

For such reasons, the Marxist-Leninist states that once tried to isolate themselves from all but strictly useful flows of information have to varying degrees given up the effort to prevent infection. Their elites and upper and upper-middle classes crave Western, particularly American goods, music, literature, and fashions. American programs are prominent on Chinese television, and China imports some 100 foreign films per year.[8] Chinese fashion models are as worldly-modern as they know how to be; Mao's mummy should quiver in its glass case. China hires American educators to advise them on overhauling their universities.[9] Even Vietnam, not long ago embattled against the United States, has in its penury admitted ballroom dancing, rock bands, Western dresses, and high heels. Its intellectuals and artists have been officially instructed to "broaden intellectual intercourse with developing countries and Western countries in order to acquaint our people with the diversified culture of the world."[10]

East European countries, especially those nearer the West, are thoroughly contaminated. The coverage of East Germany by West German television is complete; the government piped it to the few regions where it cannot be directly received.[11] But those who regularly watch the West German evening news are not likely to make good missionaries for Marxism-Leninism or to march eagerly under Soviet command in an assault on Western Europe. Instead, they march to the Berlin Wall to listen in on rock concerts. In the Soviet Union, it appeared in 1986 that 96 percent of middle-grade leaders (and perhaps more of the top level) listened with some frequency to foreign broadcasts. The best educated and best paid seem to have been the most interested because they were the most dissatisfied with conditions at home.[12] Estonians tune to Finnish television, which they understand easily; they have shown themselves the most self-assertive of Soviet minorities. The press carries schedules of Finnish broadcasts.

---

[7]*Scientific American* 258, February 1988, p. 17.

[8]*Wall Street Journal,* January 13, 1988, p. 22.

[9]*New York Times,* November 13, 1988, p. 1.

[10]*New York Times,* December 25, 1987, p. 4.

[11]J.F. Brown, *Eastern Europe and Communist Rule* (Durham, NC: Duke University Press, 1988), p. 253.

[12]James R. Millar and Peter Donhowe, "Life, Work, and Politics in Soviet Cities," *Problems of Communism* 36, January–February 1987, pp. 47, 51.

Western broadcasts to the Soviet bloc were once thoroughly jammed at great expense; in 1988 Eastern Europe gave up the effort to exclude the most hated station, Radio Free Europe. Poland, to woo viewers to the state channels, imports not only many Western features but the full programming of Italian state television. Dish antennas bring in the world's uncensored broadcasting. The Polish government reports licensing several thousand, but many people do not bother to get a permit.[13] There are also some 700,000 VCRs in Poland (and smaller numbers in other East European countries), for which perhaps 1,500 cassette titles are available, almost none of them of East European or Soviet manufacture.[14] To enter the computer age means to admit an indefinite volume of uncontrollable information; a single small disc transports the equivalent of some 200,000 printed pages.

Russia has for centuries borrowed Western culture; it has never seen itself as a separate civilization, like India or China. Italian architects designed the Kremlin, Peter the Great compelled his nobles to smoke and to adopt Western dress, and the serf-owners of the empire ate from French porcelain and spoke French. Lenin sought to implement, as he conceived it, the most modern Western mode of thought, Marxism, in the backward realm. For Russia, progress has meant catching up with the West.

In keeping with this tradition, Soviet upper class youths have been subject to a passion for things American, the prime alternative to the official tedium. They are fond of "decadent" Western music, punk hairstyles, leather pants and a wealth of practices contrary to once puritanical communist ethics. They are taking up "bezbal" in a great way. The Russian of young Muscovites—and especially the new breed of entrepreneurs—is loaded with English loanwords.[15] Leaders of the Communist Youth League are infected, too.

The Soviet Union and other communist countries are especially vulnerable because the Marxist-Leninist state has cast away much of the native tradition. The predictability of pre-*glasnost* editorials and speeches was soporific. Young people do not necessarily become democrats or antisocialists if they wear chains, T-shirts with American college slogans, or sport extravagant hairstyles; but they are not communists in traditional style.

A prime badge of elitehood in the Soviet Union is travel to the West for the cachet of having seen the sights of the world and the goods brought back. A major grievance has been deprivation of what the well-to-do elsewhere take for granted, the ability to sightsee and shop in Paris, Rome, or New York; and the number of Soviets allowed this privilege increased from mere dozens in times of high Stalinism and 3,000 in 1985 to tens of

---

[13]*New York Times,* April 3, 1988, p. 6; *Wall Street Journal,* May 1, 1987, p. 16.

[14]*Washington Post National Weekly Edition,* May 2–8, 1988, p. 10.

[15]Bill Keller, "For Russians, the Americanisms Are Coming," *New York Times,* August 28, 1988, p. 1.

thousands at the end of the decade. They include all manner of delegations, students and scientists as well as officials and tourists, but they are still only about a tenth as many as the Americans going to the Soviet Union. The potential for organized and unorganized exchanges is indefinite, as each side is curious about or fascinated by the other. If facilities are improved and Moscow becomes a magnet for tourists, the Soviet state cannot fail to be influenced by the hard currency brought by swarms of Germans, Japanese, and Americans. It will be important to make a good impression on them and to improve the Soviet image in the world.

The permeation of the world by a single culture makes nations less unlike and softens prejudices and tempers. U.S.-Soviet relations cannot be those of the dour past when there are 20 MacDonalds in Moscow, the Pepsi Generation is touted on Soviet television, Western firms advertise in *Izvestia* (paying a high price in dollars), and an American bookstore offers (for dollars) a wide and uncensored stock of books. Soviet society ceases to be so sinister when a voluptuous teenager is crowned "Miss Moscow" before a large tittering audience.[16]

Economic Internationalization

"To maintain a leadership position in any one developed country a business—whether large or small—has to attain and hold leadership positions in all developed markets world-wide. It has to be able to do research, to design, to develop, to engineer and to manufacture in any part of the developed world, and to export from any developed country to any other. It has to go transnational."[17] More and more companies acquire facilities in various countries or make partnerships or enter into close relationships with foreign companies, in both manufacturing and finance. As some go abroad, others follow, partly by force of example, partly to serve their clients, to protect against vagaries of business conditions in different countries, to have as ample a field for sales as possible, and to make use of whatever advantages various locales may offer. Even the largest nations need all manner of goods that they cannot economically produce. New products and inventions appear far too rapidly for any country to keep up with all of them.

States like to participate in the world financial system, which handles some $3 trillion yearly in international trade and over twenty times as much in exchange transactions. Securities markets are linked around the globe.

[16]David Remnick, "And the Winner Is . . ." *Washington Post National Weekly Edition,* June 20, 1988, p. 18.

[17]Peter F. Drucker, "The Transnational Economy," *Wall Street Journal,* August 25, 1987, p. 28.

Japanese investors were a major factor in the runup of the New York Stock Exchange in 1987. Corporations raise money anywhere in the developed world, and "corporate treasurers can now manage worldwide cash and investment positions from their offices, switching between currencies, cities, and countries through computer hookups with their banks."[18] The free flow of money in the modern financial markets invites nations to lure it. Investors reduce risks by spreading their holdings in different lands.

The spread of management methods and the idea of growth and power through productivity and exports affect all modern economies. The United States has been fascinated by the Japanese industrial success. The steady increase of foreign, most conspicuously Japanese ownership in the United States brings in not only capital but also expertise, technology, and, most importantly, management styles. It increases trade, as foreigners import components and use their facilities in the United States as a springboard for world exports. Incidentally, the diffusion of Japanese economic culture through the establishment of foreign branches, especially factories in Britain, Germany, the United States, and elsewhere, is essentially democratic; egalitarian approaches show good results.

There is a worldwide trend toward greater freedom to make money. The lowering of taxes in the United States leads other countries to slash theirs: why should people have to pay marginal income tax rates of 80 percent or more when the top bracket in the United States is 35 percent? All major noncommunist industrial countries have cut rates in recent years, although most remain much above the United States. Even the community- and welfare-minded Swedes slash income taxes by as much as 50 percent. In "supply side" mentality, they hope by reducing taxes to generate enough additional production (or taxpaying) to maintain the level of welfare services, which are to be made more efficient by allowing private enterprises to offer their services. If one country offers more incentives to investment, others must follow in order to keep capital from flowing where it finds a warmer welcome.

The United States has given an example of deregulation of various industries, and many European and Third World countries have undertaken divestment of publicly owned enterprises. The success of the Thatcher government in privatizing British telecommunications, automotive, and other industries has served as an example for privatization in France, Japan, Italy, Germany, Spain, and to a lesser extent the United States, which has a much smaller fraction of the economy in the public sector.[19]

The Third World has been strongly, often dogmatically, attached to economic centralization; but the state has usually failed as an engine of

---

[18]Charles J.L.T. Kovacs, *The Competitive Challenge Facing U.S. Banks* (Washington: American Bankers Association, 1987), p. vii.

[19]Steve H. Hanke, *Prospects for Privatization*, (New York: The Academy of Political Science, 1987).

modernization, and the new countries have largely lost the appetite for socialism along with the passions of the struggle for independence. Despite or because of state direction of the economy, most African countries are poorer, on a per capita basis, than in 1960. Many have taken steps—strongly encouraged by international lenders—toward selling money-losing state enterprises, plantations, factories, banks, and factories. From Mali to Botswana there is talk of private enterprise and employment growth as the means to development; even ostensibly Marxist countries such as Angola and Benin join the parade. Libya has moved partway from Islamic socialism to market economy. Latin American countries have undertaken more or less privatization, while reducing taxes and regulations to stimulate foreign investment.

Soviet bloc states cannot escape the general mode. They see themselves hopelessly outdistanced by such inferiors as Taiwan and South Korea. They must become competitive; a Soviet scholar stated flatly, "The higher the level of participation in the world economy, the higher the tempo of economic growth."[20] It would seem that the promotion of trade has become the biggest concern of Soviet foreign policy.

Foreign trade becomes ever more important, but foreign trade is even more difficult than domestic production for a political entity to handle efficiently. It also seems necessary to invite foreign participation in production, as nearly all Marxist-Leninist countries have done. Such internationalization implies a reordering of economic thinking and practice.

The Soviet Union has built up a huge merchant marine, exposing crews to undesirable ideas if they are allowed shore leave, irritating them if they are confined. To share in the opportunities of international finance, the Soviet Union has set up many banking establishments abroad, not only for transactions involving Soviet interests but to carry on normal banking business. The Soviets have shown interest in working with or joining such capitalistic organizations as GATT, the World Bank, and the International Monetary Fund. But realistic exchange rates to calculate values are necessary if the Soviet Union is really to profit from world trade; moves to devaluation go in the direction of a convertible ruble.

The Soviets seem to look to the West to finance part of the reconstruction of their economy. Having settled the once-repudiated tsarist debt, they have floated bond issues in Switzerland and West Germany, the first such since 1917; and they have piled up a respectable foreign debt, although still modest (about $40 billion at the beginning of 1989) by Latin American standards. West German banks and other European banks have been especially ready to lend them billions of dollars despite misgivings of the United States.

---

[20]Jerry F. Hough, *The Struggle for the Third World: Soviet Debates and American Options* (Washington: Brookings Institution, 1986), p. 97.

The East Bloc took no glee in the Western stock market crash of October 1987, saw nothing to gain from the troubles of capitalism, and rather feared harm to its markets in the West.[21] Times have changed since Stalin was carrying on economic warfare by counterfeiting U.S. currency.[22]

The world market also rewards freedom of creativity. The Soviet movies that bring in foreign currency are nonconformist and critical; Soviet writers are rewarded for originality by foreign royalties. Paintings that were kept under wraps are auctioned to Western collectors; they fetch enormous sums by Soviet standards, which enrich the artists even after the state takes a large cut.

Not only ministries but all Soviet enterprises, including private ones, can engage in foreign trade, although regulations are severe. Foreigners are allowed within the gates in joint ventures of many kinds; increasingly flexible terms permit foreign management and majority ownership, and sometimes profit remittances in hard currency are guaranteed. Deals made up to 1989 have not been very numerous, but their number grows steadily. They range from opening a pub to huge chemical plants. U.S. and other foreign businessmen seem mostly rather satisfied with their dealings with the Soviet Union. It is laborious to get started, but once they are in they find business steady and profitable and hope for ever better deals with what could be one of the world's biggest markets. The chief Soviet purpose is to generate exports to help the hard-currency balance of payments, but partnerships with foreign enterprises offer many possibilities of improvement of quality and variety in Soviet markets.

Perhaps the most important gain for the Soviets would be their education in business practices. Lack of training and experience is the strongest brake on the Soviets joining the world economy. Foreigners can be especially useful in helping the Soviets translate their considerable scientific and technological abilities into marketable products. Foreign trade is probably the best lever for the difficult reform of the Soviet economy.

Some rulers are prepared to sacrifice economic benefits for the fullness of power. Nicolae Ceausescu of Romania has held stubbornly to the Stalinist model, although the people shiver in overcoats in homes and offices kept at near-freezing temperatures through the winter and find little in the markets to fuel the body. Castro would like to reassert Cuban socialism after thirty years of failure to build a productive economy. But even Castro, who long decried the perversion of pleasure-seeking Yanquis, builds luxury resorts to lure tourists bearing hard currency.

For any country to cut itself off from world trade is to condemn itself to poverty. But to participate in the world economy brings change. Interna-

---

[21]*Christian Science Monitor,* November 4, 1987, p. 1.

[22]William R. Corson and Robert T. Crowley, *The New KGB: Engine of Soviet Power* (New York: William Morrow, 1985), pp. 320–21.

tional business is an excellent teacher. To earn money to buy abroad, one must sell; it is necessary to take account of foreigners' tastes and adapt their methods, and trade brings countless personal contacts. The world becomes gradually more of a single marketplace, making nations less different, not only in manners and modes but in the institutions for production and distribution of goods.

The Retreat of Socialism

Economic problems (aside from those due to natural causes) are mostly attributable to political malpractice, overuse or abuse of power. The most compelling reason for governments to sacrifice some of their power, to give more security to private property and to permit freer use of it, is to improve productivity and make the state richer. Not merely must there be some latitude for people to apply resources in order that there be more goods; in this age the ability to design and produce at a modern level is more and more essential for military strength. Dedication to authoritarian order becomes a long-term handicap for any nation concerned for its standing in the world. Hitler's Germany would surely have decayed even more rapidly than its leaders aged because of its autarchy and regimentation of production.

Authoritarian states can be organized in different ways; but they value power, not productivity. Conformity is more important than knowledge and performance; and the rulership is based on rewarding loyalists in return for unqualified support. The integrated system can function well only so far as people are prepared to accept the goals of the leadership.

The Soviet economic system, modeled on Germany's wartime mobilization, could work properly only in a warlike situation. It was put together in the civil war of 1918–1920, and it gave victory to the Leninists. It functioned very well in WW II; in wartime, the United States also used a system of priorities, price controls, and allocations. Centralization worked fairly well in the years of reconstruction as wartime habits carried over; for this reason the Soviets have worked assiduously to keep fresh the memories of their wartime glories, when the party-managed system functioned best. But people weary even of glories; and the ideal of socialism has faded as the wars have sunk into the mists of storytelling.

In decades of peace, as people looked more and more to their own well-being, the state became an ever less efficient manager; the control regime decayed into a system of organized favor. Soviet infrastructure was deteriorating from the 1970s; in the early 1980s there was little or no economic growth, perhaps an actual decline if it were realistically measured. An ever growing share of the economy was falling to the gray or black market. It became necessary, if the Soviet Union were not to sink to a Third World level, to replace political with economic motivation. The Soviet state found itself compelled to seek new methods of harnessing self-interest to production, methods not unlike the conventional ways of societies without revolutionary pretensions.

The complexity of the modern apparatus of production also makes it more and more necessary to secure the cooperation of professionals and intellectuals. But the intellectuals are the group most restive in the lack of freedom. They resent the self-righteous government of less qualified persons, and they feel entitled to the advantages of the open world system. To create an elite capable of modern production is to create an influential sector discontented with premodern political management.

For the Soviet economy and other economies organized in its image, coming to terms with modern needs implies a multitude of changes. The most basic is the partial renunciation of what was a sacred principle, the almost total monopoly of the state in production (except some private peasant agriculture), commerce, and services. Since 1987, anyone can form a cooperative, which becomes eligible for low-interest loans and can go into any legitimate business (except publishing, film-making, and a few other activities) and make money without limit, subject to moderate taxation. By the end of 1988, about 77,000 cooperatives had been registered, involving some 1.5 million persons.[23] Only co-owners are to work in the enterprise, however. Some Soviet factories, especially money-losers, are sold or leased to the workers and management to be operated as private enterprises under state overlordship.[24]

Collective and state farms are to be more or less disbanded, plots being leased for 50 years to peasants, who are allowed to buy or lease machinery and hire labor. So far as implemented, this practically reverses Lenin's nationalization of the land and Stalin's collectivization, reducing the collective farms to supervisory and coordinating organs.[25] State industry is also to be managed more like private money-making corporations. Enterprises are to be funded not by state grants but by interest-bearing loans, and Soviet industry was told to make itself "self-financing," 60 percent from the beginning of 1988, the remainder from the beginning of 1989.[26]

These inroads of capitalism can become effective only slowly and accompanied by new ways, to introduce which the devotees of economic planning study management training in the United States. Work practices must

[23]*New York Times,* March 19, 1989, p. E–3.
[24]*New York Times,* October 7, 1988, p. A–6.
[25]*The Economist,* August 6, 1988, p. 37.
[26]For a historical treatment, see Ed A. Hewett, *Reforming the Soviet Economy: Equality Versus Efficiency* (Washington: Brookings Institution, 1988); see also Jerry Hough, *Russia and the West: Gorbachev and the Politices of Reform* (New York: Simon and Schuster, 1988), pp. 85–102.

be changed to improve incentives for effort and results, vary work and permit some autonomy, provide more information for workers, give freedom to move or make changes, show esteem for the worth of people, and establish more egalitarian relations between bosses and workers. If the Soviet Union truly inaugurates a modern management style, it will have gone halfway toward a democratic society.

Other Marxist-Leninist regimes have introduced economic reforms that, without directly reducing political controls, affect the way of life of the people. Since the mid-1960s Hungary has been in the vanguard of change in the Soviet bloc. Prior to 1985 it was restrained by Soviet conservatism, but the Gorbachev semirevolution invited it to explore a new blend of communism with market economy. Hungary has partly freed prices, slackened controls over state enterprise, and reduced or eliminated subsidies for inefficient producers. Unemployment is accepted, as is the right to strike. A large part of agriculture is private. Half of the economy, by some estimates, is uncontrolled; and the head of the party urged workers to moonlight, as most of them do. Entrepreneurs are allowed to employ—"exploit" in the Marxist vocabulary—up to 500 workers. There is something of a stock market.[27] Foreigners can buy 100 percent of companies. The establishment of a school of business administration in cooperation with the U.S. government and American universities invites capitalist ideas.[28] Technological cooperation, which languishes with the Soviet Union, thrives with Western enterprises.

Poland has taken the climate of *glasnost* as license to proceed toward such changes as competitive banking, the beginnings of a stock market, considerable freedom for private enterprise with no requirement of licensing and no limitation as to size, realistic prices, and a free exchange rate for zloty. Shares in companies are sold to workers, and bankruptcy laws permit firms to be taken over or liquidated. Although practice lags behind promises, private businesses have access to hard currency loans, and access to markets for industrial materials, equipment, and labor on a theoretically equal footing with state enterprises. Rent control has been abolished for private housing, and many price subsidies have been removed. The private sector accounts for a third of employment, two-fifths of new housing, and not far from half the entire economy.[29] The regime seems to hope to undercut the demand for political reform by permitting considerable economic freedom.

Czech authorities, mindful of the disintegration of communist author-

[27]*Business Week,* October 10, 1988, p. 56.

[28]*New York Times,* November 2, 1988, p. C-1.

[29]Timothy Ash, "Trying for Thatcherism in Poland," *Wall Street Journal,* October 31, 1988, p. A-15.

ity in 1968, move hesitantly in the same direction. Dogmatic Bulgaria seeks to revamp its system of management, abolishing major control organs. Hesitantly or decisively, all Marxist-Leninist countries, including Albania, Vietnam, and Yugoslavia and excluding only the personal tyrannies of Cuba, Romania, and North Korea, retreat from the principle that socialism requires the state to manage everything.

Change feeds on change, and reform in one Marxist-Leninist state makes it harder for others to resist going the same way. After 1948 it was the Yugoslav example of reform that the Stalinists detested. In the 1970s the Hungarian "New Economic Model" had influence as far as Vietnam. In the 1980s, China has been most influential because of the incontestable success of Deng Xiaoping's far-reaching pragmatism.

For several reasons it is easier for China than the Soviet Union to move away from dogmatic Marxism and economic centralization. The command system has had only 40 years to become ingrained instead of 70 in the Soviet case. Mao put dissidents to hoeing rice and feeding pigs but usually did not kill them as Stalin did; many of them survived to return to power and change the system that had maltreated them. China, unlike the ever-growing Russian realm, has for centuries not been expansionist; it does not have to fear that a freer economy will nourish disruptive movements for minority autonomy. China has more of a mercantile, less of a militaristic tradition. Not least is the fact that Chinese in next-door Hong Kong and Taiwan, who are theoretically subject to capitalist exploitation, are at least ten times wealthier than those under the rule of the communist party. As China assumes power over Hong Kong, up to the final transfer in 1997, the need to preserve its productivity may increasingly pull the remainder of China toward free enterprise. The influence of millions of overseas Chinese is also felt, the more so since many of them have money to invest.[30]

Hence China has undergone extensive economic change under the pragmatic guidance of Deng Xiaoping. Although major state operations remain under the orders of ministries, less important enterprises work under contract, managers receiving a share of profits. State corporations, like private businesses, are permitted to engage in foreign trade on their own. Failing state firms may be consigned to bankruptcy. Some shares in state-owned businesses may be sold, and many little ones have been auctioned to the highest bidder.

Some non-state enterprises raise capital by the issuance of shares, and one firm can take over another. There is an embryonic stock market; although the Chinese seem somewhat mystified by the procedures, it bur-

---

[30]For a survey, see Harry Harding, *China's Second Revolution: Reform after Mao* (Washington: Brookings Institution, 1987).

geoned rapidly from nothing in 1986 to a turnover of some $30 million in 1987.[31] "Unregulated" markets increased to 30 percent of the economy by 1987.[32] China has about 20 million entrepreneurs and a half million cooperatives with some 4.5 million employees. Private enterprises, unlike Soviet cooperatives, can hire labor; some have 1000 or more workers. The best-selling book in Beijing in 1988 was the autobiography of Lee Iacocca.

"Special economic zones" are open to thousands of joint ventures with foreign capitalists; and China, unlike the Soviet Union, permits 100 percent foreign ownership. Foreigners are allowed to buy and negotiate land use rights. Guangdong province, next to and closely linked with Hong Kong, strives with some success to emulate Hong Kong and Taiwan.[33] Some regions have gone so far that most output is from the private sector.[34] It is proposed to make Hainan, in the extreme south, a virtual enclave of capitalism. Foreign trade has become vital to China, running over $40 billion yearly, only about 5 percent of it with communist countries. A Chinese state corporation bought a steel company in the United States.[35]

Economic reform began after the death of Mao with the dissolution of the collectively farming communes. The result was a spectacular growth of production of peasant prosperity. Agriculture was further assisted by permitting the consolidation of very small farms and allowing sublease of holdings. As use rights can be sold, there is virtual private ownership of land.[36] This increases average holdings from 1/3 ha. to 2 ha. or more and shifts labor from agriculture to rural industries. Farmers plant and sell mostly as they please, although they may be required to grow grain for sale to the state at a low fixed price. These and related reforms are to be carried out under advice of the World Bank and with a subvention of several billion dollars. The goal is to quadruple the national income from 1980 to 2000.

China, the Soviet Union, and other countries that claimed to have in Marxism-Leninism the answer to economic problems no longer stand quite apart, perhaps no longer desire to do so, as they recognize that the communist planned economy has failed. Change is slow because economic structures rest on habit and accepted ways of management, production, distribution, finance, and regulation; and they constitute a power structure. It is not possible to conjure effective new institutions into existence by fiat, in the way censorship can be ended. But economic modes are basic to the

---

[31]*The Economist,* April 30, 1988, p. 76.

[32]*Wall Street Journal,* July 6, 1987, p. 13; September 1, 1987, p. 20.

[33]Nicholas D. Kristof, "In China the Buck Starts Here," *New York Times Magazine,* December 20, 1987, p. 40.

[34]*The Economist,* December 10, 1988, p. 32.

[35]*Fortune,* July 18, 1988, p. 11.

[36]Chu-yuan Cheng, "China's Economy: New Strategies and Dilemmas," *Current History* 87, September 1988, p. 253.

ordering of society; so far as they become less sharply at odds, political institutions must be pulled along.

Obstacles to Change

Economic change is always hurtful to some and resisted by many. Even in the United States, new work styles may be hard to implement because of old habits, personality conflicts, and costs of restructuring production. In India, it is recognized that the economy functions much less efficiently than it should; yet centralized regulation is accepted as necessary to keep the very diverse country, with its dozens of ethnic groups, from falling apart. The all-Indian civil service, with the army, binds nearly a billion people; and a major reason for favoring state enterprise in principle is that it is a unifying force, whereas private enterprise is seen (perhaps erroneously) as potentially divisive. The huge officialdom that regulates or tries to regulate almost everything is not disposed to declare itself superfluous.

The problem is far more severe in countries that have made central control their major principle and the basis of the careers of a large part of the educated population. The need for reform of faltering Marxist-Leninist economies seems obvious; and there are many potential benefits, both for entrepreneurs allowed to improve their fortunes and for consumers weary of shortages and poor quality. Yet there is no straight and easy road to readjustment. In the Soviet Union, change is especially difficult, because of the long time during which the controlled economy has been consolidated—since Stalin inaugurated forced-draft industrialization in 1929—because of the near total isolation of the country until after Stalin's death and relative isolation for more than 30 years after it, and because of the equation of economic planning with Soviet greatness and leadership of the communist movement. It is not surprising that talk of reform has gone far ahead of practice.

For many reasons, remaking an economy like that of the Soviets is like moving a mountain. There is a tremendous amount of uneconomic investment in place, everyone has grown accustomed to artificial prices and markets, most of those in positions of authority have a vested interest in the system, and many people are sure to feel shortchanged or threatened by reforms, no matter how well intentioned.

The nationalized economy serves a welfare function, giving security to workers and managers almost independent of performance. Privatization permits firing people; fear of unemployment is a powerful deterrent to economic rationalization everywhere and especially in communist states, a chief virtue of which is security of employment. Workers like the leisurely and undemanding pace of communist industry and its job security; they dislike widening wage differentials and competitive pressure. In Soviet re-construction, or *perestroika,* there has been extreme reluctance to discharge superfluous personnel; and workers are retained not so much because they are needed as because they need the jobs.[37] Such tenderness cannot be rec-onciled with the requirements of rationalization; about 16 million adminis-trative jobs are supposedly to be eliminated by the year 2000.[38]

Undoing Soviet collectivized agriculture is far more difficult than dis-solving the Chinese communes. Not only are the little lords of the great collectivized estates undesirous of yielding their position and authority. The peasants have no memory of independent existence, and the more capable ones were removed in the collectivization drive of the early 1930s. For gen-erations, life has been shaped around the collective, of which the peasants were virtual serfs; and everything possible was done to undo their individu-alism and make them like factory workers. Along with a new infrastructure, a new mentality has to be created, or recreated, on the part of both village authorities and peasants. Until this can be done, peasants will be reluctant to risk leasing land they will not own to raise crops to be sold at controlled prices under the eye of persons accustomed to bossing them.

Freeing markets and prices causes inflation unless production can catch up to demand; and production is diverted from necessities, with fixed prices, to more profitable luxuries. Subsidies on bread, meat, milk, and such necessities cost the Soviets $160 billion yearly (at the official rate), the sales price being perhaps half the cost. Rents cover only 5 to 10 percent of costs. The Soviets have never ceased to lament that farmers feed bread to pigs because bread is cheaper than grain; but taking away cheap bread repre-sents a loss of one of the few real achievements of the socialist order.

When the state tries to set millions of prices, many or most of them are sure to be irrational and to invite irrational economic measures as well as profiteering. Yet it is impossible simply to step back and let producers charge as they will, because there is much monopoly and little competition or sense of competing. If state enterprises are invited to make themselves profitable, they set about doing it in the easiest way they know, and freedom may bring more abuses and confusion than innovation and rationalization of production.

More production requires decontrol, but decontrol requires more pro-duction. There cannot be proper market prices without a proper market. To solve this problem requires heroic and painful measures, which may not work. The reforms raise far more hopes than they can possibly satisfy, at least in the near term; there may well be a short-term worsening of condi-tions.

[37]Bill Keller, "Soviet Change vs. the Worker's Security," *New York Times,* May 10, 1988, pp. 1, 6.

[38]Leo Gruliow, "Laid off in the Workers' Paradise," *Christian Science Monitor,* April 18, 1988, p. 13.

There is a near-total lack of qualified private managers, and they are not encouraged. If an ambitious few are eager to work on their own account, many people resent that their more industrious neighbors profit. Ordinary people have been trained since kindergarten to despise such class-enemy cheaters. A Soviet businessman lamented, "Stop anyone on the street and ask, and you will find the general opinion is that we are thieves, profiteers, speculators."[39] People blame entrepreneurs for shortages of almost anything. Some would rather not have meat than see others making money from raising pigs. There have been reports of mobs torching their buildings and other new private enterprises.

Popular hostility may not be entirely baseless; entrepreneurs in the Soviet Union are not likely to be more irresponsible than money-makers anywhere, but they may be less restrained in view of the lack of competition and the weakness of norms. Suddenly inviting people to make money invites greed, perhaps racketeering; those who formerly pilfered materials from state stores for personal use do so on a larger scale for their new business. Gangsters also prey on private enterprises; they can do so fairly freely because the police have no interest in protecting what they see as essentially illicit business, like the black markets that have long been around. The few private restaurants have to charge high prices because they encounter great difficulties in obtaining supplies. They are correspondingly resented,[40] and local authorities try to control their charges. Capitalism cannot thrive until there is developed a culture of disciplined enterprise.

The biggest problem is that those who are charged with carrying out the reform program staff the apparatus of control. They cannot be enthusiastic for a program that threatens their careers and way of life, if indeed they understand it. Those on top see the big picture and the need for new ways; the little bosses see their own jobs. Managing the economy is the greatest occupation of the ruling party and justification for hundreds of thousands or millions of jobs. So far as there is a private economy, workers cease to depend on state jobs. The party cadres know that if entrepreneurs are allowed to accumulate wealth and to form any kind of organization, they will form an anticommunist pressure group.

The cadres see private business as a threat to their authority; they react by squeezing it. There are a thousand ways to prey on any business that is worth the attention, from endless investigations and audits to arbitrary application of rules or invention of new ones, confiscatory taxation, and deprivation of materials.[41] Simple decrees are not enough; if one form of control is abolished, the apparatus finds other ways of keeping its hold.

[39]Bill Keller, "Private Soviet Entrepreneurs, Under Fire, Try Closing Ranks," *New York Times,* November 14, 1988, p. 1.

[40]Marshall J. Goldman, "Perestroika in the Soviet Union," *Current History* 87, October 1988, p. 316.

[41]*The Economist,* May 28, 1988, pp. 63–64.

There can be substantial reform only so far as the ruling party loosens its grip on the economy, but to decree economic freedom is far from permitting it in practice. Ignorance, strength of habit, and the distance between higher authorities who see the need for change and the locals who know only their way of running things all impede rapid reconstruction. This often comes to the fore in the experience of foreign entrepreneurs, who may come to a satisfactory understanding with the ministry but encounter endless obstacles from the bureaucrats on the spot.

It is easier for other communist economies to move away from centralization in the measure that they have more memory of private enterprise and respect for it, and central planning does not represent for them a great national achievement but an importation or imposition from abroad. Yet Yugoslavia, for example, shows how hard it is, despite forty years of looking for independent ways, to untie the bonds without sacrificing the party's monopoly of power. The market mechanism is not really allowed to operate, and the ruling party finds workers' self-management politically too useful to set aside for the sake of efficiency. In some ways, Yugoslavia seems to have the worst of both worlds. Productivity is low, workers put in three-hour days, absenteeism is high, strikes are frequent, unemployment is severe, inequality increases, and inflation rolls on.[42] Incomes peaked in 1979 and have since fallen sharply. Most people seem to think fundamental change is necessary, perhaps a fully open economic system; but only token reforms are made.[43]

In Hungary, reforms made in theory many years ago are only partially implemented. Although private enterprise is freer than in any other Marxist-Leninist country, it is taxed mercilessly. State firms are not really put on their own, inefficient ones are subsidized, profits are taken away from the efficient, prices are more or less fixed, and the party continues to interfere. Despite the considerable success of its relatively open economic model, the country faces new taxes, unemployment, and rising prices.

Liberalization of the economy has been more successful in China than any other communist country, raising the national product as much as 10 percent yearly. Most of the benefit has come simply from releasing the peasant majority, however; the cities have seen less improvement. Decontrol of prices has brought inflation, and authorities have taken advantage of greater autonomy to enrich themselves. Where capitalism flourishes in southern coastal provinces there has been a large increase of inequality. In October 1988 the government stepped back, reimposed some price controls, and checked, or tried to check the provincial autonomy that has come from the free flow of money.[44]

[42]Tony Smith, *Thinking Like Communists: State and Legitimacy in the Soviet Union, China and Cuba* (New York: Norton, 1987), p. 201.

[43]*The Economist*, October 29, 1988, p. 52.

[44]*New York Times*, October 17, 1988, p. 1; *The Economist*, December 10, 1988, p. 32.

The outlook for the Soviet economy is not good.[45] The best hope would seem to be full engagement in world trade and openness to foreign enterprise; but it is very painful for inefficient producers to expose themselves to a competitive assault from abroad. Short of a revolution overturning the ruling class, deep change in the economic system can advance only as people adjust and accommodate themselves to new relations, rules, and values during a generation of developing new habits suited for a very different society. This may take 20 to 30 years in the frank estimate of Gorbachev's leading economic advisor, Abel Aganbegyan.[46] A new economy must first supplement, then slowly supplant the old.

There may be a gradual acceptance of new ways, undoing generations of indoctrination. But the crucial problem is that private enterprise needs security, and security is doubtful unless political power is limited. That is, economic reform is not promising without political reform, and it is not clear how the ruling class is to be persuaded really to renounce its authority and privileges. In many countries it has refused to do so, even though the cost has been national impoverishment.

Failure is possible. Argentina has found itself over a long period lagging ever farther behind the modern world despite many political experiments. The Soviet state needs much deeper change than Argentina to develop a competitive-economic mentality and bring its economy to the level of advanced countries.

As the modern world becomes more culturally homogenized, systems of economic management converge, and the economies of the Soviet Union and other states in its image will doubtless become more like the world majority. This does not mean, however, that their prosperity is assured; there is much uncontrolled enterprise in many poor countries. One may feel sure that an increasing share of activities will escape the grip of the incompetent state but not that the state will cease to be parasitic and burdensome.

Surely, however, Soviet-style countries can improve their economies through greater openness to the world and its markets, both for buying and selling and for the acquisition of technology; and they can improve productivity through more freedom of communication and nonpolitical management. It does not seem possible for the Soviet state quickly to make up its lag behind the Western world, a lag inherited from tsarist Russia and made worse by the gross error of Leninism. But it can evolve, and the restructuring of its economy, with accompanying slackness of controls, or a measure of cultural and intellectual freedom, can only improve prospects of a better world order.

---

[45]Robert J. Kaiser, "The U.S.S.R. in Decline," *Foreign Affairs* 67, Winter 1988, pp. 97–113.

[46]*The Economist*, April 9, 1988, p. 4; see also Abel Aganbegyan, *The Economic Challenge of Perestroika* (Bloomington IN: Indiana University Press, 1988).

Chapter 7

Easing
of Political
Differences

The Democratic Mode

If diverse peoples and states are enveloped by a common cosmopolitan culture and they manage their economies in less radically different ways, they are drawn toward a common political mode. Political institutions, like other human ways, are learned; and in a less ideological world there is less resistance to learning.

Political patterns have spread for millennia; Athens was a model for the Greek world, as was Louis XIV's court at Versailles for 17th-century Europe. British liberties and French philosophy inspired the founders of the American republic, who saw their nation as an example for the universe. It has been extremely influential since its earliest days; the French revolution would have been very different or impossible without it. From the 18th century, Britain and the United States, to a lesser extent France, have been the chief inspiration of nations wishing to adopt the best political forms. British parliamentary government has been imitated not only in former British colonies but also in European and Asian countries; the American variant of democracy has been copied widely, especially in Latin America.

The written constitution, which subjects personal power to law, is virtually an American invention. Poland and France adopted constitutions in 1791; today, almost all of the world's governments have written charters, many rather closely framed after the American, all influenced by it. Another American export is judicial review, the power of a high court to find that the legislature or executive has exceeded the authority vested in it by the constitution. British rule of law and legal style have also had great impact, as has French code law. Among other things, the United States has stood for a certain populism; a striking recent trend is the adoption of American campaign styles, frequently with professional advisors from the United States, in democratic countries around the world.

Immediately after the Bolshevik revolution of November 7, 1917, the Soviet Union set about promoting a new kind of state under a tightly struc- tured political party; the Leninists offered or demanded to lead the world to a new era in the name of the downtrodden proletariat. Their revolution has been persuasive more or less in the measure that the Soviet system has been successful. At times, especially in the 1930s, totalitarianism, Leninist- Stalinist or fascist, seemed to be the wave of the future, and the outlook for political liberalism was dark. Victory in WW II also raised the image of Soviet power as the way of the future.

The Marxist-Leninist model, however, has lost allure in recent decades because of its divisions (as in the deviations of Yugoslavia, China, Romania, and Albania), its need to use brute force to maintain itself (as in the crush- ing of strikes by police in Poland and elsewhere), and above all its failure not only to catch up with and surpass the West economically but to keep from falling further behind. Military dictatorship has also fared rather badly. As a result, there no longer is a prestigious model for economic cen- tralization, censorship, and ideological totalism. The appeal of authoritar- ianism is increasingly limited to poor countries whose rulers love total power. It does not offer real competition on the battlefield of ideas, only a rearguard resistance.

To be modern and belong to the progressive, wealthy modern world, it is necessary not only to follow consumer styles, enjoy fashionable enter- tainments, and have sufficient freedom of economic management to make these amenities possible, but also to espouse democracy. No other political system is acceptable to contemporary thought. For pride and good standing at home and abroad, rulers must at least cultivate democratic appearances.

Even the elite who profit from nondemocratic systems frequently de- sire the benefits of an open society. They see the freedoms enjoyed by their counterparts in democratic countries, and they are embarrassed to have to apologize for the political backwardness of their own country. The fact that the richest and most creative countries are uniformly democratic is a con- vincing argument in favor of that form. It is hard in the contemporary con- text to oppose constitutional government, rule of law, the right to leave one's country, freedom of speech, and election of rulers by the people. By the Helsinki agreement of August 1975, the governments of the advanced powers, including the Soviet Union and its allies, subscribed to a broad declaration of universal human rights, in effect renouncing the sovereign authority to maltreat their subjects. It is increasingly accepted that human rights are a legitimate concern of all powers.

No state can be at the same time quite modern and very authoritarian; it is not possible to have compulsory uniformity of belief and a high level of education, inquiry, and communication. Controlled information is falsifiable. Authoritarianism is anti-innovative, hence antimodern. The higher the technological level, the more necessary to have freedom of communications and predictability and responsibility of government. The modern society implies freedom to work, think, and produce.

Repressive government is under pressure in all nations sufficiently advanced to have an articulate public opinion. For example, militocracy in Latin America has ebbed to the lowest point of history, and even in grave economic distress few advocate recalling the generals to office. A large majority of Latin American countries may be formally certified as democracies. The Last Dictatorships of the old style, Pinochet in Chile and Stroessner in Paraguay, yielded to less dictatorial rule in 1988. The Mexican ruling PRI party has lost the political monopoly it enjoyed for over 60 years.

Many countries of Asia have moved toward a political opening. Turkey, for example, has ended mass trials and internal exile and gives the press free rein, although several provinces remain under emergency rule and the military is entrenched in government institutions. Taiwan has enlarged the sphere of the opposition, replaced the Mainland old guard with native leaders, and permitted broad freedom of expression.

Despite the exemplary economic success of South Korea, many of its citizens felt aggrieved to have a government imposed on them. The retreat of the regime in June 1987 and its promise of democracy showed how hard it is to sustain control of a discontented population in a country both highly dependent on foreign trade—publicity of street disturbances was causing cancellation of export orders and investment plans—and desirous of raising its place in the world's eyes by hosting the Olympic games. In December, the ruling party was able, by virtue of the division of the opposition, to win the election without gross fraud; and President Roh promised to govern with democratic propriety. Elections in April 1988 gave the opposition a majority in the legislative assembly for the first time in the history of the country. A few months later, the former dictator, Chun Doo Wha, humbly apologized to the nation for corruption and violation of human rights, returned his takings, and withdrew humbly to a monastery.

Even very poor, illiterate peoples may have strong, although naive ideas of freedom and democracy. Ugandans weary of the savage dictatorship of Idi Amin voted with great enthusiasm in 1980, only to get another dictator. Millions of Brazilians shouted in the streets for direct presidential elections in 1984, although the military government of the previous 20 years had been rather moderate and competent and had led the nation to extraordinary economic growth.

Democratic forms do not mean democratic practices, and many a dictator has proclaimed devotion to principles of popular government; but forms tend to acquire substance, at least in countries of relatively high educational and economic level. The holding of sham elections concedes that there should be responsibility of government. Promises need not be kept, but they have some effect, especially when people are aware of what the outside world says about their state.

The failure to secure consent is demoralizing and encourages corruption. To seal the frontiers is a costly admission of failure and cause of irritation. But if the borders are open, too many useful citizens take their abilities elsewhere. A great failure of military dictatorships in Latin America has been the emigration of large numbers of the most productive of their people, as from Argentina and Uruguay in the 1970s and early 1980s. Both of these countries lost about 10 percent of their population.

The compulsion for political modernization is less direct than for economic reforms. Yet it becomes even easier for nations to learn from one another, and cultural and economic integration pulls all states, despite great inertia, toward political pluralism and responsible government.

Soviet Discontent

The countries governed by political parties organized on the Leninist model and dedicated to total control of the economy, information, and political action were for a long time remarkably stable. The Soviet system was well engineered to reward absolute loyalty, to mold minds by unremitting indoctrination, and to deprive dissenters of means of promoting heresies. The monopoly of force, readiness to use it, fixed dogma, and skillful management by the ruling party made a seemingly impregnable system. With sufficient perspicacity the experts might have guessed that political rigidity in an evolving society covered a growing potential for deep change. It was generally assumed, however, that fixity was permanent.

The world failed to recognize that the communist system is artificial in that it represents a single will pretending to incorporate the real purpose of groups and people with many different purposes. It is precariously held together by an ideological fiction, and the authority of the governing party is correspondingly brittle. When the will of the central authority fails and it can no longer impose its version of the needs of society, people discover that they can assert themselves and their own interests; the ability of the party to command crumbles.

That occurred, for example, in Hungary in 1956. A harsh leader was ousted at Soviet insistence; students and intellectuals, encouraged by Khrushchev's denunciation of Stalin, began agitating; crowds demonstrated, and some of the police and army went over to them. A liberal was raised to power, and Hungary was seeking to leave the Soviet alliance when Soviet troops put an end to dreams of freedom. Events followed a similar course in Czechoslovakia in 1968. The country, in an economic slump, was so weary of an old-line leader that he had to give way to a moderate communist. Everyone thought a new day had dawned, censors stopped censoring, the dam holding back discontents was broken, and a landslide of reform was taking shape when the Russians intervened.[1]

Although Soviet forces reimposed party rule in Hungary and Czechoslovakia, the less dramatic decay of Marxism-Leninism continued. Since the death of Mao in 1976, China has been moving away from communist patterns of management. Hungary has shown some, usually growing tolerance for free expression and private enterprise from the 1970s. In 1980 striking Polish workers brought the party-state near collapse. Despite recourse to martial law and replacing the party leader with a general, it has never recovered full authority.

Communist power in the Soviet Union was more stable. Movement is slower in the bigger country; the world responsibilities of the Soviets give the rulership a stronger claim on power; and, most of all, the Marxist-Leninist state is not a foreign imposition but (at least for the Russian half of the population) a great national achievement. The Soviet people have been subject to generations of thought control and seemed quite habituated to obedience. If Polish workers protested, Soviet workers accepted what authority decreed; and Soviet patriotism required submission to the party that represented Soviet greatness.

The permanence of the Soviet system was assumed by communists and anticommunists alike for their own reasons. It seemed to be confirmed by communist practices: for decades and generations, Moscow was decorated by almost the same slogans proclaiming love for the ruling party, dedication to fulfillment of the current economic plan, and glory to the current chief. The official party organ, *Pravda,* in the early 1980s looked much as it did in the 1950s or even the 1920s (except for the name of the leader). And lesser Marxist-Leninist regimes were carbon copies of the master plan, as they took over the institutions of politburo and central committee, elitist political party, fake elections, censorship, centralized control of the economy, and political police.

Yet the history of the tsarist empire showed that Russians, like Poles and Hungarians, were quite capable of both cheating and opposing their government. No political system can escape change, least of all while under-

---

[1]Z. A. B. Zeman, *Prague Spring* (New York: Hill and Wang, 1969); H. Gordon Skilling, *Czechoslovakia's Interrupted Revolution* (Princeton: Princeton University Press, 1976).

going a social and economic transformation and coming out of times of deep disturbance. On the one hand, an urbanized, relatively educated, industrialized Russia could not be governed in the same way as the largely illiterate peasant Russia of 1917. On the other hand, the psychology and values of those who made the revolution could not be sustained indefinitely by the new possessors of power and privilege. Pressures like those in Eastern Europe were accumulating. The apparently static Soviet state of the early 1980s was overripe for change.

The most important reason that the old system had to crack was the decay of the legitimating ideology. The Soviet and other communist regimes have laid enormous emphasis on ideology and indoctrination with good reason: it is the key to making the system viable. The Marxist-Leninist state has repeatedly proved itself effective when it could point to a goal of overweening importance. It has functioned best in war mixed with revolution, when people are inspired by a common purpose, the liberation of the country for the building of a happy new society of equality. But in placid times, as years go by without bringing important improvement, the common purpose evaporates, and the communist authority loses legitimacy and becomes unstable.

In the fever of revolution, Lenin had a vision of messianic Russia, bearer of a new message of salvation, displacing the worn-out order of Europe. This vision was not insane in the context of the desperate and cataclysmic world war, the longing of peoples for a better way, and the Marxist teachings that were regarded as a new dispensation of science. The dream was both entrancing and politically useful. But it languished in failure to spread beyond the borders of the old Russian empire; and as soon as the corps of agitators around Lenin found themselves rulers of a great country, their purposes and the meaning of ideology changed.

Little spirit remained in the world-revolutionary vocation by 1924, when Stalin gave priority to "Socialism in One Country." But Stalin was able to replace the idea of utopia through revolution with utopia through state power, the building of the ideal society not by the world proletariat but by the Soviet people, organized as never before, toiling on big mechanized collective farms and in new modern factories, under the orders of the wise leader. Stalin claimed, when capitalism was sick with depression, to have found a better way to the glorious future through central planning—a coercive revolution by command to bring the new order.

The residue of idealism sufficed to make this "revolution from above" fairly successful for a few years. Former peasants won victories in the battle for socialism by building steel mills in the steppes. But morale was breaking down in abusive despotism by the latter 1930s, as was shown by the grotesque purges. The war beginning in 1941 saved Stalinism. The system of mobilization, although no longer viable in peacetime, was effective in waging war—partly because Stalin somewhat loosened the reins, allowing patriotism to replace Marxism, freeing the church, and releasing generals from labor camps to command his armies.

The messianic spirit had another partial revival in victory over Nazi Germany, the mightiest of military powers. But postwar weakness and the opposition of the United States prevented the Soviets from converting military victory into political supremacy. After the war, Stalin's prestige enabled him to put the lid back on and reimpose conformity; but by the time of his death in 1953 the country was weary and suffocated.

Nikita Khrushchev, who had risen to the top as one of the best of the Stalinists, saw the need for new beginnings and tried to inject a little life into the flagging vision, promising to outproduce America in a few years. He permitted publication of some critical books in a "thaw" that feebly presaged Gorbachev's *glasnost,* tried partially to decentralize administration, and proposed some semidemocratic reforms in the ruling party. He also claimed leadership of the less developed countries, a new proletariat of nations to overthrow the international capitalist order. On no front was he successful. He could no longer really dictate, and the party bosses who felt threatened by his reorganizations deposed him in 1964.

Khrushchev's successor, Leonid Brezhnev, was the champion of the bureaucrats. He undertook not to promote change but to prevent it. His motto, "trust in cadres," brought superficial stability as ministers and first secretaries held office indefinitely; but it entailed demoralization, corruption, and increasing incongruity of state and society.

Each effort had failed, leaving no hope of gaining sway by revolutionary agitation, by excellence in production, by military power, or by alliance with the less developed countries. The Soviet Union saw itself falling farther behind the nonsocialist world. Instead of the promised abundance, the years after the mid-1970s brought stagnation and even economic regression with growing shortages. Officialdom, supposedly composed of the best people inspired by ideological truth, was venal and extortionate. The should-be egalitarian society was riddled with snobbism and privilege. The "new Soviet man," the exalted builder of the higher order, was turning out to be a lazy drunkard. Heretical ideas filtered in, through increasingly leaky controls, not only from the idealized Western world but also from other supposedly communist societies, especially Hungary and Poland. From the latter 1970s the need for new departures was being mulled in Soviet upper circles, as it became clear that the alternative to change was perhaps irremediable decay.

The Soviet leadership was most of all moved by the malfunctioning of the economy, "the increasing discrepancy between the role the Soviet Union wants to play in the world and its growing technological backwardness combined with economic poverty . . . the system with all its economic and political rigidity and ideological dogmatism is exhausted and unable to meet the conditions required by the modern post-industrial world."[2] Post-industrial technology, unlike coal-and-iron industrialization, is not routinized and is difficult to control from a distance. The proletariat is being replaced by machines; production is based more on information than on materials and requires easy communication. Modern consumption goods require variety and flexibility to meet market demands; efficient production needs inputs from afar and international markets for buying and selling.

After the death of Brezhnev (November 1982), in the brief reigns of Yuri Andropov and Konstantin Chernenko the ice began to break. By March 1985 the old men of the politburo felt compelled by the acceleration of economic and social decay to hand power to their youngest and most forceful member, Mikhail Gorbachev, with a mandate for reform.

At first, the reformers seem to have supposed that they had chiefly to improve the organization and discipline of labor and check drunkenness. But little good came from what most workers saw as an effort to make them labor harder for no more reward, and the effort to deprive them of their vodka led chiefly to an enormous rise in production of moonshine (and an eventual retreat from semi-prohibition). Gorbachev moved on a broader front, inviting people to speak out and criticize in order to improve conditions, a policy of openness, or *glasnost,* an uncommon word that suddenly was everywhere. After a little hesitation, he and Soviet society began moving with a rapidity beyond all expectations, as long repressed ideas and feelings surged to the surface. Change was overdue, and we had forgotten the Russians' penchant for extremes, their preference for thoroughgoing revolution to modest reform.

Change was necessarily more in attitudes and ideas than in political institutions, which have the rigidity of vested interests, more in the way power was exercised than in the mechanisms of power. Repressive laws stayed on the books long after they ceased to be applied. But fissures in the control structure led to wider cracks, reforms generated demand for more reforms, and freedoms permitted bolder calls for freedom. The system that the heirs of Stalin tried to uphold for half a century after it was outworn broke down. It was time to bury the long-dead revolution.

Glasnost

Professionals and intellectuals seem to have been most receptive and eager for change, but the signals came from the elite. They doubtless felt frustra-

[2]Jiri Pehe, "Why Do Communist Systems Reform?" *Freedom at Issue,* September/October 1987, no. 98, p. 13.

tion at failing to fulfill their mission of betterment and were the more hospitable to change because the monolithic political party, with its inertia, inefficiency, and self-protective bureaucratic procedures and networks, ceased to be a readily usable instrument. If the chief is unable to achieve much through the cumbersome apparatus, there is less reason to guard its power, more reason to expose it to criticism to improve its performance and to make it more responsible. In the Soviet Union, reform (*perestroika*) means wholehearted support of the general secretary against his less cooperative servants.

Ideology and conformity were rightly regarded as pillars of the totalitarian order; typically, the communist state restricts severely the possession of typewriters and duplicating machines, and one of the greatest reproaches of the Soviets against the Czech reformers in 1968 was to have permitted freedom of the press. But the leadership could not know what directions to take without slackening of controls over expression. To repair a failing system requires knowledge of its problems, and it is necessary to have a debate to develop ideas. Without a free press, it is hard for the boss to judge the reliability of reports passed up to him.

Freedom of criticism is also the best means of moving the bureaucratic apparatus. The leader cannot simply discharge the masses of officials who prefer their own prerogatives to the progress of the state; he cannot conjure up a new bureaucracy to put his ideas into effect. At best, he can reward some who cooperate and try to jog the rest by allowing their shortcomings to be exposed. Having pretended to be competent and honest, they cannot convincingly complain when critics are allowed to show up their incompetence and dishonesty; they may, the leader hopes, be persuaded to mend their ways to justify their positions.

Those who have long suffered under the bureaucracy initially hesitate to expose themselves; but as they become convinced that it is safe to speak out, they do so, the more gleefully because they have long had to contain their thoughts and feelings. When the curtain was pulled back after 1985, the Soviet people gradually shed the apathy that had seemed ingrained, began reading the enlivened press instead of getting the news by grapevine, and watched with amazement as political differences were tossed into the public view. When the June 1988 party conference was televised, they watched wide-eyed as delegates lashed out at anyone except the chief himself; and they marched into the streets to clamor for more *perestroika*. When journalists whose entire training and career had been to serve as agents of party education and indoctrination were unleashed, they eagerly began to act like journalists elsewhere, writing for their readership and vigorously criticizing the authorities, much as people started to argue with the police as soon as they learned they could safely do so.

It became fashionable to throw convention overboard, as in the United States at the time of Vietnam protest, in giddiness from unaccustomed freedom. On one hand, soft porn thrills Soviet audiences who until recently saw nothing more lascivious than a quick kiss. On the other, Soviet intellectuals, or a large sector of them, have seemed obsessed with uncovering and denouncing or ridiculing past evils, as though seeing this as the way to salvation, democracy, and prosperity.

The press raises questions that not long ago would have been cause for forced labor: articles attack restriction of travel, controlled trade unions, the powers of the party, party privileges (such as villas and exclusive stores), powers of the KGB, and many other standbys of the Soviet way. The KGB has been subjected to criticism; and high officers, perhaps influenced by foreign duty, have denounced secrecy in the name of improving the Soviet image in the world.[3]

Stalin's image has, of course, been freely kicked around, even his alleged great achievement of the collectivization of agriculture and his record as war leader. Many of his victims have been rehabilitated after decades of denigration; much of the spirit of *glasnost* is revulsion against the barbarism of Stalinism. The 1917 revolution remains sacred thus far; but a leading economist writing in the journal *Novy Mir* virtually rejected the whole Soviet idea, the notion of the classless society and the command economy. He advocated freedom of enterprises to buy and sell, raise capital, and compete freely.[4] Gorbachev's ideological specialist, Alexander Yakovlev, asked, "Are we really the only ones who know eternal truth?"[5]

Innumerable huge banners with such messages as "Glory to the Communist Party, Builder of Socialism" have come down from buildings, with the comment that no one looked at them. Soviet television has grappled realistically with the question of human rights, to the shock of many viewers, although criticisms of Soviet practices are balanced by discussion of homelessness, inequality, and unemployment in the United States.

Foreign policy is least open to criticism in a nationalistic polity, but a large circulation paper can state that the Soviet Union bore much responsibility for the cold war. "We, advancing on the West, increased the level of military danger . . . The inept character of decisions led to our foreign policy taking on an extraordinarily expensive character . . . The interest in saving human civilization from nuclear destruction is more important than any class, ideological, material, or personal interest."[6] The Soviets no longer present themselves as makers of revolution but as promoters of human interests.

[3]*New York Times,* September 8, 1988, p. 1.

[4]Cited by *Wall Street Journal,* August 26, 1987, p. 20. For a broad treatment, see Moshe Lewin, *The Gorbachev Phenomenon: A Historical Interpretation* (Berkeley: University of California Press, 1988).

[5]*Christian Science Monitor,* December 29, 1988, p. 8.

[6]Vyacheslav Dashichev, "East-West: The Search for New Relationships," *Literaturnaya Gazeta,* May 18, 1988.

The press remains official, owned and controlled by either state or party organs; and independent publication is prohibited (supposedly to protect the state press from competition). Old habits and the instincts of self-censorship do not quickly disappear, and the conservatives growl in protest from time to time. But journals have been enlivened by competition for subscribers; in their zeal to please their much enlarged readership, editors ignore criticisms of high officials. The official policy is that freedom of speech must not be used "to the detriment of Soviet society." The limits have seemed elastic, but critics are expected to respect the basics of the revolution, Lenin's leadership, and the one-party government—although the image of Lenin has been smudged and writers have mocked the "infallibility" of the party. Soviet readers are enthusiastic, and circulation of interesting and innovative papers and magazines soared. Runs were capped allegedly because of paper shortage, but limits were lifted because of the readers' outcry.[7]

Automatic conformity is no more. There have been many protest movements against environmental threats, especially pollution, threats that have become the more grave because of lack of *glasnost* to force the authorities to attend to them. Public outcry has induced authorities to abandon nuclear power projects and various other schemes.[8] Public opinion polling has become fashionable. After mid-1988 permits were required for public demonstrations, but they have been numerous.

The atmosphere of uncontrol is general, from daring theater to freedom of modern painting and new styles of ballet. Soviet citizens, for the first time since 1917, are fairly free to travel to the West. After decades of semiprohibition of religion, the Orthodox Church—and by implication, religion in general—has been recognized. The state remains officially atheistic, but priests appear frequently on television, and the general secretary formally greets church dignitaries. A number of churches and monasteries have been returned to believers, and a new cathedral is under construction in Moscow to commemorate the thousandth anniversary of the official Christianization of Russia—which is also celebrated on a new coin. The Soviet state long exerted strict control over the Orthodox Church, severely limiting its scope and activities in order to help it die out. In the new dispensation, it is to be made an ally, like the state church of tsarist times. It is a mark of change that private charities are allowed.

It was once the iron rule of communist organization that all political affairs should be directed from a single center, there should be no independent political organization, and no party group should seek support outside the party. But the political elite has lost its unity, and institutions assert a will of their own, independent of the center. Party-run newspapers criticize

[7]*Christian Science Monitor,* October 21, 1988, p. 10.
[8]*New York Times,* January 28, 1988, p. 1; April 8, 1988, p. 3.

one another. The formerly rubberstamp Supreme Soviet rejected tax proposals of the more conservative ministry of finance.

Moscow can no long simply command local authorities. In 1987 an
old quarrel between the Soviet republics of Armenia and Azerbaijan over
the status of an Armenian enclave in Azerbaijan rose to a high pitch of
disorder, protests, and strikes. The formally supreme governmental body of
Armenia voted unanimously for the annexation of the district, a move bitterly opposed by the other republic. Armenian papers called for something
not far from sovereignty, with an Armenian division of the Soviet army.
Interethnic clashes became so violent that military intervention was necessary.

The Baltic peoples also have their own mind; communist authorities
in Estonia, Lithuania, and Latvia, with memories of independence from
1918 to 1940, have clamored for and have achieved considerable freedom,
with their own flags, financial autonomy, and preferred status for the national language. Their "People's Movements," which are separate from the
respective communist parties, are qualified to present candidates for office.
They would like to limit immigration of Russians, to have relations with
neighboring countries and ethnic communities abroad, and to form
their own units in the Soviet army; and the national authorities are more
responsive to local sentiment than to authorities in Moscow.[9] Estonia flatly
asserted the right to overrule laws of the Soviet Union; party authorities in
Moscow demurred but compromised. The Soviet Union has become subject
to ordinary political contention.

Not surprisingly, many Soviet party cadres, especially middle-level bureaucrats who are insecure and have much to lose, have been alarmed. Bureaucrats feel the rightness of that for which they are qualified and which
makes their lives. The administration is filled with narrow-minded, parasitic
little bosses, quite satisfied with the recent past and fearful of being judged
on their qualification. They are fearful of being eliminated in the massive
pruning of staffs, and they have nowhere to go.

The conservatives, admitting the need for reform, plead for caution,
decry the blackening of history, and want change to proceed under their
guidance. They cannot admit taking lessons from what they have learned
to see as the forces of evil, and they will never admit to following the example of the United States. They have to keep asserting that socialism is really
superior, pointing to the supposed or real faults of the pluralistic order.
But they have no alternative program, and everyone knows that something
different must be done.

The powerful police organs have been unenthusiastic about *perestroika,*
or reconstruction of an order highly favorable to themselves, stressing the
need for discipline, dangers of subversion, and the meddling of the West

---

[9]*The Economist,* September 17, 1988, p. 50.

in agitation by minority nationalities. The agency cannot be happy about publicity of Stalinist murder—not only were millions allowed to starve or freeze to death but vanloads were taken out and shot next to a pit prepared for them, as the police fulfilled their quotas of liquidation of saboteurs. However, its high command has been replaced.[10] The army, accustomed to being treated with reverence, has grumbled at criticism and called for more discipline.[11] Nevertheless, it has gone along with *glasnost* by allowing Westerners, official and unofficial, to inspect its installations and forces in a way that would have made the Stalinists apoplectic.

Less interested, even very humble persons are suspicious of modernity, rationality, and the corrosive values or lack of values of the West; they want the strong state to protect against immorality, pornography, and licentiousness. They see cheating and corruption unbridled as the mandates of ideology and discipline of the state retreat; some would have a new big boss to put the little bosses in their place. They have enjoyed security, albeit at a very modest material level, for many decades and fear the uncertainty of change. The myths and understandings, the clear-cut ideological answers people have grown up with have crumbled, and there is nothing solid to take their place. Trained for generations to prefer consensus to competition, they hate the anarchy of liberty, just as they have grown to esteem security of employment over productivity. There is a generalized hatred of division and fear of disorders if the binding reins are loosened and matters of public policy are left to controversy.

Distrust for freedom is traditional in the Russian mentality,[12] and it will not be soon left behind. Perhaps more than most peoples, Russians admire discipline and order, believe that justice should be given from above, and care more about national strength than their freedom to differ with political powers.[13]

Habits long and thoroughly ingrained do not disappear quickly, and there will undoubtedly be swings between more discipline and less. The de-Stalinizing "thaw" under Khrushchev a generation ago gave way in a few years to a not so deep freeze. But the recent wave of reform came because of overpowering need and was promoted within the system. A new generation will have a new mentality; Soviet education, frozen from Stalin's time, is in a turmoil of questioning as new textbooks are hastily put together. A

---

[10]Amy W. Knight, "The KGB and Soviet Reform," *Problems of Communism* 37, September-October 1988, pp. 61–70.

[11]*New York Times,* January 21, 1988, p. 3.

[12]Ronald Hingley, *The Russian Mind* (New York: Charles Scribners Sons, 1977), pp. 195–200.

[13]A survey in Moscow in May 1988 showed young people much more reformist than their elders, favoring multicandidate elections, rights for minorities, and freedom of street demonstrations. *New York Times,* May 27, 1988, pp. A-1, A-7.

school official said, "I feel my chief task is to form nonconformist minds,"[14] the exact opposite of his task a few years before.

A truly free press is distant in the Soviet Union, but dissident voices can make themselves heard, and control must be more pressure or persuasion than compulsion. Even partial and qualified freedom of expression means the end of effective official ideology and the opening of a deluge of criticism that may know no end short of admitting that the glorious revolution of November 1917 (which overthrew not the tsarist autocracy, which had collapsed in March, but a government seeking to modernize Russia politically as well as economically) was in reality a costly error.

If criticism is permitted, it becomes a habit; and it is hard to put the jinn of free thought back into the bottle of political control. The authorities learn that their state does not collapse if people are allowed to speak their minds rather freely; and a varied press, a lively theater, and interesting arts are all too much fun to be taken away without compelling reason, such as a war or a sacred revolution. It is much more useful, in any case, to co-opt artists and writers than to repress them. It is hard to compel educated people to go back to the old dull conformity and to accept the huge suffocating falsification without a compelling reason, and no strong reason is in sight. If people are told that they are free and entitled to choose their rulers, they may believe it.

For a people to break out of an imposed discipline is like a crab moulting; the old shell cannot be put back on. Once the idea of change takes hold, people to go back to the old dull conformity and to accept the huge suffo- be restored or replaced. If disorder and economic failure should lead to disillusionment, a Third World style military regime would be more probable than a revival of party autocracy. If a tight lid were forcefully clamped down, society would be left more dispirited than ever; the Soviet Union would cease to be a great power.

The Failing Movement

If the Russians leave behind a 19th century doctrine that is irrelevant to the late 20th century and outgrow political ways coming out of a rather backward country a lifetime ago, the whole movement based on the Russian revolution and Lenin's universalism is undone. Russia gave birth to the Marxist-Leninist system, and it is doubtfully viable anywhere without the support or at least the example of the homeland. That does not mean that those accustomed to arbitrary power through the mechanisms of the Lenin-

---

[14]*Time,* July 25, 1988, p. 74.

ist state are prepared to surrender them. But sooner or later they will find it impossible to maintain this unmodern system in a modern milieu without firm external support.

In Eastern Europe, the Soviet state has represented political orthodoxy, and Soviet overlordship has long restrained liberalization. It is anomalous that since 1985 the Soviets have outpaced the more reluctant of their satellites.[15] In Czechoslovakia and East Germany, crowds cheer the Soviet leader because he denounces the Brezhnev regime that the present governments of Czechoslovakia and East Germany resemble. Officials who held up the Soviet Union as their model have instead to explain that their way to socialism is different; sometimes they find it necessary to censor Soviet publications. It is dangerous for unpopular satellite leaderships to admit that they were basically wrong; for their people, communism is a foreign imposition and Leninism is easy to hate.

Most countries of Eastern Europe move faster than the Soviet Union, which is officially derecognized as ideological leader.[16] In Hungary and Poland, all manner of freethinking societies mushroom. "Class struggle" gives way to "struggle for peace," there is increased autonomy of foreign policy, and most East European countries have gone ahead of the Soviet Union in the latitude permitted for private enterprise and freedom of travel. It is no longer necessary to be a party member in order to hope for a good career. In all bloc countries except Bulgaria and Romania there is something of a pacifist movement, and an antidraft crusade inspired by the example of Western European tolerance of conscientious objectors has gained concessions from several governments.[17]

The Hungarians have admitted the most change. Political clubs proliferate, and people call openly, though quietly, for many things: control of the government by a genuinely elected body, freedom of the press, guaranteed human rights, freedom of independent associations to represent diverse interests, formation of alternative political parties, and withdrawal of Soviet troops—a veritable revolution. Censorship, which was long mild, has been abandoned. The Hungarian parliament has started acting, in a small way, like a real political body, trying to represent constituents, debating issues, and registering negative votes. In May 1988 Janos Kadar was retired from top leadership against his will by an open regular procedure, a first for Marxist-Leninist states. The ceremonial head of state is noncommunist.

Other East European countries follow at varying distances, because they are subject to similar conditions and because Czechs, Poles, and others learn about what Hungarians have attained. Dissidents confer across fron-

---

[15]For background, see Karen Dawisha, *Eastern Europe, Gorbachev and Reform: The Great Challenge* (New York: Cambridge University Press, 1988).

[16]Current events in Eastern Europe are well covered by *Eastern European Newsletter* (London).

[17]*The Economist*, July 30, 1988, p. 46.

tiers and exchange illegal publications. If the authorities make it hard for them to cross borders—sometimes it is more difficult to travel within Eastern Europe than to go to the West—they exchange manuscripts and cassettes.[18]

The fundamentalists of Prague, knowing that hardly anyone likes them, arrest dissidents from time to time; but they have felt compelled to admit a measure of freedom. Czech journalists promote an independent paper, and hundreds of thousands of Catholics demand rights for the church. Films tackle social problems, and the media investigate official malfeasance. The regime has lost confidence and the people have lost fear. A new "Prague Spring" cannot be far beneath the surface, as the Russian-imposed system since 1968 has known only how to command, not to inspire the people.

East Germany is spiritually close to Czechoslovakia, but, like Czechoslovakia, has perforce yielded ground. It has made travel to the West fairly easy, permitted more and more engagement with West Germany, and allowed some private enterprise. East Germany still stands out for rigidity, but it has come far from the grim camp of cold war years. Bulgaria has moved hesitantly, taking half a step backward for each step forward. The burgeoning of the "second economy" especially in East Germany, Czechoslovakia, Hungary, and Bulgaria, reduces dependence on the state; from a third to two-thirds of workers participate in it.[19]

The loss of authority has gone farthest in Poland, although the ruling clique refuses to legitimize the opposition and struggles to maintain their wealth and privileges.[20] The Catholic Church has come into a comfortable coexistence, even collaboration with the formally atheistic state. The great noncommunist power in the land grows stronger; over a thousand church buildings are under construction.[21] The state has virtually given up the effort to prohibit unlicensed publication. Hundreds of unauthorized books, papers, and journals appear regularly, including some 200 newspapers. Foreign travel has been made easy. Correspondingly, the government feels it must allow plural candidacies (subject to party veto) for election to weak representative bodies. Dissenters get some seats in the parliament. Political clubs are illegal but tolerated. Political powers have to deal with the Solidarity movement. Party bosses are fearful; as one remarked, "Organizations [like a recently created industrial association] have a way of making themselves independent and asserting prerogatives outside the pale of the eco-

---

[18]*The Economist,* May 21, 1988, p. 53.

[19]David Binder, "The Shadow Society: A Vital Breadwinner for Countries in the Eastern Bloc," *New York Times,* January 6, 1988, p. 7.

[20]Werner G. Hahn, *Democracy in a Communist Party: Poland's Experience Since 1980* (New York: Columbia University Press, 1987); Tad Szulc, "Poland's Path," *Foreign Policy* 72, Fall 1988, pp. 210–229.

[21]*Time,* January 11, 1988, p. 71.

nomic ... The problem for the party is that whenever you begin spreading power, economic or political, you just never really know into whose hands it is going to flow."[22]

Without a clear idea of doctrine, it is doubtful how much remains of the "limited sovereignty" of the Brezhnev Doctrine. In the new era, the in-fluence of Moscow must rest primarily on the fact that the elites of Eastern Europe need Soviet support in order to uphold their positions. The several countries, sharing something of a political outlook, are a sort of political system, like the Soviet Union itself, with its minority "republics." The needs of all the regimes are similar; as long as the Soviet Union demands little, East European governments may reinforce bonds with it to offset the West-ern magnet. Economic ties formed during many years of politically directed investment and trade cannot be quickly severed without great loss. The So-viet army remains in place, although its political effect decreases so far as people cease to believe it will intervene politically.

With little in common except unrepresentativeness of government, however, the bloc countries drift apart. For the Soviet Union, relations with West Germany, which gives billions of dollars of credits, are much more important than relations with the dogmatic Czechs, who would like to see Gorbachev removed. The Soviet leadership disclaims any intention of guid-ing its onetime faithful satellites, and they quarrel with one another. The Poles eye the East Germans with distrust, and the Hungarians and Romani-ans are frank enemies. There is little idea of collaboration; Czechoslovakia, East Germany, and Poland have engaged in a little trade war, not to exclude imports, as occurs in most of the world, but to prevent neighbors from buy-ing scarce consumer goods.[23]

For East European peoples, the retraction of Soviet power is an invita-tion to turn toward Western Europe, which they find far more congenial than the hegemony of Moscow. They want to measure up as Europeans, even dream of joining the Common Market. Young people seem especially alienated and determined to build a new life.

It remains to be seen how long Leninism can be sustained anywhere if it is left behind in its homeland. The Stalinist Romanian dictator has made it clear that he has no intention of following the example of a Soviet government that would emancipate itself from Stalinism. Castro insists that Cuba for some reason needs to remain strictly Marxist-Leninist even if the Soviet Union does not; and he has taken a number of dogmatic measures, such as closing farmers' markets, making individual home ownership more difficult, and prohibiting artisans from making things for sale. But he has released many political prisoners, refurbished tourist hotels (for guests with hard currency), and come to terms with the Catholic Church. It may be guessed that his insistence on central control, like that of the autocrats of

[22]*New York Times,* October 14, 1987, p. 4.
[23]*New York Times,* December 6, 1988, p. C1.

Romania and North Korea, has much less to do with Marxist ideals than with dictatorial egomania. And failure of Soviet backing forces even Kim Il-song toward moderation.

Xenophobic Albania began hesitantly opening doors to the world after the death of Enver Hoxha in 1985, establishing relations with Italy, France, West Germany, and others (though not yet with the hated superpowers), looking for improved technology for export industries and for markets, even allowing some latitude for foreign-trade enterprises to deal directly with firms abroad. It is doubtful that Yugoslavia can be called communist in the old sense. The press is uninhibited to the point of sensationalism and nastiness, and the central government has little control over the autonomous constituent republics of the federation. Despite having received a great deal of Soviet help, Vietnam speaks of a "neutral" foreign policy. China claims to adhere to something called "socialism," and there is no suggestion of the party's sharing power, but it is hard to imagine that a China determined to develop its potentialities and aware of its greatness will long continue to regard Marx and Lenin as great prophets.

Marxist-Leninist forms have proved useful as a means of control of less developed countries, too useful to be dropped quickly. But so far as the Soviet Union loses interest in "socialism" in Angola, Ethiopia, South Yemen, or Nicaragua, it is not important for world affairs if they call their dictatorship "Marxist." They, like all other countries, have more to gain from working with the modern world than turning their backs on it; and they have all to some extent deradicalized.

The penumbra of the Leninist movement is formed by the nonruling communist parties, the supposed vanguard of the revolutionary proletariat preparing, these many decades, for the predicted downfall of capitalism and their own assumption of power under Soviet leadership. When the Soviets confess their failures, it is nonsensical for the foreign comrades to look to them for directions. When the Soviets strongly desire cooperation with world powers, it is senseless for the parties to pretend to belong to a great revolutionary movement, and it is pointless for the Russians to pay attention to the would-be subverters of the world order.

A chapter of history comes to its close. It is remarkable for having lasted so long.

Dilemmas of the Communist State

The Soviet leadership has permitted—of necessity—considerable latitude to speak out and advocate reforms, and an unofficial society grows in the space left by the incompetence of the state.[24] But the way to a real liberaliza-

[24]S. Frederick Starr, "The Soviet Union, A Civil Society," *Foreign Policy* 70, Spring 1988, pp. 26–34.

tion of a very strong authoritarian system is long and rocky, and it could be shortened only by forcible imposition from without or much violence from within. Democratization requires turning around the habits of generations and the removal from authority of many persons now enjoying power and high social and economic position. It presupposes the development of a large new class of persons of independent standing, a powerful sector with a strong interest in free government. At present, there is only the beginning of such a class. Decades of education and social development are necessary in order to make democracy workable; until it so ripens, reform can only loosen or moderate authoritarianism, not replace it with a really open pluralistic society responsive to popular will.

Governing elites do not democratize or liberalize in order to reduce their own power and status but to improve it, perhaps to save it by making the society more efficient. They would make necessary and hopefully controllable concessions to avoid decay and/or a potential explosion. Without surrender of power they can do much to improve information and communications, to give people the feeling they are free, to attend to popular needs and demands, and to encourage criticism and initiative. It is not necessary to have genuine democracy to establish such important elements of the liberal state as rule of law, means of checking official malpractice, security for productive enterprise, and freedom for creativity.

Intelligent moderation of rulership softens or divides opponents, depriving them of a moral cause and rallying ground while giving appearances of decency and legitimacy. It improves initiative and makes the bureaucratic apparatus more responsible. It reduces discontents by concessions to popular demands, especially of the intellectuals, permitting more or less symbolic participation. But it does not propose permitting those outside the power structure to decide national directions.

The tempering of authority comes less from demands of the people than from the evolving ideas and outlook of the leadership. In communist states, habits of conformity are persistent at the lower levels; the protest of the masses is not overt dissidence but apathy, poor work, and disregard of rules. The outlying provinces in particular are inured to exploitation. So far as independent movements appear, they are less the cause than the effect of change.

It is the upper strata of the center that are aware of failure. Sensitive to comparison with life in the freer and more advanced countries, they find the ideology boring. The elite, especially of the new generation, want to belong to the modern world, not only to have fashionable goods but also to enjoy free choice of ideas, styles, and entertainments. They feel entitled to travel without restriction and to inform themselves and express their ideas and feelings.[25] Above all, they see their country failing in the world competition.

[25]As in the Soviet Union. Jerry F. Hough, "Gorbachev Consolidating Power," *Problems of Communism* 36, July-August 1987, p. 40.

Arbitrary rulers, making concessions to reduce pressures and improve the functioning of the government and the economy, seek a compromise between the needs for freedom and the demands of authority. In East Germany, for example, the aging leader, Erich Honecker, speaks glowingly of human rights and permits rather assertive youth movements, although the circles of power remain closed. Polish authorities, who have permitted much more relaxation, carefully qualify words like "democratization" and "pluralism," making it clear that they mean something other than what they do in the West.[26] Marxist-Leninist states have always claimed to be democratic at heart, and only a little amendment or reinterpretation of the typical communist constitution would make it suitable for a free society. But none wants an opposition to organize and seek political power.

Gorbachev has repeatedly affirmed that Soviet socialism is not to be displaced but improved. In his view the party knows best, individualism is bad, and the people have no right to choose their political system. Democracy is not to mean freedom of people from the state or rights against the state but the participation of the people in carrying out the purposes of the people as understood by the leadership. There should be intellectual but not political freedom. There is to be a monument to victims of Stalinism, but it is to be planned and designed not by the association of victims but by the state. Gorbachev wants such democratic values as legality, sufficient freedom of criticism, and legitimacy of government, all without the essence of democracy, freedom of political opposition to contest control of the state.

By the reforms enacted in 1988, the authority of government, which has in the past been exercised by party secretaries at each level, is vested in the soviets, bodies formed by contested but not really open elections, with freedom of nomination by "social organizations" and secret ballot. The central government is based on a huge body of 2,250 (1,500 from territorial districts, 750 from governmental and nongovernmental organizations), chosen by competitive, although one-party elections yearly. This congress elects a legislative body of about 400. It also elects the president, who, like other officeholders, is limited to two 5-year terms. The president has very broad powers; he chooses a prime minister and various other officers.[27] The courts have been made more independent; citizens have been surprised by winning cases against officials. The legal code promises real rights, including inviolability of mails and telephone communication; and the catchall crime of "anti-Soviet activity" is removed.[28]

The reformed Soviet government seeks to be respectable and legitimate, to enable the (indirectly) elected president to speak in the name of the whole people. It does not reduce the powers of the president; on paper,

---

[26]*New York Times,* October 14, 1988, p. 4.
[27]*New York Times,* December 2, 1988, p. A-6.
[28]*New York Times,* June 5, 1988, p. E-1.

they are rather greater than those of the general secretary. It is open to popular participation only at the bottom and only to the extent the authorities tolerate, but it permits some dissent and discussion at the center. A significant change is that decision-making is shifted from the party apparatus, where it has been since Lenin's time, to regularized state agencies. Formerly, the organs of state simply took their orders from the politburo.

The party continues, however, to hold the levers of all important undertakings; only some religious and volunteer or cultural organizations are independent. There is no prospect of a genuine multiparty constitutional democracy; the leader of the party will doubtless continue to be something like a dictator. If Gorbachev wants to loosen and moderate arbitrary power, there is no assurance that a successor would not do the opposite. But the party and its chief cannot rule in the old manner, lacking both an exclusive ideology and monopoly of organization.

There is no real prospect of a broad political opposition, not only because it lacks institutional expression but also because there is no clear idea of democracy. The activists of the Soviet "new left" are fractious and hesitant about the extent and meaning of the democracy they desire and whether they want to retain the essentials of the "socialist" system or change fundamentally to Western ways, whether they should try to influence the authorities or work against them. There is confusion in the Soviet press over the meaning and extent of its freedom. There is little idea of freedom for its own sake but for particular, often conflicting causes; freedom is to help the leadership revitalize and modernize. For those educated to conformity, freedom means not responsibility but doing as they please.

It is perhaps worst that Soviet society is incoherent. Oppositionists are united in little more than discontent. The party always claimed, like the tsarist autocracy before it, that the alternative to its unquestioned rule was anarchy; it has yet to be proved wrong. Not only does it confront social and economic decisions like those familiar in most of the world; ethnic divisions present perhaps unsolvable problems. They could be papered over by pretenses of revolutionary dedication; but people who can no longer regard themselves as the makers of the new society see themselves more as Russians, Armenians, or Ukrainians.[29]

Divisions are deep and passionate. On one side, there are Russian nationalists; Russian national feeling, with deep consciousness of history, sometimes xenophobic or antisemitic and sometimes humanistic, fills some of the vacuum left by retreating ideology. They use the word "Russian" in preference to "Soviet."[30] On the other side is a much-fractured non-Russian

---

[29]See Lubomyr Hajda, "The Nationalities Problem in the Soviet Union," *Current History* 87, October 1988, pp. 325–29.

[30]George Gibian, "Beneath Communism, There Is Russia," *Wall Street Journal,* March 4, 1988, p. 22.

majority of the population. Crimean Tartars clamor for their homeland, and Balts challenge the legitimacy of Soviet rule by recalling Soviet collaboration with Hitler and the brutality of Soviet intervention in 1939–1940. Peoples from Ukrainians to Moslem Central Asians have a storehouse of grievances, both against the hegemonic Russians and other minorities, as Armenians against Azerbaijanis.

The Gorbachev government seems prepared to concede some autonomy to the more self-willed peoples, not only of the nominally sovereign "Soviet republics" but areas within the strictly Russian realm, which have been placed on "territorial self-financing."[31] It is hoped that giving them freedom to move away from old patterns will help the cause of *perestroika;* peoples of the Baltic countries and the Transcaucasus are much more disposed to private enterprise than the Russians.[32] But they want not only economic but also political autonomy; and there is no reason for them to be happy with anything less than complete freedom. Affiliation with Western Europe, after all, is far more advantageous and attractive than affiliation with Russia. And if concessions are made to Estonia, why should not a dozen other nationalities demand as much? To the Central Asians, Russians can be only alien masters. And Ukrainians, 50 million strong, feel fully entitled to independence.

Everyone knows that a genuinely liberal system would lead to a breakup, so all those committed to the Soviet "union of free peoples" must be prepared to halt democratization short of risking dissolution. Those with a stake in the present system are primarily Russians. It pays to be Russian, as Russians dominate the center of power, the politburo and the party secretariat; and economic planning is advantageous for Russia proper. Conceivably, one day the Russians may decide that they would do better to release their continental empire, much as West European powers released their overseas empires after WW II; but to give up the Union means to sacrifice the glory of greatness that Russia has enjoyed for centuries.

There are many obstacles to forming a viable union of the diverse peoples. One is that the Russians, more than twice as numerous as the Ukrainians, are too dominant. A federation must bring together reasonably equal partners able to deal with one another. If a single member predominates, as Russians in the Soviet Union or Serbs in Yugoslavia, they may be in a position to exploit the others, or are perceived to do so. A second factor is the depth of differences. Languages of Soviet minorities are mostly quite different from Russian; the cultural tradition of peoples of the Caucasus and Central Asia is wholly alien to the Muscovites; many peoples, especially of the Western areas, feel that they are more European and superior to the

---

[31]*The Economist,* November 19, 1988, p. 51.
[32]Marshall J. Goldman, "Perestroika in the Soviet Union," *Current History* 87, October 1988, p. 316.

half-Asian Russians. Moreover, with few exceptions the non-Russian peoples did not elect to come under the wing of imperial Russia, just as East European nations did not elect to become satellites of Stalin. All of them have or can find countless reasons to complain of their treatment since Lenin, who was the last Soviet leader before Gorbachev to pay much attention to the feelings of the non-Russians. These handicaps might be overcome if the federal union were advantageous economically, but for a long time the Soviet economy seems likely to remain something a nation would prefer not to be a part of.

Prima facie, the Soviet Union is ungovernable. Finding means of managing it other than sheer force must be difficult at best. To permit free expression means permitting agitation and intensification of the minorities' sense of grievances. To give them political rights is to give them the means of demanding ever more. A democratic Soviet parliament, like a democratic parliament in many Third World countries, would invite a tumult of bitterly opposed groups. It would be the worse because in the socialist system everything is politicized. Reform and reshaping the economy would seem to require considerable freedom and democratization; freedom and democratization imply chaos and immobility, if not the breakup of the union.

Nonetheless, it is not impossible that the leadership can overcome accumulated ill will and make a federal structure sufficiently attractive to reconcile the nationalists to remaining tied to Moscow. It is not necessary to persuade minorities that they should join the Soviet brotherhood, only to make it impractical for them to cut themselves away from it. The Soviet Union represents power in place, with multiple levers of control and many advantages for the center. For example, it is difficult for Estonia, with population of about 1.5 million, to compete with the quality of national television. The Estonian economy, like that of all other republics, has been highly integrated into that of the Soviet Union; reorientation would be costly. Moscow does not need to use troops to coerce when it can exert pressure by simply raising the price of raw materials.

At best, the nationality problem places severe limits on the degree of political freedom that the Soviet Union can digest. In this regard, the Soviet realm is not different from many countries torn between the need for democracy and the difficulty of managing it. Perhaps the Soviet communist party can do as well as the Mexican ruling party, which maintained for 60 years an effective monopoly with democratic forms. India is a better example; it shows how a relatively slack and poorly organized party (Congress-I) can permit rather full freedoms and opposition parties without surrendering its overall leadership. It presides effectively over an extremely divided society, many Indian states being under non-Congress governments. With able and well-motivated leadership, the Soviet Union may be able to do as well. Success also depends partly on the political climate; an atmosphere of relaxation with a much reduced military burden would make the task of controlled change much easier.

Other states in the Soviet pattern face somewhat different problems in the search for viable institutions. China is less modernized than the Soviet Union, less educated, and more imbued with its own deeply authoritarian civilization; it seems to find economic reform easier but political reform more difficult. In China there is a near-balance between liberalizers, who would separate party and state functions, and conservatives, who are fearful of loss of control. The latter see basic food production neglected in favor of more profitable crops and protest the inflation that has come from removal of controls on most prices. They see market forces in publication bringing social dissolution, playing on obscenity, superstition, and immorality, all contrary either to "socialism" or to traditional values.

Passion for criticism is much less than in the Soviet Union, partly because the Chinese have more tradition of passivity, partly because Mao's errors did not approach Stalin's atrocities. Revulsion is much milder; the image of Mao is only slowly disappearing from public places. However, in the relaxation and openness to private enterprise, there is a little latitude for criticism. There is some openness after the extreme hermeticism of Mao's rule, when meetings of the party congresses were so secret that it was not known publicly that there had been a session until afterwards. Now there are dissenting voices and votes, even against nominees for top positions;[33] But "Democracy Wall," which was opened in 1978 to permit free expression by posters, was soon closed down: its purpose was to criticize the leftovers of the Maoist era, not to needle Deng Xiaoping. There is no freedom to question the wisdom of the party, and decisions are still made entirely in private.

As in the Soviet Union, there is no suggestion that the party might share political authority with any outside organization. For the Chinese, democracy is not so much freedom of opposition as the union of people and government. They do not ask that the people choose the officials but that the officials pay attention to the people. It seems, however, that the officials pay most attention to themselves; corruption, in the absence of any strong sense of direction, is said to be everywhere.

The ruling sectors in China and the Soviet Union can move in the direction of democracy if this seems necessary and desirable because the state enjoys a reasonable degree of legitimacy (except so far as Soviet minority nationalities reject central domination). Communist rule does not represent an alien imposition. For such countries as Poland, East Germany, Czechoslovakia, and Romania the contrary is the case, and the dilemma is more acute. Their governments are no longer seen as puppets, but they no longer have the excuse that they must repress dissent because Moscow

[33]*New York Times,* January 31, 1988, p. E-2.

demands it. They are still essentially antinational and contrary to traditional values. With no real claim to an ideal mission, the governments' only title to power is that they possess the state apparatus. They become much like Third World dictatorships; and as illegitimate dictatorships in the heart of Europe, they can only make delaying maneuvers.

It should not be forgotten, however, that authoritarianism has by no means lost effectiveness today. Whatever the neglect of material amenities, it may show excellent results in areas of its priorities, setting aside individual needs or wishes in favor of the works of the community. The athletic excellence of rigidly communist countries, especially East Germany, Romania, and Cuba, is familiar. East European singers, musicians, and circus artists as well as sports stars, train harder than most Westerners for more modest rewards; and they perform very well. The Soviets excel in military production (doing better in production of matériel than in management and motivation of personnel). The Soviet space program, closely tied to the military, achieves on that glamorous frontier much more for less cost than the American program, although much of Soviet technology is a decade or more behind.

The broad political movement seen as the democratic mode in much of the world is not so much for popular democracy as for more workable modern government. The state can well retain its prerogative to give technical direction of society, uphold the community purpose, keep the economy in order, and foster growth and technological change. It can impose a certain discipline and provide leadership for public morality and general community purpose. It is desirable for any state to give a sense of participation, provide outlets for antagonisms, encourage outside inputs to decision-making, and allow criticism of authorities. But there is no question of the elite's turning over effective guidance of affairs to outsiders. The mode is for elements and appearances of democracy, for quasi-democracy. This is not people-rule but a polity that pays attention to popular desires, places limits on arbitrary actions, and allows reasonable freedom of information for the benefit of the state as well as the people.

This is true not only of countries of the Soviet model but also of many countries of the Third World that have moved toward democracy, especially former military dictatorships of Latin America. That such countries, in which a small minority have traditionally held nearly all economic and political power, should rapidly become genuinely democratic by virtue of holding elections is an illusion. But they are more open and probably have better growth prospects than under dictatorship.

The compromise of authoritarian reality with elements of democracy, in one variant or another, can produce a workable modern government. Singapore has shown a phenomenal growth rate while having strictly controlled elections, an official monopoly of the media, and extensive regulation of citizens' lives. A strong commitment to capitalist development and export orientation does not mean that the masses are invited to decide anything of consequence. To the contrary, the ruling Singaporese seem to feel that real democracy would introduce uncertainties hurtful for business confidence. Taiwan edges carefully toward a more open political system, yielding by degrees enough to defuse most of the potential opposition of the Taiwanese to the mainlanders, but at a pace not likely to lead to a popular democracy for many years.

The steady Japanese rise in the postwar period possibly owes much to the fact that a single party, closely linked with the highly qualified bureaucracy, has been in charge. The government has been subject to periodic accountability to the voters, and it has maintained a high degree of competitiveness in the economy. But the contest for power has been basically contained within the ruling sector, and government and business have worked together to advance productivity.

The semitotalitarian Marxist-Leninist systems start from quite different conditions and are under somewhat different pressures; how they can evolve is one of the most critical questions of world order. Neither the Chinese nor the Soviets seem to have a clear idea of the goal of reforms, of a state to replace the tight party-run regime of these many decades. They are venturing into new terrain, and much depends on what they are able to construct. Concessions made in timely and controlled fashion, like reforms in China and the Soviet Union, may make party rule more acceptable. One can hardly guess whether they may foster the growth of stronger independent sentiments in the longer run or find an acceptable compromise.

Without becoming a Western-style democracy, the Soviet-style state can move in the direction of Hungary, toward a general relaxation of controls; or in that of Poland, toward military rule with acceptance of considerable independence of citizens; or in that of Yugoslavia, toward a sort of federal compromise; or, of course, in a mixture of two or more of these. Of these, none is encouraging. The best, the Hungarian example, is darkened by gross inefficiency, declining health standards, and reemerging poverty.[34] The Polish government is half at war with its people, and Yugoslavia is bogged down in ethnic division complicated by bureaucratic regulation. The Soviet Union, whatever its course, cannot come closely to resemble a Western power in the near future; it will continue to be a different society with different strengths and weaknesses.

Some of the change will be more form than substance. Russians have long been more tolerant of pretense than Americans, and the Potemkin village is a work of the Russian genius.[35] But the Soviet Union of Gorbachev

---

[34]George Schöpflin, Rudolf Tökés, and Ivan Völgyes, "Leadership Change and Crisis in Hungary," *Problems of Communism* 37, September–October 1988, pp. 23–28.

[35]Hingley, *Russian Mind*, pp. 90–104; Jerome D. Frank, *Sanity and Survival: Psychological Aspects of War and Peace* (New York: Random House, 1967), pp. 106–7.

differs importantly not only from that of Stalin but from that of Brezhnev, just as the nondemocratic China of Deng is far from that of Mao and is more promising for the well-being of the Chinese people, although formally it is ruled in about the same way. Without censorship, an obligatory ideology, and fully centralized economic management, the state is no longer communist in the old way.

Although less at odds with the modern world, the Soviet party will continue to be the heir of its past. But it is easy to forget how far the Soviet state has moved since Stalin's government by terror, which relied on constant fear to make blind obedience. The extent of change in China since 1976 and in the Soviet Union since 1985 has exceeded any reasonable expectation.

Weakening Antagonism

The competition of the cold war was intense because it combined the question of power and the question of political philosophy. The Soviet Union feared, or claimed to fear, that its great class enemy, the United States, was trying to master the globe and might turn on the countries, the Soviet Union and its friends, that resisted its sway. The United States saw the Soviet Union as binding more and more peoples—a big chunk of humanity when China seemed to be a close ally—into a closed and aggressive power bloc with limitless ambitions. The danger was magnified because the enemy represented a hateful antithetical political philosophy, submission to which would be a tremendous and irreparable tragedy.

In both these aspects, the conflict has tended to subside since the beginning of the cold war around 1947. The division of Europe became fixed and was hardly at issue after 1955. The outcome of the Korean war seemed to indicate the same of East Asia. The split of China from the Soviet camp at the beginning of the 1960s made the communist threat seem less apocalyptic to the United States and hopes of world victory much more distant to the Russians. It appeared at first that the newly independent countries coming out of the breakup of colonial empires in the 1960s might go in either direction. It is not very long since Nikita Khrushchev was pointing to the growing "camp of peace" under the Soviet aegis as proof that the future belonged to "socialism;" and the United States was worried that he might be right. But only a few unimportant countries were lured to the Soviet side.

The Cuban missile crisis of 1962 was the last really acute confrontation of the superpowers. The United States fell into a costly and prolonged engagement in Vietnam, which it professed to see as part of the bipolar struggle; but it was remarkably insulated from the potentially more dangerous U.S.-Soviet antithesis. The rivalry became less intense; the United States did not pay much heed as the Soviets gained positions in Africa, mostly as a result of the effort of Portugal to hold its empire by force. The American preoccupation with Marxism-Leninism in Nicaragua and El Salvador in the 1980s was only a feeble echo of the stiffer contests of the 1950s and 1960s and seemed to be generated more by personal antagonism than antisovietism.

The United States does not seem to hope for geopolitical gain from Soviet problems in Eastern Europe, and the Soviets are not visibly much interested in trying to extend their sway anywhere. No modern country and no democracy is a subject of superpower contention; and the troubles of Third World countries in recent years seem to have taught even the more optimistic that there is little to be gained by intervention in them.

The ideological confrontation has also eased during several decades. Revolutions are events, not permanent conditions; and the rationale of the Leninist revolution has been long outdated. The fundamental idea of the Marxist philosophy on which the Soviet Union was theoretically based, class conflict growing into proletarian revolution, may have seemed to have some validity when Marx formulated it in mid 19th century; but it was outmoded for the West by the time Lenin made it the rationalization of a radical coup in 1917. Lenin's notion of a special right of factory workers, who are usually a small minority, to govern all (through the self-appointed agency of the communist party) in the name of their historical destiny might have been slightly relevant for coal-and-iron industrialization, but it has become more and more hollow ever since the Bolsheviks pretended to apply it. It would be more rational to give the honor to the service workers, who are much more numerous in the modern economy. Or the computer-feeders might more realistically than the coalminers or steelworkers claim to be the vanguard of history. Since Marx wrote well over a century ago, there has never been a revolution remotely resembling what he postulated as the goal of history. In fact, there has been no revolution in any even moderately advanced country except as the result of defeat in war.

The infant Bolshevik government thought that it could overturn capitalism in the West by passing out incendiary pamphlets. But the very idea of revolution, the intoxication of the making of a new society, coming down from the American and even more from the socially more radical French revolution, has wilted. It belongs to the repressed classes of the traditional society and to the intellectuals who feel for them, to those who hope to build a new society of pure justice on the wreckage of the old. Life is already being revolutionized by technology, and we know of the future only that it is likely to be tumultuous. The idea of turning society upside down to save its soul has become farfetched. The democratic society is in any case much more open to change than the monopolistic party system. It is ironic that the chief Soviet excellence, military strength, was not in the revolutionary canon.

The Russian revolution maintained some force and appeal only so far as it fortified its claim of worldly salvation with evidence of material success or military victory. But its impetus has been declining since shortly after the Second World War, when the United States undertook to halt its expansionism by "containment." For a decade or more, the Soviet state has been on the defensive, ideologically and politically.

Not only the revolution but the great war is far behind, and the Soviet people take both stability of the social order and peace for granted. Not only has the dogmatism of Marxism withered; the old Russian messianism seems to have gone. For centuries, Russia saw itself as something like the center of the universe, destined to redeem mankind, an idea that suited the stupendous territorial expansion of Russia and its relative isolation. The Russia of the tsars was not a country but a faith, as it should be in the spirit of Leninism.[36] A new reality has ground away the faith.

As long as Russia-Soviet Union was growing more powerful, a policy of strength made sense. But it lost meaning when shrinking resources could no longer support it. Expansionism has ceased to be rewarding, and it is no longer a privilege for Russians to stand over a host of lesser nationalities. The old ethnocentrism seems moribund as upper-level Russians crowd the visa offices of the American embassy, the weary slogans are ignored, and the land is flooded with messages of the materially superior outside world. It is a mark of change that the great Soviet Union asked, welcomed and gave thanks for assistance from a host of onetime class-enemy capitalist states after the Armenian earthquake of December 1988. The revolution, too, ceases to be the dawn of a new age and becomes an event of history; tsarist aristocrats can publish their memoirs in Soviet journals.[37]

The old Russian authoritarian, or autocratic pattern, which was refurbished and modernized by Lenin, is worn out, like authoritarianism in all advanced countries. It was based on the rulership of a large number of smaller and weaker nationalities; tsarist Russia, like the Soviet Union, was an essentially military multinational empire. But the reforms of General Secretary Gorbachev amount to a recognition that total rulership is no longer sustainable. Sustaining Soviet purposes requires compromising Soviet principles. This is fortunate: if modern weaponry is inordinately destructive, it also requires high technical sophistication, to achieve which the mobilizational system must partly demobilize itself. Modern civilization is viable only because, in order to keep abreast technologically, a power must open its system and liberalize, if not ultimately democratize its structures.

[36]Robert Wesson, *The Russian Dilemma* rev. ed. (New York: Praeger, 1986), pp. 9–13.
[37]*New York Times*, November 11, 1987, p. 1.

Like it or not, Soviet leaders admire the United States; and they no longer hope to overthrow it but to come alongside it. The Soviets have never been able to gain recognition as equals of the real superpower; the nearest they have come was with the Nixon-Brezhnev Basic Principles Agreement of 1972. They are chagrined not to be able to participate fully in all international questions.

Although it maintains airs of socialistic progressivism, the Soviet Union, as a settled authoritarian power, is inherently conservative. The Soviets seem to feel more kinship with politically center-rightist West Germany than with any other Western power, and they have turned from courting the German Left to smiling on the Right—with much success. In 1988 they preferred the more conservative American candidate for the presidency.

In Stalin's time, Soviet envoys were rude and reclusive. From Khrushchev's day they began to learn better manners and became more effective, but until the days of *glasnost* they seemed to think it more important not to divulge anything than to make a good impression. Gorbachev and his cohorts gave an example of how to use the media, with skill like that of experienced American practitioners. Freeing dissidents, permitting open discussion and criticism, getting away from paranoid secrecy, moving toward political and economic reform, and calling for cooperation instead of hostility between the great powers gave Gorbachev high popularity ratings around the world.

If ideology was once important in building up animosity between the United States and the Soviet Union, its downgrading marks the end of an epoch. In 1988, the new chief ideologist, Vadim Medvedev, called for a new and flexible concept of socialism, with borrowings from capitalism and an economy based on supply and demand.[38] Soviet writers argue for retrenchment and abandonment of unpopular regimes and movements,[39] and underline interdependence of nations and cooperation in the solution of common problems. Gorbachev, although maintaining the sacredness of 1917, has come close to saying that the whole course of Soviet development has been wrong, admitting that troubles come from within, not from an alien enemy. "Today we face a different world."[40] He told the United Nations, "The new phase also requires deideologizing relations among states. We are not abandoning our convictions, our philosophy or traditions, nor do we urge anybody to abandon theirs . . . let everyone show the advantages of their social system, way of life or values . . . That would be a fair rivalry of ideologies. But it should not be extended to relations among states." Lenin's

---

[38]*New York Times*, October 6, 1988, p. 1.

[39]Alexei Izunov and Andrei Kortunov, "The U.S.S.R. in the World," *International Affairs* 1988 no. 8 (August), p. 54.

[40]*New York Times*, December 9, 1988, p. A7.

mummy should have squirmed when he called for a "world community of states based on the rule of law," ensuring the rights of the individual, and renounced the basis of the communist party's claim to power: "We are, of course, far from claiming to be in possession of the ultimate truth."[41]

Distrust for the Soviet Union has naturally run deeper in the United States than in any other major country, as the leader of the Western world has taken on—sometimes seemed to enjoy—the responsibility of opposing Soviet power and influence. The cold war is the profession of many, and they are not easily convinced that their profession is obsolete. But attitudes change, often quickly. Americans are probably more curious about the Soviet Union than about any other nation, and vice versa. In 1940–1941, when Stalin was trying to crush Finland, the United States detested no power more than the Soviets. But after the American entry into the war, the Russian soldiers battling the Nazis became heroes, and Stalin was seen as a genial fellow, probably a democrat at heart. The turnaround to cold war again was rapid, as the Soviet Union was transformed in two years from ally to a menace to world order. The reverse turning has also been rapid; by the end of 1988 Americans were so impressed with Gorbachev's message of cooperation instead of conflict that he was rated the second most popular person in the United States, following President Reagan but ahead of President-elect Bush and the pope. That the American administration at the end of 1988 accepted in principle the long-standing Soviet proposal for a conference on human rights in Moscow shows a remarkable change of attitude.

The example of China is instructive. A generation ago that power, which is considerably more alien in tradition to the United States than is the Soviet Union, was excoriating its Soviet ally as bourgeois and weak-kneed; the Maoists shouted for revolution at home and abroad, calling for sharing of nearly everything in "People's Communes" and smashing oppression throughout the world. They ranted ferociously against "American imperialism." The U.S. administration seemed to regard the "Chicoms" with much more bitterness than the more subdued communists of Moscow. Potential Chinese domination of Southeast Asia was a major justification for war in Vietnam. But Nixon's 1972 opening to China was generally welcomed, and since then relations between the United States and China have warmed to reasonable cordiality. There remains some potential for misunderstanding, as the values of a still essentially closed society and an open society differ; but both sides see the utility of cooperation.

The cold war was mostly the responsibility of the Soviets, at least in the sense that they could bring it to an end by desisting from supporting subversion and eschewing a threatening military stance. The United States for its part never demanded that the Soviet Union do anything contrary to

[41]*New York Times*, December 8, 1988, p. A6.

the material well-being of its people. It rather urged that the Soviet leadership adopt roughly the policies espoused by the Gorbachev semirevolution, or counterrevolution.

If political differences diminish, economic cooperation advances; and the Soviets become increasingly dependent on foreign trade, investment, and ideas. The Soviet Union through the 1970s was the world's second economic power; in the 1980s it has fallen to third place and faces the likelihood of being surpassed by China. No longer an economic rival, the Soviet Union remains a trading partner, buyer of agricultural products (especially grain) and capital equipment and an attractive field for investment.

The cold war was a time of problems and dangers. They are replaced by less dramatic problems and more insidious dangers.

Chapter 8

Friendly Relations

Complex Relations

It is a gross oversimplification to deal with international affairs as though they consisted of the dealings of abstract entities called "nations" with one another as individuals. Relations of governments and peoples are inseparable, and their interactions are increasingly in matters such as trade, capital movements and exchange rates, communications, economic development, propaganda or enlightenment, publications, information, travel, disease control, drug trafficking, terrorism, legal and illegal migration, and environmental problems. Except at the time to pay taxes, such matters have more impact on most people's lives than what carries the aura of "high" or power politics. Many things also have more long-term effect on the strength of the nation and its ability to compete in the world than the complications of deterrence, alliance, and influence.

Even State Department officials in Washington and in the field spend most of their time on unexciting matters such as visas, passports, arranging visits, commercial formalities, and economic and cultural relations; and seventy percent of U.S. government personnel abroad are non-State Department. The Departments of Commerce, Treasury, Agriculture, and Labor represent the interests abroad of business, finance, farmers, and workers. Agencies to a total approaching 40—including Justice, Housing and Urban

Development, Health and Human Services, along with others from the CIA through the Agency for International Development, Drug Enforcement Agency, Federal Aviation Administration, United States Information Agency, and so forth—carry on their own activities, sometimes virtually their own foreign policies, around the globe. Such splitting of foreign activities is common in other countries as well. For example, the Japanese Ministry of International Trade and Industry (MITI) is almost a rival foreign ministry.[1]

There are official and unofficial dealings, moreover, not only with other governments but also with hundreds of organizations, from the United Nations to charitable foundations. States of the United States have foreign offices and send missions, mostly to lure investments. Cities have "sister-cities" abroad, many of them in the Soviet Union or China, mostly for cultural exchanges. Or they may take a stand against administration policy by friendly gestures toward the government of Nicaragua or pronounce themselves by referendum on nuclear policy. In 1988 Texan authorities consulted with OPEC about raising the price of oil, contrary to the interests of the U.S. government.

In a sense, most of the foreign relations of a pluralistic society are carried on by private persons and enterprises, sometimes coordinated with official policy but much more often on their own and serving their own purposes. Relations of one complex and open society with another include not only trade and financial operations but activities of professional organizations, groups devoted to causes, visitors and tourists, movement of students, study of one country by persons of the other, cultural exchanges, and religious activities.[2] So far as force becomes less relevant in international affairs, the role of non-state actors rises.

Such matters are mostly unnoticed and nonpolitical. In the rivalry of power, issues are usually inseparably linked; in the pacific relations of pluralistic nations, issues are usually independent. There may be linkage, because, for example, bad political relations deter trade, as between the United States and Romania. Nonpolitical relations between American and Soviet citizens are hostage to the political background. Dozens of joint U.S.-Soviet projects in fields such as medicine and science languish or flourish when relations are chill or warm. Even between friendly powers, politics sometimes get in the way of business or vice versa. In 1971, friction over Japanese textile exports led Nixon to snub the Japanese by declining to consult them before his dramatic opening to communist China.[3]

---

[1]R.P. Barston, *Modern Diplomacy* (New York: Longman, 1988), p. 21.

[2]As noted for India by Norman D. Palmer, *The United States and India: The Dimensions of Influence* (New York: Praeger, 1984), p. 245.

[3]Chae-jin Lee and Hideo Sato, *U.S. Policy toward Japan and Korea: A Changing Influence Relationship* (New York: Praeger, 1982), p. 188.

Such linkage is unusual between friendly countries, however. Canada does not overtly tie discussions of acid rain across the border or questions of industrial subsidies to its cooperation in missile defense; the disparate matters come together only in broad attitudes of willingness to collaborate. Economic frictions between the United States and Japan do not interfere with close military-political collaboration. On the other hand, the United States presses hard in trade questions against politically very friendly countries, South Korea and Taiwan. In economic bargaining, the importance of political strength is doubtful.[4]

Economic issues are likely to be linked with political in dealings with governments that closely control the economy. For example, trade concessions for the Soviet Union are made contingent on observance of human rights, especially freedom of emigration (by congressional insistence, contrary to the wishes of the executive). Japanese cooperation in the development of Siberia is conditioned on settlement of Japanese demands for the small islands north of Hokkaido occupied by the Soviets. Anger at the Soviet invasion of Afghanistan kept the United States from participating in the Moscow Olympic Games of 1980, and the Soviets in reprisal boycotted the 1984 Los Angeles Games. It also led the United States to decree an embargo on grain sales to the Soviets, although this was rescinded in little more than a year, not because of the illogic of trying to impoverish the Soviet diet as punishment for the sin of the government but because it hurt American farmers. However, politics does not stand in the way of cooperation where interests strongly coincide. For example, the cold war did not keep the United States and the Soviet Union from joining to check nuclear proliferation, for example, or to demand freedom of navigation for their navies in opposition to Third World demands regarding law of the sea.

A fundamental difference of nonsecurity from security affairs is that the former, unlike the win-lose or lose-lose games of power, are of mutual benefit. No country is compelled to belong to an international organization or to permit trade or to allow sports teams to leave or enter its territory. Whatever is done in such matters must be agreeable to all parties.

For the most part, nonpolitical relations reduce political asperities. This is sometimes their purpose; for example, groups arranging citizen exchanges between the United States and the Soviet Union feel that they are contributing to goodwill, peace, and disarmament. Political effects are usually, however, an unintended by-product. The mere fact that many people become personally acquainted across political lines and find each other human has some effect on national policy. Those engaged in sundry foreign business, from tourism to trade to scientific exchanges, are impatient with political interference. Desire for gain erodes political prejudices; commerce

---

[4]Robert O. Keohane and Joseph S. Nye, *Power and Interdependence* (Boston: Little Brown, 1977), pp. 207–8.

is open and tolerant. South Korea, not long ago anathema to the Soviet bloc and China, has gained acceptance by the importance of its trade; China buys more than twice as much from it as from North Korea.

On the other hand, it sometimes seems that trade between the United States and Japan is an irritant, even as it creates mutual dependence. Nations are, of course, competitors as well as partners. But the competition is seldom sufficiently acute to cause much ill will; and if nonpolitical relations are sometimes contentious, they are likely to have diverse and balancing effects. If some are hurt by imports from Japan, larger numbers profit. Moreover, good business diminishes political antagonisms; attractiveness of the Soviet market makes Soviet power somewhat less menacing.

Modern Diplomacy

The diplomats empowered to meet regularly with foreign authorities have lost much of the importance they had when they were the chief means of communication among powers; their autonomy and responsibility in negotiations have nearly disappeared. But personal representatives are still their government's principal source of information about the world. The Department of State, for example, receives more than a million dispatches per year. There are more than a thousand personnel at U.S. embassies in major capitals such as Bonn (with the largest staff), London, Rome, Paris, Mexico City, and Cairo (because of big aid programs). Career foreign service officers are the professionals of foreign affairs; roughly 4,000 are stationed abroad. Diplomacy is important in terms of human contacts; there are some 35,000 foreign diplomats in New York City alone.[5]

Diplomats symbolize the nation abroad; wooden or suave, adept or naive, they still do much to make or unmake relations. Although dramatic affairs of state have been taken away from them, ambassadors preside over a wide range of activities, supervising all government personnel stationed in the country. They inform their hosts and settle many minor conflicts. The personalities of the ambassador and his aides contribute to the understanding of needs and attitudes; they convey the outlook and philosophy of their country and government better than any written communication.[6]

Diplomatic representation between such friendly countries as the United States and Canada, is likely to be mostly a matter of formalities, social affairs, and routine business. The American ambassador to a Third World country, on the contrary, is frequently a powerful figure; in some

[5]*New York Times*, May 9, 1988, p. A–14.

[6]For a general treatment, see R.P. Barston, *Modern Diplomacy* (New York: Longman, 1988); Hedley Bull, *The Anarchical Society* (New York: Columbia University Press, 1977), pp. 162–83.

cases, as in Central America, he has been a proconsul. The respective ambassadors do much to set the tone of relations between the United States and the Soviet Union. Diplomats also work in and with international organizations; the position of the American ambassador to the United Nations is sometimes treated as cabinet-level.[7]

Diplomacy contributes to peace and good relations, and it is a poor idea to seek to isolate regimes. For some years after the revolution, the young Soviet state was ostracized by the powers; the apparent result was the narrowing of Soviet mentality in its formative years. A number of countries, including most of those of Central America and of the Arab Near East, shun relations with the Soviets to this day, with the encouragement of the United States.

The Federal Republic of Germany for decades after WW II not only boycotted the German Democratic Republic but also did its best to prevent diplomatic relations between East Germany and nations outside the Soviet bloc. But in 1969, under Willy Brandt, the Federal Republic reversed its policy and worked to open and expand relations with the East; in 1972 it recognized the government it had so strained to prevent other governments from recognizing. Since then, it has gone to considerable expense to build bridges, seeking with some success to enmesh the government of East Germany in a cooperative network. Similarly, the South Korean government endeavored by all means to isolate North Korea from the end of the war until 1988, when the more democratic leadership of Roh Tae Woo, expressing confidence in its economic and military strength, decided it was better to seek broad ties and to help bring the North into the international community.[8] At the request of the South Koreans, the United States in 1988 slightly relaxed its prohibition of trade with North Korea. It is possible that the United States would do more to reduce terrorism by encouraging relations with Libya and between Libya and conservative Arab states than by trying to bar them.

Some small nations are prepared to sacrifice the advantages of diplomatic relations for the satisfactions of ideological self-assertion against the United States. Albania, Iran, and South Yemen have made that choice. It is fairly understandable that they wish to avoid contamination; it is less logical that the United States would negate its influence by refusing relations with unsavory regimes. In the cases of Cuba, Angola, Mozambique, Vietnam, and North Korea, it is the United States that rejects formal relations. But the prospect of diplomatic relations is used, rather vaguely, as an incentive; for example, the United States hints that formal relations with Vietnam could follow withdrawal of Vietnamese forces from Kampuchea. The Soviet

---

[7]On diplomatic maneuvering, see Paul Gorden Lauren, ed., *Diplomacy: New Approaches in History, Theory, and Policy* (New York: Free Press, 1979).

[8]*New York Times,* July 7, 1988, pp. 1, 5.

Union is readier to have its representatives in any capital that will receive them. The United States ended its influence in Vietnam by cutting off contacts with the communist victors; the Soviet Union seeks to maintain standing in Afghanistan, where it is much more disliked than the United States ever was in Vietnam, by dealing with Afghan guerrilla leaders.

To some degree, diplomacy remains what it has traditionally been, a very prestigious occupation, dominated by an elite. The foreign services of most advanced industrial countries are a branch of the professional civil service, usually requiring training in special schools and high qualifications. Some 50 nations have academies for the preparation of diplomats like those for army officers.[9] In some countries, foreign service professionals become top level advisers; longtime Soviet ambassador to the United States, Anatoly Dobrynin, for example, became one of the chief counsellors to General Secretary Gorbachev. Third World nations, not expecting their envoys to accomplish much in any case, often send inconvenient persons into dignified exile as consuls or attachés.

It has long been an American custom to appoint amateur ambassadors for political reasons, especially to elegant posts, such as London or Rome—career foreign services officers can go to Guinea or Paraguay. Recently about half of U.S. ambassadors have been noncareer. Formerly an ambassadorship was commonly the reward for a large campaign contribution, but this consideration has been eliminated by the limit ($1,000 per person) on gifts to presidential candidates, and the principal qualification for noncareer envoys has become political zeal. Nonprofessional diplomats may be very effective, but they frequently are not, and they reflect something of the abiding American casualness toward foreign relations. The president also frequently names a personal envoy to deal with special problems, such as conflict in Central America or the Near East.[10]

Closely related to conventional diplomacy is the ceremonious visitation of influential persons. Meetings of high-ranking leaders seem usually to have positive results. They are mostly enjoyable, as important people journey here and there, intersperse their meetings with golf or sightseeing, and are treated as befits their rank. Not only is what the high personalities tell each other about their views important, but also the much publicized social interaction and the atmosphere of friendly get-together make for good feelings. People are likely to take a more kindly view of those by whom they have been graciously entertained, just as in Arab custom it was held improper to murder a man with whom one had broken bread. Rather frequent travels of Indian prime ministers to Moscow and of Soviet general secretaries to New Delhi have done much to promote cordiality between the

---

[9]Barston, *Modern Diplomacy*, p. 251.

[10]On the diplomatic profession, see Martin Neyer, *The Diplomats* (Garden City NY: Doubleday & Co., 1983).

two countries. Influential non-heads of state are also pleased to be invited to meet and discuss with the chiefs of a great power. A visit to Moscow by Franz Josef Strauss, once perhaps the strongest of West Germany's hard-line exponents of anti-Sovietism, was a Soviet triumph.[11]

In earlier generations, state visits were a function of monarchs. The crowned heads of European states all knew each other well, and many of them were related. In 1903 Edward VII did much to cement British-French relations by his amiability in Paris. As late as the beginning of this century, German Kaiser Wilhelm II thought that by getting together with his cousin, Tsar Nicholas II, he could restore good relations between their countries despite membership in opposing alliances. The agreement they signed had to be undone by ministers more cognizant of their obligations or more settled in their prejudices.

Modern leaders meet far more frequently because of the ease and rapidity of travel and the fact that they can remain in close contact with the home office wherever they may jet. Personal meetings and top-level discussions also have the advantage of putting foreign affairs closely in the hands of the chiefs and backstaging everyone else. Becoming personally acquainted, they can speak of fellow heads of state as "my friend;" and they learn to think of both allies and antagonists as people with problems and weaknesses as well as strengths. Chemistry of personality does a great deal; how the British prime minister or the American president takes to the Soviet general secretary can make a real difference in the way their governments treat one another. Good feeling between Ronald Reagan and Margaret Thatcher did much to keep the U.S.-British relation special. On the other hand, if the American chief has an antipathy for a certain dictator, this becomes a sort of ideological commitment to his destruction.

Many conflicts can be solved by skill and will; and negotiation is still an uncertain art, especially when the two sides do not understand each other well. If it had occurred to Carter to let Brezhnev know how he would react to the invasion of Afghanistan, when the United States was aware that something like this was in prospect, it might not have occurred; and the history of U.S.-Soviet relations would have been different.[12]

The acme of diplomacy is the get-together of heads of state, or summit, of the superpowers. Such a meeting of American president and Soviet general secretary is much inflated in the age of image and is commonly viewed as a climactic negotiating session, at which weighty issues are to be decided. But decisions have to be based on negotiations carried on patiently by delegates in advance. If the chiefs strike out on their own—as when, at Reykjavik in 1986, they subscribed to unprepared disarmament ideas—the result is embarrassment. The great issue at the summit is how the principals impress

---

[11]*New York Times,* December 28, 1987, p. 7.
[12]Thomas T. Hammond, *Red Flag over Afghanistan* (Boulder CO: Westview, 1984) p. 124.

one another. The visitor is engaged in a huge public relations display; so far as successful, he achieves on a larger scale over a few days approximately what the ambassador should on a much smaller scale over a longer period. He learns from direct contact about important people in the host country, and he presents an image of his government. The heads of state are ordinarily tactful, those to whom they speak are usually hospitable, and feelings between the two powers are warmed in the euphoria of mostly avoiding tough issues and stressing the positive, joking and feasting together as well as exchanging bargaining statements.

The effects of getting personally acquainted may be negative, as when in 1961 Nikita Khrushchev tried to bully, or at least antagonized, the young new American president, John Kennedy, fresh from the humiliation of the Bay of Pigs. But usually personal encounters tend to soften differences, ideological and national, and contribute to easing of attitudes. Feelings of President Reagan were clearly modified by his several meetings with General Secretary Gorbachev, which played a major part in softening the posture of his administration toward the power he had set out to combat energetically. Gorbachev also probably enlarged his ideas about the United States and gained confidence in his ideas for reform.

The summit meeting is also a vehicle for many subsidiary interchanges. It gives each side unaccustomed access to the media of the other. Hundreds of those accompanying the chief find an opportunity to meet and perhaps deal with persons and organizations of the host country; it is a small scale peaceful invasion. Each side also has its best opportunity to present its views in a favorable context; people at least listen politely to their guests. The United States has big advantages as an international host, with an abundance of interesting persons to meet and from whom to get the most diverse views; and New York is well ahead of Moscow as a shopping center. The euphoria of the summit fades in a few weeks, as old problems and conflicting viewpoints reemerge; but regular summits might make the world less dangerous.

In the pluralistic society, many nondiplomats act in one way or another as representatives of their country. For example, since the American Congress is responsible for appropriating the funds needed to carry on any foreign activity, its members, especially but not only those of relevant committees, take an active interest and may practically carry on negotiations. If the president needs backing for an agreement, he is well advised to consult congressional leaders in advance, perhaps to include them in discussions. Foreign rulers may use contacts with senators or representatives to push their desires, and legislators may step into a gap left by the executive. For example, when the White House declined negotiations with the Sandinista government of Nicaragua, Speaker James Wright of the House of Representatives became for a time its chief contact with the American government. Congressional travellers go to countries, such as the Philippines, El Salvador, or the Soviet Union, talk with leaders, and come home with recommendations. Such activities can be combined with interesting travel.

Traditional diplomacy has tended to recede, but the personal meetings of representatives and dignitaries of different states will continue to do much to set the tone of relations between powers.

Image-Making

Governments endeavor systematically to promote their views and image; speaking over the heads of other governments, they try to gain the admiration or affection of foreign peoples. Official self-advertising was once considered unseemly; but since the world wars raised political stakes and passions, propaganda, as it is somewhat pejoratively called, has become a major undertaking.

Important states want not only to convince others of the rightness of their ways and policies but also to give the world the benefit of their cultures, in a sort of gentle imperialism. Hence they have large and multiform foreign information programs, whether from pride in the national achievements, which may be the chief motivation of Germany and France, or to make a favorable impression on customers, a purpose that seems to influence the Japanese.

The Soviet Union has the biggest program of all, including more hours of broadcasting to the world than any other nation, cheap books and magazines, and free travel to the land of the Soviets. A huge Festival of the Soviet Union in New Delhi (in exchange for an earlier Festival of India in Moscow) brought 1,400 Soviet circus artists, dancers, musicians, and other performers under banners proclaiming Soviet-Indian friendship.[13] Ballet troupes, especially the celebrated Bolshoi, display their graceful beauty to hundreds of thousands of nonproletarians in many lands. The Moscow Circus delights and amazes multitudes; in 1987 it helped the Nicaraguans briefly forget their material misery. Glossy Soviet magazines in English and other major languages, distributed at low cost, give a glowing image of Soviet life and invite people to Intourist offices. Soviet books enlighten millions of readers in the Third World who cannot afford much more expensive Western books. Soviet icebreakers free whales trapped by ice off Alaska, to the plaudits of the world.

The Soviet Union has been more conscious than most powers of the political importance of its message ever since Lenin, a professional political agitator, brought about a revolution in 1917 by convincing people that his

[13]*New York Times*, November 27, 1987, p. 8.

party offered a better way to the future. Only since 1985, however, have the Soviets tried very much to appeal to foreign governments and peoples by speaking in realistic terms; and their public relations have become far more sophisticated and effective. It is indicative of their success that West Germans, despite skepticism about the Soviet political system, seem to have been fairly well persuaded that the Soviet Union is morally at least level with the United States.

The United States, relying primarily on private enterprise, finds it more difficult to mobilize its immense cultural resources and employ them systematically to build American prestige and win affection for this country. Neither the Congress nor the presidency is greatly impressed with the utility of such activities, the effects of which cannot be measured or perceived directly. However, the U.S. Information Agency (USIA) carries on multiple labors of information, such as participation in international fairs, broadcasting the Voice of America, satellite television broadcasts, lectures, cultural exchanges, libraries and cultural centers, and feeding programs and information to the media of scores of countries. Its worldwide television service ("Worldnet") offers five to ten hours daily, by cable and satellite, of free programming that is especially attractive for impecunious Third World broadcasters. American musicians give concerts in countries of all political colorations.[14]

Although the cultivation of the American image is worldwide, it is most important in addressing itself to people who have relatively restricted access to foreign media. The number of persons in the Soviet Union and the bloc who try to inform themselves from abroad is—or was, prior to *glasnost*—far higher than in opener societies. The Voice of America, with Radio Liberty (broadcasting to the Soviet Union) and Radio Free Europe (broadcasting to Eastern Europe), plus the BBC, the Deutsche Welle, and others, deserve some credit for change in Soviet society.

American policymakers, however, do not take much notice of the state of opinion abroad until it erupts in violence and seems to pose a security threat. It is assumed that this great nation should be admired, and the wrongheaded persons who do not like it may ordinarily be ignored. If a government, like that of Honduras, is cooperative, there is little concern about the feelings of the people; the State Department is surprised by anti-U.S. riots and dismisses them as the work of agitators. The fact that the United States is rich and visible means that it has to exercise more tact; the extent and depth of anti-Americanism in the world—directed against

[14]There is a dearth of recent writing. See John W. Henderson, *The United States Information Agency* (New York: Praeger Publishers, 1969), and Paul J. Braisted, ed., *Cultural Affairs and Foreign Relations* (Washington: Columbia Books, 1968). On the objectives of the USIA, see Leo Bogart, *Premises for Propaganda: The United States Information Agency and Its Operating Assumptions* (New York: Free Press, 1976).

the government, not the American people—contributes greatly to the problems of U.S. foreign relations.[15]

A controverted question is whether the agency that acts as salesman of the nation should try to press its values on its hearers or pay most attention to its reputation for candor—and the nation's reputation for objectivity and impartiality—by giving the bad news with the good. There is much to be said for the latter course. People learn negative things in any case, and it is much better that they be told frankly by spokespersons of the nation. The British Broadcasting Corporation has earned the best reputation for factuality, thanks to an impartiality that comes easier because Great Britain is more a bystander than a participant in many of the world's clashes.

What a public relations agency can achieve is limited by facts; nations speak to the world most persuasively through their deeds. The best information program can only partially compensate for actions that contravene common ideas of international order and decency, especially actions that threaten the dignity or independence of other states. The national image is the product less of the media than of national conduct.

The leading nations could reasonably do very much more to win the world's appreciation or understanding; they spend much less on selling themselves than do the manufacturers of automobiles and beer. Appropriations for the U.S. Information Agency have grown in the 1980s to about $800 million yearly, the largest fraction of which goes for broadcasting. This is about 1/360 of the defense budget. It is ironic that, when West Germany, one of the most important allies, was smiling at Moscow, the United States ended support for binational cultural centers in seven German cities.[16]

It is predictable that in the future the United States and other nations concerned for status in the world will consider it one of their principal functions not only to promote tourism, trade, and investment, but to strengthen national security by persuading other peoples of the good character of the nation and its way of life.

The government, however, is a cramped and stumbling advocate of itself. The bulk of the influence of a democratic nation is the work of private persons and organizations, mostly little concerned with image, that make an impression on foreigners, from journalists and entertainers to businesspeople. It is to the disadvantage of the Soviet Union and countries of similar organization that their cultural relations have been almost entirely official. So far as Soviet producers of books and movies see them as an expression of creativity and a source of foreign currency, their work will attain far greater impact, like that of less politicized societies.

American cultural exports frequently give foreign audiences an exag-

---

[15]Cf. Alvin Z. Rubinstein and Donald E. Smith, *Anti-Americanism in the Third World: Implications for U.S. Foreign Policy* (New York: Praeger, 1985).

[16]*Wall Street Journal*, June 3, 1988, p. 1.

gerated idea of the violence, hedonism, and amorality of the society that they depict; and they may cause envy of American affluence. But their over-all effect is certainly positive; it is hard for the viewers of American cinema or television to regard this country as basically evil. The cultural production of the United States is so massive and manifold that it would be difficult for a government like that of the United States to screen or direct the flow for foreign policy purposes. It is not feasible to select movies for export to give a nice impression of the United States, and it would be contrary to American political principles to try to do so. Yet it should be possible, without any political censorship, to assist the distribution abroad of many attractive works that do not quite have the guaranteed mass appeal for commercial outlets. Similarly, it would be simple and inexpensive to make it easier for foreigners to obtain books and journals from this country, often badly needed but unobtainable for lack of foreign exchange.

The effects of travel are not dissimilar to those of cultural exports. Foreigners form ideas of the character of America (or France or Britain) from those who come to their country as tourists or business travellers, or who take up residence there, and from those whom they meet in the United States. The effect may be negative; the "ugly American," coarse, patronizing, and insensitive, is not mythical. Large numbers of British soccer fans who followed their teams to the Continent to make trouble (until banned) gave their country a bad image by drunkenness and extraordinary rowdiness. But most persons who go abroad are decent, spend money, and make themselves welcome.

There have been purposeful efforts to organize people exchanges with the Soviet Union for political purposes.[17] The Soviets are usually more eager for such exchanges than the American side, not only because they hope to influence American public opinion but also because the Soviet elite longs for opportunities to travel abroad. The Soviets make much more effort than Americans to impress foreign tourists favorably, giving them priorities for scarce desirables, from food to theater tickets. They have also spruced up Moscow for big gatherings, like the Olympic Games, temporarily banishing from the city undesired persons, from hippies to prostitutes.

A class of travellers formerly of great importance in the relations of the advanced countries with the less developed was that of missionaries. Supported by the donations of millions, especially in Britain and America, they promoted their faith among the heathen of many lands and indirectly the interests and standing of their country in the world. Evangelists of various churches, and also persons devoted to medicine or education, at one time played a major role in relations of China with the West; they were among the most humanitarian Westerners whom the Chinese knew, and

[17]Gale Warner and Michael Shuman, *Citizen Diplomats: Pathfinders in Soviet-American Relations and How You Can Join Them* (New York: Continuum, 1987).

their mark has not been erased. Missionaries, Christianizing and educating, have also exercised a great deal of influence in Africa. They are still active in some places, especially Latin America, where they have converted an important fraction of the population in such countries as Guatemala and Brazil to evangelical faiths. Organizations that they have founded have taken root and grown under native leadership.

The images of outstanding individuals also contribute to the image of the nation. Many Third World countries have high regard for such figures as Washington, Jefferson, and Lincoln. Franklin Roosevelt and John Kennedy gave the United States a good name in many lands. Thomas Paine has been taken as a journalistic model for the Indian press. Lenin still stands for the Soviet Union; Stalin was the symbol of communist discipline and power but has come to symbolize tyranny. Mao, displaced from his position as the demigod of China, still appeals to the imagination of sundry rebels. Fidel Castro has been a hero for mostly youthful radicals in numerous lands, along with Che Guevara, killed (martyred?) in the cause of revolution in Bolivia. Mahatma Gandhi incarnates the spirit of India.

The heroic figures of history were mostly military, from Alexander the Great and Julius Caesar to Napoleon. In the middle part of this century, revolutionaries were overrepresented. In the new age, however, builders and creators will probably be most prominent. It is probable that most of them will be produced by the open societies, like the overwhelming majority of recipients of Nobel Prizes, and that the United States will have more than its share.

It is in creativity that the democratic society shows most superiority to the authoritarian society; and through its music, writings, drama, styles, designs, and science, it compensates for political errors. It may even be claimed that the loosely structured American society excels in comparison with the democratic but tighter-knit Japanese. The United States leads much more as purveyor of news, styles, television programs, movies, and books than it does as producer of high-tech manufactures, pouring out good, bad, and indifferent in unsurpassed abundance.

The greatest impact that a modern nation has on the world is cultural, in a broad sense, the effect of its ideas, institutions, and inventions as well as its arts, literature, and other forms of entertainment and instruction. For the rather estimable role of cultural imperialist, the United States has unique advantages. Diversity of population and backgrounds, although in some ways disadvantageous, raises creativity. The loosely structured, immensely pluralistic, uninhibited society, spending a great deal of money on entertainment and rewarding its creators and practitioners far beyond any other nation, offers the peoples of earth an incomparable cultural smorgasbord. So far as this is an American century—as was eagerly prognosticated in the euphoria of WW II—it is culturally Americanized.

International Organization

This is an era of multiform globalization but not of world political organization. The victors of WW I formed the League of Nations, which might have become a major factor in stabilizing the world but for U.S. abstention. The memory of blissful noninvolvement was strong and the recognition that the world had become more dangerous was weak, so the only power that could have effectively led the League declined the honor. In the 1930s the League had neither the will nor the capacity to check Japanese, German, and Italian aggression. It did only enough to irritate these powers, the withdrawal of which left the League a hollow shell.

The United Nations was an extension and perpetuation of the wartime antifascist coalition, formalized and reshaped into a slightly improved version of the League. The victors desired both to maintain something of their wartime unity and also to do better than their predecessors of 1919 in establishing a framework for world order. The organization they put together under the name of their coalition was an expression of the cooperation of the great powers, then the United States, Britain, and the U.S.S.R. They assumed that they would continue to work together for world order as they had cooperated in war; the United Nations Organization was not designed to handle quarrels between them.

In its early years, the United Nations enjoyed something of the prestige of the victorious alliance and was assumed to be the appropriate agency to deal with almost any kind of minor world problem; the ready answer to almost any political problem was, "Let the United Nations handle it." Support for the U.N. was especially strong in the United States, which had the honor of hosting its headquarters in New York, in contrast to the European locale (Geneva) of the League.

Faith in the United Nations was still high in the 1950s. The zenith of its ability to serve collective security came in Korea. Because the Soviet Union carelessly boycotted a crucial meeting of the Security Council, at which it could have exercised its veto, the Council gave its sanction to military action to halt the North Korean attack. Sixteen nations sent contingents to Korea, mostly token, in 1950–1951; and General Douglas MacArthur was formally chief not of an American but a United Nations force.

After the 1950s, the United Nations became incapacitated, from the point of view of the United States and the prevalent world order, by the growing influence of both the "nonaligned" nations and the Soviet bloc. The U.N. as originally constituted was made up overwhelmingly of nations friendly to the United States or dependent on it; the Soviet Union could count only on a handful of satellites (augmented by the votes for two Soviet "republics," Ukraine and Belorussia, a concession made to Stalin in recognition of Soviet war losses). As late as 1959, the elected members of the Security Council included one communist state, two neutralist, and seven members of the Western alliance system. The Soviets repeatedly used their veto in the Security Council to thwart measures approved by the majority, and this was regarded as evidence of their reprobation by the world community.

But many new nations, mostly coming out of the breakup of the old colonial empires, were admitted to membership; the 51 founding members had become 159 in 1988, including all sovereignties except ever-neutral Switzerland, divided Korea, and miniministates such as Monaco. Most of the newcomers were less than friendly to the United States. From the 1970s, this country was having to use its veto from time to time against a majority of the Security Council, while the General Assembly gradually became dominated by Third World states with varying grievances against the West or demands on it.

Willingness to support the U.N. financially also declined. The Soviet Union led the way by declining to help pay for peacekeeping operations of which it disapproved, and various other states followed. In the 1980s the United States fell deeply in arrears. The United States has much leverage from the fact that it contributes 25 percent to the U.N. budget or about $800 million, more than the next two, Japan (about 11 percent) and the Soviet Union (about 10 percent) together.

The Congress has been even less enthusiastic about financing the United Nations than the administration. The United States objects to the extravagance and bureaucratism of the body and demands economies. Probably more significant has been annoyance with the influence of a Third World-Soviet coalition in the U.N. administration (the Secretariat), and the use of the U.N. as a forum for attacks on the United States. In the past, the Soviet Union has been more skillful in political maneuvering in the U.N. than the United States, as the former has identified itself with the aspirations of the Third World majority. But the United States has a large advantage in economic power and ability to dispense favors, while the fact that the principal activities of the U.N. are centered in New York helps the United States to influence delegates and present its views.[18]

The formal governing body of the United Nations is the General Assembly of the entire membership, although security affairs are the province of the 15-member Security Council (5 permanent, 10 selected by respective regions for 2-year terms). The Assembly is a world forum, a sort of town meeting of the planet, where the feeblest have voice and vote along with the mightiest. Unrealistically, however, it gives all member states equal authority to control spending irrespective of their financial contribution; states paying four-fifths of the expenses have voted (in vain) against the

---

[18]Thomas A. Franck, *Nation Against Nation: What Happened to the U.N. Dream and What the U.S. Can Do* (New York: Oxford University Press, 1985), pp. 254–69, argues that the United States should use its power of the purse more effectively to shape U.N. policy.

budget approved by the majority. Half the members pay only the minimum dues, 1/5,000 of the budget, or less; the 80 poorest nations together contribute little more than 1 percent of the total. The United States has sought to have a veto over the budget through a provision that approval had to be unanimous, on the supposition that nations paying very little would be morally unable to hold up the budget.

The U.N. is also unsound in that it gives equal standing to states that are responsible to their people and to those that are not. The fact that the large majority of governments represented in the General Assembly are more or less self-appointed deprives it of moral authority, so the democratic powers are justified in giving little weight to its views and decisions.

On the other hand, the structure and procedures of the United Nations and affiliated bodies are democratic. In them, authoritarian positions have to be argued on grounds of equality and rights of the less privileged peoples and nations. For example, UNESCO (United Nations Educational, Scientific, and Cultural Organization) long sought to promote governmental control of media on grounds that it was necessary to protect Third World peoples from monopolistic Western news agencies; censorship was only indirectly implied. The U.N. must have some effect, how much can only be guessed, in the diffusion of ideas of legal and democratic politics to Third World elites.

The United Nations is valuable as almost the embodiment of international law and the principle of equal sovereignty, which, however unrealistic, is the formal basis of international order. Above all, it lends moral support to the prime rule of the international system, that the boundaries of sovereign states are sacred; and it has defended this principle with great consistency throughout its history.[19] However incapable of dealing with great power confrontations, it serves as a nonpartisan world political body. The U.N.'s top administrator, the secretary general, is a respected figure, as neutral as may be found, an advocate of peaceful settlement and an arbiter. No one else is so well placed to sponsor negotiations in difficult areas, as the Iran-Iraq war and the war in Afghanistan.

No other organization can field a small army so respected that hardly anyone shoots at it. The U.N. has been able to send small detachments from nations not suspected of great ambitions, such as Finland or Norway, to trouble spots, mostly to support cease-fires by a symbolic neutral presence. It has fielded 13 peacekeeping forces, the greater number in the 1960s, more than half to Israel or its neighbors. In 1988, there were U.N. forces in place in Cyprus, on the frontiers of Israel (3), along the Iran-Iraq cease-fire line, between India and Pakistan in Kashmir, and in Afghanistan, ranging from 50 to several thousand personnel. It is not easy to pull out; the U.N.

[19] Tom J. Farer, "International Law: The Critics Are Wrong," *Foreign Policy* 71, (Summer 1988), pp. 25–26.

has been in Kashmir since 1949, in Cyprus since 1964.[20] The UN has been helpless in many crises, from Berlin (1948) through Suez and Hungary (1956) to the Biafran civil war (1967–1970), Soviet intervention in Afghanistan (1979–1988) and the Iran-Iraq war (1980–1988).

In 1988, the U.N. revived and showed itself more useful than for many years past. It played a major part in the implementation of the plan for Soviet withdrawal from Afghanistan, and it provided the mechanism for bringing a truce in the Iran-Iraq war; it also undertook negotiations to solve the complex problem of the Western (formerly Spanish) Sahara. It has also taken a hand in the Greek-Turkish standoff on Cyprus, the restoration of independence of Kampuchea, and the Angolan-South African conflict.

This resurgence of U.N. activities was made possible by the improved climate of international relations. The Soviet Union decided in 1987 to strengthen the U.N. as a peacekeeping organization for Third World conflicts, and it paid up arrears for peacekeeping operations, which it had boycotted. It also reversed previous practice by permitting some of its citizens to remain permanent international civil servants with the U.N. instead of simply being delegated for short periods by the Soviet state. Soviet cooperation with U.N. peacekeeping efforts led the United States to be more forthcoming toward it also. The world body may revert to some extent to its original purpose.

The U.N. also serves as umbrella for many useful specialized organizations. They include the International Labor Organization (ILO), the Universal Postal Union, the Food and Agriculture Organization (FAO), the United Nations Childrens' Emergency Fund (UNICEF), and the United Nations High Commission for Refugees. The United Nations Council on Trade and Development (UNCTAD), endeavors to coordinate the plans and pleas of the needier countries and was the chief spokesman for the proposed New International Economic Order. It is also spokesman for the "Group of 77" (actually over 120), the brotherhood of the "developing" nations. The World Health Organization (WHO) marked up a signal victory in 1971 by the elimination from the earth of one of the classic plagues, smallpox. It plays an active part in narcotics control.

Such bodies, little celebrated and mostly unpolitical, are trusted where a program sponsored by the United States would be suspect. In the Third World, they save the lives of hundreds of thousands of refugees, give technical assistance in agriculture, improve health care, do something for economic growth, and sponsor worthy projects. If swarms of locusts appear in Africa, the battle against them is organized in the name of the FAO.

The United States has ordinarily been the mainstay of the specialized U.N. organizations. However, it has reduced support not only for the political activities of the U.N. but for its humanitarian roles as well; for example,

[20]On peacekeeping and other missions, see Franck, *Nation Against Nation*.

the World Health Organization (WHO) was penalized, apparently in retaliation for its campaign for breast feeding (to the detriment of manufacturers of infant formula) and its efforts to promote control of sales of pharmaceuticals.[21] The United States has also withheld its dues to the Food and Agriculture Organization (FAO) in an effort to force administrative reforms. Withdrawal of financial support by the United States and Britain brought about changes both of leadership and policy in UNESCO, probably the most important of the affiliated bodies.[22]

There is also a set of financial organizations loosely affiliated with the U.N. Much as the victory of 1945 provided the occasion for setting up a world political body, it made possible the establishment of a new international financial regime, the key idea of which was to overcome the economic nationalism held partly responsible for the war. The United Nations Monetary and Financial Conference, meeting at Bretton Woods, New Hampshire, in July 1944, established several bodies: the International Monetary Fund (IMF), to smooth and control the exchange rate fluctuations that caused much trouble in prewar years; the International Bank for Reconstruction and Development (IBRD), usually known as the World Bank, intended first to finance the rebuilding of devastated countries and subsequently the development of less developed countries;[23] and the General Agreement on Tariffs and Trade (GATT), to facilitate international trade, especially by reducing discrimination and increasing multilateralism.[24] Unlike the United Nations, the IMF and the World Bank are controlled by those who pay the bills. The United States, with nearly 20 percent of shares, has a veto in both, although the head of the IMF has traditionally been a European. Perhaps because the World Bank has an American chief, there has been some rivalry between the two. Japanese participation in both is growing, despite U.S. reluctance to allow them a larger role.

These agencies and others related to them played a great part in the extraordinary expansion of world exchanges from 1945 until the 1980s, and especially in the period until the American economic primacy was visibly waning, around 1970. The IMF oversaw remarkably stable exchange rates. The World Bank, granting concessional loans to the poorer countries, contributed to the good growth rates of that period. And the GATT was for many years the focus of reduction of tariff barriers.

These are not far from being universal organizations, including nearly

---

[21]*Wall Street Journal,* April 7, 1988, p. 1.

[22]S. Nihel Singh, *The Rise and Fall of UNESCO* (Riverdale MD: Riverdale Co., 1988).

[23]On the IMF and World Bank see Irving S. Friedman, *Toward World Prosperity: Reshaping the Global Money System* (Lexington MA: Lexington Books, 1987).

[24]Robert Gilpin, *The Political Economy of International Relations,* (Princeton: Princeton University Press, 1987), p. 191; Gardner Patterson, "The GATT and the Negotiation of International Trade," in *Negotiating World Order,* ed. Alan K. Henrikson, (Washington: Scholarly Resources, 1986), pp. 181–98.

all important trading nations except the Soviet bloc. GATT has 95 members; the IMF, which has money to lend, 148. They are capitalist-oriented, designed to make workable an international economic order based on market principles and free exchanges. To belong to them is to belong, at least partially, to the free-market world economy. Consequently they were long anathema to the Marxist-Leninist countries, which were excluded from membership not only by ideological repugnance but by their disinclination to furnish information on their finances. However, the needs of the Soviet Union, East European countries, and China have risen, their ideological scruples have waned, and a number of them have applied to join. United States policy has been skeptical, particularly toward Soviet membership, fearing that it would be disruptive.

There are hundreds of other international organizations of various kinds, mostly informational, without formal powers or consequential financial resources. They are overwhelmingly of postwar origin, a majority having been founded in the past twenty or thirty years; one of the notable developments of the contemporary era is the proliferation of multilateral forums and meeting grounds. Many of them are consultative economic organizations, in which governments or enterprises may be members. Typically, the Organization for Economic Cooperation and Development (OECD) groups the European democracies, the United States, Canada, and Japan in efforts to liberalize world trade and coordinate economic aid to less developed countries. The OECD is a successor to the organization set up in 1948 to oversee European recovery under the Marshall Plan. It has a council and a secretary general; but its work is mostly to facilitate communications regarding common problems.

Numerous even more loosely structured groups carry on negotiations and decision-making informally with minimal organization, at most a small secretariat. For example, the Paris Club of creditor governments has no fixed membership and no budget. It was born of a 1956 meeting of governments to negotiate debt relief for Argentina. Open to all creditors, it has "headquarters" in Paris, with facilities provided by the French government. It works with major banks, the IMF, and other agencies to alleviate the debt problem. It can do nothing except reach understandings with debtor nations; its consensual decisions have to be put into effect by bilateral agreements.[25] Nonetheless, it is quite influential and has brought about scores of settlements. Even more informal is the Group of Seven (G-7), which exists when delegates of the United States, Japan, Canada, Britain, France, Italy, and West Germany meet to discuss currency and related matters.

Many other international organizations, mostly private, work with governments or supplement their activities. The International Civil Aviation

[25]Alexis Rieffel, "The Paris Club, 1978–1983," *Columbia Journal of Transnational Law* 26, 1984, No. 1, pp. 83–108.

Organization efficiently regulates international air traffic. Amnesty International is the premier world watchdog of human rights, in the spirit of the Helsinki agreements; the governments that it scolds pay tribute to its importance by their objections. The Red Cross, which is over a century old, is universally seen as an agency of mercy in battle and relief of suffering. Care International also helps the suffering, as do numerous other organizations, many with a religious affiliation.

International organizations not only perform useful tasks but also lubricate international interactions and understanding. They are meeting grounds where influential persons of many nations get to know one another, forming something of an international class of educated and dedicated persons, whose loyalty is to some extent transferred from the sovereign state to humanity.

Shared Concerns

It is a by-product of modern technology that problems spill over national borders. For example, organized crime has become highly internationalized, giving the Paris-based Interpol, formed by 140 countries, more and more to do. It tries to trace criminals around the world, and also takes interest in the laundering of money, a necessity for the modern gangster. The United States has also undertaken increasingly to indict and prosecute persons abroad for acts committed abroad, such as conspiracy to violate U.S. law.

The business of narcotics is thoroughly multinational. The raw material is grown in one country, processed in another with chemicals from a third, shipped through one or two more, and retailed in a fifth or sixth. Profits, which come to tens of billions of dollars, may be laundered and invested elsewhere. It has been proposed that an international agency assist the drug enforcement agencies of poorer countries.

There being none, American enforcement authorities attempt to attack the sources in countries such as Mexico, Jamaica, Colombia, Peru, and Bolivia. Far-reaching control programs have been attempted, from uprooting coca bushes in the Andes to searching out processing facilities, with some transgression of the sovereignty of drug-producing nations. This policy of interdiction abroad has not been successful and may even worsen the problem. After years of anti-drug warfare sponsored and supported by the United States, the price of cocaine has remained little changed, and the output of opium and hashish in Asia and of coca and marijuana in the Americas continues to rise. The cost to the producer countries of the United States' attempt to get them to solve its drug problem is enormous, as they cannot contend with the corruption fostered by huge illegal funds; yet the

United States achieves little or nothing.[26] At best, the problem requires broad international cooperation.

Many other common concerns increase steadily. Science and medicine are international by nature, and cooperation among the specialists of all nations is essential. Consequently, scientists are usually instinctively internationalist, impatient with the senseless parochialism of nations; they oppose the armaments that absorb resources needed for better purposes (sometimes to a degree that more "realistic" folk find naive). U.S. and Soviet scientists have long worked together amiably in Antarctic research, and teams of experts from the two powers cooperate against alcoholism. Such cooperation increases so far as political relations permit because the two nations have the largest corps of investigators and the most to gain from joint research.

Very high technology becomes so expensive that it is beyond the capacity of all but the richest nations. Only the United States and perhaps Japan are equipped to develop modern airliners; the leading European nations had to form a consortium to produce the Airbus (at a considerable loss). If there is to be a new supersonic transport, it apparently has to be an international endeavor. Space research has been mostly national because of the competitive spirit in which it began in the 1950s, but it lends itself to multinational collaboration. Japan is rapidly getting into space orbit, partly in cooperation with the United States, partly in competition.[27]

The Maltreated Earth

The cooperation of many nations is imperative to meet growing environmental problems, mostly related to exponential population growth in the parts of the world least able to accommodate it; about 80 million people are added to the earth's multitudes every year. The crowding of many Third World countries threatens exhaustion or destruction of agricultural land and water resources, and frustrates efforts to alleviate world poverty. Extirpation of Amazon jungle is a threat to world climate. Deforestation in Nepal and India causes calamitous floods in Bangladesh. Some countries face desertification and pauperization, while poverty makes population growth ever more difficult to control. Migratory locusts are a persistent plague in Africa.[28]

[26]Ethan A. Nadelman, "U.S. Drug Policy: A Bad Export," *Foreign Policy* 70, Spring 1988, p. 84; Bruce M. Bagley, "The New Hundred Years War? US National Security and the War on Drugs in Latin America," *Journal of Interamerican Studies and World Affairs* 30, Spring 1988, p. 166.

[27]James Yue, "Japan's Space Effort," *Harvard International Review* 10, November 1987, p. 39.

[28]*Time,* January 2, 1989, is dedicated to "The Endangered Planet." The yearbook edited by Lester R. Brown, *State of the World 1988, World Watch Institute Report* (New York: Norton, 1988) covers environmental issues in detail.

The desire for more goods implies more pollution. One nation's acid fumes become another's acid rain. It is convenient to throw garbage into the sea or the atmosphere. If the ozone layer is depleted by industrial chemicals, there is a problem not only of (relatively benign) skin cancer: an increase of 10 percent in ultraviolet radiation reaching the earth might have large effects on crops. We may be doomed to swelter under a blanket of carbon dioxide produced by burning fossil fuels; and lowlands may be flooded by the melting of icecaps. Unfortunately, improvement of the composition of the atmosphere will require even more time than its gradual deterioration.

Irreplaceable resources are also destroyed for small short-term gain. Destruction of rain forests, especially in Brazil, makes low-grade pastures at the cost of releasing large quantities of CO_2, reducing humidification and production of oxygen, and wiping out uncounted and unrecorded species of plants and animals. It represents little gain for Brazil and a loss for all nations, just as when migratory birds are slaughtered in passing over a nation. The overutilization of ocean fisheries, like the overgrazing of common pastures, is ruinous. The chief but perhaps insufficient hope for the conservation of irreplaceable resources is enlightened self-interest. Tourist revenues have been a strong incentive for nations, especially of Africa, to protect assets of flora and fauna; safaris in their magnificent parks bring in a large part of the revenues of Kenya and other East African countries. Gorilla-watchers make it worthwhile for Rwanda to protect the gentle apes. Pride plays a part; Madagascar, for example, finds its lemurs a national treasure.

International cooperation, however, is indispensable. Many world conferences have been held to deal with environmental and related problems. Nations are rather remarkably ready to cooperate for respected causes even at some sacrifice of material interests. The enclosed Mediterranean was becoming miserably polluted; the 18 riparian nations got together, despite their great political diversity (Albania halfway participating), to clean it up; by 1988 most beaches were swimmable. In 1987, 49 nations agreed to freeze and eventually reduce the production of chlorofluorocarbons, which are destroying the ozone layer protecting us from damaging ultraviolet radiation. The U.S. Senate ratified the proposed treaty with rare unanimity. The only flaw was that the proposed reduction was far from enough to stabilize the O^3 blanket. In November 1988 the industrial nations agreed to freeze emissions of nitrous oxide, a cause of acid rain and other ills; but the United States refused to go along with a cutback.

The success of the International Whaling Commission, despite economic interests of some nations, has been striking. Founded in 1946 with no enforcement powers except the pressure of world opinion, the commission gradually obtained more and more support to reverse the threatened extinction of many or most species of the great mammals. It was able in 1986 to declare a moratorium and bring commercial whaling virtually to a halt.

The Soviet Union cooperated with the United States, despite the large investment of the former in a whaling fleet. The leading holdout was Japan, which has a taste for whale meat; the United States took the issue seriously enough to threaten economic reprisals if the Japanese proceeded with plans to take some hundreds of whales allegedly for "research" purposes.[29]

Much depends on the climate of opinion. It should also be possible for the richer nations to provide incentives for cooperation in causes that are of interest to them and for which they may bear some responsibility. In this spirit, the World Bank has tried to use its lending power to impose environmental standards on otherwise careless nations.[30] But frictions are sure to arise as the necessary sacrifices become more serious. How, for example, should the costs of cutting down consumption of fossil fuel be allocated? What if some countries prefer a warmer climate? Can nations be punished for "environmental aggression" against the world's air or waters, or for destroying resources of which they are sovereign owners?

There is a certain inconsistency in the willingness of nations to get together to protect the ozone layer or the whales even while they pile up the means of murdering the entire human population. However, an ever growing number of shared problems will threaten human welfare if technological civilization continues to develop and expand. For their prosperity if not their survival, the sovereign nations must learn to work together to keep the planet livable. So far as they become conscious of this need, the temper of relations among nations changes. Politico-military competition is based, after all, not on material but psychological needs; and the psychology of cooperation overtakes power rivalry.

Nonviolent Power

In the game of nations, it is commonly assumed that a democracy, with its checks on executive action, the publicizing of all important moves, and the need for broad consent, is at a serious disadvantage. Foreign policy in a democracy is inconsistent, untidy, and unsteady. Public opinion swings, interest groups contend, and leaders are replaced. The strategists of the democratic power may envy their authoritarian counterparts for their ability to plan a steady course. But it is not entirely negative if foreign policy is a bit indecisive in use of power; indecision may allow economic or social forces to solve the problem.

For many ends, from the understandable desire to be well regarded to the promotion of trade and industry, the democratic power has advantages.

[29]*New York Times,* January 22, 1988, p. 5.
[30]*Wall Street Journal,* July 3, 1987, p. 1.

It should, by taking informed opinion into account, be able better to formulate intelligent approaches than less open authoritarian powers. It has greater capacities in the private and unofficial realms, in cultural, economic, and social endeavors, everything that is better carried on nongovernmentally. As J. William Fulbright, longtime chairman of the Senate Foreign Relations Committee, wrote, "The nation performs its essential function not in its capacity as a *power* but in its capacity as a *society*."[31]

Unofficial influence can be strong even when policy is against it. Thus, despite a generation of official efforts to cut linkages, Cuba is permeated with American influence through radio and the personal contacts of Cubans with friends and relatives in the United States. Cubans long to travel, chiefly to Florida; and many are passionate for U.S. comics, baseball teams, and musical stars.[32] They flock to (pirated) American movies, and their sometimes truculent leader is said to be an avid watcher of U.S. television. The Vietnamese are apparently better disposed toward Americans, memories of the war and lack of formal relations to the contrary, than toward the Russians, who give large-scale economic assistance.[33]

It is an advantage of the democracy that the government is not the sole representative of the nation and people. Consequently, the nation as such is not much hated. If the government is disliked, the people are likeable. Many years of propaganda never turned Soviet citizens against the United States or things American, although they were at times afraid of association with Americans as potential spies. Iran has been saturated with denunciation of the "Great Satan" and an unremitting Hate America campaign of long duration, yet Iranians are said still to like American styles and to welcome American visitors.

Restricting exchanges diminishes the largest U.S. influence. Less self-confident nations are less inclined to give themselves this luxury. The government of China, for example, hates the Nationalist regime on Taiwan; but it would like to bring the two into a closer union in which the larger would dominate. Consequently, it demands that Taiwan permit trade. Taiwan, fearful of the influence of the much larger China, steadfastly refuses, although it bows to necessity by closing its eyes to smuggling and indirect trade. There is much to be said for the Japanese approach of dealing with everyone and offering technical and economic aid, while bargaining for whatever advantages may be obtained. In this situation, no one threatens Japan in any way, and there is no apparent reason why anyone would.

Foreign leaders are more likely to be hostile than their peoples. But it is not to be assumed that they are immune to education and persuasion. For example, Soviet First Secretary Khrushchev was much influenced by his

[31]J. William Fulbright, *The Arrogance of Power* (New York: Vintage Books, 1967), p. 258.

[32]*Time*, September 21, 1987, pp. 46–47.

[33]James Fallow, "No Hard Feelings?" *Atlantic* 262, December 1988, p. 78.

exposure to the United States in 1959; for the son of Russian peasants, it was an eye-opener to see how American farmers lived and worked. If the goal were to influence Cuba, Castro would be invited to come to the United States and talk with Americans. The American president would urge him to open his country to U.S. exports, tourism, and so forth; exchanges would be maximized.

It is useful to have friendly leaders in general come to the United States, but it is more desirable to have as visitors those most in need of education regarding this country and its purposes. One might hope not only to enlighten the adversary leader and his entourage; a foreign leader visiting this country is sure to be proud of being received by the great power. There is no need for unmerited favors or praise—although American presidents have often pinned medals on coarse dictators.

If a nation is unfriendly, this is the more reason to attempt to change its feelings. Could a great power have such a "soft" approach to international affairs? It would spare itself much trouble by doing so. A nation is likely to turn against the United States only in the emotional heat of revolution, and then only so far as convinced that this country is hostile. There would otherwise be little reason to do so, and good relations are usually far more important for the lesser power. If a truculent leader takes an anti-American stance from personal bias, the most effective response is probably to ignore it and assist reason to prevail.

Unfortunately, however, much of foreign policy is made for satisfactions at home. Calm is by definition undramatic. Leaders like to act forcefully, much as angry parents like to punish their children. Many people would be happy to use force with their fellows; they enjoy it when their nation does so, at least if the costs and risks are low, the cause sounds noble, and the victim is despicable. But if the purpose is to change behavior, incentives ("positive reinforcement") are usually more effective in the long run than threats or punishment; this is as true of international politics as it is of child training.

So far as foreign policy makers are sophisticated, we will see less use of force. If democracy progresses, foreign policy will be increasingly democratic. That is, it will make more use of the means appropriate to a democratic society, from diplomacy to multinational cooperation, and will operate less as power, more through the thousand nonviolent interactions of interdependent states and societies.

Chapter 9

Economic Politics

Trade and Political Relations

The greatest impact nations have on one another is usually economic, and the United States has become painfully aware how crucial for its livelihood are international capital flows and foreign trade accounts. Production and finances are intertwined around the globe, and exchanges are linked from Frankfurt to New York to Tokyo. A Japanese market crash could bring a painful rise of U.S. interest rates and a selloff on Wall Street, and vice versa.

The modern democratic countries form something of an economic whole, the parts of which increasingly share troubles and prosperity. Third World countries may suffer economic collapse despite normality in most of the world, but no part of the Western world has a severe recession by itself. The stable democracies of the West come toward a common level; with roughly similar capacities and institutions and easy flow of capital and methods of production, lower wages favor the less prosperous. Negotiations among the advanced countries, moreover, are rather egalitarian; it does not matter greatly that New Zealand is more comparable in economic dimensions to Oregon than to the United States.[1]

---

[1] For a general treatment, see Robert Gilpin, *The Political Economy of International Relations* (Princeton: Princeton University Press, 1987).

Only the Soviet bloc remains partly self-excluded from the global community. The major industrial economies, including Japan, Germany, France, and Britain, carry on less than 4 percent of their trade with the militarily second superpower, and the United States only 1 percent (mostly grain exports). Finland alone, among developed countries, depends heavily (although decreasingly) on Soviet trade, because of location and relations established by post-WW II reparations. The fact that 60 percent of Soviet trade is confined to the bloc and flows at more or less irrational prices is doubtless an important cause of the relative backwardness of the socialized economies. Even for the Soviet bloc, however, foreign commerce is vital and becoming more so. It is no longer possible to dream of autarchy, as Stalin once did.

Strictly political issues are usually left behind in the dealings of the industrial powers. For example, what the United States and Canada have to talk about is mostly trade-related, secondarily dealing with such matters as U.S. acid rain in Canadian lakes. Defense issues, such as the level of Canadian expenditures, access to Canadian territory for early warning of missiles, and the like, require much less attention. With Japan, likewise, a large majority of sometimes rather acrid discussions deal basically with the U.S. trade deficit.

Yet politics remain inseparable from economics, and foreign trade problems are injected directly into the political process of both richer and poorer countries. Economic bargaining has political overtones, and it may be assumed that leaders enjoy exerting economic influence in the same way as they enjoy political influence. There are victories to savor and defeats to rue, principles to be asserted for the sake of principle as well as material interests to be defended. For example, American insistence on the right of American firms to participate in Japanese construction projects bears no relation to the slight interest of American firms in doing so. The U.S. trade representative will probably have a gala the day the Japanese rice barrier is cracked.

Economic interests also enter politics, although there is no contemporary parallel for the way powerful multinational corporations at one time dominated several countries of Central America. Foreign interests cannot be excluded from domestic politics in the United States, since a large number of foreign as well as domestic lobbyists promote or oppose legislation or administrative regulations regarding taxes, tariffs, and concessions, not only of the federal government but of states. Foreign political action committees (PACs) contributed $2.3 million to 1986 congressional campaigns.[2]

---

[2]Martin and Susan Tolchin, "Foreign Money, U.S. Fears," *New York Times Magazine,* December 13, 1987, p. 63. For a general discussion, see Martin and Susan Tolchin, *Buying into America: How Foreign Money Is Changing the Face of Our Nation* (New York: New York Times Books, 1988).

Japanese firms spend millions lobbying the U.S. Congress, and U.S. corporations hire retiring Japanese bureaucrats to gain access to officialdom.[3]

Economic questions are most politicized in relations with states with politically controlled economies. In commerce with communist states, trade barriers come into question on only one side, tariffs and quotas having no meaning for sales to Soviet state enterprises. On the other hand, the United States makes favorable or unfavorable conditions for imports from the Soviet Union on political grounds. Their volume is seldom great enough to raise a clamor for protection, but the Jackson-Vanik Amendment (1974) made most favored nation (MFN) status for communist states conditional on freedom of emigration. This might have been successful if the conditionality had been quietly applied; publicity led the Soviets to refuse, bringing a setback to relations and reduction of the Jewish emigration the amendment was intended to facilitate.

American allies have been much readier than the United States to do business with the Soviets, just as they are less eager to spend for defense. The most forward are the West Germans, who on the front line are most aware of what a war would mean to them, who see the softening of East-West differences as movement toward reunification of Germany, however distant this prospect, and who have a long tradition of economic penetration of Eastern Europe. The Germans officially encourage trade in both directions and are the largest noncommunist buyers of Soviet exports; they are engaged in more joint projects than any other country and have led in giving credit to the Soviet Union. Japanese, French, and British banks also compete for Soviet business, while American banks shy away.

The United States has never decided how far to encourage trade with the Soviet Union, which is desirous of maximizing sales in order to be able to buy technical goods. Some Americans have feared that almost any trade would add to Soviet military capabilities, feeling that if the Soviet Union wants something it must be bad for the United States. Export-Import Bank financing is denied for exports to the Soviet Union, although the purpose of the bank is simply to promote U.S. exports. In this mood, President Carter cut off grain sales after the invasion of Afghanistan, although it was difficult to argue that less feed for Soviet cows and pigs would incline the Kremlin to desist from the attempted Sovietization of Afghanistan, and the Soviets could fill their needs from Argentina at small additional expense. In this case, the conservative pocketbook proved weightier than conservative politics, and the embargo was revoked by President Reagan shortly after taking office.

It is not certain whether it is more suitable for the United States to try to compel the Soviets to make their own personal computers (if allies could be persuaded to join in refusing to sell) or to encourage them to depend

---

[3]*Wall Street Journal,* August 5, 1988, p. 14.

on foreign suppliers. It may be desirable for the Soviets to become more involved with the outside world, maximize contacts, and develop a vested interest in good relations. There is some fear that a Soviet presence in such bodies as GATT would be disruptive; yet participation in a world trade organization may have some effect on Soviet conduct.

A typical question was whether to permit the sale of aircraft to Soviet bloc countries. For political reasons, they have used only Soviet planes, which are noisy, fuel-inefficient, slower, and more in need of upkeep and repairs. But by 1988 the atmosphere had changed sufficiently to permit Eastern Europeans to turn to the West and the Western powers to authorize sales to them. The fact that the Soviets can learn a good deal from modern European and American planes, especially their electronics, was outweighed by the profits from a potentially large market and also the political point: that officially Marxist-Lennist countries have to have Airbus or Boeing planes instead of Ilyushins underlines the technical inferiority of the Soviet aircraft industry, which has not produced a new airliner for twenty years. It was once trying to compete in world markets and even produced a supersonic rival for the Anglo-French Concord; it has long since abandoned the field.

The political usability of trade is diminished by the rising ability of Japan and Western Europe to furnish almost anything that the United States can and their unwillingness to forgo sales unless they see good reasons to do so. When martial law was decreed in Poland in 1981, the United States adopted several punitive measures; but no other powers joined, and they did not have much effect beyond somewhat increasing Polish dependence on the Soviet Union.[4] Only an economic hegemon is in a position to apply trade sanctions effectively; and the United States is no longer hegemonic.

The position this country enjoyed in the postwar era, like that of Great Britain in the 19th century, has been satisfying, beneficial to the U.S. economy, and a means of holding together an anticommunist alliance system. It is very convenient that the international reserve currency, the currency for the bulk of international transactions, was and is the dollar. Yet the open trading system has not prevented, indeed has fostered the rise of other economic giants. Correspondingly, the United States has in the 1980s encountered growing and politically controversial problems of unbalanced accounts, both domestically and internationally. This has brought a new awareness of limitations and the need to take other powers into consideration and has turned attention toward world markets. The U.S. role has become shaky; it is not politic to press Japan very hard on minor issues while

---

[4]David Leyton-Brown, ed., *The Utility of International Economic Sanctions* (New York: St. Martins Press, 1987); Miroslav Nincic and Peter Wallensteen, eds., *Dilemmas of Economic Coercion: Sanctions in World Politics* (New York: Praeger Publishers, 1985).

depending on Japanese support for the dollar. This country cannot continue to be the world economic leader without making more sacrifices than it seems prepared to make.

Trade Barriers

Economic controversies arise between nations, as they do in domestic politics, from conflicting material interests; they are made worse by the fact that political systems do not smoothly adjust the needs of the community but respond variably to demands of different sectors. If each government could arrive at clear-cut policies for the general welfare, agreement would come much more easily, exchanges would proceed on principles of relative advantage, and all would be better off. But no state is so rational.

Maximum liberalization of trade is generally in the interest of all, except so far as political interests contradict economic ones. It is advantageous for the nation to be able to buy and sell as freely as possible. A case can be made for temporary protection to permit infant industries to gather strength or to enable stricken ones to adjust. But to allow free trade is to increase competition, with multiple benefits; and the chief reason to export is to be able to pay for imports. Yet the emphasis is the opposite. Nations strive, often energetically, to promote exports; and they virtually always (Hong Kong and Singapore perhaps being exceptions) do something, sometimes a great deal, to hinder imports. Japan has purposefully expanded exports with marvellous success,[5] while restraining imports in many, sometimes subtle ways. European countries, having largely eliminated barriers among themselves in the European Economic Community (EEC), are overtly protectionist against the outside world.

Walls around national markets are age-old. In the 18th century, governments wanted to maximize exports in order to pile up stocks of gold to finance wars; nowadays they like to see foreign exchange reserves accumulate for economic leverage. From the point of view of national authorities, an export surplus is desirable, because it maintains the value of the national currency and makes foreign exchange available for whatever purpose may be desired. A country with a positive trade balance improves its economic standing because it invests surplus funds abroad and becomes an international creditor or rentier. There is also a sense of power and security in having a strong position in world markets. Japanese automobiles bring not only money but also prestige.

It is also a fact of politics, democratic and nondemocratic, that pro-

---

[5]James Fallow, "Japan: Playing by Different Rules," *Atlantic* 260, September 1987, pp. 22–32.

ducers, representing concentrated interests, are more influential than consumers, representing diffuse interests. This is not usually beneficial for the
economy as a whole; when governments erect barriers to imports or give
incentives to exports, they ask whether an industry needs it, not whether it
is good for the country. Extra costs to the consumers add up to much more
than extra profits for the producers. If duties are lowered, the gain for consumers may be more than fifty times the cost of retraining workers and
making other adjustments.[6]

The sheltering of uneconomic production also causes rigidity and inefficiency. Coddling a weak industry ordinarily does not give it strength to
become competitive but removes the need for efficiency. Many sheltered
industries of the Third World, like some of the United States, have become
an economic burden. On the other hand, the drive to improve and modernize production in competition with the world builds productive strength.

Bargaining about conditions of trade and related matters, such as the
U.S. demand that Germany and Japan stimulate their economies in order
to absorb more U.S. goods, occupies much attention of the foreign policy
establishment. Complaints of those hurt by imports are never-ending, and
economic affairs increasingly claim the attentions of statesmen. Since 1975
the leaders of the United States, Canada, Japan, Britain, France, Germany,
and Italy have met yearly to talk about economic growth, subsidies, tariffs,
interest rates, exchange stabilization, and the like; they have economic, not
political summits.

Protectionism abroad is probably the greatest preoccupation of Japan;
its diplomats are said to be exhausted by endless wrangling over issues of
access to markets, and they have developed a ramifying lobbying network
in Washington. Trade becomes a bigger political issue whenever demand
stagnates or shrinks, making imports more damaging to native industries.
The American Treasury Department has chastised not only Japan but also
Taiwan, South Korea, and Singapore for their large trade surpluses, warning that "unfair trade practices" would be subject to penalties,[7] although no
one claims that the United States does not engage in similar practices.

The United States can congratulate itself, however, on having taken
the lead in promoting freer trade in the postwar period. Its interest initially
stemmed in large part from the conviction that hindrances to international
trade had been a major factor in the tensions of the 1930s leading to WW
II. However, the opening of the international trading system has continued
to be a major interest of the United States in accord with its political and
economic outlook.

Efforts have been relatively successful. Successive negotiating confer-

---

[6]Theodore H. Moran, *Multinational Corporations: The Political Economic of Foreign Direct Investment* (Lexington MA: Lexington Books, 1985), p. 273.

[7]*Wall Street Journal,* November 18, 1987, p. 39.

ences cut down barriers rather remarkably through the so-called Kennedy Round of 1967, which made average cuts of 35 percent in duties on nonagricultural commodities. As a result, during most of the post-1945 period international trade grew twice as fast (8 percent) as production (4 percent). Since the early 1970s, however, there has been creeping protectionism in the United States and many other countries. There are several reasons: floating and unsteady exchange rates, making economic calculations more difficult; the rise of OPEC and sharp increases of fuel costs, with pressures on the balance of payments of many countries; difficulties of adjustment to the rapid rise of Japanese competition, followed by that of Taiwan, South Korea, and other "New Industrializing Countries;" and the global economic slowdown appearing in the late 1970s.[8] The European Economic Community has tended to compensate for removal of internal barriers by more protectionism against outsiders. Most important for the United States has been the shift from a strong creditor position in 1981 to an even stronger debtor position.

Consequently, trade imbalances have become increasingly controversial and politicized, and countries have taken shortsighted measures to protect special, that is, basically uneconomic interests. In theory, freer trade is still the goal, and bargaining over concessions always goes on, but the political pressures to do something for producers commonly prevail. The executive, representative of the whole country, is likely to be more in favor of trade liberalization, whereas legislators, elected from individual districts, are responsive to producers' interests. The American trade bill of 1988 placed emphasis, however, not on protecting domestic producers but on forcing other countries to open their markets.

Agriculture is most troublesome because of the political clout of farmers, and trade negotiations are tied up with touchy questions of subsidies. The Japanese standard of living would be much raised if the governing party could set aside the interests of a relatively small number of farmers (overrepresented in the Diet), who receive several times world prices for rice and many other products grown on their small plots. The cost of living in Western Europe could likewise be much reduced by ending the generous subsidies given farmers, especially in France. They have had the odd result of making the highly industrialized EEC, with a shortage of arable land, the world's second largest agricultural exporter.

The consequent reduction of U.S. food exports has been severe, and the United States has pressed for a general agreement to bring agricultural subsidies to an end. Farmers of the EEC, half of whose income may come from the taxpayers, have blocked the effort; but it is not clear that American farmers would permit any such utopian outcome. American practices, in any event, are irrational. A few sugar producers keep up a fence around the

[8]Gilpin, *The Political Economy,* pp. 191, 193, 204.

American sugar market, with narrow gates, and thereby work great harm on impoverished friendly sugar-producing countries that the United States would like to help—at the same time forcing American consumers to pay several times the world price of sugar. It is impossible for Argentina to come near servicing its foreign debt while the United States and the EEC subsidize exports in competition with Argentina's chief reliance, grain. Subsidized agricultural exports hurt many Third World nations, the development of which the industrial nations wish to promote by economic aid.

Controversies over agricultural barriers, with their political overtones, cause most acrimony. Nothing that the United States has demanded of Japan has aroused so much protest as rather trivial demands for freer entry for citrus fruit and beef, while raising the issue of an open market for rice is like hitting politicians with a hot poker. The ease with which good friends can quarrel is shown by the controversy that arose over beef imports to the European Common Market in 1988. Having prohibited the use of hormones in raising European beef, on doubtful grounds of alleged health hazards, the EEC authorities banned the import of American beef grown with hormone stimulation. The American authorities, unable to outlaw the use of hormones in this country, regarded this a simple protectionism (although it is not dissimilar to the prohibition of Argentine beef exports to the United States on alleged sanitary ground) and imposed prohibitive duties on a series of European food exports—grounds, in European eyes, for reprisals, and so forth.

Industrial subsidies are also a perennial issue; and as straight tariffs become old-fashioned, "anti-dumping" is a common excuse for protectionism. Producers claiming to be injured by the competition of subsidized foreign goods demand help; protracted negotiations follow, sometimes leading, when patience runs out, to countervailing duties, theoretically to equalize costs. The United States claims that the European airplane manufacturing consortium, Airbus Industrie, offers unfair competition because it is subsidized by the European member-governments, and threatens to halt sales to this country; Airbus retorts that Boeing is subsidized by the U.S. military.

The charge of dumping is usually a specious pretext and a screen for protectionism. Unless governments provide a subsidy, producers rarely wish to sell below cost. No one could afford to do so very extensively for long; dumping could hardly be more than a temporary weapon in an intraoligopoly fight.

Antidumping measures may turn out badly. The United States objected to Japan's selling computer chips too cheaply ("dumping"); prices were raised, and American producers using chips, who are more numerous than chip makers, were injured. The American trade representative also demanded that the Japanese government compel Japanese electronics firms to give American producers a fixed market share, something the United

States could not possibly undertake for the sake of foreign sellers. The overall result was to increase Japanese market dominance.

When tariffs are scaled down, nontariff barriers (such as quality restrictions) tend to take their place. Although quotas are contrary to the principles of GATT, which is dedicated to nondiscrimination, it has seemed more acceptable to negotiate a "voluntary export restraint" or to set up an administrative barrier than to put a tariff in place. Only a very small percentage of goods produced in the United States were protected by nontariff barriers in the early 1970s; the proportion had risen to about one-third by 1987.[9] It is estimated that half of the world's $3 trillion of international trade is negatively affected by cartel-like deals, quotas, regulations on imports, and subsidies.

The internationalization of production makes impediments to trade increasingly unrealistic. Goods are made in one country in a factory owned in another, using components from third countries, and are assembled and sold in still other countries; they are both imports and exports for several economies. To help Detroit, Japanese automobile exports to the United States were subjected to quota; the result was increased prices for American buyers and increased profits for Japanese producers, who shifted to more expensive models, sharpening the competition for American makers in the more remunerative sector of the market. Meanwhile, Japanese firms establish branches in the United States, American cars contain more and more Asian parts, and American manufacturers go into partnership with Japanese. Much of the output of American electronics firms is produced in East Asia, not only Japan but Hongkong, Korea, Taiwan, and Singapore, while the largest exporter of computers from Japan is IBM Japan.[10] Production facilities being placed wherever advantageous, not much less than half of international trade is intrafirm.

It does not help much if countries move toward democracy, because this permits pressure groups to assert themselves more vigorously. For example, as Taiwan has opened its political system, it has become more stubborn on trade issues, especially agricultural interests. The democracies understand one another's problems, as economic rationality yields everywhere to politics; but understanding does not mean sympathy. Japanese rice farmers burn the American president in effigy.

There is little coordination of foreign trade policies with other economic policies. For example, duties on Brazilian exports conflict with the desire that Brazil should earn an export surplus in order to be able to pay at least part of the interest owed on its enormous foreign debt; but nearly

[9]Robert B. Reich, "The Economics of Illusion," *Foreign Affairs* 66, no. 3, 1987/88, p. 521; Ralph Landau, "U.S. Economic Growth," *Scientific American* 258, June 1988, p. 52.

[10]Robert B. Reich, "The Trade Gap: Myths and Crocodile Tears," *New York Times*, February 12, 1988, p. 27.

half of Brazilian exports encounter tariff barriers. The United States specifically rejects any linkage of trade and debt questions, presumably because they are detached in the American political system. From the viewpoint of the debtors, however, they are very much related.

When the industrial nations feel some moral obligation to uplift the impoverished part of the world and are willing to expend respectable sums for that purpose, it would seem that they would favor both their own consumers and the incipient industrialization of the Third World by opening markets to their products. Governments are not so sensible or consistent. They will accept raw materials, but they show little mercy toward manufacturers that compete with higher-cost domestic products. Rich nations demand that poor nations cut their exports and receive more goods that they do not need, such as cigarettes. It is easy for Third World countries to conclude that the richer nations are not much interested in their economic development, certainly not in their industrialization.

Trade in services, such as telecommunications, insurance, and banking, has been much less discussed than exchanges of goods but has become increasingly important. The United States has advocated openness and non-discrimination, with special feeling because the United States is more competitive in services than in goods. Other nations, on the other hand, feel that they should get into lucrative services but need to shelter their enterprises to give them a chance to break into the market. The extension of the rules of the GATT to services would improve world economic prospects.

Intellectual Property

As the share of commodities in commerce decreases because of the growing sophistication of manufacturers, the misuse or theft of rights of inventors and designers becomes an ever greater problem.[11] The pirating of artistic productions, music, books and the like, has long been a major business in some countries, especially Taiwan; the pirating of high-tech wares has come to loom larger, as much of their value lies in their engineering, design, and planning. There are many complicated questions arising from imitation or counterfeiting of trademarks, the copying of drugs, the uses of bioengineering, and techniques of production. Computer software is pure information, subject to easy duplication; damage to the software industry is billions of dollars yearly. The United States is the chief loser from infringement of intellectual rights; its losses were recently guesstimated between $43 and $61 billion per year.[12]

[11]Helena Stalson, *Intellectual Property Rights and U.S. Competitiveness in Trade,* (Washington: National Planning Assoc., 1987).

[12]*New York Times,* November 20, 1988, p. E-24.

The development, testing, and licensing of a new drug probably cost well over $100 million; the cost of producing large quantities may be slight. Developed countries, especially those with a strong pharmaceutical industry, feel that developers should have maximum protection. Less developed countries regard the drug companies as simply selfish in denying them the ability to help their ailing citizens by making any drugs they can. Brazil, having the capacity to imitate but hardly to innovate, takes this position, that public health needs override the rights of invention; in reprisal, the United States imposes penalty duties on Brazilian exports, to the outrage of the Brazilians.

Respect for industrial patents is also variable, and there is the same conflict of interests. A developing country wants maximum freedom of utilization at minimum cost. It may insist, in return for registering a patent, that the owner produce the product locally, or owners of patents may be required to license them on possibly disadvantageous terms.

While Third World governments theoretically disapprove infringement of intellectual property rights, they may do little to stop what can be an important source of income. Smuggling is a major world industry; and unauthorized copies of popular movies and cassettes, both audio and video are abundant in many places.

The Soviet Union and other Marxist-Leninist countries formerly appropriated intellectual property quite freely, but they have bowed to international usage and have entered the relevant agreements. All countries now belong to the international conventions protecting intellectual property, the watchdog for which is the World Intellectual Property Organization. The United States takes the lead in seeking to tighten standards for protection of patents, copyrights, and designs through multilateral negotiations, with hopes of cutting its trade deficit. It is remarkable that disputes are not more numerous and more acrid in view of the opportunities and temptations for cheating and the stakes involved.

Capital Flows and Exchange Rates

Money flies around the world at electronic speed, seeking the big profits of tiny percentage gains on enormous sums; daily transactions approach $200 billion.[13] Capital flows acquire an importance comparable to trade in merchandise. The importation of capital into the United States, financed by the huge trade deficit, led the nation after 1981 to become dependent on foreign capital, especially Japanese, to finance the federal deficit in a noninflationary manner. Foreign central banks committed $140 billion to shoring

[13]Susan Strange, *Casino Capitalism* (Oxford: Basil Blackwell, 1986), p. 11.

up the dollar against the selling wave of late 1987; and they were said to be assisting the candidate they favored, George Bush, in the election year of 1988 by keeping the dollar steady. Failure to do so would have caused interest rates to leap up, possibly triggering a recession. Foreign banks—mostly Japanese and European—are also a vital source of commercial credit; by 1988 they were making a quarter of business loans in the United States, and they held over a fifth of banking assets and deposits in this country.[14]

The United States' big excess of imports over exports in the 1980s entailed large-scale borrowing from the rest of the world. The U.S. national position changed from creditor by $181 billion in 1981 to debtor by approximately $600 billion at the end of 1988, and this figure grows over $100 billion yearly. Interest and profits will be increasing foreign-held assets by a figure approaching $100 billion per year even if the trade deficit were ended, which cannot be done quickly. Correspondingly, Japan has a huge surplus available for investment worldwide, especially in the United States; its overseas assets are in the range of $1 trillion, bringing in perhaps $100 billion in investment income, added to the continuing Japanese trade surplus of similar magnitude. Little Taiwan in 1988 had $80 billion in reserves. The import of capital is useful if it is applied to financing production, as occurred in the United States in the 19th century and in Japan in the 1950s; it is negative if it serves to finance ultimately unsustainable levels of consumption, as in the United States in the 1980s.

Exchange rates affect the profitability of exports, hence the flow of trade. They were kept steady, based on gold under Bretton Woods arrangements, from 1945 until 1971, when pressures on the U.S. balance of payments became excessive. Since then, there has been no stability but sometimes disconcerting movement, with swings accentuated by speculation. The dollar rose through 1984, not only hurting U.S. exports and underpricing imports but also drawing capital into the United States. The dollar began an overdue slide in February 1985, until by late 1987 it had lost about half its value in terms of currencies of leading trading nations. The inertia of commerce was such, however, that the American trade deficit shrank only belatedly and very slowly.

Business-minded exporting nations like their currency to be undervalued in order to cheapen their exports. Most Third World countries tend to keep their currency overvalued by controls, sometimes to an exaggerated degree, in order to facilitate imports, both luxuries for the elite and necessities for the cities. The United States is pulled both ways. It wants the dollar to be cheap to improve the trade balance; on the other hand, a cheap dollar raises import prices and contributes to inflation. Exchange rates are closely linked to interest rates, which attract funds seeking a maximum return.

[14]Kerry Knobelsdorff, "Foreign Banks Mine Lucrative U.S. Markets," *Christian Science Monitor*, May 16, 1988, p. 16; *New York Times*, April 10, 1988, p. 3.

Stable exchange rates are essential for economic integration, but they are not easily maintained without undesirable controls. The countries responsible for the bulk of world financial flows, the Group of Seven (United States, Japan, West Germany, France, Britain, Italy, and Canada) meet frequently, most commonly to consider and tinker with exchange rates. But the central banks' chief method of intervention is to buy and sell foreign currency; to do this in opposition to market forces can cause large losses, because the money available for speculation is much more than any central bank can match. Speculation feeds on itself; if the conviction spreads that the dollar is going to fall, traders sell dollars, leading to further pressure on the dollar. The banks can also influence exchange rates by raising or lowering interest rates, to make a currency more or less attractive for investment; but it is difficult to manipulate interest rates very much because of their effect on national economies.

Exchange rates cause controversy. Treasury Secretary James Baker's threat to drive down the dollar helped panic the U.S. stock market in October 1987, and his vehement demand that West Germany permit monetary expansion was characterized by Germans as "stupid and arrogant."[15] The Europeans blame the United States for the low dollar, and the United States presses Korea and other countries to raise the value of their currencies, to their annoyance. The Japanese feared that the rise of the yen after 1985 would bankrupt their export industry, but they adjusted extraordinarily well and maintained a very large export surplus.

Relations between exchange rates and trade are complicated not only by capital flows and speculation but also by differing rates of inflation. Higher inflation in one country than another makes fixed exchange rates unrealistic and eventually unsustainable; if this was unsettling for the United States in the early 1980s, it has had disastrous results for Third World countries with immoderate inflation.

Ideally, an international monetary system should be self-regulating; that is, an imbalance should bring about changes in prices, especially of different currencies, that would correct the imbalance. If a surplus on foreign trade could be used only to buy goods abroad, that would presumably occur, and the system would function smoothly. But if the trade surplus is invested in the country with an excess of imports, it rather finances expansion, more imports, and more imbalance.

Some yearn for the traditional gold standard of the 19th century. It prevailed generally until the First World War and was upheld by the United States until the depression of the 1930s; gold was kept as a means of international settlement until 1971. It had the virtue of imposing a stiff impartial discipline on national currencies, preventing inflation, and keeping exchange rates stable. But it did not prevent maladjustments and panics, and

---

[15]*U.S. News and World Report,* November 16, 1987, p. 61.

nostalgia cannot resurrect a premodern standard of value. Governments are not willing to give up their authority to manage, or try to manage, their currencies. The result is a slightly anarchic condition, and there is little idea how the nations are to collaborate more consistently.

Multinational Corporations

Foreign investment in capital-needy countries brings more political complications than in industrialized countries, because of inequality of conditions; but it may usually be deemed positive and desirable.[16] The practice of corporations establishing branches overseas is very old, and it was long associated with European emigration. Until fairly recently capital went mostly into plantation agriculture (such as tea, sugar, or rubber), mining, or oil production. Foreign branches of great manufacturing enterprises became prominent after WW II, especially in the 1960s. They have been growing more rapidly than international trade, and they constitute an expanding fraction of the world economy. This is a direct result of technological development: ease and rapidity of travel, perfection of telecommunication, and improvements of transportation all make it easier and more attractive to locate productive facilities where firms can take advantage of low labor costs or access to markets or both.

In the 1960s, the bulk of the surging multinationals were American; and there was an outcry that American corporate monsters were taking over the globe, threatening economic independence and the viability of nation-states. From the early 1970s, however, European and especially Japanese investments have grown more rapidly than those of the United States. This country remains the largest single holder, but its preponderance has markedly diminished both in the developed countries and in the Third World, where U.S. firms represent under half of direct foreign investment.[17] A few Third World-based enterprises, chiefly Korean and Brazilian, have gone transnational. Movement sometimes goes by stages: Japanese firms are driven by labor costs to set up operations in Singapore; Singaporean firms are pushed by rising wages to branch out to Thailand.

Protectionism contributes to the growth of multinational enterprise. When barriers rise, producers seek to leap over them by establishing branches; the movement of capital takes the place of the movement of goods. For example, imposition of quotas on Japanese automobile exports

---

[16]For general studies, see Moran, *Multinational Corporations;* and Rhys Jenkins, *Transnational Corporations and Uneven Development: The Internationalization of Capital and the Third World* (London: Methuen, 1987).

[17]Jenkins, *Transnational Corporations,* p. 50.

to the United States led to the location of Japanese factories in the United States; and U.S. computer producers, finding difficulties in exporting to Japan, set up shop there. Although governments may be protectionist, they can hardly exclude foreign enterprises that promise employment and technology transfer.

The great corporations are transnational or multinational in the sense of operating in and profiting from many countries, both in manufactures and sales. Yet the large majority of them are effectively national, having headquarters in one nation and being staffed at the top largely or entirely by nationals of one country. This is not inherent in their nature but results from growing up in a single country and having the bulk of their operations there. The entrepreneurs are not necessarily patriotic when business decisions are made; they have little desire to serve anyone. On the contrary, so far as they look to a world market and to profits from foreign operations, they more or less escape control of the home government. As business becomes cosmopolitan, its management likewise will surely become more multinational.

Although nations have frequently forbidden foreign acquisitions that seemed injurious to pride or economic independence, foreign investment in advanced countries is generally seen as productive, making jobs and increasing exports. Most American automobiles sold in Japan, for example, are made by Japanese-owned factories or joint enterprises. For such reasons, multinational operations by corporations of industrial countries in other industrial countries have grown rapidly. In 1986 they came to $50 billion, or five times more than fifteen years earlier.[18] From 1974 to 1987 $1.3 trillion came into the United States.[19]

Branch plants and joint enterprises transfer technology and ideas more effectively than does trade. They inject a new competitive impulse, increase employment, and stimulate ideas of management; the effect of Japanese factories showing Americans how to operate has been salutary. The mobility of capital favors market economies and gives an incentive for economic policies favorable to production. The exported enterprises, moreover, acquire a growing stake in the well-being of the countries where they become established.

On the other hand, direct foreign investment in the Third World has increased much less since the late 1960s.[20] There has been much criticism of the effect of multinational corporations (MNCs) on weaker and less developed economies. They are often seen as imperialistic, monopolistic, and exploitative.[21] It would appear, however, that many of the problems, such

[18]*The Economist,* November 26, 1988, p. 73.

[19]Martin and Susan Tolchin, "Foreign Money," p. 63.

[20]Jenkins, *Transnational Corporations,* p. 7.

[21]For a negative view, see Volker Bornschier and Christopher Chase-Dunn, *Transnationals and Underdevelopment* (New York: Praeger Publishers, 1985).

as the increase of inequality allegedly brought by the foreign enterprise, are normal to the development process; and foreign enterprises do not usually behave much differently from domestic ones.

The foreign corporation in a less developed country is expected to pay better wages than local employers; it will also probably meet its tax obligations and obey laws more carefully than national entrepreneurs because of its vulnerability. However, it is distrusted as alien; and its economic power and sophistication may lead to abuses. A sin commonly imputed to the multinationals is that they support undemocratic governments willing to make deals disadvantageous for the people, repress unions and strikes, and keep wages low. Something such has doubtless occurred with some frequency, but it is not usually clear whether a government favoring foreign investment is selling out the interests of its people or does so for the sake of economic growth.

Especially in the 1960s, the activities of MNCs in less developed countries and attacks on them were the subject of international friction. In an extreme case, Castro's takeover of U.S. investments in Cuba was the principal cause of the break of relations in 1960–1961. In many countries, quarrels arose over concessions of mineral resources, which nationalistic parties denounced as a giveaway of the national patrimony. Initially welcomed for the investment they brought, the alien enterprises found themselves resented and sometimes expropriated; they would then go to the home government for support, which that government, somewhat unwillingly, might give. Under the Hickenlooper Amendment, the United States government was required to end assistance to governments that nationalized American holdings without prompt and adequate compensation. This has been applied only once (against Ceylon in 1963), but expropriation of American properties has caused much bad feeling and has evoked reprisals.

Nationalizations peaked in the mid-1970s, with 83 cases in 1975,[22] and have since declined to very few. For several reasons, friction over MNCs has greatly diminished. The most valuable foreign holdings, those in mining and petroleum, have generally been nationalized, often retaining the former foreign owner as contracted manager. Oil companies, for example, provide technical and marketing services for a fee or a share of profits instead of producing and selling oil themselves, leaving the host country the satisfactions of ownership. U.S. firms seem less imperialistically threatening as more Japanese and European competitors enter the markets. It has become more difficult politically for home governments to intervene visibly on behalf of business interests; and the corporations, without support from home, have adjusted their relations with host countries. Many Third World countries have developed industrial capacities of their own and are less jealous of foreign holdings.

---

[22]Jenkins, *Transnational Corporations,* p. 179.

Both sides have learned that they can gain from the relationship. Developing country governments, advised by United Nations and other international organizations, have become more sophisticated in their attitudes; they have found that they can extract benefits from foreign corporations in many ways: by requiring them to bring in technology, educate local workers and professionals, involve local enterprises, buy local products, reinvest profits, and export a certain proportion of their production. More sensible than to nationalize foreign enterprises is to get them to serve the national economy.

The corporations, on the other hand, have become more cooperative and less intrusive. Instead of the traditional wholly-owned subsidiaries, closely managed from a distant headquarters, they have increasingly formed joint ventures or made licensing or franchise agreements, or entered into management contracts in lieu of ownership.[23] For economic as well as political reasons, they minimize the number of foreign employees, even at upper levels.

Corporations are ready or eager to go wherever there are attractive conditions: political stability, moderate taxation and regulatory policies, skilled or at least educable labor, efficient communications, good transportation, and access to markets. The usefulness of foreign investment is shown not only by such booming economies as Singapore but also by the rapid growth of Brazil (until checked by foreign debt), which has skillfully coordinated foreign with state and private Brazilian capital. The advance of Taiwan and South Korea is even more impressive; Japanese investment has been particularly useful for the latter.

Despite political shortsightedness and uneconomic barriers, business has become more international because of the demands and possibilities of ever-changing technology; and it internationalizes the world.

The Global Community

Governments, like other strong organizations, are inward-looking, competitive, and desirous of underlining their separate values. But whether they work for it or not, the erosion of differences among nations brings hope for a better international order. The ever growing ability of peoples to exchange goods and ideas makes political differences less relevant.

Tariffs are anachronistic, like the tolls levied by medieval barons. It is no more rational to impede the shipment of goods from Asia to California

---

[23]Gilpin, *The Political Economy*, p. 256; see also Adeoye A. Akinsanya, *Multinationals in a Changing Environment: A Study of Business-Government Relations in the Third World* (New York: Praeger, 1986).

than from Kansas to New York. No country can economically supply nearly all that it needs, while numerous items can hardly be produced economically unless they can be sold globally. Trade barriers also interfere with production, which becomes internationalized by finding sources or placing facilities wherever is most advantageous. The broader the market, the more useful specialization becomes.

The European Economic Community shows the extent to which historically self-centered but democratic powers can be drawn together by economic needs. Their steady economic growth would not have been possible if the countries had retained their old walls. The EEC has been hamstrung by special interests and problems, especially related to agriculture; however, tariff barriers have been torn down and virtually all remaining impediments to intra-European trade are to be eliminated by the end of 1992, permitting goods, capital, and people to travel freely. Restrictions on services are to be eliminated, and regulations are to be made uniform. Integration tends to grow; the EEC has a "European currency unit," or "ecu," which it is proposed to make into a common currency, to be administered by a European central bank.

If a hundred special interests can be overridden, this will make a single market of 320 million customers with as much purchasing power as the United States.[24] The exports of this area in 1987 were 60 percent greater than those of the United States and double those of Japan. European producers, in a bigger and more competitive market, will become more competitive in the world.

Taking a lesson from the European success, the United States and Canada agreed in 1988 to remove all tariffs between the two countries in ten years, also to ease barriers in most service sectors, liberalize controls on U.S. investments in Canada (except for "cultural" industries such as broadcasting and publishing), and to remove many other restrictions on exchanges. Most trade between the two countries was already free; opening the door wider is even more beneficial to Canada, which gains freer access to a larger market, than to the United States. Such free trade areas will doubtless grow. There has been discussion of extending the U.S.-Canadian arrangements to more or less of Latin America and Japan or other Asian countries.

There is some danger, however, that the elimination of some barriers will lead to raising others. The United States and Japan are apprehensive that European unification may mean fencing off Europe for the benefit of Europeans.[25] European producers are not eager to see American or Japanese producers take advantage of the newly broadened market, entry into

[24]*The Economist*, February 13–19, 1988, p. 45; *New York Times*, May 22, 1988, p. F–1.

[25]Stephen Greenhouse, "The Growing Fear of Fortress Europe, *New York Times,* October 23, 1988, p. F–1.

which they regard as a privilege for which they want reciprocal concessions. Moreover, there are protectionist sentiments in the growing Eurobureaucracy.

It can hardly be doubted, however, that the results of eliminating trade barriers of any kind are on balance positive. Although integration does not rapidly decrease nationalism,[26] it not only raises production and lowers prices but brings the multiplication and interweaving of relations of all kinds. It makes a mixture of adversary with mostly cooperative issues and replaces singular hatreds with numerous annoyances and a multitude of gains.

This implies a reduced role for the state. As the economic separation of European nations is erased, part of their sovereignty is transferred to the Community, and the European Parliament slowly adds to its powers. So far as the world is united economically, corporations extend themselves beyond the jurisdiction of the state, which loses control of both markets and productive units. Political authorities have the task of fostering and guiding production in the competitive arena, as the Japanese have done best.

International agencies strive to do for the world something of what the EEC bureaucracy does for the European nations. The GATT and the international financial agencies, among many formal and informal organizations, help to reduce frictions over investment and exchange issues. Understandings also grow in importance in regard to many affairs of common interest, mostly economic, from air traffic to customs procedures. Such understandings, or "regimes" as they are called,[27] are a kind of latter-day international law. Qualified, incomplete, and without formal enforcement, they grow up from and are enforced by practical necessities in the density of international intercourse. Nations observe them in the usually justified belief that others will do likewise.

Economic integration and the lessening of the artificial separation of peoples represent not only the hope of better relations among the industrial nations but also the hope of reduction of world poverty. Not much can be expected from aid programs; the most effective way in which the leading economic powers can help the poorer countries is by encouraging them to enter fully into the world economy. There is no good reason for any advanced country to restrict the sale of products of the developing nations. At present, raw materials and commodities produced by less developed countries have free or nearly free access to markets of the rich countries, but their industrial products are penalized. It is as though there were a

---

[26]Robert O. Keohane and Joseph S. Nye, *Power and Interdependence* (Boston: Little Brown, 1977), p. 210.

[27]Discussed by Stephen Krasner, ed., *International Regimes* (Ithaca NY: Cornell University Press, 1985).

conspiracy—and Third World nations are willing to believe there is—to keep them from advancing beyond the stage of primary producers serving the industrial interests of the advanced countries. A better integrated world economy would not only open countless opportunities for production but would imply freer flow of investments and would tend to raise earnings toward the level of the real value of labor.

Chapter 10

Inequality
of Nations

Unequal Conditions

Poverty has many faces: poor health care and malnutrition, with life expectancy under 50 years; illiteracy and ignorance, with severe shortage of skilled or technically trained personnel; large families in poor housing; and simple lack of everything except absolute necessities or subsistence. By 1986 figures, 39 countries, with population of 2,493,000,000, had per capita incomes under $450; there were 48 countries in the range between $450 and $4000; 21 Western industrial countries with population of 741,600,000 had per capita incomes from $4860 (Spain) to $17,680 (Switzerland).[1] Those near the bottom live in a very different world from those near the top. The gap comes (in 1986 figures) between per capita product of $3000 and $6000; hardly any countries fall in this range.

There is a tendency for growing separation of rich and poor. At the upper level, economic and cultural differences are diminishing. It is remarkable how close to the same level such countries as France, Japan, Sweden, Italy, Germany, Britain, and the United States stand. In 1929 the Euro-

---

[1]*World Development Report,* World Bank (New York: Oxford University Press, 1988), pp. 222–23.

pean income level was only about half that of the United States, and the Second World War caused further unequalization. But by now, the differences among the Western democracies, from Austria to Finland to Britain, along with Canada, Australia, New Zealand, and Japan, are less than between regions within the United States or Britain.

Their way of life is increasingly cosmopolitan; and as the modern world spreads its cultural blanket, people everywhere become more alike. The dress, entertainments, and to some extent the mode of thinking of those who fully belong to the modern world becomes similar around the world. Yet in a fundamental way the world becomes worse divided. The economic gap between the advanced nations and those left behind by the scientific-industrial revolution does not shrink but for the majority widens. Latin America and Africa, along with a number of countries of Asia, have generally grown poorer in relative terms, in many cases in absolute terms, in the 1980s. The world community increasingly splits between nations that look down on the misery of the majority and those that can only envy the rich.

It may seem remarkable that material progress is not universal; after all, any country needs only to look how the more prosperous ones manage their affairs and do likewise as best it can. A vast reservoir of technology is available at little cost, often furnished gratis by international agencies and economic aid programs; capital is happy to go anywhere that it can be profitably applied with reasonable security; Africans, Asians, and Latin Americans make perfectly competent workers happy with a small fraction of what their counterparts in the industrialized countries receive. Yet many countries stagnate or go backwards. In the 1980s most African countries have had negative growth rates, like such more or less resource-rich lands as Argentina, Uruguay, Chile, Guatemala, Bolivia, Philippines, Peru, and Venezuela.

The case of Argentina is especially striking. It has all the ordinarily esteemed advantages: excellent resources, a largely homogeneous and well-educated population, and a tradition of constitutional government; and it made remarkable progress after the disorders of mid-19th century. By the 1920s, it had taken its place among the elite of nations. But after an incompetent president was removed by a military coup in 1930, the road has been downhill through a long series of corrupt governments, military dictatorships, and unstable democratic regimes that have done little better than efforts at authoritarian discipline.[2]

Less familiar is Suriname, which in 1975 was one of most prosperous countries of South America; a dozen years later it was beset by shortages of almost everything, soaring inflation, unemployment, the breakdown of its

[2]See Carlos H. Waisman, *Reversal of Development in Argentina* (Princeton: Princeton University Press, 1987).

modest industrial production, and civil conflict. It subsists thanks to charity from the Netherlands.[3]

The more productive and advanced nations have more intense relations with the world cultural and economic centers and they are also more stimulated by international competition. There is no indication of retrogression in any of the advanced industrial democracies. But if Guyana plays no role in world affairs, this does not much trouble the rulership or prevent it from preferring exploitation to development. It feels reasonably secure; and no one, not even Venezuela, which claims much of its territory, is going to attack it as long as the Guyanese injure only themselves.[4]

In Haiti, a gangsterish group finds it more important to keep themselves in power than to make Haiti attractive to foreign investment, tourists, and donors of aid. If nine-tenths of Haitians with professional qualifications forsake their country,[5] this makes it easier for the exploitative elite to stay atop the passive many. Many African countries are poorer than they were as colonies.[6] Factories and schools are abandoned; two-thirds of the roads that Zaire, a land of great mineral wealth, possessed on obtaining independence in 1960 were impassable a generation later,[7] although the population had more than doubled.

There have been countless examples of economic retrogression in the past, or more often stagnation, which might last for centuries. The West— that is, the nation-state system of Western Europe plus its overseas extensions since the 17th century—has had the unique good fortune that for about a thousand years it has been tending to pull ahead of the rest of the world. But until the 16th century, the differences of technical and economic capacity between Europe and such venerable centers of civilization as India and China were not extreme.

The gap began to widen sharply with the scientific revolution beginning in the 17th century and the industrial revolution that took hold late in the 18th century and has been quickening ever since. Even in the latter 19th century, the difference in material standards between the masses in the West and much of Asia was not outrageous, a ratio of perhaps five to one. But the technological explosion of recent decades has increased the gap between cash incomes (excluding goods that do not enter the market) to a hundred to one in the case of the poorest countries, the so-called "Fourth World."

The explosive expansion of technology makes it more difficult to nar-

[3]*New York Times,* July 13, 1987, p. 25.

[4]Chaitram Singh, *Guyana: Politics in a Plantation Society* (New York: Praeger, 1988).

[5]Roger C. Riddell, *Foreign Aid Reconsidered,* (Baltimore: Johns Hopkins University Press, 1987), p. 254.

[6]Riddell, *Foreign Aid,* p. 272.

[7]Blaine Harden, "Journey out of the Heart of Darkness," *Washington Post National Edition,* December 21, 1987, p. 13.

row the gulf. Modern production techniques are out of reach of the poorer countries, except as introduced by foreign entities. A generation or so ago, it was not difficult for a less developed country to install a textile plant or even a steel mill and congratulate itself on industrialization. Nowadays advanced foreign technology and a leap of management and skills are necessary in order to produce even bicycles competitive on the world market, much less the sophisticated devices of the computer age. Only countries that work very closely with the United States or Japan (such as South Korea and Taiwan), that invite foreign corporations to do the job, or that can afford large expenditures and have a big protected market (such as Brazil and India) can make a start. Microelectronics and bioengineering are for the few. Not only do the less advantaged countries lack supercomputers or the capacity to make use of them; they can hardly afford a good industrial laboratory, and they do not have the conditions and institutions that would encourage anyone in the modern world to install one.

Paradoxically, the technological advances that bring the world into a single cultural sphere cause maladjustments and problems that increase the differences between peoples.

Causes of Inequality

In the contemporary world, inequality of nations results from many things, advantages and disadvantages in the complex agglomeration of different societies. Mostly, however, it is the result of the better adaptation of some than others to the needs and opportunities of modern production and their ability to work with and profit by the international system. The difficulties of the poorer countries in many ways no doubt elude our understanding. However, they seem to include the following:

1) Technology feeds on technology, and the more advanced a nation is, the better equipped to utilize the cornucopia of technical knowledge. Development proceeds where the informational, personal, and material resources are present; to shift to new regions is hard. A high-tech firm may use cheap labor in a Third World country for part of the production process, but it naturally keeps at home its research facilities, its planning, and its basic capacities, not from chauvinism but because its leading personnel prefer to work there and can be more productive in the better conditions. Because of poor infrastructure, lack of support facilities, and shortage of managerial and other skills, it costs more to apply advanced engineering in a poor country than a rich one. Low wages of unqualified labor do not help much, as unskilled or semiskilled labor has a decreasing role in production.

2) Wealth generates wealth and poverty reproduces poverty. Some countries have surplus agricultural capacity; in others, soils are degraded

and eroded, or denuded by gatherers of firewood.[8] If the government plants trees, they are cut down or eaten by goats. Desertification advances in many countries, as growing populations overuse the land.

3) The poor countries have less to put into productive enterprise, they invest a smaller share of the national product in the future, and their investments are probably less remunerative than those of more advanced countries. The poorer countries not only spend a smaller fraction of their small incomes on research and development but apply it less efficiently.

4) The modern centers attract more capable persons from the less developed countries as travel becomes easier, people are better able to inform themselves, and nations become less dissimilar. Education, laboratories, and opportunities for creating or earning wealth are in the wealthy countries; they draw the ambitious, those who have skills valuable anywhere (such as engineers and scientists), and those who have independent resources. Those who feel discontented with a less than modern life-style or frustrated and suffocated in the less dynamic society look to a better existence elsewhere; the young people who are most needed for the future find it easiest to emigrate. Their countries are robbed of skills not only of this but of future generations; and as some go and the national prospects worsen, others find it easier to follow.

5) Poorer countries have weaker educational systems, and the results of their education may be partly negative. Teachers, lacking political influence, are miserably underpaid. Large or huge Third World universities, with mostly amateur, ad honorem faculties, give little useful training. Many of them are politicized into nonfunctionality. Their graduates, with diplomas coveted as entitlement to government employment, add more to discontent than to productivity.

6) Chronic disease and parasitic infestation reduce physical and mental capacity, affecting a large part of the population in poorer countries, especially children. Malnutrition, verging on starvation, afflicts perhaps a third of the world's people and diminishes their ability to work. Poor hygiene and weak physiques demoralize the masses and deepen their separation from the more fortunate.

7) The division of the world may be summarized as between the countries of rapid population growth, which have difficulty supporting present numbers, and those of slow or no increase of numbers, which can provide their people with increasing material abundance. There are few nations between. Those in the first group divide slowly rising output among more and more persons—in most countries, populations double in less than 35, often 25 years. The poorer country, with the larger families, is less capable of raising its children to be productive citizens, while ever larger invest-

---

[8]Lester R. Brown, "Analyzing the Population Trap," in Lester Brown ed. *State of the World 1987* (New York: W.W. Norton, 1987), pp. 22–36.

ments are needed even to maintain economic and social infrastructure, especially in overcrowded cities.

8) The economically weaker countries are disadvantaged, for political, cultural, and psychological reasons, in dealings with the modern world. In buying and selling goods and services, those with the greater resources inevitably get somewhat the better of the bargain. The financial burden is worse, as rulers of poorer countries would relieve present problems by mortgaging the future. Political leaders use foreign loans more or less for their own benefit; the nation, in due course, is expected to repay, and capital is drained out. Foreign borrowing, unless better managed than usual in less developed countries, demoralizes, increases economic and psychological dependency, impoverishes, and compounds itself as more is borrowed to service the debt. The indebted Third World can expect little or no economic improvement until the debt issue is resolved.

9) The less developed countries offer little security and predictability for investment. Despite the fact that capital is relatively scarce in them and potentially should have—often does have—a higher return, it takes flight from political uncertainties to the refuge of the United States, Western Europe, or other stable countries. When natives take money out, foreigners hesitate to put it in.

10) Most less developed countries receive low prices for raw material exports because of overproduction and because technology accounts for an ever larger proportion of the value of finished goods. But their low-tech manufactures are seen as unfair competition in the industrial countries and encounter barriers; they have little bargaining power in seeking better conditions.

11) The military establishment, which has some influence in advanced countries, in less developed countries either holds power directly or keeps watch over the civilian administration. In many, it uses its power for its own benefit. But the military is not usually very progressive; it represents waste, not production. It may exceptionally be concerned for economic strength, but its mentality is not conducive to development.

12) Unproductive institutions perpetuate themselves. Prominent among them is state management of the economy, which may function tolerably well in advanced countries but is almost always inefficient in less developed countries, sometimes very wasteful and exploitative. Pressure groups dependent on state enterprises and controls are usually able to prevent measures to rationalize the economy.

13) There is a general demoralization. National pride has little appeal for the educated. Native cultures are being buried under imports, mostly of uninspiring quality. Superstition and mysticism flourish, from anomic fatalism to belief in witchcraft, with consequences for the economic and political structures. To modernize requires willingness to adopt foreign ways and to surrender a large part of native habits, values, and culture,

guiding modernization to preserve essentials. Only a very self-assured culture can accept extensive loss of institutions without demoralization. Few can emulate the Japanese success. But to try to go backwards to traditional values, as in Islamic fundamentalism, invites weakness.

14) Societies are poorly integrated, divided between the rich (by local standards, sometimes by world standards) and the medium to very poor. They are also usually split along racial, ethnic, or religious lines. Most new countries lack a significant national history. There is little sense of national community; different groups feel entitled to get whatever they can for themselves.

15) Most less developed countries are ruled by more or less parasitic groups using their position for their own benefit. Poor and rich share the idea that befits the static society: if you go up, I go down; or I am down because you are up. One does not come near understanding Third World politics unless one understands the charms of aristocracy, the abundance of servants, the possession of modern luxuries when the surrounding masses have nothing, the pleasure of jetting around the world when most people are confined to the village.

Any of these handicaps would burden a developing society; unhappily, most or all of them occur together.

The Political Incubus

The heaviest of the chains holding nations back is the failure of government to work for the general wellbeing. Sometimes government is incredibly bad—stupid from the point of view even of the masters. The Khmer Rouge went far toward destroying Cambodia as a civilized nation. The military clique governing Burma since 1962 has less dramatically but effectively demodernized the country. The Soviet Union decided in the latter 1980s that it had been badly governed through most of its history under the brutal tyranny of Stalin and the dull tyranny of the Brezhnev era, and for this reason had achieved little for immense sacrifices. The corruption that afflicts most nations is not only a burden on the economy but a symptom of the rot of the political system.

The self-management of society is a problem for which the most modernized and educated nations have no adequate answer, but it is axiomatic that bad government is characteristic of less developed countries. If a country were organized in an efficient manner favorable for production, it would surely rise rapidly. But bad government is self-perpetuating. It closes down freedom of information and criticism that would facilitate reform. It maintains or increases the inequality of classes and the social divisions that are a major cause of bad government. It rewards politics more than production, cheats its people, discourages planning and saving, and develops character traits ill suited for a modern economy.

The modern industrial nations give the less developed countries a model (however far they fall short of it in practice) of reasonably responsible government. But in some ways modernization makes political improvement more difficult. Traditional standards are weakened without being effectively replaced by more modern ones. Modernization ordinarily tends, especially in the more backward countries, to increase inequality, as a few gain far more than most, and those on top acquire tools of oppression. There can be no well-integrated society of the near-modern and the premodern.

As economies become more complex, political structures become more crucial and misgovernment more damaging. Problems of modernization exceed the capacities of the rulership of the traditional society. It lacks expertise for a thousand new tasks, from providing education at all levels to managing exchange and interest rates, guiding labor relations, investment policy, and a host of needs for regulation in the uncertainties of rapid change, all inviting official intervention and offering opportunities for corruption.

The political struggle is usually chaotic; crude and brutal characters come to the top. There is no tradition of moderation and compromise. Sophistication of decision making may be low; inflation rates of hundreds of percent or more in many countries testify to institutional incapacity and incompetence. Through ignorance and shortsighted greed many countries have ruined agriculture by requiring farmers to sell their produce to the state much below market prices.

Rulership may be of poor character or incompetent. Bolivia was governed by a narcotics dealer, General Luís García Meza, 1980–1981. The Nicaraguan Sandinistas have grossly mismanaged the economy, for example by prohibiting private sale of foodstuffs that the state could not handle, thereby wasting produce while people went hungry. Argentina, a relatively sophisticated nation, decided in 1987 to move the capital from Buenos Aires to Patagonia at enormous expense when the country was nearly bankrupt; the supposed benefit was to facilitate trimming the bureaucracy because civil servants would refuse to leave the comforts of the metropolis. The project was soon forgotten. Afghan authorities, boasting of the entry of an armored column into the beseiged city of Khost in late December, stated that joyous residents "showered the armored convoy with flowers,"[9] presumably taken from the local greenhouses.

Leaders also have shown egregious incompetence in foreign relations. It is difficult to see how the dictator of Iraq could have calculated in 1979 that he could overcome Iran, a richer country with a population three times

[9]*New York Times,* January 1, 1988, p. 2.

larger than Iraq's. In December 1987, the Nicaraguan leaders, for no evident reason but bravado, spoke of plans for a huge military buildup, including armed forces of 600,000 and much Soviet armor, at a time when the U.S. Congress was considering support for their enemies. They also gratuitously stated that they would not recognize electoral results unfavorable to themselves. A few days later, probably having gotten better advice, President Ortega made some reasonable proposals.[10]

Political leadership in the poorer countries is also handicapped by class and ethnic differences. In Belgium, the differences of Walloons and Flemings lead to democratic powersharing; the opposition of those of African and East Indian origin in Guyana is the basis of oppression, like the differences of Europeans and Blacks in South Africa. Such divisions in a host of countries make democracy unworkable, as freedom of agitation of political parties equals freedom of demagogic if not violent agitation for a particular clientele.

Bloody political extremism is not absent in Europe (as shown by terrorism in Northern Ireland and the Basque region), but it has been exceptional in the West since WW II. In the Third World it is all too frequent. Thus "Tamil Tigers" randomly murder humble Sinhalese; gunmen will enter a theater to shower death on the audience. Sinhalese extremists kill those of their own nationality who favor compromise. In India, Sikh radicals shoot up a wedding party. In the 1960s Liberal and Conservative peasants in Colombia gunned down tens of thousands of peasants of the opposite affiliation (while the leaders of the respective parties, more attuned to the modern world, socialized in the capital). In the 1970s, military authorities in relatively advanced Argentina "disappeared" thousands of those suspected of radical affiliation. The Khmer Rouge in Kampuchea, 1976–1978, tried to liquidate anyone who could read, wore glasses, had a profession, or owned a home, and went on to kill those guilty of Vietnamese or Chinese ethnicity and suspected members of their own party. Between a quarter and a third of the total population were murdered.

Death squads and terrorism are a regular part of contemporary politics in several Latin American countries. Political slayings, by leftist guerrillas, rightist gangs, security forces, or drug traffickers, are a daily occurrence in Colombia; although the higher authorities have seemed to have good intentions, there have been no prosecutions. Human life—or that of the "lower classes" or of political enemies—is not much valued in a large part of the world. But without respect for people as people one cannot build a progressive economic and political order.

Bad government makes poverty, ignorance, and amorality, all of which produce bad government, just as good government brings prosperity, education, and civic feelings, leading, it may be hoped, to better government.

[10]*New York Times*, December 20, 1987, p. E 2; January 14, 1988, p. I-31.

An incompetent civil service is a political power blocking the reform of the civil service. If the police are abusive and extortionate, only persons of such inclinations enter the profession, and they will make it difficult for honest individuals to work with them. It is hard for higher authority to cleanse the forces, because they are needed to keep order, and the police are called upon to discipline the police. President Miguel de la Madrid of Mexico, on taking office in 1983, promised and seems to have really intended a "moral revolution" to root out corruption, especially in the police; he gave up long before the successor he picked promised to root out corruption. Decent and educated people at the head of the government cannot check death squads when, as in Brazil and Colombia, the uniformed forces are part of the problem.

Whether in hopes of promoting development or to please political interests, the state usually assumes control of much of the economy. State enterprise is not necessarily inefficient, but it is almost certain to be when the political system is troubled, and its wastefulness keeps the economy backward. Having nationalized, the state cannot easily denationalize, partly because of a shortage of capitalist-managers to take over, more because of political interests. The circle is hard to break: Edward Seaga became prime minister of Jamaica in 1981 with a program of economic liberalization; despite much foreign assistance, political pressures led him to expand state intervention in agriculture, tourism, and bauxite mining.

Democracy, or quasidemocracy, does not work much better than dictatorship. Habits of authoritarianism are not set aside as soon as elections are held; the respect for law is slow to build. Some interpret democracy as license not to pay taxes; it is estimated that in democratic Argentina less than half of should-be taxpayers even file returns, and value-added tax is 70 percent evaded.[11] Patronage becomes the chief rationale of political parties; many public servants, very likely a large majority, have little or nothing useful to do. Typically, in Calcutta there are 35 employees to handle each municipal bus. A government job, probably paying several times the average income, is a precious possession, in return for which the public servant conforms to whatever political superiors require.

Where there is an excess of bureaucrats there follows an excess of regulations, many or most of which hamstring production so far as applied, if they do not give openings for corruption. The mass of regulations being unenforceable, they are irregularly enforced or ignored in the interest of practicality. The result, as in Argentina, is a half-functioning economy, where power lines short-circuit, telephones are unobtainable and usually do not work anyway, the state oil company is the only petroleum producer in the world that regularly loses money, income taxes are a joke, the mails are abominable, and hyperinflation makes economic calculations impossi-

[11]*Wall Street Journal,* March 20, 1987, p. 11.

ble. But business and labor alike block change in a system they find comfortable.[12]

The state, whether quasidemocratic or dictatorial, is clientelistic, power flowing downward through leaders and their followers at several levels. The essentially oligarchic regime is little capable of formulating, much less implementing the kind of resolute policies needed to reshape the social order and the structure of power. Unable to make hard choices, the government mostly seeks to avoid injuring any strong group in a society of vested interests. The goal of politics is not to achieve anything for the community but to get benefits for office-holding.

If the system of clientelistic or corporatist controls weakens and democratic institutions become more effective, it encounters other troubles. Politicians propose and the people call for more concessions than the state can afford or the upper classes care to concede. From the point of view of the elite, the virtue of democracy should be the right of private property, which under a dictatorship may be insecure; any attack on property rights (such as land reform) is held antidemocratic and an abomination. Unions and sundry organizations that in the well-functioning democracy would be agents of pluralism, intermediaries between people and state, turn into additional contestants in the struggle for privilege. Labor laws become means of extortion. If anyone really moves to carry out a program of popular benefits, the likely result is overspending, economic disequilibria, failure of confidence, recession or depression, and corresponding discontent. It is worse if, as usually occurs, the redistributional movement is accompanied by radical agitation; the tone of threat to the social order is as important as the substance of "progressive" legislation.

Government by the majority in most of the world would mean government by the poor. This is unacceptable to the nonpoor minority. Any program really beneficial for the masses is suspect of demagogy, and the elite give priority to the preservation of status, the elevation of the possessors above the propertyless. Measures proposed for social justice, which may be of more benefit to political operators than to the truly needy, alarm the better-off; they react defensively, decrying, with some justification, corruption, atheism, and communism. Economic troubles, political strife, and tensions follow.[13]

No one has devised a system whereby highly unequal countries can gradually grow into democratic attitudes and institutions while avoiding the abuses of a populist democracy. It may be impossible as long as there is a wide gap between those who participate in the modern world and those

---

[12]Tyler Bridges, "Argentina's Underground Economy May Dig Deeper," *Christian Science Monitor,* January 5, 1988, p. 11.

[13]On populist democracy, see Robert Wesson, *Democracy in Latin America* (New York: Praeger, 1982), Ch. 4.

who do not. The fantastic technological advance of civilization brings peoples together but also separates them and troubles their relations.

Weaker Powers Among the Strong

Weaker powers want above all to be treated as important in a world inclined to ignore them. As would-be equals, they jealously guard their dignity. Thus they will not allow their people to sell blood to hospitals in the rich countries because this would be demeaning, and they reject the dumping of garbage on their territory, even for good pay.[14] They detest anything suggestive of coercion, not only because of whatever injury it may bring but because it reminds them of their vulnerability; and any visible pressure is resented.

They most of all desire to reaffirm the national sovereignty. They are zealous in defense of the equality of all states under international law, which is an artificial extension of the almost universally accepted principle of the legal equality of persons. They reject any intrusion across borders, such as the right, as asserted by Israel and the United States, to seize wanted persons in other countries.[15] They are also eager advocates of international organization, to which they cannot contribute much but from which they benefit. They find their best forum at the United Nations and affiliated bodies, where they have their turn at the podium along with powers perhaps thousands of times weightier in world affairs.

The uninfluential have their own league, the organization of the non-aligned states, sometimes called the Group of 77. The group was started with 23 members in Belgrade in 1961; it has grown to over 120, but it has almost no formal organization. The demands and complaints of the "Non-Aligned" (which can include such a committed state as Cuba because it does not have a formal military alliance) are primarily directed against the richer states with which they have most to do and from which they may hope for favors.

A large majority of Third World states, despite or because of their dependence, vote contrarily to the United States in the U.N. For example, such generally good friends of the United States as Mexico, Brazil, and Argentina agree with their superpower in only about one-sixth of votes taken in the General Assembly.[16] So far as they are free to do so, they seek to diversify relations to reduce dependence. Latin Americans cultivate trade

---

[14]Guinea-Bissau, one of the poorest of nations, rejected $600 million for taking 15 million tons of refuse. *Christian Science Monitor,* July 11, 1988, p. 8.

[15]Tom J. Farer, "International Law," *Foreign Policy* 71, Summer 1988, p. 29.

[16]Abraham F. Lowenthal, "Rethinking U.S. Interests in the Western Hemisphere," *Journal of Interamerican Studies and World Affairs* 29, Spring 1987, p. 7.

with Europe and Japan, if not the Soviet Union. Similarly, Romania has promoted relations with China, to the annoyance of the Soviets.

Mexico, to compensate for economic dependence, decries interventionism and imperialism; it has regularly taken positions contrary to the United States regarding Cuba, Central America, and other matters. For the United States to favor a policy is to turn Mexicans against it.[17] No Mexican politician can afford to speak English in public, although he may (like President Salinas de Gortari) have graduated from Harvard. There is a culture of anti-Americanism, as in the National Museum of Intervention in Mexico City, entirely dedicated to the wrongs inflicted by the United States. Chief of these was the annexation of a large part of Mexican territory in 1847, the infamy of which is taught to all schoolchildren. According to a British scholar, Mexican anti-Americanism is less a grassroots sentiment than "a formal knee-jerk phenomenon, the work of political elites who need a rallying cry. It is a manipulated ideology, a ploy to rally support, done just as much by the Right as by the Left."[18]

Typically, Colombian foreign policy is pulled toward the United States by a high degree of dependence but pushed away by the urge for national autonomy and memories of Colombia's independent history and U.S. support for the separation of Panama (1903). The nation would like to win international kudos and respect as an independent force for peace, in the face of economic problems reducing its freedom of action.[19] This implied bettering relations with Castro's Cuba, despite its sometimes unpleasant behavior toward Colombia, and support for peace initiatives for Central America, to the displeasure of the Reagan administration.

The thrust of nonalignment is generally anti-U.S. because this country impinges much more on the Third World than do the Soviet Union, Japan, or European countries. Latin American foreign ministries and that of Canada have failed to see the bipolar contest in the same way as the United States. Brazil, for example, under conservative military regimes was not bothered by the official Marxist-Leninist orientation of Angola or the presence there of Cuban troops; the Brazilians wanted to develop their own influence and did so rather well.[20] Nearly all Third World nations were angered by the Soviet invasion of Afghanistan, but hardly any were willing to

[17]George W. Grayson, *The United States and Mexico: Patterns of Influence* (New York: Praeger, 1984), p. 193.

[18]*New York Times,* January 7, 1988, p. 4. For a Mexican view, see José Juan de Olloqui, "On the Formulation of U.S. Policy toward Mexico," in *Mexico in Transition: Implications for U.S. Policy,* ed. Susan K. Purcell, (New York: Council on Foreign Relations, 1988), pp. 109–19.

[19]Bruce M. Bagley and Juan G. Totkatlian, "Colombian Foreign Policy in the 1980s: The Search for Leverage," *Journal of Interamerican Studies and World Affairs,* 27 (Fall 1985), pp. 27–62.

[20]Alexandre de Barros, "Defense and Security Issues: Implications for the New Atlantic Triangle," in *Latin America, Western Europe, and the U.S.: Reevaluating the Atlantic Triangle* ed. Wolf Grabendorff and Riordan Roett (New York: Praeger, 1985), p. 172.

join the American embargo on sales of grain and the boycott of the Moscow Olympics.

Latin Americans would rather tolerate dictatorship, rightist or leftist, than see the United States intervene in any but the most benign fashion, nonintervention being more important than form of government. There is more anti-U.S. feeling in the Caribbean-Central American area, where U.S. influence is very strong, than in South America, where it weighs less heavily. There is little gratitude for the protection so generously given: the United States becomes unpopular where it expends (and hence intervenes) the most, as in El Salvador and Honduras. Third World peoples are prepared to give credence to almost any tale about the United States, such as that the CIA invented AIDS or that the United States imports Third World children for medical experiments. Africans suspect that a "safe sex" campaign is a Western device to reduce their population and potential power. Pro-U.S. feelings are apparently strongest in Eastern Europe, where Soviet pressures are greatest.

Self-assertion includes economic nationalism, and small powers are often protectionist; to open the national market seems to invite dominion. This has led to many uneconomic efforts for self-sufficiency. Saudi Arabian wheat costs twelve times the world price.[21] Formerly any self-respecting country wanted to have a steel mill. This has gone out of style, but it is probably held necessary to have a modern air force. It is also probably uneconomic to have a national airline, which every slightly ambitious nation boasts, although it may possess only two or three aged planes. It at least stands for modernization and advertises the country.

In one way, it is useful to be small and weak; generally speaking, the smaller the population the more foreign aid per capita. China and India, with 75 percent of the low-income people of the world, receive only about 10 percent of the economic assistance handed out. But assistance implies dependence, and the smaller low-income countries face a more difficult dilemma in admitting a foreign economic penetration that they are less able to resist. They want foreign investment, technology, and perhaps management; but these make their sovereign independence hollow.

Poorer states often see themselves as less responsible and independent than they are, attributing their problems to superpower greed or domination. Client states, such as the Philippines or South Korea, blame the patron for anything short of earthquakes.[22] Just as politics in the Third World country is commonly personal with a touch of the conspiratorial, people see events in the outside world as the result of mostly malevolent wills. They believe prices of their exports and imports to be fixed not by impersonal

---

[21] *Wall Street Journal*, September 3, 1987, p. 18.

[22] James Fallow, "Korea: The Burden of Omnipotence," *Atlantic* 260, October 1987, pp. 20–25.

market forces but by hidden agencies, just as political affairs are dictated by the CIA or the Trilateral Commission.

Economic conditions being caused by the stronger powers, the less developed nations feel that they deserve more consideration. They want better prices, more investments, and credits on easier terms. The clamor for reform of international interchanges, the New International Economic Order (NIEO), was much heard in the 1960s and 1970s. The want list included price supports, tariff preferences, foreign aid amounting to at least 0.7 percent of the GNP of industrialized countries, debt relief, freedom of nationalization of foreign investments, more technological transfer on better terms, better terms of trade, and more voice in the International Monetary Fund and related agencies.[23] The economic agenda of the less developed countries was largely abandoned in the 1980s because of nonsuccess and the unwillingness of conservatively-minded powers, the United States and other OECD members, to intervene against the market or to make important economic concessions. It was also sidetracked by the problem of the foreign debt and regional issues.

Not getting much sympathy for their broad agenda, producers of many commodities—tin, nickel, coffee, cocoa, natural rubber, bauxite, and others—have formed alliances to restrict marketing. The major consuming countries have been unenthusiastic, although they have sometimes cooperated in the interest of price stability to protect the economies of commodity producers, which are often dependent on one or a few crops. One of the few marketing arrangements to show some success in fixing quotas and prices is the International Coffee Organization. The weakness of would-be cartels is inability to control production. The dumping of sugar, for example (for which the EEC must bear some blame), has depressed the world price well below the cost of production even in efficient producers.

The most important producers' cartel has been the Organization of Petroleum Exporting Countries (OPEC). Founded in 1960, OPEC was enabled by Arab solidarity in the 1973 war with Israel to quadruple crude petroleum prices. It thereby became a significant factor in world affairs, petroleum being by far the most important commodity traded. The war between Iran and Iraq permitted it to triple prices again in 1980. But importing countries were driven to conserve, non-OPEC producers stepped up production, and prices settled down after 1981. The only sword that OPEC has, the cutting of production (so far as members can be persuaded to observe quotas) is two-edged. The OPEC share of world production fell from 56 percent in 1973 to 33 percent in 1988, and dreams of great riches for a contingent of lucky countries evaporated.

The bargaining position of the less developed countries is weakened

---

[23]Robert Gilpin, *The Political Economy of International Relations* (Princeton: Princeton University Press, 1987), p. 299.

by the fading of U.S.-Soviet hostility. When tensions were high in the 1950s and 1960s, countries on the sidelines were favored by competitive wooing; news that the Soviets were offering a project or extending a loan to some country automatically triggered moves by the United States to offset it. Recently Arab countries have been able, by making gestures of turning to the Soviet Union, to exert some pressure on the United States to provide arms. Mostly, the less developed nations have to claim attention on humanitarian grounds or because of the complications they cause in world affairs.

Complications of Inequality

There are many positive effects of the intensive interaction of nations. For the most part, the transfer of technology is a boon. Everyone approves of the spread of hygiene and the reduction of death rates in poorer countries; in some of them, life expectancy is 60 years or more, as high as in the industrial countries a generation ago. Life almost everywhere has become more varied, opening more possibilities of human fulfillment, whether or not it has become happier.

Yet the worsening inequality of nations, whereby most of humanity lives practically in a different world from the prime beneficiaries of the industrial-electronic revolution, causes many social, economic, and political problems for both poor and rich. Some are environmental, such as lower priority poorer peoples give to protecting rainforests and endangered species and their relative reluctance to pay the costs of preventing pollution in their desire for industrialization. Some are social, such as immigration changing the social fabric and politics of the more prosperous lands. Others are political, as their instability confounds the purposes of great powers.

Economic exchanges between poor and rich countries must be considered mostly beneficial for both sides. Without markets abroad, the Third World would be poor and primitive indeed, while the industrial countries need both markets and materials. But economic relations between rich and poor are troubled. Foreign investments in less developed countries are helpful for economic development and the diffusion of technology, but they generate frictions. The wealthy can hardly avoid taking advantage of their superior resources and bargaining power in dealing with the impoverished. Lending is especially subject to abuse; indebtedness has become a curse of most Third World countries.

Illegal commerce also presents grave problems; the poorer countries are the chief source of narcotics for the richer. Andean or Burmese peasants earn ten times as much from coca bushes or opium poppies as from coffee or beans, and there are huge expanses of suitable land. Consequently, narcotics amount to well over half the exports of Bolivia, Colombia, and Peru, and are not much less important for several other countries. From the view-point of the consuming countries, this is an attack on their societies; for the exporting countries, the responsibility lies with the buyers, whose money is irresistible.

The effects are more devastating in the producing than in the consuming countries. The traffickers form the most powerful criminal organizations ever known, with resources exceeding those of some of their governments. Efforts at repression lead not only to bribery but to murder. The drug lords become a major power in the land, or part of the government; they also collaborate with guerrillas, who share their interest in undermining the legitimate state.

Economic inequality also causes pressures of immigration. The flow, legal and illegal, from poorer to richer countries has been increasing rather steadily for a long time and seems impossible to halt. The enormous difference of earnings, along with growing awareness and ease of travel, is an irresistible magnet for both the educated and the uneducated. From the point of view of the poorer countries, it is good and bad. Mexico and the Dominican Republic, for example, would be far worse off if there were not an outlet in the north for surplus labor, from which remittances come to alleviate village misery. On the other hand, they lose not only surplus hands but needed skills. There are interests in the industrial countries desirous of cheap labor; however, labor unions and professional organizations see their standards undercut.

Recent emigrants from Third World countries to West Germany, Britain, France, the Netherlands, and various other countries form a considerable fraction of the population; displaced or seeming to displace native labor, they provoke a rightist-extremist antiforeign backlash. Italy's new prosperity has made it a haven for immigrants from Africa and even Eastern Europe, generating problems Italy had never known. Even exclusive Japan is troubled by a small but ever-growing tide of illegal entrants, mostly from the impoverished Philippines.

The United States is the great magnet, drawing as many foreigners as all the other rich countries combined. Convenient as this is for filling jobs natives will not take, it raises social problems, increases inequality, and burdens the political process. Mexicans flooding into the United States create communities of second-class noncitizens. The flow will not cease: the population of Mexico grew from 25 million in 1950 to 85 million in 1988, and the rate of increase has moderated only slightly. Many migrants also arrive from Central and South America and the Caribbean, mostly illegally. Asians, a much smaller fraction of the undocumented, come in large numbers from Vietnam, Korea, and the Philippines.

In 1988 the United States half surrendered to illegal immigration, more than two-thirds of it from Mexico, by amnestying two million "undocumented" residents. In a not distant future, the new arrivals will have achieved substantial political power in the democratic state. For better or worse, it will have powerful effects on U.S. foreign policy, at least in regard to Latin American and Third World issues.

What poorer countries lose by the "brain drain" the richer ones gain. The contribution of foreigners to the American economy is immeasurable; Asians have especially moved into professions to which one gains entry by education. A large fraction of the American sick are attended by foreign, typically Indian physicians. Without foreign engineers and technicians, high-tech industry would be paralyzed. Nearly half of first-year graduate students in mathematics and physics in the U.S. are foreigners, and it is predicted that in a few years a large majority of engineering professors in this country will be foreign-born.[24] Asians, more disposed than traditional Americans to battle the complexities of exact sciences, do much to maintain American competitiveness.

A more disagreeable export of Third World countries is terrorism. Stimulated by the disturbance of traditional societies by alien models and values, terrorism has a largely Third World base. It is conditioned by the low valuation of human life, deep discontents, and the intensity of political and ideological causes. Most international terrorism occurs in or flows from the Near East, where the Western powers confront more wounded pride than anywhere else and where "holy war" has been traditional since the Islamic expansion of the 7th and 8th centuries.[25]

Radicalism and political tensions within the affluent democracies are also nourished by the misery of poor countries so far as people feel broad responsibility, uphold humanitarian values, and despair of change within the framework of conventional politics. The strength of Marxism in the American academic community results much less from pity for the ground-down American worker (who is likely to earn as much as the professor) than from shame for the exploitation of the masses of Latin America. This is the biggest reason for revulsion against "imperialism," which is associated with capitalism, a repugnance that easily turns into an attack on the democratic order as a system giving undue riches and power to the few.

Third World Debt

International lending is convenient. It temporarily and for a goodly fee transfers money from those who have more than they need to those who would like to spend more today at the price of a promise to pay tomorrow.

[24] *Time*, January 11, 1988, p. 65.

[25] For a survey, see Christopher Dobson and Ronald Payne, *War Without End: The Terrorists, an Intelligence Dossier* (London: Harrap, 1986); William Gutteridge, ed., *Contemporary Terrorism* (New York: Facts on File Publications, 1986).

But it has created problems ever since medieval monarchs defaulted their pledges to Italian bankers. In the 19th century, there were occasional debt crises and defaults, but they were surmounted fairly soon as economic growth provided the means of at least partial payment. After WW I, international debts became a major subject of contention. The United States loaned the allied European powers large sums, by the standards of the day, both before the United States entered the conflict in April 1917 and afterwards to assist first the war effort, then reconstruction. After the war, the debtor nations, chiefly France, Britain, Italy, and Belgium, met difficulties in repayment. Much of the diplomacy of the 1920s revolved around the war debts and the related problem of the even more unpayable reparations owed by Germany under the Treaty of Versailles. In the depression of the 1930s, a moratorium was declared; and the debts were forgotten in the turmoil preceding WW II. They were not quite forgiven; the United States still keeps the old obligations on its books with eternally accumulating interest, because writing them off would nominally increase the federal deficit.

The depression of the 1930s also brought the default of many bond issues of less developed countries, chiefly in Latin America. Thereafter, private lending to governments went out of fashion. Banks extended commercial credits, and they occasionally underwrote investments, usually on a modest scale, in Latin America and the new countries emerging after WW II; but governments wanting money went to other governments and international institutions such as the World Bank. The official lending that took place was mostly modest in scale and caused no great problems in the decades of expansion into the 1970s. The International Monetary Fund occasionally helped out when exchange rate problems occurred. The World Bank made loans on favorable terms to developing countries, especially for economic infrastructure (transportation facilities, power production, etc.) and agriculture. This was an inexpensive form of foreign aid, since the bank usually recovered its costs without difficulty.

In the 1980s, however, the foreign debt of the Third World—Latin America, Africa, and a number of Asian countries—turned into an enormous problem, an oppressive burden on economic and political development, and an irritant in international relations. This development was probably inevitable, as there had been a long-term trend toward increased indebtedness of less developed countries, with pressure on their balance of payments as loans matured. But the burden mounted acutely during the 1970s. The oil price increases of 1974 and afterwards and the greatly increased earnings of the oil-producing countries generated a great volume of floating international funds, especially eurodollars (dollars held on accounts outside the United States). At the same time, oil-importing nations faced heavy deficits and shortages of foreign exchange.

The response was an outburst of international commercial lending by the multinational financial community, working rather closely with international agencies, especially the International Monetary Fund and the World Bank. The big transnational banks, followed by hundreds of smaller ones, in Japan and Europe as well as the United States, loaned freely and abundantly as never before to the thirsty countries. Banks actively competed in pressing huge amounts of money on borrowers about whose financial capacity they hardly inquired. Their primary motive was the expectation of higher profits where capital was more needed than in the advanced industrial countries and where they could charge higher interest and collect more fees. They were also encouraged by governments; the "recycling" of petrodollars was somewhat like an extension, on a much larger scale, of official economic aid; and it earned praise at the time, however unsound in business terms.

They loaned with special enthusiasm to Latin America, regarded as the most promising less developed region. Disequilibria because of oil prices worked both ways: hardpressed countries borrowed to keep up imports; oil-producing countries suddenly made affluent, like Mexico, saw their riches as license to borrow and spend the more freely. Most African countries were too poor to interest the commercial banks, but they became heavily indebted, relative to their resources, mostly to official lenders. A number of Asian and East European countries were also caught up in the credit lark. The amounts laid out far exceeded any previous international transfers; the total Third World debt passed $1.3 trillion in 1988.

The large capital flow created a brief economic euphoria and financed some growth where a substantial fraction was well applied. But not surprisingly, the monies had been in most cases poorly applied; and they seldom produced the export income to permit payment of interest, much less repayment of principal. It soon became necessary to borrow not for investment but to keep up debt service. The problem became acute with the semidefault of Mexico, one of the biggest borrowers, in August 1982.

There followed countless negotiations and renegotiations between bankers and debtor countries, with the IMF usually participating and governments looking on and admonishing. It became customary to postpone payments on principal and to extend new loans to assist in keeping interest payments current, an unsound practice forbidden in domestic banking but more or less mandatory in international lending. The result was gradual increase in the amounts outstanding despite net capital outflow.

The IMF kept the process going by making substantial loans for the purpose not of stabilizing exchange rates, as was the original purpose of the Fund, but of staving off widespread default and a serious threat to the viability of big banks, especially in the United States. The IMF also hoped or pretended to hope to solve the problem by conditionality, that is, making its loans conditional, more in theory than practice, on the adoption of economic reforms by the debtor nations. The World Bank did its part by lending not for projects to improve the economic capacities of the recipients, as had been its function, but to help them stay current, more or less, in debt service.

This approach worked reasonably well for the creditor institutions for several years, although profits were partly fake and they found it necessary to set aside increasing reserves for largely valueless debt portfolios. The debtor countries squeezed their economies to pay out more interest than they received in new loans. Net transfers from the Third World debtor countries came to $43 billion in 1988, dwarfing the total of economic aid. As a result, they suffered varying degrees of inflation or hyperinflation, unemployment, shortage of investment, capital flight, cramping of health care and education, growth of parallel economies, and lowered real incomes. Economic problems brought political unrest, and the new democracies that came to power in the early 1980s suffered severe malaise.[26]

There is no pleasant answer to the trillion dollar question. The Third World borrowers cannot transfer to the financial institutions year after year a large part of their receipts of foreign exchange, in many cases 5 percent or more of the GNP. The principal creditors cannot afford quickly to accept the loss of assets or even to forgo interest payments; they feel compelled to defend the book value of the loans, which are of the order of magnitude of their total capital. They consequently resort to something of a scam, providing most of the money needed to keep payments coming more or less as contracted. On the other hand, it is very difficult for debtor countries, even the largest, to repudiate the debt because doing so raises the cost of trade credits, excludes refinancing of obligations, hurts their position in world markets, and shuts off foreign investment.

U.S. policy has rather successfully defended the interests of the creditors, acting with little regard either for the needs of the debtors or the broader and longer-term foreign policy interests of the United States. As long as the debt overhangs the debtor economies, there can hardly be a return of confidence and investment. Sensible persons with funds in Peru or Argentina, perhaps Mexico or Brazil, will keep them there only if interest or profit rates are very high to compensate for insecurity. The promising economic development of the 1960s and 1970s has given way to stagnation, widening of the gap with the developed countries, and potential political instability.

There have been put forward a "menu" of remedies, including conversion of debt obligations into equity holdings in the countries concerned, the issuance of "exit bonds" to turn debt into tradable securities, and various plans for giving some relief through special agencies. An imaginative

---

[26]See, for example, William A. Lovett, *World Trade Rivalry: Trade Equity and Competing Industrial Policies*, (Lexington, MA: Heath, 1987), pp. 137–60; Alfred J. Watkins, *Till Debt Do Us Part* (Lanham, MD: University Press of America, 1986); Robert A. Pastor, ed., *Latin America's Debt Crisis: Adjusting to the Past or Planning for the Future* (Boulder CO: Rienner, 1987); and Robert Wesson, ed., *Coping with the Latin American Debt* (New York: Praeger, 1988).

partial answer is to apply part of the debt, duly discounted, to environmental improvements. For example, arrangements have been made whereby European governments help Bolivia to buy back part of its debt at a deep discount in return for the setting aside of forest reserves. But no scheme can eliminate the pain.

For the health of the world economy, it must be realistically recognized that, so far as debts are truly unpayable, the sooner they are written off the better. European creditors have moved in this direction, at least in regard to destitute African countries. Although the Reagan administration took a firm stand of principle against any such impairment of contracts, reality gradually penetrates perception.

For the future, it would seem essential to separate business from politics, that is, to end the practice of private lending to governments. Although it may seem convenient and profitable, making unsecured loans to politicians or political interests is to invite trouble. So far as the amounts are large, the practice is injurious, economically and also politically, to the should-be developing nations. The financing of commercial transactions can be accomplished on a strictly commercial basis. So far as projects are useful and potentially productive, private interests handle them on the basis of rational economic calculations, or they can be undertaken by international agencies or governments as a frank contribution to development. But general loans to weak governments become an abuse of financial power.

The debt issue is a major problem of world order, basically a political problem. It came about because the multinational or "money center" banks, probably without being clearly aware of it, took advantage of the political weakness of less developed countries, with the willing consent of their government. The dimensions of the problem arose from the carelessness of the lenders combined with the incompetence and corruptness of the borrowers. It is not surprising that politicians should be willing to sell the future for a pot of gold. They receive; those later called upon to meet the charges will view the matter differently. Lenders should not be shocked to learn this fact of life.

Irresponsible lending/borrowing is an unfortunate aspect of the integration of the world economy and the development of the world financial-economic system, along with the stark inequality of rich and poor nations. That is, it results from the contrary trends toward global integration and the growing separation of rich and poor nations, coupled with mismanagement and corruption. Moreover, the mentality of development financing, along with the idea prevalent in economic aid that money equals growth, has made unsound practices seem respectable. At the same time, the difficulty of rebelling against the international financial community has largely deprived the borrowers of their ultimate defense, default.

The plague of debt sickens not only the less developed countries of Latin America and Afro-Asia, but afflicts many others such as Denmark,

Iceland, Poland, Yugoslavia, and Turkey, which have taken advantage of the modern fluidity of money to ease current problems by undertaking future obligations. The United States is by no means exempt, as it has financed much of the prosperity of the 1980s by an excess of imports over exports and reliance on foreign buyers to absorb a large part of the fiscal deficit. To restore health to the system and to the debt-encumbered nations is a challenge to the imagination, goodwill, and self-discipline of the leading financial powers. Unless they can rise to this challenge, hard times are in the forecast.

Development Aid

An urgent common task of the industrially developed nations is the amelioration of the extreme poverty of the great majority of humanity. If this seems mandated by morality, it is imperative in order to reduce tensions and problems arising from the excessive differences of rich and poor.[27] Like many international concerns, it mixes competition with cooperation.

Concern for the well-being of distant and alien peoples is a historically new phenomenon. There have always been impulses to save the souls of nonbelievers, but in the 19th century a famine killing millions in China hardly stirred the Western world. The great wars made disaster relief a duty of civilization. Food and other emergency help, largely from the United States, saved tens of millions of lives in the aftermath of WW I, especially in Eastern Europe and Russia. After WW II, the United States again kept huge numbers of destitute people from starvation.

It was more of a novelty that in 1947, as recovery lagged and radical parties swelled, the United States inaugurated a large scale multiyear program of reconstruction of Europe, the Marshall Plan. All countries suffering from wartime devastation were invited to participate. Some nations under Soviet influence, Czechoslovakia, Poland, and Finland, accepted; but they hastily withdrew under pressure from the Soviet Union, which would not have its satellites participating in what it called an imperialist conspiracy. If the Soviet Union had not reacted thus negatively, the United States would very likely have done little more for the stricken continent in the 1940s than it did in the 1920s; however, thanks to Soviet opposition and apprehension of the then strong and militant communist parties in Western Europe, the large expenditures won hearty congressional approval.

Good administration, clear purposes, generous funding, and most of all the abilities and willingness of Europeans to work hard to rebuild their

[27]Riddell, *Foreign Aid Reconsidered*, pp. 12–26.

countries made the Marshall Plan a huge success. It laid the basis not only for rebuilding of the wasted continent but for an unexampled upsurge of production and trade. It became a model; for any great economic need since then, there are calls for a new Marshall Plan.

Since 1947, American foreign economic aid has retained much of the basic character of the Marshall Plan, a mixture of anticommunist politics and humanitarianism. It is at once a balm of conscience and an adjunct of foreign and military policy, a way to spread modernization and democracy and the means of winning or holding allies.

As recovery progressed and the communist threat receded in Europe, attention shifted to nations of the Third World that suffered not war damage but economic backwardness. It soon became apparent, however, that development of the less developed countries was more difficult than rebuilding the battered. Much less was achieved toward modernizing traditional economies than hoped, and enthusiasm waned. Expenditures on the Marshall Plan were 2 percent of U.S. GNP; after it, foreign aid spending gradually tapered off and recently has been only 0.2 percent of GNP. This remains a fairly respectable $9 billion per year; it would be hard to imagine the Congress appropriating anything approaching the equivalent of Marshall Plan years, or $90 billion dollars yearly.[28]

Total aid to developing countries has been maintained or gradually increased, however, as other countries, with less anticommunist motivation than the United States, undertook assistance programs in accord with their resources. For some, such as France and the Netherlands, aid programs were mostly a continuation of responsibilities in formerly colonial territories become independent. For others, especially Scandinavian countries, motivation was broadly humanitarian. A number of countries spend a larger proportion of their GNP on foreign aid than the United States, specifically (in declining order in 1986) Norway, Denmark, Netherlands, Sweden, France, Belgium, Finland, West Germany, Italy, Canada, Australia, Japan, Switzerland, Ireland, and New Zealand.[29]

Spending little for armaments, Japan has undertaken to dedicate an increasing fraction of its huge trade surplus to helping poorer nations; and it has surpassed the United States in total outlays. The Japanese began by offering reparations for injuries caused by the imperial armies in the war, especially to soften bitter memories in Southeast Asia. They went on to a successful program for promoting exports and developing sources of raw materials and advanced to cooperation with ASEAN (Association of Southeast Asian Nations) countries for regional security, development of democracy, and economic growth. For example, Japan has earmarked substantial

---

[28]David R. Obey and Carol Lancaster, "Funding Foreign Aid," *Foreign Policy* 71 (Summer 1988), pp. 141–55.

[29]*World Development Report 1988*, p. 262.

funds for land reform in the Philippines. American officials propose cooperation whereby they would help to spend Japanese money.[30]

After the Soviet Union entered the competition for Third World influence in 1955, it undertook to rival American and other Western generosity. It made substantial expenditures, mostly in large and spectacular projects, such as the Aswan Dam on the Nile. The refusal of Western powers, principally the United States, to finance this Egyptian aspiration provoked Nasser to nationalize the Suez Canal in 1956. By taking over the task, the Soviets won considerable credit and influence in Egypt. Many less grandiose Soviet projects followed in Africa and Asia. Since the 1970s, however, the Soviet Union and its allies have retreated from economic assistance; Soviet bloc aid, which was 31 percent of the total in 1961, dwindled to 8 percent by 1984.[31] Recently Soviet aid has gone almost exclusively to dependents, such as Cuba and Nicaragua, largely in the form of favorable pricing for imports and exports, not projects, least of all grants of money. East European countries, especially East Germany, have provided modest but sometimes conspicuous aid to various countries, such as constructing a stadium or a food processing plant.[32]

Aid is disbursed not only by national governments but also by international agencies. The International Monetary Fund tries to relieve financial stringencies, but the terms of its loans are not generous, and in the 1980s its resources have been strained by the debt problem—something much beyond the management of exchange rates, which was its proper purpose. The World Bank is more dedicated to charitable or developmental functions.[33] It funds worthy projects not attractive to commercial lenders, especially for economic infrastructure; its largest areas of lending are agriculture, rural development, and energy. Its concessional loans may be practically gifts, with (for example) a ten year grace period, forty years to pay, and interest of 2 percent. Outright gifts are made by an arm of the World Bank, the International Development Agency (IDA). In the 1980s, World Bank resources, like those of the IMF, have been diverted unproductively to trying to alleviate or postpone the debt burden crushing most Third World nations.

Smaller international lenders, such as the Interamerican Development

---

[30]Steven R. Weisman, "U.S. in India: Less Aid, Less Influence," *New York Times*, April 21, 1988, p. A-4.

[31]Paul Mosley, *Foreign Aid: Its Defense and Reform* (Lexington KY: University Press of Kentucky, 1987), p. 240.

[32]Some relatively poor countries have modest foreign aid programs for political purposes; Brazil, for example, spends a few million dollars yearly on small nations it considers in its sphere, Paraguay, Bolivia, and Suriname.

[33]Barend A. de Vries, *Remaking the World Bank* (Cabin John MD: Seven Locks Press, 1987); Richard E. Feinberg et al., *Between Two Worlds: The World Bank's Next Decade* (New Brunswick NJ: Transaction Books, 1986).

Bank, the African Development Bank, and the Asian Development Bank, are oriented to the needs of the respective regions; in them, the recipient countries have a larger representation.[34] Affiliated agencies of the United Nations, such as the Food and Agriculture Organization, furnish several billion dollars of aid or assistance in various forms.

Aid for less developed countries has become an apparently permanent part of the world scene, partly charity, partly a worthy use of power with economic and political returns. Foreign aid assuages feelings of guilt; in democratic countries, the plight of the poor majority, not only at home but abroad, cannot fail to touch consciences. There is no logical reason, in the intercommunicating world, that democratic and moral values should stop at the frontier; and many persons in the rich countries blame their own nations for the sad condition of those hungering while food surpluses pile up in affluent countries. It is in the Third World that the wealthy can be most effectively charitable for the smallest cost; $10 feeds a child for a month.

There have been real successes, projects that have done what they were intended to do to the general satisfaction, such as rural electrification and irrigation.[35] Smallscale, people-to-people developments have transferred useful technology, brought new ideas, and changed the ways of many villages. The Green Revolution raised yields greatly in many countries, especially of Asia, mostly by superior varieties of rice and other cereals. India, for example, moved from severe shortages to a surplus of grain.

A program of the U.S. Agency for International Development (AID) with private voluntary organizations for giving microloans to small entrepreneurs and would-be entrepreneurs seems to be an unalloyed success at minimal cost. Several million entrepreneurs have been furnished up to a few hundred dollars capital at low interest, enabling them to buy a few sewing machines, get tools to make furniture, or set up a little shop. A small U.N. agency, the International Fund for Agricultural Development, makes loans to villagers who have never seen a bank, to buy livestock or weaving machines or equipment to make pottery, and so forth, at almost no net cost, because the repayment rate is almost 100 percent.[36]

Such direct-to-people aid is not bureaucratically or politically attractive. Largescale aid goes to governments, and it is difficult to be sure that its purposes are well served; confidence in the efficacy of aid has decreased markedly in the 1980s. An infusion of capital brings little benefit to coun-

[34]Lending capacity of the World Bank is about $12 billion yearly; of the IADB, about $4 billion; Asian Development Bank, $2 billion; African Development Bank, $1 billion. Irving S. Friedman, *Toward World Prosperity* (Lexington, MA: Lexington Books, 1987), p. 199.

[35]Riddell, *Foreign Aid Reconsidered*, p. 190.

[36]*Christian Science Monitor,* January 11, 1988, p. 10; Clyde H. Farnsworth, "Micro-loans to the World's Poorest," *New York Times,* February 21, 1988, p. 1 F; *The Economist,* August 20, 1988, p. 70.

tries whose finances and priorities are not well organized and managed. Those most in need of assistance are least prepared to make good use of it.

In some dictatorships, such as Haiti under the Duvaliers, aid has served to finance corruption and to keep mean and unscrupulous rulers in power. Technical progress, so far as achieved, has often proved superficial. After a village has been persuaded to adopt new and supposedly much better crops or ways of planting, the foreign volunteers go home and the villagers often revert to the old ways. The Peace Corps, a noble program mobilizing volunteers to improve living conditions of needy peoples, teaching, digging wells, and the like, has been only a qualified success. Many intended beneficiaries have found the program offensive, and it has been withdrawn from a majority of the countries where it was engaged. When in 1987, 600 American soldiers were sent to Ecuador to rebuild jungle roads, opponents claimed that they were merely carrying out military exercises.[37]

It is difficult enough for an entrepreneur within an advanced country to coordinate properly all the factors that go into a successful enterprise, including infrastructure, available materials and supplies, qualified management and labor, transportation, public acceptability, markets, and buyers' preferences. It is much more difficult for outsiders in a less developed country to do this successfully. Uneconomic projects may be worse than nothing, as the country is saddled with an enterprise not easily abandoned, for reasons of prestige and politics, but costly to maintain.

An aid program, being formulated in and by the donor nation, is likely to serve the purposes of the latter as well as or possibly more than the needs of the recipient. It is usually tied to purchases from the donor. To some extent, aid programs of different countries are politically and economically competitive, although there is some effort toward coordination among Western donors through the Development Assistance Commission, an agency of the OECD.

The fact that U.S. aid is largely guided by political strategy is a guarantee of economic waste.[38] Food aid may be better for the farmers of the exporting countries than for those of the countries receiving it. The Swiss and Swedish governments, probably among the more enlightened, promoted a steel mill in Togo, which had neither the resources to produce steel nor a market of consequence; it became a white elephant, never operating at more than 20 percent of capacity and raising the price of steel to Togolese users.[39]

Even if the project is suitable, the technology may well not be. Industrial nations wish to do things in the ways with which they are familiar and

[37]*Mensajero* (San Francisco), November 30, 1987, p. A–5.

[38]Bernard D. Nossiter, *The Global Struggle for More: Third World Conflicts with Rich Nations* (New York: Harper and Row, 1987), p. 111.

[39]Steven Mufson, "White Elephants in Black Africa," *New Republic,* December 29, 1986, pp. 18–20.

the recipients want the most advanced methods regardless of costs relative to the price of labor. Official aid programs are pushed by administrators, national and international, who are convinced of the total worth of their profession, a little like the administrators of the defense establishment. The bigger the loan or the project, the better for the career of the person organizing it. Projects are almost always evaluated by agencies with an interest in their continuation.

Aid is tangled with politics not only on the side of the donors but also of the receivers. Donors of aid deal with the bureaucracy; and it is not easy for outsiders to be sure that the benefits go to the needy, who are very weak in most Third World societies. It is nearly impossible to keep aid from serving the priorities of corrupt or at least self-interested establishments. Even if it is tied to definite purposes, it is difficult to assess the effect, because money is fungible; by financing a worthy purpose, the donor may facilitate waste elsewhere. Disaster relief has repeatedly relieved the powerful and greedy. It would be sensible to direct aid to the countries most competent to make use of it; but the countries most in need are the least competent.[40]

There is consequently a growing inclination to administer aid through private voluntary organizations dedicated to Third World development, of which there are scores. They become less than private as the bulk of their funding—up to 80 percent by U.S. law—comes from public sources; but they seem to be generally better able to reach down to the people than official agencies. They operate less bureaucratically and their motives are not so easily impugned. The "trickle up" sought by private organizations is probably more effective over the long run than the "trickle down" of massive, capital-intensive projects; and the social effects seem more salutary. When U.S. aid to the Haitian government was cut off after the frustration of elections, it was continued only through voluntary organizations helping the people directly, mostly in health and agriculture.

Only a small fraction of aid is disbursed in this way, however; and it does not solve the deeper problem that aid creates dependence. The national psychology cannot escape injury when a nation comes to rely on foreigners and their money. An unearned income is a disincentive for sound economic practices. Contrary to the ideals of most donors, aid programs strengthen the bureaucratic apparatus, making it more difficult to escape the trap of statism.[41]

Instead of the government undertaking a project with borrowed or

---

[40]Nossiter, *Global Struggle*, pp. 141–42; Mosley, *Foreign Aid*, p. 240.

[41]For assessments of development aid, see Riddell, *Foreign Aid Reconsidered;* Mosley, *Foreign Aid;* Robert Cassen, *Does Aid Work: Report to an Intergovernmental Task Force* (Oxford: Clarendon Press, 1986); Nossiter, *Global Struggle*, pp. 107–45. For a discussion of the problem when it seemed simpler, see Robert S. McNamara, *One Hundred Countries, Two Billion People: Dimensions of Development* (New York: Praeger, 1973).

donated funds, it may be well to arrange for private enterprise to "build, operate, transfer," a procedure dubbed BOT.[42] Under BOT, a foreign contractor constructs a facility at its own risk, operates it for profit under franchise for a fixed period, and turns it over to the host government or native interests. There is no charge to the national budget, and the government can be sure that the project will be calculated to be economically sound. There are complications, but many a fiasco could have been avoided by this simple approach.

The record of development aid has been poor in Africa, mediocre in Latin America, better in Asia. It can help to modernize and raise productivity, but it can also cause economic and political distortions; the correlation of aid and growth is not strong. Whatever the judgment, however, the affluent countries have undertaken a duty imposed by global interdependence. Despite problems and doubts, assistance for the less fortunate majority of the human species has been assumed as a moral, economic, and political obligation; if better managed, it might do much to relieve the inequality of peoples that is a curse of modern civilization.

Socio-Political Inequality

Generous as they may be, efforts of the richer countries to assist the poorer can have only limited effect unless there is political development. Economic levelling and the improvement of understanding among nations presuppose political levelling and movement toward pluralism and democracy, changing the psychology of the Third World and replacing indifference or despair with hope.

Change can only be gradual; the first requisite is the improvement of the human capital of poorer countries. People earn respect as well as money by education and training, especially the specialized training that the modern world demands and rewards. It is a hopeful fact that the increase of literacy and education in the less developed countries has gone forward even when standards of living have stagnated. The growing sophistication of peoples, such as those of Latin America, about family planning, ideas of hygiene, and the desire for education has not been undone by the depression of the 1980s.[43]

There is a great desire on the part of young people even in quite poor countries to learn a profession and qualify themselves. The son of peasants becomes a taxi driver; his son can study to be an engineer. Knowledge, growing faster than the economy, should eventually pull production behind it.

[42]*The Economist,* September 17, 1988, p. 20.

[43]Albert Hirschman, "The Political Economy of Latin American Development," *Latin American Research Review* 22, October 1987, p. 11.

Alongside education, improvement of health is a necessity for many populations afflicted by high incidence of chronic disease, malaria, helminthic parasites, and dysentery. Care of children's health is indispensable for the well-being of society tomorrow, but hundreds of millions grow up undernourished and physically and mentally impaired. Unhappily, in many countries of Africa and Latin America expenditures on health and education have been cut in the past decade by as much as half because of economic depression.

Whatever can be done for health is also undercut by the fact that the world remains divided into the countries that have population growth rates under 1 percent and those that have rates over 2 percent. Those with small families acquire more wealth for fewer people; those with large families have ever less to sustain them. Both education and healthcare become problematic; and in many lands a majority of children are noneducated in nonfamilies without the benefit of the transmission of skills from a father.[44]

The outlook is not good, but it is not hopeless. Values change; literacy, television, and urbanization, even something so simple as rural electrification, all have their effect on family size. Economic security reduces the compulsion to have large families; for example, small pensions for those who have one child or none would amount to compensation for not burdening the state with costs of education and other social services, ultimately of finding a job for the young. The problem has receded from attention since the 1960s, but it is grave. Decline of fertility has been less than expected, and most growth has been in areas least capable of supporting it. Economic development was to take care of the growth of population, but for many countries there has been no economic development. The world, which had 3 billion persons in 1960 and 5.4 billion in 1989 would be weighed down by 80 billion by 2100 if present rates were to continue.[45]

China has reined in its population growth by stern, unpopular measures; and it may stabilize about 1.2 billion in the first part of the 21st century. Few if any other countries have an equal capacity to handle the problem, but awareness of the need seeps into traditional societies and the idea that large numbers mean power or influence may be left behind. Control of population growth is a legitimate concern of all countries. By enlightened policies, the industrial democracies could do much to encourage restraint.

The democratic governments can also do much to encourage responsible government. Arbitrary dictatorship should increasingly be regarded as backward and senseless. Material and psychological rewards would help to persuade elites of the desirability of human and civil rights; it is legitimate

[44]On implications of the population problem, see Daniel Chirot, *Social Change in the Modern Era* (New York: Harcourt Brace Jovanovich, 1986).

[45]For a survey, see Jodi Jacobson, "Planning the Global Family," in *State of the World 1988*, ed. Lester R. Brown (New York: Norton, 1988), pp. 151–69.

to link aid for governments to decent treatment of their people. The multilateral promotion of democracy is preferable so far as it can be organized; it is much less suspect of self-interest of a powerful nation and is less distrusted. It has been proposed that there should be an international electoral commission, whose observance of elections would not be intrusive like that of a foreign power.[46]

The deemphasis of force in international relations would do much to discourage military politics. It has often seemed that the United States looked with favor on Third World dictators as being more amenable to its purposes; but since the United States saw the wisdom of going with the popular currents in the antidictatorial uprisings in Haiti and the Philippines in 1986, it has been hard to deny the longtime American mission of supporting popular government for both idealistic and practical reasons. Dictators are inclined to be unscrupulous, ready to deal with anyone for gain; and repugnance for American-supported dictators has motivated most anti-U.S. movements.

It is futile to suppose that popular democracy can quickly reshape traditional societies accustomed to the politics of force and abuse. In the mentality of the age, it is necessary to give everyone the vote and to base government on elections. But functional democracy requires many things together, such as independent and informative media, a nonpolitical civil service, well-organized political parties, nonpolitical police and military organizations, impartial and educated judges, a reasonable degree of honesty, respect for legality, familiarity with democratic procedures, and broad agreement on the meaning and desirability of democracy. These cannot mature rapidly, and the establishment of a genuine democracy requires a long transition.

Democratization, moreover, requires not only formal structures of government but also the strengthening of social forces on which the democratic order rests. These include more or less independent professional and middle classes, free and competent print and broadcast media, and organizations able to speak for different sectors of the population. The greatest obstacle, more difficult to overcome than ignorance and inertia, ingrained ways and antidemocratic structures, is the high degree of inequality in the Third World.

To overcome the many handicaps of the Third World is difficult, perhaps impossible. The best efforts can bear fruit only slowly, and those who would remake the afflicted nations may well despair. It is hard to be optimistic if one contemplates the immense and ever growing slums around the world, where millions live without sewers, clean water, health facilities, or jobs, where home is a propped-up metal sheet, or for many a place on the sidewalk.

---

[46]Andrew B. Schmookler, "Needed: An International Elections Commission," *Christian Science Monitor,* January 4, 1988, p. 16.

Yet change is stirring and showing many signs of material progress. Calcutta, whose name is synonymous with filth, crowding, and misery, built a modern subway, to the amazement of its citizens. It is clean and orderly; the modern technology is a symbol of progress.[47] In Latin America, the two most populous and self-confident nations, Brazil and Mexico, have the basis for modern industrial development, as does India; such nations have a sense of destiny.

The growing awareness of opportunities and the possibility of building a fuller material existence is strongest in Asia, where it has spread from Japan and Hong Kong to Taiwan, South Korea, and Singapore, all of which have reaped rewards of creating favorable conditions for production. Since the passing of Mao, huge China has had one of the world's highest growth rates. Thailand and Malaysia may follow in turning their underemployed labor force into an asset. If countries feel they must be able to do what their neighbors can, this offers the best hope of overcoming monstrous division of humanity.

It is a hopeful fact that the non-Western world has largely—by no means entirely—given up its effort to find a different way to a better future. This effort was spearheaded, in a vigorous counterattack against the Western economic and cultural as well as political assault, by the Russian-shaped and Soviet-sponsored communist movement. This has failed. Various less aggressive efforts of Third World powers to promote different ideologies have also failed. No longer thinking in terms of finding a different path to the future, the less developed states can more easily join the universalized modern world.

The world is becoming more one, despite the excessive inequality of nations. Within this one world, the salvation of the Third World has to come from its peoples, their hopes and willingness to work for improvement. But the most advanced, intellectually active, and confident nations can contribute ideas, leadership, and material help. Their own well-being and security require that they do so.

---

[47]Mary Walsh, "Letter from Calcutta," *Wall Street Journal*, May 6, 1987, p. 20.

Chapter 11

The World Panorama

Trends

Seemingly random events and circumstances can turn the world in unforeseen directions. There probably would have been no World War I if the assassination of the archduke had not presented the Austro-Hungarian court what seemed to be a golden opportunity to crush Serbia; and without a great war, there would have been no communism or fascism. If Lenin's brother had not been hanged as a subversive, the Russian revolution would very likely not have been turned from a pro-Western to an anti-Western movement. If President Wilson had been in better health and had used a bit of tact to secure ratification of the Treaty of Versailles, the influence of the United States might have spared Europe the storms of the 1930s. If President Hindenburg of the German Weimar Republic had not been senile, he would hardly have named Adolf Hitler chancellor, and there would have been no second chapter of the great war, without which the Soviet Union would never have raised a challenge of world power.

Yet the principal trends of the modern world are strong and enduring. Accidental events shift them, slow them, or accelerate them, but seem hardly to change them over a long period. The principal aspects of our world, as it completes its recovery from the traumatic decades, may not be very different from what they would have been if no world wars had intervened. The violence and disorder of 1914-1945 hastened some developments that were on the way and set back others; but the effects of the scientific-industrial-electronic revolution went on, just as the political evolution of Europe continued despite the victory of the conservative powers in the Napoleonic wars. The cultural and economic homogenization of the world has been gathering momentum for centuries, although rulers have tried from time to time to oppose it; and well over a century ago, civilization was heading in the general direction of an international system somewhat like the present one.

By the middle of the 19th century and the introduction of the machine gun in the U.S. civil war, warfare had become an unsuitable mode of interaction of nations. For many decades, this fact was hardly recognized, but it was made clear by the futile slaughter of WW I. The makers of WW II were vainglorious enough to hope that by mechanization they could have the benefit of war without the price in lives. They were proved wrong, and the nuclear bomb climaxed the progression toward making war obviously insane.

The world of 1914 had been moving for a century in the general direction of constitutional or democratic government. Nineteenth century observers such as Jeremy Bentham and Giuseppe Mazzini saw the lack of self-determination of peoples as a cause or the cause of war.[1] Educated opinion on the eve of WW I was confident that responsible government was the way of the future. President Wilson pressed the idea that doing away with discontents of alien-ruled nationalities should be central in making peace; and the Allied victory seemed to be a great triumph for democracy.

It is arguable that democratization might have escaped the setbacks of the interwar years if the United States in the 1920s had taken an interest in sustaining the libertarian movement it promoted at the Paris peace conference. If the peace failed, it was not because the principle was invalid but because it was not or could not be consistently applied. The triumphs that gave Hitler great prestige and confidence—the annexation of German-speaking Austria and Germanic areas of Czechoslovakia—he owed to the principle of national self-determination.

Whether democracy is more prevalent now than it would have been without the wars one can hardly guess. War and violence are unhealthy for democracy, because they engender extremist thinking and sanction absolute power, yet they break down traditional authoritarian structures and open the way for popular government.

Although colonialism was outworn and generally unprofitable at least from the beginning of this century, the wars hastened its end. The breakup of the empires had been on the way since the principal British colonies in

---

[1]Kenneth Waltz, *Man, the State and War: A Theoretical Analysis* (New York: Columbia University Press, 1959), pp. 143–44.

North America won independence in the 1770s and the Spanish empire in the Americas broke away in the first decades of the 19th century. In India, the Congress began agitating for rights in 1885 and was soon calling for self-rule. Few, however, saw any need to apply the principle of self-determination to the colonial peoples until the wars undermined imperial dominion. The victors upheld libertarian principles; and many soldiers from Africa and Asia, having fought for freedom in Europe, went home wanting freedom for themselves.

The United States had the material capacity for global leadership long before 1914; the world had only to wait until increasing involvement or national ambition led this country to exercise its might. The relative decline of Britain and France was inevitable because of the spread of the industrial revolution, with or without the disaster of the wars. Except for the setbacks in two wars, Germany has been on an ascendant curve since 1870. The rise of Japan has been almost continuous since it undertook modernization in mid-19th century; defeat in WW II brought only a few years' interruption of its progress. Russia was a rising power, with population dwarfing that of West European countries, prior to 1914; its contemporary standing is probably not much different from what it would have been if Lenin had never schemed revolution. Except that European integration could hardly have come without the prostration of war, the world might well have assumed the broad contours we see today.

Trends that have been strong for a century are fairly reliable today, because the basic factors of change, the multiplication of technological capacities and cultural development, are now more compelling than ever. Moreover, in the modern world, there is probably less danger that a deviant personality will upset or turn around the general course of development. In the huge highly structured modern state it is harder for any individual decisively to change the course of history. There is not likely to be a dictator in the United States, with its multiple checks and controls. No contemporary Soviet leader could wield the kind of personal power that Stalin had. Gorbachev may be able to undo something of the Soviet deviation, but he cannot make it into a really new country. No gifted or erratic individual can change fundamental directions in Japan. The rulership of major European countries appears generally levelheaded and lacks power to make radical changes in either internal or external politics. If there are some unpredictable personalities in less developed countries, they lack power on the world scene.

The future will surely see a continuation of technological improvements and increasing capacities in production, communication, travel, and transportation; and the world will be brought ever closer together. The cornucopia of invention will not cease to flow, and the process of homogenization would continue for a long time even without new inventions. It becomes more difficult for nations to manage the economy effectively, and arbitrary government has to seek legitimation in the information age. Conflictive interests—whereby one state gains from harming another—tend to recede and become mostly symbolic, while costs of conflict bear ever less relation to possible gains. The great tension-building antimodern movements have had their day. Governments give more and more attention to domestic management, while shared international concerns dispose them to more cooperative attitudes.

Yet it can never be assumed that humans will behave rationally. Within the state there are opposing trends toward better civic order or toward disorder; similarly, on the international stage trends to integration and equalization are countered by trends to division and unequalization. The degree to which tendencies toward easier and mutually beneficial international relations, with innocuous and many-sided competition, prevail over more antagonistic relations depends largely on the satisfactions felt by peoples and leaders.

Concord comes easily in prosperity; in times of hardship, it is natural to blame others and to try to improve conditions at their expense. Bad times cause countries to turn inward, to exclude foreign goods, to assert rights against outsiders, and to listen to the preaching of hostility. The huge postwar expansion of trade was made possible by relative stability and prosperity. In a depression, trade questions that at present have no political importance could become passionate issues. Protectionism might well cause a severe shrinkage of international exchanges and further economic decline, while political extremism in any major power would stimulate extremism everywhere.

Whether it will be possible to continue the generally upward course of material welfare or whether institutional or other failings will overtake us is crucial for the future of international relations. Financial breakdown, economic conflicts, or institutional failure of any kind could make the world more dangerous. Strains could be cumulative if enmities increase, anxieties rise, the economy recedes, and good relations with other countries become less valuable. Such dangers and potential tensions are accentuated by the division of the world between the relatively advanced and the backward, or between the wealthy and the poor.

Although Western society seems to be increasingly wasteful and incapable of converting improved technology into improved welfare, more fortunate regions have seen a remarkably prolonged period of economic expansion. The split of the world into the rich and the poor, on the other hand, is growing deeper. The differences are deep and persistent. Bad goverment is self-reinforcing. A power-holding apparatus frustrates changes that have no great driving force behind them, and a political machine cemented by corruption can keep an alternative from being put together. The vices of political management of the economy seem irremediable. The international financial system contributes to impoverishment; the nations can be divided into those handicapped by unpayable foreign debt and those free of this burden. The poorer countries are further impoverished because they have little to offer the educated and ambitious people whom they most need, those who can improve their lives by removing themselves to countries that will better reward them.

The forces of equalization can prevail only if states, organizations, and peoples recognize the desirability of breaking down differences by the better spreading of information and culture, the reduction of barriers to trade, and the encouragement of more effective political institutions.

Rivalry

It may be, as Spanier states, that "conflict and the possibility of war can never be abolished."[2] "Never" is unknowable, but for a long time force will play some part in the interaction of sovereign states; and by virtue of the fantastic progress of physics, chemistry, and engineering, the world is inherently dangerous. This is the price of technological advance in the absence of overriding law.

Yet, as the unusability of modern weaponry is assimilated into thinking, the powers may increasingly express their rivalries nonviolently. Yearnings for prestige and sway do not necessarily generate war, just as many animals are territorial without being combative or have only symbolic duels. There is no evidence of an ingrained human instinct to extend the dominion of one's state; if there is congenital aggressiveness, it does not necessarily pertain to the artificial aggregations called governments and does not have to be expressed by mass slaughter. Competitiveness may be expressed at any level, as individuals or as members of families, teams, clubs, corporations, agencies, or whatever; the identification with the nation may be strong or weak.

The energizing effects of contestation among nations, moreover, are counterbalanced under modern conditions by its divisiveness: not everyone is convinced that there is much to gain from hostility to a foreign power that does not obviously reflect a direct threat. Competition and conflict of nations cannot be eliminated, but they can be checked. If the institution of war could be moderated in the 18th century, it can be left behind in the 21st.

Recognizing that they have little to gain from the use of force, nations may take more pride in cultural, scientific, or economic achievements, Nobel prizes and Olympic medals, standard of living, and worldwide prestige.

[2]John Spanier, *Games Nations Play* 6th ed. (Washington: Congressional Quarterly Press, 1988), p. 644.

Sports, for example, are an outlet for aggressivity and are at the same time a common interest of different nations.[3] The Americas Cup yacht competition excites millions who have never been sailing, while it brings yachtsmen of different nations into friendly contact. Latin Americans, with little military-political competition, are enthralled by soccer rivalries, the excitement of which reaches hysterical levels. In many countries, an important match brings business practically to a halt, and other news is relegated to the back pages.

The Olympic Games mix athletics and politics. The spectators cheer more for the nationality than the personality of competitors; and the media reporting them play up the flag, not only in the politically-conscious Soviet Union but in the publicity-conscious United States. But the original Olympic Games were one of the festivals uniting the quarrelsome Greek city-states; they were a time of truce and secure travel. They were revived in 1894 explicitly to promote peace.

East Germany, having no real economic weight in the world and being politically impotent, has gained much prestige from its dedication to athletics. By systematic training and great effort it regularly figures as a superpower in the international arenas of swimming, track, and so forth.[4] Like East Germany, Cuba spends much of its scanty resources on winning medals at international meets, ranking ahead of far larger and richer nations. The government picks out promising children, trains them assiduously, rewards them generously, and gives them fame, relative freedom, and the good life.[5] This self-advertisement would seem much more cost-effective than the making of revolution abroad.

Another area of friendly, sometimes cooperative competition is space exploration.[6] It is marginal for the United States but central for the Soviet Union, being the latter's chief area of real excellence apart from the military, a way to longed-for international recognition. It is necessarily a governmental activity, hence relatively well-managed in the soviet system. Space heroes and feats are much glorified in Soviet media, museums, and art. As Gorbachev stated in 1987, "[Here] one experiences a sense of pride in the intellect and achievement of the Soviet people. . . . We do not intend to slacken our efforts and lose our vanguard positions in the conquest of space."[7] Political and organizational strength compensate for technological

[3]Konrad Lorenz, *On Aggression* (New York: Harcourt Brace and World, 1966), pp. 282, 287.

[4]Michael Janofsky, "The East German Sports System," *New York Times*, July 3, 1988, p. 1.

[5]Frederick C. Klein, "Cuba Adds Punch to Its Politics," *Wall Street Journal*, December 18, 1987, p. 20.

[6]See Walter A. McDougall, *The Heavens and the Earth: A Political History of the Space Age* (New York: Basic Books, 1985).

[7]*Washington Post National Weekly Edition*, January 11–17, 1988, p. 17.

deficiencies to give an inspiring goal, especially for the technically minded youth.

The shock to Americans of early Soviet successes in space from 1957 into the 1960s (first satellite, first man in space, early moon probes) stimulated an American project to send astronauts to the moon. After this was triumphantly achieved, the American space program flagged. Meanwhile the Soviet Union, although trailing the United States in electronics and computers by a decade, moved steadily forward with a broadbased program, reaping scientific and political rewards. No other country can compete with the Soviet Union in number and reliability of launchings, price for putting packages into orbit, and cheap satellite photography. The Soviets even have a look-alike to compete with the U.S. shuttle. Reports that the Soviets might be on the way to Mars injected new life into the American space effort.[8]

Yet the space rivalry hardly creates animosities. Although it is an outlet for competitive impulses, it generates mutual respect and offers opportunities for each side to learn from the other. Data gathered from Venus or Saturn are freely shared. Although American corporations are barred from renting space on Soviet vehicles, both sides have gained from cooperation. It becomes more necessary as missions become more ambitious; an excursion to Mars, for example, would be much delayed without mutual help.

Such innocuous competitions would be more engrossing if sums devoted to them were comparable to those spent on means of destruction. But they can hardly serve as the "moral equivalent of war," of which William James wrote,[9] because there is no sense of danger. A contest is the more thrilling as it represents a threat to pride, power, or prosperity, conceivably to national existence. A military defeat is a powerful stimulus to reform; a shortfall in technology leaves most people indifferent.

The United States was stirred by the Soviet technological-educational challenge in the latter 1950s mostly because of the military implications of Soviet space triumphs. Predictions of Soviet industrial superiority by the 1970s, based on extending graphs of national production in the 1950s, caused less excitement than the specter in the early 1960s of the Soviets gaining control of the steamy jungles of the Congo and from there reaching out to swallow up Africa.

Yet competition in capacity for genocide is surely not needed, and the character of rivalry changes as the actors change their values. The Soviet Union set itself, in fulfillment of Lenin's revolution, on an ideologically charted course contrary to historical directions of modernity—responsible

[8]Kathy Sawyer, "A Red Star Rises in Space," *Washington Post National Weekly Edition*, August 3, 1987, pp. 6–7.

[9]*William James: The Essential Writings*, ed. Bruce W. Wilshire (Albany: State University of New York Press, 1984), pp. 349–61).

government, legality, freedom of information, and most of what goes under the name of democracy. Since consolidation of the state and especially since WW II, the Soviet Union has been adapting itself to the modern environment. The post-1985 Gorbachev reforms are based on the realization that the old patterns were leading to a backwardness threatening the dreams of greatness that are the true essence of Soviet and Russian ideology.

The totalitarian or near-totalitarian state has turned out to be a failure; the Gorbachev refashioning seeks to save a system threatened by decay, at the price of giving up most of the ideas of the revolution. The large majority of radical parties in the Third World as in the industrial countries are unaffiliated with what remains of the Soviet-led movement; the issue of international communism is dead. The Russian Revolution set out to destroy the international system; having failed, the Soviet state seeks to improve itself within the system. It cannot aspire to more.

It is to be expected that the Soviet Union will continue to represent authoritarianism, and this will increasingly be the conservative side. The Leninists and Stalinists claimed to stand for authoritarian revolutionism, but in a stable universe this is a contradiction in terms. The old left-right dichotomy of politics, invented in the French Revolution, is outworn. The stronger division is between the pluralistic and the centralized, the individualistic and the communitarian. What may be called the "communitarian" approach, with flexible guidance of the economy, can be effective.[10] This was apparent in the success of very limited democracy of Singapore and of South Korea before 1988.

It is possible that the traditionally rival superpowers will become more cooperative. Their economies are complementary; so far as the Soviet Union really joins the world economy, it will be more attractive than Japan for American enterprise. The two peoples find each other congenial, and Americans tend to admire a big country suggestive of their own in its dimensions and variety. If the Soviet Union casts xenophobia entirely aside and develops its touristic facilities, millions of Americans may be drawn to its sights. And the two big multiethnic powers may feel something in common in relation to hard-driving, homogeneous Japan.

Japan becomes a leading contender in world affairs, and China may be on the way to greatness. A uniting Europe will doubtless play a growing role, as competition becomes increasingly economic. More exactly, the essence of the new kind of rivalry lies in modernization, the ability of nations to make use of and contribute to the human capacities created by intelligence. This may become more intriguing for the peoples of the world than the arms race.

[10]George C. Lodge and Ezra F. Vogel, *Ideology and National Competitiveness* (Boston: Harvard Business School Press, 1987), p. 321.

Economic Competition

The idea of 19th-century Social Darwinists that nations were engaged in a bloody struggle for survival of the fittest was wrong, but there is a real contest among nations in the increase of their productive capacity. Economic superiority is no less real than military or political might and is more enjoyable for most people; economic decline is harder to confront, but it becomes painful. Perceived economic threats have in the latter 1980s, for the first time in the postwar era, led Americans to doubt the primacy of military dangers in the world. A 62 percent majority was reported to believe that economic power was more important in determining a country's influence in the world than military power, and 57 percent saw Japan as posing more of a threat to U.S. national security than the Soviet Union.[11]

The Department of Defense might not agree, but the citizens polled are not unrealistic, as the Japanese make themselves the lords of world finance and buy up not only the Hawaii they once bombed but Los Angeles skyscrapers. Economic defeats hurt not only pride but pocketbooks, while no one really knows whether there is a military danger. The Soviets have taken nothing American and have little capacity to injure the United States (short of an unthinkable nuclear assault), but the Japanese have conquered many American industries.

Tanks and planes quickly become obsolete, and they give no return for tomorrow, but economic investment builds still higher productive capacity. Spending on economic progress brings greater economic progress; spending on military power reduces potential future economic and military power—a problem particularly for the United States, which among Western industrial nations devotes the largest percentage of its product to defense. Military competition is pointless for the overwhelming majority of nations; their means to national pride and respectability is economic growth, to catch up with the most modern states or at lease reduce their lag and to outdo their rivals. The old idea of making the state powerful through trade and the accumulation of gold to pay soldiers has found a more sophisticated expression in the modern competition in productivity.

The United States, long complacent about its wealth and industrial prowess, cannot sustain its place among the nations without greater efforts. H. Ross Perot has pleaded, "When we go to our jobs each day, we are playing in an international economic superbowl where the best product wins—and there is not even a red ribbon for second place. The losers lose their jobs, not just a game ... The only way to succeed is to unite as a team, take on the world, and win."[12]

[11]Monica Langley, "Protectionist Attitudes Grow Stronger in Spite of Healthy Economy," *Wall Street Journal*, May 17, 1988, p. 1, 6.

[12]H. Ross Perot, "How our Credit-Junky Nation Can Get out of this Mess," *Washington Post National Weekly Edition*, November 9, 1987, p. 21.

Not many Americans are deeply stirred by such a call. The Japanese are more purposeful. Having come to grief as military empire builders, they have pressed for greatness in production and exports, a determination shared by not only political and industrial leaders but the ordinary citizen, who works overtime and reads economic and technical books.

With almost no raw material resources and little arable land, Japan has made itself the prime example of the ability of a not very numerous people to raise themselves to preeminence by hard work, education, and good organization. The huge Japanese trade surplus seems likely to continue, along with Japanese technical virtuosity. With half the population of the United States, Japan has expanded its presence everywhere, while that of the United States has gradually shrunk.[13]

The United States finds its advantages melting away. For a century, until perhaps the 1970s, it had the world's best educated work force, thanks to high quality compulsory mass primary education and an unparalleled system of higher schools. Now it has more functional illiteracy and a larger proportion of school dropouts than its competitors. International ratings and competitive tests show that American students have fallen behind those of nearly all Western and many Third World countries, especially in the subjects most important for modern productivity, mathematics and physical sciences. Half of U.S. engineering doctorates go to foreign students, and the proportion of engineers to population is six times higher in Japan than in the United States. Much of the superiority of human capital that carried the United States to the economic summit has been dissipated, and inferior education today means inferior performance 10 or 20 years from now.

There is satisfaction to be taken in the variety and creativity of American higher education, which is still the world's finest. To build up excellent graduate schools and scientific laboratories is much more difficult and time-consuming than to set up high-quality primary and secondary schools, and the looseness of the American social-political fabric favors the freedom and variety productive of science. Japanese basic science is held back by rigidity of academic administration, dislike for individualism, a calcified bureaucracy, underequipped and underfunded universities, and rote learning education. Japanese scientists are said to do better work at American institutions than at home.

Americans still did 55 percent of world research and development in 1985;[14] but the Japanese share rose to 20 percent in 1985 from 5 percent in

[13]For a critical view, see Clyde Prestowitz, Jr., *Trading Places: How We Allowed Japan to Take the Lead* (New York: Basic Books, 1988); for a more admiring view, see Ezra F. Vogel, *The Impact of Japan on a Changing World Order* (Hong Kong: Chinese University Press, 1987). For an alarmist view, see Daniel Burstein, *Yen! Japan's New Financial Empire and Its Threat to America* (New York: Simon and Schuster, 1988); more optimistic is Joel Kotkin and Yoriko Kishimoto, *The Third Century: America's Resurgence in the Asian Era* (New York: Crown Publishers, 1988).

[14]*Fortune* 117, February 1, 1988, p. 49.

1965, when the United States had 70 percent. Relatively few Americans study science, and earnings of physicists, biologists, and chemists average about a third of those of lawyers and physicians. A majority in the former category work in the defense industry; three-quarters of U.S. research and development is military. The United States, with twice the population, spends less on civilian research than Japan, graduates fewer engineers (and a hundred times more lawyers), and produces less new technology.[15]

Japan is ahead of the United States in most areas of high technology except some branches of computerology, including software;[16] and the United States is losing ground on almost all technical fronts, gaining on none. Japan has well-planned and -financed programs in supercomputers, genetic engineering, and semiconductors, and looks to preeminence in artificial intelligence, nuclear fusion, space colonization, and hyperspeed travel.[17]

Having long been superb imitators, the Japanese have become the foremost innovators. They did not share in the discovery of superconducting ceramics, but they took the lead toward their exploitation. They obtain a fast-growing share of U.S. patents; in 1987, the three leading recipients were Japanese firms. Nearly half of U.S. patents were for foreigners, a fifth for Japanese.[18] The principal new consumer electronic products of the past ten years, such as camcorders, compact disc players, and digital audio tape, have all come out of Japan.[19] The United States led the world in the introduction of color television; Japan leads in high-definition television.

It is the strongest asset of the United States that its society is the most open in the world, in marked contrast to the Japanese, the most ethnocentric of major nations. Class barriers and cartel mentality are weak; mobility is high. Nowhere else is it traditional for the young genius with an idea to start a high-tech business in the garage; nowhere else do little companies with new products and grandiose dreams burgeon so abundantly.[20]

Shortfalls in American education are partly made good by the ability to attract skilled persons. The "brain drain" from countries badly needing talent is widely regarded as undesirable, and the United States requires students to leave this country after completing their studies. On the other hand, the demand that the Soviets permit more emigration amounts, as

---

[15]Charles H. Ferguson, "Obsolete Arms Production, Obsolescent Military," *New York Times*, April 11, 1988, p.A 19.

[16]*Wall Street Journal*, November 14, 1988, p.R–6.

[17]Ronald A. Morse, "Japan's Drive to Pre-Eminence," *Foreign Policy* 69 (Winter 1987–1988), p. 10.

[18]*Time*, March 21, 1988, p. 50.

[19]*The Economist*, March 12, 1988, p. 66; Leonard H. Lynn, "Research and Development in Japan," *Current History* 87, April 1988, pp. 165–68.

[20]On economic growth, see Dale Jorgensen, Frank M. Gallop, and Barbara M. Franmeni, *Productivity and U.S. Economic Growth* (Cambridge: Harvard University Press, 1987).

Soviet spokesmen complain, to a demand that they let highly qualified persons transfer their abilities to this country. If any country sought purposefully to build up its technical and scientific abilities and thus its long-term economic capacity, the best expenditure it could make would be to endow laboratories and lure the best scientists and engineers with large salaries to use them.

Competition in national productivity has many aspects, mostly difficult to define clearly or politically impossible to change. Investment depends on national savings, but Americans are less prone than citizens of other industrial countries to save for the future, and no one proposes a means of altering their values. U.S. corporations, compared with Japanese, seem more focussed on the latest financial returns and on dividends rather than investment. The Japanese are more competitively avid to raise market share, which means long-term profits; Americans seem to prefer raising prices and profits instead of going after more sales. This may have been a major reason that U.S. producers were very slow in responding to the radical fall in the dollar after early 1985.

Good relations between labor and management or ownership are crucial, but they are problem-laden in modern societies. Labor strife, often motivated less by concern for workers' welfare than by union politics or jurisdictional disputes, contributed to Britain's relative decline through most of the postwar era. Tenseness and uncertainties of industrial relations have been a disincentive for investment in the United States as well. Japan, on the other hand, has given an example of improved management, giving workers security and consideration, making them more like partners in a shared enterprise and correspondingly willing to work for its progress.

Japanese institutions favor better cooperation between private enterprise and government. In the Japanese view, the two sides ought to have the same broad objective of promoting the national capacities; and there is little of the adversarial approach common in the United States. In this country, it seems to be assumed that the function of the government in regard to business is simply to prevent abuses. Tax laws and regulations have hardly been designed to encourage enterprise, innovation, and expansion.

Social order and government determine productivity. The questions of the future are whether the society rewards efforts directed to improvement and how far the nation gives official and unofficial authority to persons best qualified by ability and character. The Japanese have done well in both of these aspects, through their feeling for social responsibility and their selection by impartial examination for the academic tracks that lead directly to high status in both business and public service.

The United States has no real strategy in world competition; it is contrary to the American way to have one. The inventive but chaotic American society rises to grapple with problems if it becomes thoroughly aware of them and sufficiently dissatisfied. It may or may not be farsighted enough.

It is hard to get away from the predilection to borrow for today's enjoy-
ments and prosperity without much thought of paying tomorrow. American
management has repeatedly left innovation to the Japanese. The wasteful
litigiousness of the United States is a symptom of maladjustment, as is the
fact that this country imprisons a much larger proportion of its population
than other industrial nations. Conceivably, the American political system is
less equipped for the twenty-first century than that of some of the competitors.

The U.S.-Japanese Competitive Symbiosis

The most modern international relations are those between the most modern countries. Japan and the United States, the world's foremost economic
powers, have come into a novel coexistence of deep significance for world
order. Although the union has never been consecrated formally, it is a sort
of marriage of convenience, dictated by economics but not graced by much
affection.

One dimension of the relationship is investment. The Japanese stake
in American industry is large and promises to grow indefinitely; and as
Japanese plants are located in the United States, their suppliers follow.
Many localities are eager for the jobs Japanese investment promises; states
compete with offers of tax holidays and special facilities for the privilege
of hosting Japanese enterprises. It may be that Japanese firms, as their
American branches mature, will become the first true multinationals outside of Europe. Honda U.S.A., for example, would be an equal partner of
Honda Japan.[21]

U.S. firms are much more conspicuous in Japan, especially in consumer products changing the Japanese way of life, from breakfast foods and
pizza to bandaids and credit cards. There are a growing number of
Japanese-American joint ventures on both sides of the Pacific, since each
wants access to the markets of the other. American brokerage houses enter
the Tokyo stockmarket (the nominal value of which is much larger than that
of the New York Stock Exchange), and Japanese brokers are prominent in
New York. The Japanese being the world's leading bankers, Americans must
become accustomed to dealing with them. However, the yen is only beginning to challenge the dollar as world reserve currency; and the Japanese are
highly dependent on the U.S. market, which takes about one-third of their
exports. They cannot afford to see the U.S. economy shaken.

For most of its history, the United States focussed on Europe as the
fountainhead of culture, styles, science, and art, the great financial and in-

[21]*The Economist,* February 20, 1988, p. 18.

dustrial center. But Asia outdoes Europe, and a greater volume of trade flows across the Pacific than across the Atlantic. For both the United States and Japan, the European market is secondary. The strongest foreign cultural influence in the United States is Japanese.

There are many areas of cooperation; for example, Tokyo and New York consult on dealing with drugs, garbage, and other problems of great metropolises. The United States wants Japanese assistance in regard to economic aid and the Third World debt, despite reluctance to relinquish authority. After the U.S.-Canadian free trade pact was negotiated, there was talk of such an agreement with Japan. Military cooperation is good, and the Japanese contribute generously to the cost of keeping American forces in their country. In a unique collaboration, the United States and Japan are to build a new fighter plane.

For those who remember Pearl Harbor, it is ironic that American authorities urge the Japanese to forget the American-dictated constitutional prohibition of armed forces and devote more to defense. Without considering long-term consequences, the United States would like Japan to take a more active military-political role, at least in Asia; but the Japanese, having barely passed the 1 percent of GNP long regarded as the limit, are hesitant to undertake an ambitious military buildup. The less China and other Asian countries are afraid of Japan, the better for business. Japanese foreign policy is denominated in yen.

The two societies are mutually stimulating; no others learn so much from each other. Yet it is in spite of themselves that the two nations are drawn together. They do not communicate easily. Their ways are very different; their people do not get along so easily as Americans with Germans or French, not to speak of Britons. The difference was shown after Pearl Harbor, when American citizens with even a small fraction of Japanese blood were interned en masse, although there was no evidence that they represented a danger, while German- and Italian-Americans, even citizens of the respective countries, were not so treated.

Respect for the Japanese has grown greatly since then, and victims of relocation have received an apology and modest compensation, but the potential for prejudice has not been entirely overcome. Although Japanese investment is eagerly sought and owners of real estate are happy to have Japanese buyers, there are protests that Japs are buying up the country; almost no attention is given to the larger European investment. Despite great interest in things Japanese, from sushi to the educational system, the number of Americans fluent in Japanese, although growing, is tiny compared with those having a command of French or German. Even the American Embassy in Tokyo has hardly any officers who can speak Japanese easily and correctly. Despite their concern with Japanese technical competition, Americans pay little attention to Japanese research.

Success nourishes Japanese confidence and resentment of American bossiness and superior manners. Good relations have rested largely on the forthcomingness of the Japanese, who become more self-assertive. They take pride in their institutions, including their remarkable ability to combine governmental guidance with competition. They see themselves as helping to cover American deficits, making the concessions in trade negotiations, and humbly following the American lead. In the American view, they are a bit arrogant in their technical confidence. In the Japanese view, Americans want them to take on more financial responsibilities but to remain subservient.

The Japanese situation is delicate because of their vested interest in easy access to the American market and their growing investments in it. But Japanese purposes are sure to diverge from those of the United States.[22] Nationalism is not far below the surface. A Japanese cabinet minister, Seisuke Okuno, declared publicly that the Japanese occupation of much of China in the 1930s was not aggressive, since "The white race had turned Asia into a colony. Japan was by no means the aggressor nation."[23] Okuno was compelled to resign, because the Japanese value relations with China highly; but he did not retract his sentiments, which are widely shared. Many Japanese doubt that Japan was an aggressor in WW II, that its leaders deserved to be hanged, and that they have to keep an American-drawn and imposed constitution.

Japanese society is more exclusive, in pride of race and homogeneity, than that of any other major nation. Relatively egalitarian among themselves, they are reluctant to accept foreigners. One reason that they can be democratic is that they live within a psychological fortress of their own and are not far from regarding all Japanese as superior to all non-Japanese.

The self-esteem of the Japanese rises more rapidly than the willingness of Americans to accept them as full equals. It is hard for those who not long ago considered the Japanese inferior Orientals and hated them bitterly in the war to feel comfortable in partnership with them. In endless controversies over trade and other matters, it is assumed that the Japanese are at fault. The Japanese regard many American actions as poorly considered and find American negotiating tactics incomprehensible. The Americans demand that Japan raise prices for computer chips because they are hurting American producers; they want prices reduced for the sake of American chip users. They insist on U.S. participation in Japanese projects in which no U.S. firms are interested.

The Japanese regard Americans as prejudiced, quick to censure them for faults that would be pardoned in Europeans. The United States refuses

[22]Morse, "Japan's Drive to Pre-Eminence," pp. 4, 6, 11, 18.
[23]*New York Times*, May 11, 1988, p. A 9.

on grounds of secrecy to sell its Japanese ally an air defense system that Europeans are welcome to buy;[24] it compromises with Iceland over continued whale fishing but threatens Japan with sanctions.[25] They see themselves unfairly blamed for the American trade deficit.[26]

It is difficult for Americans to blame the Japanese very much for things that Americans traditionally admire—education, business management, and generally getting rich—but the flood of Japanese goods is an insult to American prestige and pride. In political rhetoric, Japan-bashing may be more profitable than Soviet-bashing. Many Americans find the Japanese a more obvious threat than the invisible Russians; and sledgehammering a Japanese automobile seems appropriate, despite the political importance of the alliance with Japan. If they had an authoritarian government instead of an American-drafted constitution, it would be much easier to blame them; but the fact that they have succeeded with political principles like America's does not save them.

To improve their image, the Japanese endow American cultural programs and such worthy aims as cooperation in biological research; and they send television programs to the United States to portray their country favorably. In 1986, Japanese firms gave $100 million to U.S. nonprofit organizations.[27] But nothing can erase the fact that Japan is a homogeneous, family-like society, proud of ethnic purity, with currents of xenophobia. The Japanese mentality and values, like Japanese manners, although slowly changing, are very different from the American. Japanese go to the United States in large numbers to do business or to study technical subjects, but they send their children to Japanese schools.

The unique cooperative-conflictive relationship between the world's leading economic powers may be showing the way to the international relations of the future.[28]

World Leadership

The United States has been the preeminent power in the world since 1918, although it rather loftily held itself apart from European quarrels until WW II. The Germans under Hitler's irrational leadership challenged it, with the

[24]*New York Times,* February 5, 1988, p. 29.

[25]*New York Times,* January 24, 1988, p. 10.

[26]For example, Prestowitz, *Trading Places,* would attack U.S. trade problems by getting tough with Japan.

[27]*Washington Post National Weekly Edition,* June 27–July 3, 1988, p. 23.

[28]See Karel G. van Wolferen, "The Japan Problem," *Foreign Affairs* 65, Winter 1986/87, pp. 288–303; George R. Packard, "The Coming U.S.-Japan Crisis," *Foreign Affairs* 66, Winter 1987–1988, pp. 348–67; Ellen L. Frost, *For Richer, For Poorer: The New U.S.-Japan Relationship* (New York: Council on Foreign Relations, 1987).

support of Japanese militarists; but they were cast down by its industrial might. In 1945, the United States had the means of dominating this planet as no power in history; but it was not prepared to turn this strength into permanent empire. Since 1945, the American position has been slipping, sometimes rather rapidly, sometimes imperceptibly. This was for a long time the predictable result of the recovery of Europe, the Soviet Union, and Japan from wartime devastation. This recovery having been long since completed, the standing of nations continues to change because of differences in their capacity to make use of the fruits of modern technology.

Some countries have done poorly. The Soviet Union set itself up against the American-led world with an ideological claim backed by the Leninist political organization. This bid for leadership caused considerable anxiety—mixed with hopes—but it ultimately had to be relinquished. Latin America seemed likely in the 1960s and 1970s to play a more prominent part in the world, but in the 1980s it lost ground. India has struggled to keep pace, but its principal growth is in population.

For a generation, there has been talk of China as one of the big players in world politics, a pole of a tripolar or quadripolar world. It has advanced remarkably since the demise in 1976 of Chairman Mao, who retarded it for many years by giving ideology priority over rationality. In the outlook of Deng Xiaoping's China, neither military power nor ideology is very relevant; the big issues are economic. But it is unclear whether China has achieved a viable solution for its political problems or whether the will to foster modernization will take second place to the imperatives of rulership. China's tasks of combining order and freedom are easier than those of the Soviet Union, but they are formidable, and it cannot be a major actor for many years.

For the near future, the European Economic Community, led economically by the West German powerhouse, is a far stronger contender. So far as the economic amalgamation promised for 1992 succeeds, it is sure to act more effectively in the world. It may be expected to find more political purpose so far as decisionmaking is shifted to the center and the European Parliament becomes an effective all-European body. The Community is already the economic equal of the United States, and it may be enlarged by such countries as Austria and Sweden, conceivably one day by countries now of the Soviet bloc. The Community can hardly dream of a very active political role because of its diversity and cumbersomeness, but it becomes less amenable to U.S. leadership.

The most dynamic candidate for a larger world role is Japan. Unimpressive and unfearsome because of its size (about that of Montana) and its population (about 125 million), it has steadily increased its economic power and promises to continue to do so. The inflated prices of the Tokyo stock market—price/earnings ratios four times as high as in the United States—reflect enormous optimism.

In a mere ten years Japan has surged to a leading place in the world economy. The Japanese credit balance in the world is far larger than that of the United States has ever been; and it continues steadily to grow, while the U.S. balance remains deeply negative. The 10 biggest banks in the world are Japanese, 7 of them being more than twice as large as America's Citibank.[29] Of the 26 biggest corporations, as measured by assets in 1988, 19 were Japanese, 3 American, and 4 European.[30]

The percentage of international banking deposits in dollars was still over 50 percent in 1988, but it had fallen from 75 percent in a mere six years.[31] The share of the yen in international banking and bond markets, on the other hand, has risen steadily. As the yen appears more reliable than the dollar, with the sound backing of the Japanese trade surplus and powerful creditor position, its role in world trade grows. It is advantageous for the United States that trade is conducted in dollars, giving greater predictability and avoiding exchange commissions; it becomes advantageous for the Japanese so far as trade is conducted in yen. The Japanese, dependent on foreign markets and especially the United States, are cautious; but they gradually play a larger part in international financial management.

The Japanese economic offensive is more promising than the military or political-ideological offensives of ambitious powers of the past. The United States did not use its immense financial strength after WW II to tighten its grip but permitted Japan and West Germany—indeed, helped them—to rise in the American shadow and grow out from under it. The Japanese are more resolute, and financial power grows on itself. The larger their holdings, the more income they bring in, additional to the large trade surplus. The world becomes more indebted to them, and money is modern power. If the Japanese stake in the IMF and World Bank surpasses that of the United States, so will Japanese influence. As the Japanese acquire holdings in the United States and Western Europe, they also acquire ability to support political parties and sway decisionmaking. As they have the capital others need, their word is heeded.

How far this gathering of economic power can go one cannot guess. It is difficult for a democratic state to muster resolve to counter it; it does not galvanize like a military threat, and action is never urgent. Will is decisive; and the clannishness of the Japanese, in some ways a handicap, is an asset in this regard. On the other hand, the ability of the United States to draw foreign talent has negative as well as positive aspects. The United States and other countries can try to copy Japanese methods, but this is never fully successful; they cannot undo the fact that their societies are less

[29]*New York Times,* July 20, 1988, p. C 1.

[30]*Fortune,* November 21, 1988, p. 195.

[31]Carla Rapoport, "Will the Yen Push the Dollar Aside?" *Fortune,* December 5, 1988, p. 156

coherent and less dedicated than Japanese. So far as one can project the future, Japanese economic and financial power will continue to grow as long as the national will and drive remain strong.

The emergent panorama is very different from the military bipolarity and economic one-sidedness to which the world became accustomed in the postwar period. The United States feels itself slipping, although it remains extremely strong. The Soviet Union strives to maintain a standing appropriate to its territorial immensity and the historic greatness of Russia but finds it very difficult. China promises to enter from the wings. A semiunited Europe is the greatest of economic powers with little political power or purpose. Japan, the most successful modern economy, becomes the world's leading financial power. As military power recedes and "alliance" takes on new meaning, their interactions belong to a new era of international relations.

World Order

A universal political organization, the Peoples' Republic of Planet Earth, would seem logical. So far as competition among nations becomes less bitter, a supranational order should grow. But it is hardly possible to supersede independent sovereignties; humanity must find a way between dangerous anarchy and unattainable order. The political union of nations has been an everlasting dream, but only despotic universal empires have come near realizing it.

Thinkers have from time to time schemed some sort of international concord. Immanuel Kant, for example, before the French Revolution projected a league of virtuous states; he believed it could be brought about by convincing rulers that war was wrongful and harmful.[32] But a universalist organization to subdue the international anarchy seems to become a possibility only in the wake of the losses and griefs of a big war. The peoples then long for a more secure order, and the victorious powers wish to consolidate their victory. They are better able to do so because they come out of the war with a common purpose and the contest has eliminated the contrary forces. The great powers have not been willing, however, to relinquish any important part of their freedom to injure one another.

In this regard, the United Nations was no great advance over the League of Nations; it could not be, because one of the most important of the founding nations was politically very different from the Western powers and correspondingly distrustful. The U.N. is consequently no embryonic world government. It no longer represents a glowing ideal, and hardly any-

---

[32]Immanuel Kant, *Eternal Peace* (Indianapolis: Liberal Arts Press, 1957).

one would make an important sacrifice on its behalf. The United States has become weary of acting as its chief financial support. It is a largely symbolic organization, upholding the principle of independent sovereignty and the sanctity of national territories. It is an excellent meeting ground where representatives of all nations can communicate, and it can facilitate the resolution of local conflicts. But it may be as much an impediment to the formation of a new and more perfect union as a step on the way.

Without another disastrous conflict, there is no prospect of establishing any institution that deprives the sovereign states of important powers or control of policies or resources. The incentives are feeble, and mistrust is great. And even if there were a demand to develop a stronger world body, it seems impossible to devise even theoretically any generally acceptable scheme of government. It would have to suit small powers (which stand for equality of sovereign rights), very populous countries (which would like representation corresponding to population), wealthy powers (which wish to have influence proportional to their contribution, not to be saddled with expenses beyond their own consent), and very strong powers (which are not disposed to bow to the will of the weak simply because these are gifted with the half-mythical condition called "sovereignty").

Strengthened international law may offer more hope of improvement of international order. But it is most effective where least needed, in regulating pacific relations of friendly nations. It fails where most needed, in regard to big issues and when nations are seriously at odds; and states acting for their interests do not give much thought to the effects of their actions on the international regime.[33]

Much of international law is a residue of the age when international relations were the concern of chanceries and diplomats, not of countless governmental and nongovernmental agencies and actors. It says nothing about the liability of one country for acid rain on another, about denial of trading rights, or the destruction of a social order by the demand of another for narcotics. However, customs and understandings of international behavior grow along with interdependence. The rules of behavior among states should be like traffic laws. Because they are essential to reduce frictions, keep traffic flowing, and avoid collisions, upholding them should be the concern of all drivers.

The idea of international jurisprudence has declined from the vogue it enjoyed in the first half of this century, when many people thought that formal arrangements would settle political and economic differences. Rigid rules lacking clear-cut sanction or means of enforcement are much less helpful than recognition of mutual interest, and it is questionable for a dignified body to lay down judgments that cannot be enforced. The Interna-

---

[33]For a detailed discussion, see Gerhard von Glahn, *Law among Nations* 5th ed. (London: Macmillan, 1987).

tional Court of Justice, whose 15 judges are elected by the General Assembly and Security Council of the United Nations, hears hardly any cases and has been able to achieve practically nothing. It gives an impression of futility of internationalism.[34]

In the more tranquil atmosphere of the latter 1980s, the World Court regained some stature, as the United States and the Soviet Union proposed giving it compulsory jurisdiction under some treaties. So far as the interest in international order rises and the interest in getting the better of other powers decreases, it should be possible to find means of giving force, by nonviolent means, to a world legal order.

International organization of the future, however, seems likely to be mostly ad hoc, consisting of a multitude of bodies for different purposes, private, semiofficial, or governmental, with little power but the reaching of agreement, acting not to command but to enable states to find acceptable solutions for common problems, to come to understandings, and to work for common ends. It should be something like what the anarchist would like to see take the place of the state, a set of arrangements to improve coexistence, with powers resting on the usefulness and persuasiveness of cooperative action.

It is hardly desirable that there be any strong universal political authority. The competitive anarchy is positive. Domestic pluralism rests on international division; the open, competitive international system is the backdrop of national freedom, just as the fluidity of pluralism underlies the democratic order. In the age of mass production and overwhelming organization of increasingly homogenized societies, the existence of strong independent entities is the bulwark against total stultification and stagnation. Without something like independence of sovereignties, the further progress of civilization would be dubious.

But no power should be dangerous to others if the trends of the last generation continue much further, with the growth of shared interests and the weakening of aggressive ones. Humans, like animals, repeat behavior that is rewarding; but recent important exercises of violence have been unrewarding: Germany, Italy, and Japan in WW II; Britain and France at Suez in 1956; the United States in Vietnam; the Soviet Union in Afghanistan; Iraq in its war with Iran. Japan, which amiably does business with anyone, like the European Community, is the model of an economic superpower almost without political purposes. The nations are competitive, but they do not have to be injurious; their competition may be increasingly in production, education, and science, by which none can feel injured. The nations are not on seesaws, sending one down as another goes up; improvement of the well-being of one usually adds to the well-being of others.

---

[34]For a survey, see Thomas M. Franck, *Judging the World Court* (New York: Priority Press Publications, 1986).

In the words of Richard Falk, "We are entering a poststatal period, although its character remains highly conjectural."[35] It may be, as the president of South Korea, Roh Tae Woo stated, "Today the world is entering an age of reconciliation and cooperation, transcending ideologies and political systems."[36] As boundaries come to mean less, to have less effect in defining and restricting activities, the special rights of sovereign states must come to seem contradictory to the global realities of culture, production, and thought. The nation, which grew up in war and was shaped by needs of defense, must change as the needs of physical defense recede. Its claims and attitudes have to evolve, although perhaps subtly and imperceptibly. In particular, it may become more of an administrative unit, necessary but not dominant, no longer asserting supremacy based on needs of national security but still serving as the primary focus of the community, expressing a people's sense of oneness and belonging.

The ability of the nation-state to behave as it pleases shrinks with the integration of the world; even on its own territory it becomes less sovereign. It is agreed that all nations can legitimately take an interest in human rights anywhere, although no one is likely to mount an invasion to force a government to be decent to its people. No country can indulge in unrestrained production of narcotics, however profitable it might be; there would certainly be reprisals if any tried to assert that sovereign right. The freedom to pollute oceans and atmosphere is questionable; the measures to be taken against violators may become a subject of major controversy. Whether a country can increase its population without restraint and cause problems of immigration to less crowded lands is potentially a matter of international concern, at least if the world undertakes to feed the famished poor. If the leading military powers manage to end the nuclear arms race, they may find the manufacture and possession of nuclear and chemical weapons by smaller and perhaps less responsible powers a reprehensible danger to humanity, an infraction of the world moral order, which they could outlaw if they would. They may also be able to act in concert against the terrorism that is a menace to civilized peoples and prevent less responsible countries from providing arms, materials, or training for terrorists.

All modern nations are increasingly constrained in their conduct by the advantages of international cooperation. No nation can really afford to engage in conduct offensive to a majority of the world community. The leading nations can, so far as they agree, coerce offenders against international mores pacifically by denying them the benefits of the international system.

The international system, like technological society, is in a state of

---

[35]Richard Falk, "Anarchism and World Order," in Richard Falk and Samuel Kim, eds., *The War System: An Interdisciplinary Approach* (Boulder: Westview, 1980), p. 47.

[36]*New York Times*, July 7, 1988, p. 1.

rapid and unforeseeable change; the best prediction is that it will be quite different in the 1990s from what the 1980s knew. A new society requires better management of power and resources. How change comes about depends partly on conditions beyond the grasp of individual humans, but it is also to some extent within the powers of intelligence to shape, for good or ill the future of humanity, a major determinant of which will be the way sovereign states deal with one another.

Index